KU-771-918

ı ... 1862   Dent Blanche ... 1863   Dent d'Hérens ...

3adile ... 1868   Kazbek (Caucasus) ... 1869   Gspaltenhorn ...

ıteau ... 1874   Elbruz (Caucasus) ... 1875   Sass Maor ...

8   Grand Dru ... 1879   Matterhorn Zmutt Ridge ...

Face ... 1883   Schreckhorn NW Ridge ... 1884   Adai Khokh (Caucasus)

tnuld (Caucasus) ... 1888   Dych Tau (Caucasus) ...

t Ridge ... 1892   Pioneer Peak (Karakoram) ... 1893   Dent du Requin ...

shi (Caucasus) ... 1897   Tupungato (Andes) ... 1898   Illimani (Andes) ...

boine (Canada) ... 1902   Columbia (Canada) ...

esthorn NW Ridge ... 1906   La Perouse ... 1907   Trisul ... 1908

V Face ... 1911   Pawhunri (Sikkim) ... 1912   Kangchenjau (Sikkim)

1919   Mont Blanc Innominata Ridge ... 1920   Breithorn N Face ...

Ober Gabelhorn S Face Direct ... 1924   Everest? ...

Face Red Sentinel ... 1928   Brenva Face Route Major

Aiguilles Rouges du Brouillard E Face

936   Nanda Devi ... 1937   Chomolhari ... 1938   Alphubel NE Face

tian N Face ...

THE
ALPINE JOURNAL
2007

The sculpture unveiled on 22 June 2007 in the centre of Zermatt during the Alpine Club anniversary meet. Marking 150 years of friendship between the resort and the Club, the work was commissioned by the community of Zermatt and created by the sculptor Stefan Mesmer. (*John Cleare*)

THE
ALPINE JOURNAL

2007

The Journal of the Alpine Club

A record of mountain adventure
and scientific observation

Edited by Stephen Goodwin

Assistant Editors:
Paul Knott and Geoffrey Templeman

Production Editor: Johanna Merz

Volume 112

No 356

Supported by the
MOUNT EVEREST FOUNDATION

Published jointly by
THE ALPINE CLUB & THE ERNEST PRESS

THE ALPINE JOURNAL 2007
Volume 112 No 356

Address all editorial communications to the Hon Editor :
Stephen Goodwin, 1 Ivy Cottages, Edenhall, Penrith, CA11 8SN
e-mail : sg@stephengoodwin.demon.co.uk
Address all sales and distribution communications to:
Cordée, 3a De Montfort Street, Leicester, LE1 7HD

Back numbers:
Apply to the Alpine Club, 55 Charlotte Road, London, EC2A 3QF
or, for 1969 to date, apply to Cordée, as above.

© 2007 by the Alpine Club

All rights reserved

First published in 2007 jointly by the Alpine Club and the Ernest Press
Typeset by Johanna Merz
Printed in China through Colorcraft Ltd., Hong Kong

A CIP catalogue record for this book is
available from the British Library

ISBN 978 0 948153 88 4

Foreword

Alpine Club members present at the gala weekend in Zermatt last June will not quickly forget the moment a helicopter hovered between the Grand Hotel Zermatterhof and the parish church and hoisted the cover from a sculpture marking 150 years of friendship between the AC and the Valaisian resort. It was a splendid *coup de théâtre* by our Zermatt hosts. Though they had turned to me for some suitable words for the stone, its form, Stefan Mesmer's bronze mountaineer, and the dramatic means of the unveiling had been kept a secret.

The mustachioed figure, raising his hat towards the Matterhorn, spoke of the Club's early days in the Alps, while the rough boulder beneath the mountaineer's feet and the clean slab recording our 1857-2007 anniversary lent the piece a contemporary tone. The balance between past and present was well judged. We are, after all, still here, and for a Club that had its beginnings in the year of the Indian Mutiny and during Palmerston's first government that is not bad going.

On the stone, I had described our AC forebears as 'the pioneers of alpinism', a phrase I had hesitated over at first, thinking it might sound immodest or presumptuous. One glance around the Zermatt skyline, however, was enough to dispel any doubts about the claim; against peak after peak, ridge after ridge, one could write an Alpine Club name.

There above us was the magnificent Zmutt ridge, first climbed by Mummery and party in 1879. Those two names, Zmutt and Mummery, together embody the spirit of alpine-style mountaineering that still imbues our Club – Mummery the exploratory mountaineer and the Zmutt, a demanding route where retreat is problematic and the sense of commitment and uncertainty remains acute. It nearly wasn't so on the Zmutt. Thankfully plans to tame this icon of alpinism have not come to pass, at least not yet, as Doug Scott explains here in a conscience-prodding essay on ethics.

This 112th volume of the *Alpine Journal* is a special issue marking the Club's 150th anniversary. However, the temptation to dwell on AC history was largely removed by the publication in autumn 2006 of *Summit: 150 Years of the Alpine Club* by George Band (HarperCollins). The *AJ* was thus free to wander more widely and get writers to consider some of the issues that swirl around contemporary mountaineering. Thus Ed Douglas reflects on our unease when climbing is marketed as a 'lifestyle' sport and Robert Macfarlane on our ambivalence to wild places. Peter Gillman examines some very questionable ascents while Scott rails against the dumbing down of classic routes by bolts and sundry ironmongery.

Debate about the future direction of mountaineering is hardly new. Nor even is the fear of a kind of creeping urbanisation, both in the mindset of a growing number of climbers and in our physical subjugation of the crags and alpine ridges. In an introductory essay to *Alpine Centenary 1857-1957*

John Hunt spoke of the spirit of adventure being increasingly coloured by competition and the mastery of artificial techniques. 'As increasing numbers look for outlets among the hills, from the growing artificiality of civilisation, there is a tendency, slight as yet but noticeable, to translate to this realm of lasting values some of the false values from the cities.' Hunt's language may be distinctly of the 1950s but half a century later there is no doubting its force and presentiment. Regrettably the 'tendency' he warned of is no longer slight.

As to the business of alpinism itself, Hunt was writing, as he so perfectly put it, at 'a time of poise' in the history of mountaineering. In the previous four years, seven of the world's highest summits had been climbed and what followed would inevitably be on a descending scale, he said. Nevertheless he believed much scope for true pioneering remained in the Himalaya, the Andes and Alaska, and still more should the Iron Curtain be 'lowered'.

As important as the reflective pieces in this anniversary journal, are the opening articles that show mountaineers doing just as Hunt hoped and treading new ground, much of it ferociously steep and frighteningly loose, in the very ranges he identified. As for venturing behind the Iron Curtain (not so much 'lowered' as torn down), Hunt would undoubtedly have taken particular pleasure in reading of the achievements of the AC's expedition last year to the Pamirs and the exploits of other AC members in the Tien Shan. No clouding of the spirit of adventure hereabouts.

Hunt may also have underestimated how much remained to be done on the Himalayan giants. In a revealing set of tables, Ken Wilson has detailed the most notable climbs on four of the world's highest massifs, starting with Everest. The result is a reminder, simultaneously, of some extraordinarily bold and well-planned ascents but also of the high human cost of mountaineering at the extreme. There is plenty of scope for analysis and debate. Even at first glance it seems there is a slowing down of outstanding new climbs at the highest altitude. Perhaps that shift down the scale is inevitable, but has just arrived a bit later than Hunt predicted.

Putting together the 112th *AJ* has, as ever, been a team effort. This year it seems to have been more time-consuming than ever, but perhaps that was due to the distractions of a succession of anniversary events, notably the Zermatt gathering. In consequence, I'm sure Johanna Merz's task as production editor became even more taxing than usual. I am immensely grateful to her. Thanks also to Paul Knott, Area Notes editor, who has efficiently put together another comprehensive record of climbs around the globe, to Geof Templeman for compiling the obituaries and reviews, to our publisher Peter Hodgkiss of the Ernest Press, to Andy Parkin who has enriched this journal with cartoons and paintings, and to each and every one who has contributed. Thanks again to you all.

Stephen Goodwin

Contents

CLIMBS   1

Silent Scream ~ A year in the life of ...   *Nick Bullock*   3
Confounding the Colonel on Kedar Dome   *Ian Parnell*   17
Top Marx in Pamirs for AC climbers   *Tim Sparrow*   26
Haizi Shan ~ A lot to be grateful for   *Malcolm Bass*   40
The Ascent of South Walsh   *Paul Knott*   46
Celestial Touring. Ski-mountaineering in the
    Tien Shan   *Dave Wynne-Jones*   54
Lhotse South Face Winter Ascent
    ~ The Dream Comes True   *Osamu Tanabe*   61
A Good Day   *Simon Yates*   68

ANNIVERSARY   75

Resisting the Appeasers   *Doug Scott*   77
Recent Himalayan History. The Highest Peaks:
    notable attempts, ascents, repeats, trends, incidents *Ken Wilson*   84
The Crux. Great moments or turning points
    in British climbing history   *Gordon Stainforth*   93
Soul Traders: 150 Years of Peddling Adventures   *Ed Douglas*   124
Climbing Controversies   *Peter Gillman*   131
'All one might wish of wisdom'   *Robert Macfarlane*   137
The Rise and Fall of the Working Class Climber   *Dennis Gray*   142
Scottish Winter Climbing: the last 50 years   *Simon Richardson*   147

JOURNEYS & RANGES   159

Further Travels in Eastern Tibet
    By foot, horseback and Land Cruiser   *Tamotsu Nakamura*   161
Mad Dogs?   *John Starbuck*   172
Cordillera Central, Argentina   *Evelio Echevarría*   184

ARTS   195

A Night on Les Droites   *Andy Parkin*   197
Preserving our Mountain Art.
    Digital Technology: a new imaging landscape   *Tony Riley*   204
'The Charged Silence of a Summit'
    in Contemporary Mountaineering Poetry   *Terry Gifford*   211

HISTORY 227

The 'Eiger of Africa'.
 First ascent of the east face of Mawenzi *John Edwards* 229
Testing Mallory's Clothes on Everest *Graham Hoyland* 243
Prophets of Pyrénéisme *Kev Reynolds* 247
One Hundred Years Ago *C A Russell* 256

AREA NOTES *Edited by Paul Knott* 261

Alps 2006 *Lindsay Griffin* 263
Russia & Central Asia 2006 *Paul Knott* 272
Greenland 2006 *Derek Fordham* 279
Scottish Winter 2006-2007 *Simon Richardson* 283
Wadi Rum & Jordan *Tony Howard* 288
Turkey 2002-2006 *Geoff Hornby* 291
India 2006 *Harish Kapadia* 296
Nepal 2006 *Dick Isherwood* 305
Pakistan 2006 *Lindsay Griffin* 308
China & Tibet 2006 *John Town* 315
New Zealand 2006-2007 *Mark Watson* 318
Bolivia 2006 *Eric Monasterio* 323
North America 2006 *Ade Miller* 330

Mount Everest Foundation:
 Expedition Reports *Summarised by Bill Ruthven* 336
Reviews *Compiled by Geoffrey Templeman* 344
In Memoriam *Compiled by Geoffrey Templeman* 381
Alpine Club Notes 406
Contributors 419
Index 425
Notes for Contributors 434

Illustrations

ront cover: The Matterhorn from Sunnegga. Watercolour, 23 June 2007. (*Rowan Huntley*)

ıck cover: Kurt Diemberger in animated conversation with Walter Bonatti; Peter Mäder, ̣wiss Alpine Club general secretary, stands behind; Doug Scott is interviewed for Swiss TV ̣1 the summit of the Breithorn (*photo: Stephen Goodwin*); Stefan Mesmer (*right*), who created ̣e sculpture commissioned by Zermatt, and Stephen Goodwin, *AJ* editor, who instigated the ̣thering at Zermatt and provided the words of friendship for the stone (*see frontispiece*); AC ̣embers and guests on the terrace of the Riffelberg listening to speeches prior to the celebration ̣nner; AC president Stephen Venables receives the gift of a painting, *The Finsteraarhorn*, from ̣AC president Frank Urs Müller; Anna Lawford, curator of the ACL photo library, and Toto ̣ronlund, committee member and heroic administrative 'Sherpa' for the Zermatt event. ̣(*ll photographs by Bernard Newman, editor of Climber magazine, except where stated.*)

The sculpture unveiled on 22 June 2007 in the centre of Zermatt during the Alpine Club anniversary meet. Marking 150 years of friendship between the resort and the Club, the work was commissioned by the community of Zermatt and created by the sculptor Stefan Mesmer. (*John Cleare*)   *Frontispiece*

                                                             Page

Andy Parkin, *Cerro Torre*, pastel.
Winter solo trip 2000.   1
Nick Bullock on the crux pitch of the first winter ascent of *Travesty*.
(*Libby Peter*)   4
Nick Bullock on the crux of *Slanting Gully* on Lliwedd, North Wales.
(*Libby Peter*)   6
Matt Helliker traversing beneath an ice umbrella on *Death or Glory*, Peru.
(*Nick Bullock*)   8
Nick Bullock on the summit of Huantsán Sur after making the first ascent
of *Death or Glory*. (*Matt Helliker*)   9
Jon Bracey below the north face of Phari Lapcha, Nepal. (*Nick Bullock*)   13
Snotty's Gully, Phari Lapcha (Machermo Peak), Nepal. (*Nick Bullock*)   14
Jon Bracey entering *Snotty's Gully* on day 2. The first pitch from the bivvi.
(*Nick Bullock*)   15
. Jon Bracey on the last steep pitch of *Snotty's Gully* before the final headwall
pitch leading to the ridge before the summit. (*Nick Bullock*)   15
. Tim Emmett beneath the giant east face of Kedar Dome. The left-hand line
shows their new route up the south-east pillar. (*Ian Parnell*)   18
. Day 3. 5600m. Tim following across the perfect granite slabs that
characterised the central section of the route. (*Ian Parnell*)   21
. Day 4. 5700m. Tim leading against a backdrop of blue skies. Although by
afternoon this would be filled with clouds, the weather held throughout
their climb. (*Ian Parnell*)   22
. Day 4. 5800m. Tim starting a typical pitch, weaving through ice pitches
before heading across blank slabs. (*Ian Parnell*)   23

15. Day 6. 6250m. Tim following the twin corner which was the only real weakness through the steep blank final wall. (*Ian Parnell*)
16. Map: the Shakdara range, south-west Pamirs, Tajikistan. (*Sketch map by Tim Sparrow redrawn by Gary Haley*)
17. Looking across the Wakhan valley to the Hindu Kush. (*Tim Sparrow*)
18. Base Camp in the Nishgar valley with Pik Karl Marx looming beyond. (*Tim Sparrow*)
19. Piks Karl Marx and Nikoladsye, looking up the East Nishgar glacier. (*Tim Sparrow*)
20. Alex Rickards and Steve Hunt at their top camp on the East Nishgar glacier. (*Tim Sparrow*)
21. Alpenglow on the west face of Pik Tajikistan. (*Tim Sparrow*)
22. West flank of Pik Karl Marx. (*Derek Buckle*)
23. Kai Green crossing a snow bridge on the west face of Pik Karl Marx. (*Derek Buckle*)
24. Alex Rickards and Steve Hunt camping below the Far East Nishgar glacier. (*Tim Sparrow*)
25. Alex Rickards and Steve Hunt descending the south ridge of Nikoladsye South. (*Tim Sparrow*)
26. On the summit of Pik Karl Marx. *From left clockwise*: Alex Rickards, Steve Hunt and Tim Sparrow. (*Tim Sparrow*)
27. The north face of Haizi Shan. (*Malcolm Bass*)
28. The last pitch before the west ridge. (*Malcolm Bass*)
29. Pat Deavoll on the west ridge of Haizi Shan. (*Malcolm Bass*)
30. The west ridge of Haizi Shan from the top of the north face route. (*Malcolm Bass*)
31. Malcolm Bass on the west ridge approaching the summit. (*Pat Deavoll*)
32. Aerial view of the Walsh massif from the south. (*Graham Rowbotham*)
33. The west face of South Walsh. (*Paul Knott*)
34. Base camp and the Walsh massif. (*Paul Knott*)
35. Graham Rowbotham traversing into the couloir on the south face. (*Paul Knott*)
36. On the corniced section of the south-west ridge with the upper south face behind. (*Paul Knott*)
37. Passing towers on the south face. (*Paul Knott*)
38. Graham Rowbotham on the summit of South Walsh with Mt Lucania in the haze behind. (*Paul Knott*)
39. Kara-Say valley. Anna Seale crosses the meltwater torrent on the ebb. (*Mike Sharp*)
40. Camp Day 3 in the stony waste of the river valley nearing the junction of two glacial valleys ahead. (*John Goodwin*)
41. Heading up the left fork to the Kara-Say glacier. (*Mike Sharp*)
42. Lizzy Hawker gaining the summit of Pik Karga. (*John Goodwin*)
43. Dave Wynne-Jones on the summit of Pik Koyon. Behind are Pik Kyrgyzia (*left*) and Pik Karga (*right*). (*Mike Sharp*)
44. Climbing the upper part of the couloir at 8300m. The yellow rock wall at the top of the couloir was detoured around to the left. (*Osamu Tanabe*)
45. Overall view of the Lhotse south face. (© *The Chunichi Shimbun Ltd*)

. The same view of the Lhotse south face depicted as a diagram
showing the 2006 route and heights of camps. (*Diagram by Gary Haley*) 65
. Everest viewed from the summit ridge of Lhotse at 8475m
after the ascent of the south face. (*Osamu Tanabe*) 66
. Traversing a fragile rock wall at 8350m to detour around the
uppermost part of the couloir to the left. (*Osamu Tanabe*) 66
. Our 'rescued' route diagram. (*Simon Yates*) 69
. Seña Pia from "Cabbage Daisy" meadow. (*Simon Yates*) 70
. The south faces of Monte Iorana I & II. (*Simon Yates*) 73
. Andy Parkin on the summit of Monte Iorana I. (*Simon Yates*) 73
. Marcel on *Iorana* heading for the pick-up. (*Simon Yates*) 74
. Andy Parkin, *Chogolisa*, acrylic on canvas. From K2 base camp at 5200m, 1996. 75
. A cannonade on the Matterhorn, July 1862. (*Freda Raphael Historical Archive*) 95
. Beatrice Tomasson and her guide, Arcangelo Siorpaes, in the Cortina
Dolomites, 1898. (*Bâton Wicks Archive*) 97
. *Central Buttress*, Scafell, Easter 1915. George & Ashley Abraham.
(*Bâton Wicks Archive*) 99
. Siegfried Herford and George Mallory at Pen y Pass, December 1913.
Geoffrey Winthrop Young. (*Alpine Club Photo Library*) 101
. The last picture of Mallory and Irvine, Camp IV, Everest, 6 June 1924.
(*Mountain Camera Picture Library*) 101
. Edward Norton at 28,100ft on Everest, 4 June 1924. T Howard Somervell.
(*Somervell family*) 102
. Joe Brown making the first ascent of *The Right Unconquerable*, Stanage,
April 1949. Ernest Phillips 104
. Rustie Baillie starting up *Cenotaph Corner*, Dinas Cromlech, Llanberis Pass.
John Cleare 107
. John Streetly on the first ascent of *Bloody Slab*, Clogwyn d'ur Arddu,
10 June 1952. E A Wrangham. (*Bâton Wicks archive*) 109
. Layton Kor on the Central Pillar of the *Eiger Direct*, 5pm, 19 March 1966.
Chris Bonington 111
. Rusty Baillie at the crux on the first ascent of the Old Man of Hoy,
18 July 1966. Chris Bonington 113
. Ed Drummond and Dave Pearce pioneering *A Dream of White Horses*,
Craig Gogarth, October 1968. Leo Dickinson 114
. Doug Scott on *The Scoop*, Sron Ulladale, June 1969. Ken Wilson 116
. Ian Clough on the South Face of Annapurna, May 1970. Chris Bonington 118
. Dougal Haston arriving at the summit of Everest, 6pm, 24 September 1975.
Doug Scott 119
. Tasker, Boardman and Renshaw on the NNE ridge of Everest, 5 May 1982.
Chris Bonington 121
. Leo Houlding on the crux of *The Passage to Freedom*
El Capitan, October 1999. Andrew McGarr 122
. Macfarlane illustration. (*John Beatty*) 138
. Mitre Ridge, Garbh Choire, Beinn a'Bhuird. (*Simon Richardson*) 149
. John Ashbridge climbing *Parallel Buttress* (VI,6), Lochnagar. (*Simon Richardson*) 149
. Approaching the great North-East Corrie of Lochnagar. (*Niall Ritchie*) 151

77. *Albatross* (VI,5) on Indicator Wall, Ben Nevis (climber unknown).
      (*Simon Richardson*)   1!
78. No 4 Buttress, Core an Lochain, Northern Corries. (*Niall Ritchie*)   1!
79. Halvor Hagen climbing *The Hoarmaster* (V,6), Coire an Lochain,
      Northern Corries. (*Simon Richardson*)   1!
80. Andy Parkin, *The Dru, Chamonix.* Acrylic on canvas.   1!
81. North face of the holy mountain Hayungarpo 6388m. (*Tamotsu Nakamura*)   1(
82. Dawn over the Lhagu glacier and east face of Hamogongga 6260m
      seen from Lhagu village, Kangri Garpo East. (*Tamotsu Nakamura*)   1(
83. Map: Kangri Garpo East. (*Sketch map by Tamotsu Nakamura*)   1(
84. Lhagu glacier, Lhagu lake and east face of Gonyada 6423m and Zeh 6127m
      viewed from Lhagu village, Kangri Garpo East. (*Tamotsu Nakamura*)   1(
85. North face of Gemosongu 6450m and Midoi glacier, Kangri Garpo East.
      (*Tamotsu Nakamura*)   1(
86. A bridge over the Parlung Tsangpo near Mimei village, Kangri Garpo East.
      (*Tamotsu Nakamura*)   1(
87. Map: Botoi Tsangpo. (*Sketch map by Tamotsu Nakamura*)   1(
88. West face of unnamed shining peak c5800m and glacier in Linzhou Longba
      to the east from Yuri village, Botoi Tsangpo, north of Bomi, Nyainqentanglha
      East. (*Tamotsu Nakamura*)   1*
89. North face of Dojiza 6250m and Juxi glacier, Botoi Tsangpo, north-west of
      Bomi township, Nyainqentanglha East. (*Tamotsu Nakamura*)   1*
90. Map: Watkins Mountains, Greenland.
      (*Sketch map by John Starbuck redrawn by Gary Haley*)   1*
91. Paul Walker and John Starbuck ascending the final section of the NE ridge
      during the first summit attempt on Gunnbjørnsfjeld (3693m).
      4 March 2006. (*Adrian Pedley*)   174-1*
92. Paul Walker and John Starbuck approaching the platform during the
      first summit attempt. (*Adrian Pedley*)   1*
93. John Starbuck approaching the summit of Gunnbjørnsfjeld during
      the first summit attempt. (*Barry Roberts*)   1*
94. Looking up the flank of the NE ridge during the second summit attempt,
      on Gunnbjørnsfjeld, 9 March 2006. (*Paul Walker*)   1%
95. Douglas Gurr climbing beside the fixed rope on the NE ridge steepening
      during the second summit attempt, 9 March 2006. (*Adrian Pedley*)   1%
96. Map: Cordillera Central, Argentina. Province of San Juan.
      (*Sketch map by Evelio Echevarría*)   1%
97. Map: Cordillera Central, Argentina. Province of Mendoza.
      (*Sketch map by Evelio Echevarría*)   1%
98. Cerro Tolosa (5317m) seen from the south. The south face of Aconcagua
      in the background. (*Evelio Echevarría*)   1%
99. Mendoza: the upper Las Cuevas valley, looking north, with Cerro Piloto
      (5064m) in the background. (*Evelio Echevarría*)   1%
100. Nigel Gallop in the southern Cordón del Portillo, 1955.
      (*By courtesy of Nigel Gallop, London*)   1%
101. Cordón del Portillo, with the Tres Picos del Amor (5000m), ascended in 1954.
      (*By courtesy of Nigel Gallop, London*)   1%

2. Andy Parkin, *Mont Maudit, Chamonix*. Pastel. From Fouche bivouac hut. 195
3. Cartoon: *Preparation. Winter and spring, running out to work at Eyam ...* (*Andy Parkin*) 197
4. Cartoon: *The summer and en route for the Alps. Hitch-hiking, a pretty girl stops and I discover Annecy ...* (*Andy Parkin*) 198
5. Cartoon: *A few weeks later, one dark and moonless night. Bivouac opposite the dark mass of the mountain ...* (*Andy Parkin*) 199
6. Cartoon: *The weak light from my headlamp, its battery nearly dead, only lights a feew metres in front of me ...* (*Andy Parkin*) 200
7. Cartoon: *My idea, at the start, had been to climb the classic route – La Davaille – and to follow the best line ...* (*Andy Parkin*) 201
8. Cartoon: *The climbing continues to be hard and delicate. But I'm starting to relax and the top is in sight. I can definitely get off this thing now.* (*Andy Parkin*) 202
9. Cartoon: *Daybreak. I'm sat on the summit, peaceful and calm ...* 203
0. Diagram: Digital images now provide greater control over colour. (*Tony Riley Collection*) 204
1. Diagram: Noise in a digital image. (*Tony Riley Collection*) 205
2. Clearing Winter Storm in Yosemite Valley (*Photo © Joseph Holmes*) 206
3. Edward Norton at 28,100ft on Everest, 4 June 1924. T Howard Somervell. (*Somervell family*) 208
4. Andy Parkin, *Lhasa detail*. Pastel, 1991. 227
5. Harry Archer and Porter M'Shauri at the cairn built on our recce to indicate the descent point down from south wall into the Great Barranco. (*John Edwards*) 231
6. Map: Profile of the east face of Mawenzi, Tanzania. (*Sketch map by John Edwards redrawn by Gary Haley*) 232
7. Mawenzi's east face from south wall with clouds boiling up the Barrancos. (*Tommy Thompson*) 233
8. John Edwards deciding it's time to rope up on Day 1 on the east face. Barranco south wall in the background. (*Tommy Thompson*) 235
9. John Edwards climbing the basalt rock, Day 1 on Mawenzi's east face. (*Tommy Thompson*) 236
0. John Edwards in 1962 holding the Duke of Abruzzi's ice axe, together with a note dated 1906 concealed in a tin. (*Harry Archer*) 238
1. 'Out of Africa': Leaving Two Tarn Hut to climb Mount Kenya in 1964. *Left to right*: Harry Archer, Pete McGowan, John Edwards, Tommy Thompson. (*Peter Scott*) 238
2. John Edwards on the summit of Mawenzi (Day 3) – Kibo in the background. (*Tommy Thompson*) 240
3. Primitive gear used by Edwards and Thompson on the east face climb. (*Ben Osborne*) 241
4. Similar to 123 but showing climbing belt, ex WD crampons, small petrol stove and our only emergency gear. (*Ben Osborne*) 242
5. Jean & Pierre Ravier on the south face of the Doigt de Pombie (Pic d'Ossau) 1956. (*Jean & Pierre Ravier collection*) 249
6. The Esparrets Buttress, on Mont Perdu, August 1973. (*Jean & Pierre Ravier collection*) 250

127. Pierre (*left*) and Jean Ravier in the family home at Tuzaguet, 2006.
(*Jean & Pierre Ravier collection*) 2:
128. Pierre and Jean Ravier with Kev Reynolds at Tuzaguet in June 2006.
(*Jean & Pierre Ravier collection*) 2:
129. Members of Tom Longstaff's party on the summit ridge of Trisul, 12 June 1907.
(*T G Longstaff*) (*Alpine Club Photo Library*) 2:
130. Andy Parkin, *K2 south face*. Pastel on paper, 1996. 2(
131. The south side of the 4208m Grandes Jorasses, with Phantom Wall.
(*Antonio Giani*) 2(
132. The north-west face of Pik Vektor, in the Mushtuairi valley west of Bielukha,
first climbed in 2005 by Vitaly Ivanov and friends via the centre of the face.
(*Mark Brits*) (See *AJ* 111, 273, 2006). 2'
133. Mikisfjord, East Greenland. The sailing vessel *Dagmar Aaen*, expedition vessel
of Arved Fuchs, has been used for Arctic and Antarctic expeditions since 1991.
It is a wooden boat, built in 1931. (*Arved Fuchs*) 2:
134. Blair Fyffe on the first winter ascent of *The Knuckleduster* (VIII,9)
on Number Three Gully Buttress, Ben Nevis. (*Steve Ashton*) 2:
135. View west from Jebel um Ejil to Rum village and the east face of
Jebel Rum. (*Tony Howard*) 2:
136. Peter Bishop on the first ascent of *Adam's Rib*. (*Geoff Hornby*) 2'
137. South and east faces of Dedigol Daglari, showing route lines of *Freya Face*
and *Adam's Rib*. (*Geoff Hornby*) 2'
138. A helicopter comes to the rescue. Yonggyap La behind. (*R Wani*) 2'
139. The Stremfelj–Zalokar route on the south face of Janak Chuli (7044m).
(*Andrej Stremfelj*) 3(
140. Sunrise from Yazghil Sar (5964m) in the Shimshal region. (*Lee Harrison*) 3(
141. Mayan Smith-Gobat on *Shadowlands* (27), Sinbad Gully headwall,
Fiordland, during the first free ascent. (*Craig Jefferies*) 3'
142. *The Mutant* (6+) on the west face of Lendenfeld. Allan Uren, Julian White
and Tim Robertson, December 2006. (*By courtesy of Adventure Consultants*) 3:
143. The locations of Long Laguna Glaciar and *Fly the Crack* on Pico Gotico,
and of the *Flyvbjerg-Monsterio route* on Rumi Mallku. (*Erik Monasterio*) 3:
144. The McNeill-Nott Memorial route on Mt Foraker (Turgeon-Mayo 2006).
(*Maxime Turgeon*) 3:
145. Bradford Washburn 1910-2007 3:
146. Gill Nisbet 1951-2006. (*Ted Maden*) 3'
147. The old AC logo. 4'
148. The current AC logo. 4'

Climbs

Andy Parkin *Cerro Torre*
Pastel
Winter solo trip 2000

NICK BULLOCK

Silent Scream
~ A year in the life of ...

Wind whipped snow against the thin metal skin of the Leschaux Hut. I lay fully clothed and covered in thick woollen blankets. A shaky forecast and New Year celebrations had no-doubt kept other climbers away. Tim Neill and I had climbed *L'Oeil au Beurre Noir* on the Petites Jorasses, a wave of water-ice leading to a steep silver pencil compressed by overhanging granite, and as 2006 slipped into 2007 I thought it fitting that my most prolific and successful year of climbing had finished with a great route.

The rock and ice up high had been generous in 2006, and the crumbling, vegetated sea cliffs of Gogarth forgiving. Experiences were racked, ready to be pulled from a crammed memory. Images, people and moves flitted in and out of my head. Pulling the blankets around me, flushed on success, warm for a while, until the thought of what I had lost in 2006, and that question I was so frequently asked, quelled my fire.

'Good to see you're still alive, when are you next going to try and commit suicide?'

Why was it that people appeared to think me reckless? Holding down a relationship appeared impossible; who wants to be with someone who is going to die sooner rather than later? But I couldn't live nervous of the 'what ifs'; I couldn't live life with longing.

2006 started with a fierce struggle on a little dark crag in North Wales. Snow swirled around the heavily hoared crag and butted up to the base. Libby Peter and I wallowed our way through deep powder armed with a rock-climbing guidebook and open minds. *Travesty*, a summer E1 5b, was judged worth a look.

Swinging, pumped, hanging from picks slotted behind flakes, I looked around the arête and knew the corner I had to pull into and traverse was going to be difficult. Llyn Idwal, white and frozen, looked a thousand miles away. The arête was overhanging and undercut with exposure like a big alpine face. Teetering, pressing front points onto tiny rugosities, quivering, sideways, slow and delicate. Axe picks placed on edges held me in balance. The wind blew snow up the face, stinging. Expecting to slip and fall, a creeping, calculated journey ended with me in the corner system waiting for Libby. The first winter ascent of *Travesty* was nearing completion.

On a roll, both in climbing and with life, Libby and I returned to Clogwyn Du two days later. *The Crack*, an overhanging off-width, another summer rock climb, was the obvious prize. Two hours of battling resulted in a big

3.   Nick Bullock on the crux pitch of the first winter ascent of *Travesty*.
      (*Libby Peter*)

fall, exhaustion, and time running out before picking up Libby's girls from the childminder.

Adam Wainright, Noel Crain, Graham Desroy, Mayers, Helliker...I called all the usual suspects later that evening, the list like a *Who's Who* of climbing. And one by one they rang or sent text messages declining the offer. I was desperate, knowing that Ian Parnell and Rich Cross were in the area and on the hunt.

Finally, James McHaffie returned my text and agreed to come out the following day so long as he was back by four to start work.

'No problem, how long can a two pitch climb take?'

Large wet flakes of snow swirled around the cwm. Caff sat in the snow beneath Clogwyn Du, removed his round, wire-framed glasses, cleaned them of snow and replaced them. Pulling a thick sandwich from his rucksack he devoured with vigour. Duct tape covered his salopettes and his cotton hoody was more suited to the base of a boulder. I was interested to see how Caff, one of the best trad' rock climbers in the country, went on.

'Good to see you're still alive, when are you next going to try and commit suicide?'

Arms straight, gripping axe shafts harder than ever, I struggled, body taught, shaking with effort. Two falls already and after each a return to the ground. Again I was at the point where a slip of the axe from the rounded edge, or feet from the smooth wall, would result in a big fall.

'Go on Nick!' Caff's scream from below mingled with the wind whistling.

The thought of success drove me on. Failure threatened. Failure had dogged me in 2005. Driven to the point of destruction, I was on a mission of success in 2006. Fifteen years of working with some of the worst individuals in Britain had given me this chance for a 'dream' existence. Failure will occur, but acceptance is never easy.

Reaching right, an edge for the point of a crampon, slipping, moving, sliding...

The sun sets, a bright-red glowing blaze, dipping into the sea. Snow falls, fresh and deep. Racing from the top of the crag, covered in powder, laughing, joking, red hues reflect from the surface of the shimmering sea. Waves pound and lap against the snow-covered sand dunes. Caff has already missed one climbing lesson he was due to instruct.

Success. I felt justified in my decision to give up work. Focusing and acting on my decisions has always been my way. Grey is not a part of my life. Maybe that was the problem in relationships. Partners saw this in me and knew that my living to the full was something I would find difficult to change.

Success was more to me than seeing my name in a magazine or writing an article. I had set out to climb. The climbing and the experience were the important factors. I hadn't given up work and a wage for an extended

4.   Nick Bullock on the crux of *Slanting Gully* on Lliwedd, North Wales.
      (*Libby Peter*)

holiday. This was a chance I had made for myself and I was determined. The freedom allowed me to be in the right place at the right time. It allowed me to travel, meet up with the right partners, be persistent and wait for the right conditions.

Leaning into the deep stone surround, looking through the rain streaked glass; a wet Llanberis Pass had put a stop to the climbing. Obsession whispers continually. Obsession drives me on in times of tension, pain and hunger. Obsession takes me to summits and plunges me into despair. Throwing kit into the van, I drove to Scotland.

Scotland gave three routes in four days, including a new line on the Ben. Returning to North Wales, the situation had improved. A simul-solo in the crisp cold afternoon on Snowdon, side-by-side, firm névé and smiles. Taking Libby's girls to ballet on a Saturday morning, racing along wet winter pavements. Bangor pier, laughter and weak winter sun. Lying on damp wood, spying through the gaps watching the sea lapping corroded iron. The last routes of a fickle Welsh winter were some of the best, *East Gully* and *Slanting Gully* on Lliwedd, a feeling of closeness. A feeling of belonging.

'You're still alive then?'

The prospect of Peru in July forced me now to reach a level of fitness high enough to attempt the Welsh rock climbs I coveted. Going to Peru in the middle of summer had always seriously affected my rock climbing. Pushing to my limit in the mountains set rock climbing back a long way, but the mountains call.

Obsession is a curse.

Pushing hard, slapping, fighting, running it out. *Me* on Yellow Wall at Gogarth, overhanging rubble, big air-time, flying, hanging, wrecked and rain soaked, I closed my eyes, imagining what could be if only I could ease up, if only partners were not scared of committing to someone who was going to die early. Spinning. Crumbling rock, clouds, lonely late nights, waves pummelling the cliffs, conversations pummelling my mind. Reflections. I needed to hurt. I did hurt. Tim Neill and I had another adventure racked and it felt good, but was it worth it?

The flight, the taxis and the eight-hour bus journey to Hauraz in Peru felt long and arduous. Snow, battering wind, rain and thick cloud caused frustration in our little camp tucked away from everyone. Matt Helliker and I had travelled around the range to the east side of the Cordillera Blanca, walked six hours to the head of the valley, stashed kit and prepared. Our chosen route, a splitter couloir between Huantsán main summit and Huantsan Oeste was not going to happen. No way after four days of snow would either of us contemplate entering a 1000-metre couloir topped by a loaded sérac. A line spotted on the third of Huantsán's three peaks offered hope. At the first opportunity we would try it.

5.   Matt Helliker traversing beneath an ice umbrella on *Death or Glory*,
      Peru. (*Nick Bullock*)

6. Nick Bullock on the summit of Huantsán Sur after making the first
ascent of *Death or Glory*. (*Matt Helliker*)

'Good to see you're still alive, when are you next going to try and commit suicide?'

The snow stopped on the morning of day five. Helliker, young and keen,
bounded ahead as we walked towards Huantsán Sur. More talented than
most, he lacked the selfish drive that affected me, but there was a lot of grey
and anguish in Helliker's life because of this. Was being focused to the
point of obsession wrong? Probably, if someone else was involved.

We began on rock, soloing, staying close; loose blocks teetered and
swayed. Crashing, tiles flew. Helliker moved with a flowing ease that I always
found difficult. The afternoon sun shone as we aimed for creaking, towering
séracs, wilting like flowers starved of water.

At the top of the rock section we donned crampons and roped up. This
middle section of the climb proved the most testing as we sneaked and
sprinted, passing beneath, on top of, and around the countless séracs.
Climbing runnels of deep snow we moved together towards massive
umbrellas of wind-blown ice overhangs. The dipping sun began to turn a
deep red. Nearing the biggest of the overhangs, we found a ledge and
arranged a bivvi. Brooding in the dark, shuffling on a cold stone ledge, the
night was tense. A sérac high on the face calved and we cowered as the first
lumps hit us.

'You're still alive then?'

For once, starting early was not a problem. Helliker traversed the length of an umbrella of ice so big an articulated lorry could have parked beneath it. The climbing was pitched as we were in fear of being hit by debris. We crossed a furrow, freshly cut by the newly calved sérac, with blocks of pure blue ice embedded deep into the snow. Questioning and thinking were not an option. I did not look up once.

The climbing became more technical but more safe as height was gained. Route-finding was the key now, and as Matt climbed out of the runnel above I knew by his shout we had made it and it would only be a matter of time before the summit was reached.

'This is going to be very serious!'

When we started on the *Maze*, a girdle traverse of Right-Hand Red Wall at Gogarth, we both knew the easy pitch, the last pitch, would be the crux. The guidebook description of 'impending and loose', told us everything. 'Impending and loose' on Red Wall is serious, no matter what the grade.

I left Toby Keep attached to five pieces of gear, cams in clay, wires sunk deep into moving blocks. Toby wanted a pleasant day, a warm up. The sea crashed into the zawn a hundred feet below adding to the exposure, and we both knew this was no warm up.

My return from Peru had been fraught and after a day another relationship was over.

'Don't fall off Nick.'

Inching along a small ledge with no gear between Toby and myself, I had no intention of falling off; unfortunately the quality of the rock had other ideas. Inching, knocking, carefully weighting. Slow. The ledge broke, crumbling rock, dust, spiders and fear. The block detached from the cliff. Twisting in a slow, mesmerising dance, the block turned, end-over-end, plummeting, crashing into the rocks at the base of the zawn and rousing the seagulls, shocked, a frenzy of white wings, screaming, circling. The crowd on the promontory overlooking Red Wall murmured in anticipation. A handhold ripped. I reversed, gasping.

'This is very serious Toby.'

I was scared. The wall overhung and I was going to have to pull at some point. Obsession doesn't allow backing off.

'Good to see you're still alive, when are you next going to try and commit suicide?'

It was ludicrous. I was about to rip both Toby and myself off the wall and all I could think about was the end of the relationship. Was it my fault? Did my lifestyle have to lead to loneliness?

Edging once more along the gangplank, a large plinth like a traffic cone poked up. I wanted to stand on the point to reach some handholds, but I couldn't commit. The thought of balancing on the top of the cone was sickening. My stomach churned, twisted guts, tight, almost as tight as the night I left her house for the last time in the dark and the pouring rain.

I kicked the plinth and it swayed – swayed like I had when I let her go from that last fierce embrace. Walking from the door in the dark, stinging eyes, the rain washing away the tears pouring down my face. I kicked for a second time and the rock separated and fell. Inching higher, I placed a wire behind a creaking flake and lunged for a jug. Catching the hold, gripping hard, fighting for the relationship, the fear coursing through me subsided for a second until the foothold broke, my body turned, spinning on an axis. I saw Toby pulling ropes and bracing himself. Hanging from one hand, I pulled and lunged again. The rock held as I pulled and flailed, squeezing, hoping for strength, pleading for a change. I saw myself walking in the dark and the rain. The crowd had long gone by the time I pulled over the lip of Red Wall.

Orange, red and white; dust, laughter and light. Jostling. Tourists in baggy ethnic clothing. Bumping shoulders with locals, skin weathered and creased with the intense sun. Kathmandu had always felt good, but now it felt safe, a million miles from my failed relationship. Mountaineering gave an escape and time for recovery. Yes, I would get over this, time would heal, but memories of passion, tenderness, touching and tears, still tortured. Failure felt as sad as a wilting bouquet of flowers wrapped in cracked cellophane at the site of a car crash.

Bracey and I had spotted the gully on the walk to Gokyo village in the Khumbu, Nepal. Originally we had intended to climb on Phari Lapcha's north face but an unclimbed gully between its main summit and west peak stood out and demanded attention. Perfect ice plastered to the back of a deep cleft leading to a knife-edge ridge and an unclimbed summit.

'It's always good to see you as it may be for the last time.'

Stumbling over another ice-covered boulder, forcing myself on, trepidation, excitement and fear. The steel grey of the early morning, the eerie light and solitude, brought back the 40-watt illumination of the 'long-leg' landing of a high security gaol. Imagination ran riot. The smell of sweat, shit, and wasted life filled my mind. Maybe witnessing that waste had fuelled my drive and made me unwilling to compromise. Bracey was in front picking his way toward the next challenge, that perfect gully. Everest was behind, a massive dark bulk, intimidating like some of the inmates from my previous life. Or maybe not. With its fixed rope, vanity, litter and oxygen, the street-fighting days of Everest were over long ago.

Crash...steel penetrated bubbled overhanging ice. The rucksack on my back pulled. Thin air burned. The steep, chandeliered entrance to the gully pulled the mind's eye.

Crash...ice splintered. I had boasted how light my rucksack was as we started walking, but already it weighed heavy, like the memories. Lungs sucked, wanting more.

Crash...another placement.

Crash...I imagined my axe as a wooden stave breaking bone in the prison.

Crash...one hit is self-defence, the second is assault. Stalking the landing one New Year's Eve, I was convinced at any moment a 15-stone drugged psychopath would break through steel; I held my stave aloft ready to strike.

Crash...kick kick, nose, ice, shoulder, ice, skull, brittle, swing, show no fear...crash.

Safe...

Bracey continued, following a shallow corner until he stood belayed beneath a sheer wall. Icicle draped, the wall surged upwards like a knife driven into the massive blue sky. I revelled in my nomadic life. I had escaped from the Prison Service to space, light, freedom and fresh air. It must be difficult for another to contend with that, knowing I have no ties, knowing I could leave at any time.

'Someone else has taken your place, someone who may live to old age.'

'It should go but it looks hard.'

Bracey's shout floated from his hidden position. This was the crunch pitch, the part of the climb we could not see from the valley. I followed with excitement and anticipation. Was it easy after all? His 'It should go,' sounded good, but I wondered what the Bracey version of 'hard' would entail. He and I had not been on a climb together since I broke my ankle, falling from *Omega* on the Petites Jorasses in 2003. Since then Bracey had honed his skills to become one of the best. We shared a lengthy history, brought together for the first time by our late and close mutual friend Jules Cartwright. Bracey had grown up, once the homeless climbing and skiing bum, now he was living in Chamonix with his girlfriend and working as a mountain guide. I was a climbing hobo, homeless, poor, but rich in experience.

Panting, I peered up. Bracey stood, hidden, belayed in a cave beneath a flowing cascade of icicles. To the left, fluted ice led to a steep, mixed corner. Relieved, I grabbed the gear and pushed on. Squeezing into the back of the corner-crack, pressing down with the palm of a gloved hand, bridging. The corner was vertical and strenuous but my axe picks stuck like chewing gum. The debilitating rucksack had been hung from an ice-screw at the beginning of the corner, to be pulled as Bracey seconded. At least I wasn't aiding. Aid climbing on an alpine-style route really gave me a feeling of not being good enough.

7.　Jon Bracey below the north face of Phari Lapcha, Nepal. (*Nick Bullock*)

Bracey disappeared, traversing right and down-climbing over thin, ice-covered slabs, cunning in his esoteric protection – a thread, a stubby screw and faith. At the foot of a vertical off-width, a hex was persuaded into the crack before venturing into the corner. Fortunately, good hooks, torques and technique helped with upward momentum.

At the top of the snowfield and about to enter the couloir we thought it prudent to consider our options. Floundering and digging a bivvi in the dark, confined and covered with spindrift belching from above did not appeal. An early finish seemed best, even if a feeling of being useless and slacking ran through both our heads. A bucket seat was cut and the long night endured.

'Ten metres left, Jon.'

The rope moved up until there was no more to give.

'Strip the belay and move up, I'm on some pretty steep ground,' called a perturbed voice.

Sick of waiting, we had started to climb early, Bracey entering into the icy-confines of the deep cleft. It was magnificent, a meandering river, iron hard, rippled, vertical. A search for slightly more forgiving ice, with calves and shoulders fatigued with the constant bash and crash, proved fruitless. Swelling finger-joints filled with fluid from the pounding ached like my heart with the memories.

8.   *Snotty's Gully*, Phari Lapcha (Machermo Peak), Nepal. (*Nick Bullock*)
     Nick Bullock and Jon Bracey made the first ascent of the west peak of
     Phari Lapcha via the prominent gully, naming the route *Snotty's Gully*
     (M5 WI5 1000m) in memory of the American Sue Nott who perished
     with Karen McNeill (New Zealand) on Mount Foraker in June 2006.

Left
9.   Jon Bracey
entering *Snotty's Gully*
on day 2. The first pitch
from the bivvi.
(*Nick Bullock*)

10.   Jon Bracey on the last steep pitch of *Snotty's Gully* before the final
        headwall pitch leading to the ridge before the summit. (*Nick Bullock*)

'Someone else has taken your place, someone who may live to old age.'

Shutting my eyes to escape the surroundings for a second, I thought of what could be if only I slowed.

Reaching the end of the gully, deep unconsolidated snow, loose blocks, crumbling rocks, all led to the crest running between Phari Lapcha's main and west summits. The views were spectacular, Everest white and shining, a snow plume reaching high into a cold clear sky. The belay bringing Jon to the ridge was non-existent.

'Good to see you're still alive, when are you next going to try and commit suicide?'

At midday Bracey and I stand on the pointed, rocky west summit trying hard not to overbalance and fall. The release is tremendous, I feel justified. The loss and loneliness is worth this feeling if only for the few minutes it lasts. Anti-climax sets in as we turn.

Acknowledgements: Thanks to DMM, Vasque, Mammut, Patagonia and Lekki and to the MEF and BMC/Sports Council of Britain. Your financial help and assistance is invaluable.

IAN PARNELL

Confounding the Colonel on Kedar Dome

'Where are the rest of your team?' asked the Colonel.

'Er…there are just the two of us,' I hesitatingly replied.

'I see,' said the Colonel in a manner that made it plain that all he saw were two fools lost in the Himalaya. He continued his interrogation.

'How many bolts do you have?'

'Bolts?' I was really confused now.

'The Hungarians used 10 bolts and 95 pegs.' The Colonel was referring to Atilla Ozsvath and Szedbo who in 1989 had been the first team to breach the great east face of Kedar Dome in India's Gangotri region.

'I have their topo here, I think you should look.' The Colonel's finger jabbed triumphantly at the gear list. We'd only brought a couple of pegs and as for a bolt kit, if we'd brought that along we'd be banned from drinking in our local pub for life.

'The Hungarians fixed one thousand metres of rope. How many ropes do you bring?' The Colonel was playing his final ace and he knew it.

'We only have two, we try to climb alpine style,' I tried to explain.

The Colonel nodded his head and smiled as though he'd solved the final question in this puzzle.

'We will return next year to make second ascent of the Hungarian route. We have 14 members in our team. I do not think east face Kedar Dome is possible alpine style. But I wish you good luck.'

The first time I saw a picture of Kedar Dome's east face was in Jan Babicz's neat little guidebook *Peaks & Passes of the Garhwal Himalaya*. The photo was relatively dark and indistinct but there was no doubting the sheer bulk of the granite face rising more than 2000 metres in height. Even more striking, however, was Babicz's comment, 'The massif seems to be most interesting from the side of the Ghanohim glacier above which rises, the only one of this kind, the monolithic east face of Kedar Dome. It probably constitutes the biggest alpine problem in the Gangotri region.'

I knew about the Hungarians Ozsvath and Szedbo's 1989 route, a superb near-free climb up the central spur of the face, and hoped to head out there to attempt my own line. But as the years ticked by I got side-tracked by other mountains. In the meantime the strong Polish trio of Jacek Fluder, Janusz Golab and Stanislav Piecuch added a big-wall style route on the blank right-hand side of the face. Largely serious aid climbing, like the Hungarian, the Polish route ended at the top of the rock difficulties, leaving

11. Tim beneath the giant east face of Kedar Dome. The left-hand line shows their new route up the south-east pillar. The other two lines are 1. Hungarian 1989 and 2. Polish 1999. (*Ian Parnell*)

the 500m corniced ridge untouched to the summit. Finally my chance came when a fellow Brit, Kevin Thaw, invited me to join him on an attempt in the autumn of 2006. Unfortunately, within weeks of the invite, Kevin had to pull out with work commitments.

Every other Himalayan partner I could think of seemed to be booked up when fate stepped in. Visiting my friend Tim Emmett, I began moaning about my lack of partners when Tim piped up that he would like to go. I must admit I was initially taken aback. Tim's alpine climbing resumé amounted to one single route. A solitary one-day ascent in the Alps seemed little preparation for something this big in the Himalaya. But then Tim is no ordinary climber. He seems to be able to excel in whatever vertical discipline he turns his hand to. Onsighting 8a sport climbs, dodging death on E9 gritstone routes, taking deep-water soloing ever and ever higher and floating up mixed and ice routes around the world, little seemed to slow him down. Crucially, rather than these high numbers, Tim's attitude reassured me that he would be a solid partner. If ever there was an Olympic competition for most motivated person, Tim would run away with the gold medal; he's surely the most psyched climber in the world. I knew his positive attitude would be a real benefit, particularly when the going inevitably got tough as it always does on any big climb.

Arriving at Sudoban, our base camp a day's trek beyond Tapovan, it was easy to see why Kedar Dome has been largely overlooked in recent years in favour of the higher profile Gangotri testpieces of Meru's Sharksfin and Thalay Sagar's north face. From this angle Kedar looks little more than an oversized snow dome, in fact its *voie normale*, the west face, is a fairly popular ski descent. A four-hour walk further up the glacier reveals Kedar's split personality. Roughly 2000m high, the east face is the antithesis of its snowy west side. Frankly, it is brutally intimidating and I began to wonder whether the Indian Army colonel might have been right to doubt my alpine-style plans. Surely I should have been here with a large team of Himalayan veterans, not a complete alpine novice? Viewing that great bulk of granite through binoculars, desperately trying to piece together a route from its half cracks, bulging arêtes and smooth walls, it gradually became obvious that Tim's mountain naivety would prove to be a great asset rather than a hindrance. Where I saw gaps in our line Tim saw possibilities and where I could only spot time-consuming aid, he saw exciting freeclimbing challenges. Tim convinced me that our proposed line would go free, although deep down I still harboured doubts. The final section of the central 800m granite wall, in particular, looked overhanging in places and if the crack systems didn't link up, the face was so blank there would be no other options but retreat from 1600m up – a descent which we wouldn't have enough equipment to manage safely.

After one false start, when snow started to fall as soon as our alarm went off at ABC, we finally set out in early evening for the face. The late start was planned, hoping that climbing in the cool of the night would ensure the long initial ice couloir was properly frozen and aiming to minimize any stonefall from the face above. What we hadn't realised, however, was that just getting to the start of the couloir would prove to be one of the crux sections of the climb. Hidden from our previous recce, the first 200m of the climb involved rock so bad you'd hesitate to use it for kitty litter. Loose and rotting scree had to be climbed with a pedalling motion just to stay stationary on this continually moving slag heap. Gear was virtually non-existent, with the hardest section having to be climbed without belays. It was just as well we were climbing at night because if we'd been able to see the full reality of how serious this section was we would have given up there and then.

Things calmed down when we finally accessed the couloir and the icy mush allowed progress closer to 'normal' alpine climbing. Still dawn light was breaking when we finally reached a spot where we could get the tent up. Above the couloir the fun really began. Pure rock climbing on excellent granite led us into the heart of the wall. At first easy, we followed huge flakes 30 or 40 metres long but at times narrowing to only three or four centimetres. Gradually piecing together these features involved more airy friction climbing, padding across blank slabs. As the wall steadily steepened, finding these connections became more of a challenge but moving methodically and patiently we'd always find the missing links. After two days and about 600 metres of ground rarely harder than French 6a, we swung round into the upper bowl of the face. It was here that the face began to show its teeth. Above us the upper wall reared vertical, or in the case of one possibility we'd spied, an arête took on the form of a huge ship's prow, overhanging on all sides. I was beginning to wonder if my trust in Tim's enthusiasm that the line would all work out had perhaps been misplaced when we spotted a solitary weakness to the right. Two slim corners pierced the blankness, seemingly linked by a huge hanging icicle. It looked like it might go. We had no option left but to try as neither of us even wanted to contemplate a descent from this height.

The turning point of that top wall came on pitch 20 as Tim headed up toward a blank corner capped by a huge hanging icicle that wouldn't be out of place on some M route in Cogne. I pondered on whether we could give our Kedar line a grade of M25, the longest hardest mixed climb in the world? We might get away with it, as surely you wouldn't get the mixed boys hobbling in their fancy modern ice boots all the way to this corner of India for the repeat. It's a strange experience belaying on a pitch like this. For the first 20 minutes or so, there's a relief that you're not on the sharp end, and rather than having to face the fear, you can look around, snap away with your camera and soak up 1500 metres of exposure. Then gradually the novelty of your surroundings begins to pale as the circulation to your legs is cut off by the hanging belay. The rope's progress stalls to mere centimetres every other minute while perversely the cold shadows race towards you as the sun dips out of sight.

12.   Day 3. 5600m. Tim following across the perfect granite slabs that characterised the central section of the route. (*Ian Parnell*)

13. Day 4. 5700m. Tim leading against a backdrop of blue skies. Although by afternoon this would be filled with clouds, the weather held throughout our climb. (*Ian Parnell*)

14.   Day 4. 5800m. Tim starting a typical pitch, weaving through ice pitches before heading across blank slabs. (*Ian Parnell*)

15. Day 6. 6250m. Tim following the twin corner which was the only real weakness through the steep blank final wall. (*Ian Parnell*)

In between belay aerobics I often fell into the temptation of cursing Tim. Why was he taking so long? How hard could it be? And why didn't he just grab the gear, cheat and get us out of here? What I didn't know was that Tim was battling his way up what would prove to be the hardest pitch of the climb. Perhaps at the local crag in pleasant sunshine you'd give this pitch French 6c but here with frozen fingers, a rucksack on and fighting for breath at 6150m, it was to quote Tim 'the hardest pitch I'd ever on-sighted'.

The sun had long left the face when I eventually joined Tim at the belay. Groaning under the weight of our 'followers' rucksack, I had at least warmed up a bit. Tim was gradually turning into a human icicle. Up until this point the route had been remarkably kind to us. While all day we'd climb through smooth walls and steep cracks with few ledges even to squat, each evening would find us finishing next to a reasonable snow patch or flat piece of gravel on which we were able to hack out decent tent platforms. This fifth night, however, we weren't to be so lucky. Tim, an open-bivouac virgin, began to panic, wondering out loud about hanging all night in his harness. But with an hour's digging we eventually excavated two scoops about 6m apart. Tim was really earning his Himalayan apprenticeship on this route.

I've heard it argued that due to some unknown law of alpinism, climbers get the pitches they deserve. Our Kedar climb could give credence to that theory. While the day before, Tim, the rock technician, got the beautiful intricate crux, I was left with a series of grovelling corners, made even more entertaining by the increasing quantity of ice that was building up on the rock. To cap it all, not only did I have to slither my way up something perhaps closer to a mixed climb in rock shoes, but with Tim's great lead on the crux, we'd managed the route so far all free without falls; the pressure was on for me to keep up the clean sheet.

Knees have always been important in my climbing. They're something you rarely see mentioned in the text books but I feel are seriously underrated for those crucial moves, the 'emergency udge' and 'the last-second scrabble'. Those last pitches required all the desperation techniques I'd learnt over the years and by the time I'd managed the final jams between ice and rock my knees were cut raw. But somehow I hadn't fallen off and we'd climbed the full 1500m wall free and on-sight.

There was only the 'minor' matter of 500m of corniced ridge left to the summit. It's tempting to dismiss this section of many routes. After all, such snow plodding is technically trivial compared with the rock climbing that had gone before. Both the Hungarians and Poles had reached this point and called it good; 'lowering off at the end of the technical difficulties' seems to be the usual phrase. But the fact that these final metres come at the end of the climb, after all that cumulative effort and fatigue, means that even seemingly easy ground can prove very taxing. Just below the summit, the ridge opened out offering us a quicker option to access our descent down the west flank. I guess this was where the difference between myself as old style mountaineer and Tim as young gun alpinist showed a little as I insisted on dragging my tired partner over a long succession of false summits to finally reach the very top of Kedar Dome. We had been lucky enough to be the first to reach this summit from the east side, the first to climb successfully in pure alpine style and the first to climb all free. I'd love to have met the Colonel on the summit and asked him what he thought?

Summary: An account of the first ascent of the south-east pillar of Kedar Dome (6830m), Garhwal Himalaya, India, 2-8 October 2006.

Acknowledgements: Ian Parnell and Tim Emmett would like to thank the BMC, the Mount Everest Foundation, Arcteryx, Mountain Hardwear and Lyon Equipment for their support which helped make this expedition possible.

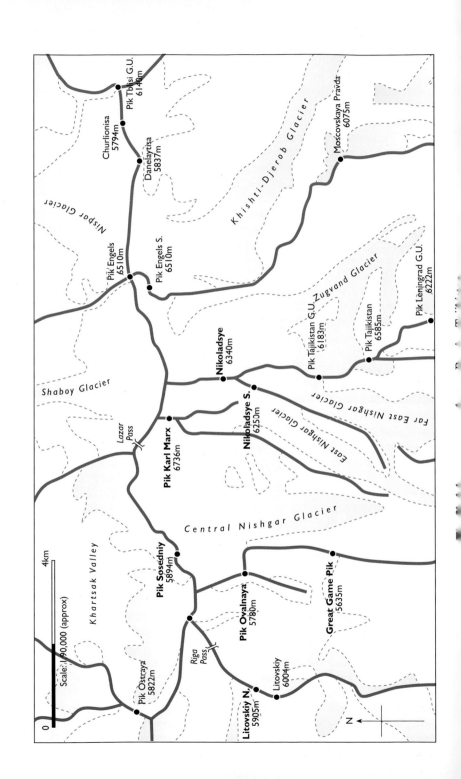

TIM SPARROW

Top Marx in Pamirs for AC climbers

A s my last foray abroad into the Greater Ranges finished with a painful poke between the eyes from a rifle muzzle, along with being relieved of money and gear, I was somewhat apprehensive to read internet reports shortly before leaving that Osama Bin Laden was reputed to be lurking somewhere in the Pamir mountains of Tajikistan. The Tajik government were quick to dispel this as a myth, though wife and family took some convincing, especially as we were to visit the Wakhan valley, along which runs the Afghanistan border. The only barrier to passage was a shallow river. However, the area was politically safe, we were assured, and no problems would be encountered with trigger-happy locals wanting to acquire some Western goods. Thankfully, this proved true.

17. Looking across the Wakhan valley to the Hindu Kush.
(*Tim Sparrow*)

Historically, the valley is very rich, with the remains of ancient castles and vestiges of civilisations covering three millennia. In the late 19th century the Russian Empire pushed south through here in a vain attempt to wrest control of India from the British. The famed meeting of Captain Younghusband with Colonel Yanov at the height of the 'Great Game' took place in this valley, with both convinced they were well within their own country's domains. Owing to the superior Russian numbers, Younghusband retreated gracefully, Yanov apologetically sending him back south with a haunch of venison. Shortly afterwards, the Pamir borders were drawn up, with a narrow finger of Afghan territory following the Wakhan valley, across which the two sides agreed not to venture.

With enticing pictures of rarely visited peaks, Phil Wickens tempted Club members to join him; like the other six members of the trip I was hopelessly ensnared and unable to say 'no'. We were aiming to make first British ascents in the rarely visited Shakdara range of the Pamirs, including Pik Karl Marx (6723m) and Pik Engels (6510m). Karl Marx, formerly known as 'Peak of the Peacemaker Tzar', was first climbed in 1946 via its snowy west face by a Russian team led by Beletski. Pik Engels, formerly 'Queen's Peak', was first climbed in 1954 by a team led by Gvarliani.

The range was very popular with Soviet climbers in the 1960s through to the 1980s. In 1982 the annual Soviet mountaineering championships resulted in many hard, mixed routes on some of the awesome north and east faces. However, the collapse of the Soviet Union and the civil war that ravaged Tajikistan put an end to this activity and the range sank into quiet obscurity until recently. In 2004 a Russian group made a traverse of most of the range and in 2005 a multinational group of western NGOs working in Dushanbe visited the Shaboy valley from the north, hoping to climb both Engels and Marx. Finding the glacier approach extremely hazardous, they nearly reached the summit of Engels by a new route but were unable to access Karl Marx. As no British climbers, and seemingly no non-Soviet climbers, had climbed these mountains we were in an enviable position.

Arriving in Dushanbe's sizzling summer temperatures by the only Tajik Airline plane allowed to fly in Europe gave us our first headache. We had a five-week invitation but could only be granted a four-week visa at the airport. This would curtail later activity. Rick Allen, now resident in Dushanbe, collected us and took us to his Great Game travel company's guesthouse where most of us simply slept and sweated. All our food, except dehydrated hill food, was purchased in the bazaars of Dushanbe. Buying 50 loaves of bread and sealing them in plastic bags was not a good move in the prevailing temperatures.

The two and a half day journey, via Khorog, would be considered one of the great road trips of the world if it were better known and more accessible. The road for the most part followed the gorge of the Panj river, which drains the entire southern half of the Pamirs before its waters evaporate in the Aral Sea. For a whole day we bounced along rough dusty roads, gazing open-mouthed at Afghanistan across the rough, silt-laden river. The contrast between the countries left a deep impression. The Tajik side had a road, electricity and the ability to travel freely; the Afghan side had no electricity and only a narrow donkey track, which spectacularly forced a way through sheer cliffs along suspended walkways above the river.

Having arrived in Iniv, from where our maps indicated a herders' path leading into the Nishgar valley, we hired donkeys or 'Pamir Jeeps' to carry our supplies to Base Camp (excluding 50 loaves of fermenting bread). We sited this in a pleasant grazing meadow at 3800m, below the junction of the branches of the Nishgar valley. First impressions indicated a lot of scree.

18. Base Camp in the Nishgar valley with Pik Karl Marx looming beyond. (*Tim Sparrow*)

19. Piks Karl Marx and Nikoladsye, looking up the East Nishgar glacier. (*Tim Sparrow*)

Exploration of the West Nishgar glacier

Altitude headaches attended our arrival at Base Camp but did not prevent an exploratory visit up the West Nishgar valley where we hoped to acclimatise. Indistinct tracks led over loose, interminable boulders to a gear stash at 4725m from which we returned nursing worsening headaches. Two days later the whole party relocated to scratch a camp out of the boulders before dividing into three groups. From here, some decided on a single carry to a higher camp on the glacier at 5174m, while lesser (or more cunning) mortals opted to do this in two stages.

Heavy overnight snow on 12 August forced a switch of plans, so instead of attempting Ovalnya, Phil, Rick, Derek and Kai set off in mist to explore the Riga Pass. In brightening conditions they reached a small top at 5685m, overlooking the pass, which provided excellent views towards Litovskiy to the south and Karl Marx to the east. An easy descent led back to the camp in deteriorating weather.

Meanwhile Steve, Alex and I came up from the lower camp having climbed high and slept low. With a break in the poor weather, it seemed wise to gain a bit more acclimatisation, so we headed for a rounded peak labelled only as 5635m. Simple snow slopes led to a ridge followed southwards to the summit, graced with a prominent boulder. Having no name, we christened it Great Game Peak. Others proposed a Soviet-style name, 'Peak of the Glorious Committee of the 150th Anniversary of the Alpine Club', but it wouldn't fit on the map. With no record of any ascent or cairn it may have been a first ascent but it seems unlikely.

Poor weather on 14 August sent all but Derek and Kai scurrying back to Base Camp. The pair still harboured the hope of climbing the impressive south-east face of Litovskiy's north summit. Despite overnight wind and snow, it was calm the next day and Derek and Kai set off. Arduous postholing led to moderately angled snow gullies (30°) then upwards through several small rock buttresses to the broader, 70° upper slopes. A leftwards traverse on snow and ice gained the compact, corniced summit at 5905m. The continuing traverse to the higher south summit looked an interesting proposition. The pair abseiled their ascent route and returned exhausted to Base Camp that evening.

Exploration of the Central and East Nishgar valleys

On 16 August, Phil, Rick, Steve, Alex and I headed up the Central Nishgar valley, turning a rocky bluff (nicknamed 'The Beast') which barred access via a slog up steep scree on its west side. Camp was made on a sandy plateau at 4430m. Next day, Phil and Rick headed up the Central Nishgar, heading for the west face of Karl Marx, leaving Steve, Alex and me to find a route up the East Nishgar and the south ridge of Karl Marx. A moraine ridge on the true left bank of the glacier led to a boulder plateau and a crossing of the Far East Nishgar glacier. We found a surprisingly easy route through the ensuing icefall, leading to monotonous slopes and eventually a camp at about 5300m. Next day, easy glacier slopes led to a camp at 5800m below an impressive bluff, at the end of the south ridge of Karl Marx and the junction of two steepening glaciers.

Early starts were not our forte, and we were reluctant to stir before the sun warmed the tent. So it was about 8.30am when we set off to investigate the eastern branch of the glacier, the western branch having fresh sérac debris. We continued our investigations unexpectedly all the way to the summit. Once through the initial icefall, Alex led a plod through a cwm to a wall of steep snow and a col at about 6200m. Claiming fatigue, he handed the lead to Steve who ploughed up the broad east ridge until he too ground to a halt about 250m higher in the soft sugary snow. I took up the baton and ploughed on until I crested a cornice guarding the south ridge. The grind continued up the easy ridge until I too weakened. But by then there was no further to go, the view to the northern Shaboy and Khartsak valleys opened between the snow flurries and we claimed the first British ascent of Pik Karl Marx – disrespectfully ahead of the expedition leader! Descent was by the same route. From near the summit we spotted Phil and Rick as two tiny dots arriving to camp on a col at the top of the west face.

20. Alex Rickards and Steve Hunt at their top camp on the East Nishgar glacier. (*Tim Sparrow*)

Left
21. Alpenglow on the west face of Pik Tajikistan. (*Tim Sparrow*)

After a rest day, Steve, Alex and I reascended the eastern glacier to attempt the peak Nikoladsye. We gained its north ridge by a long ice slope of about 60° in the middle of which my arms and legs decided to stop working, necessitating a switch of lead. When Alex reached the ridge he began squawking excitedly, having been confronted with a near vertical drop of unfathomable proportions on the other side. Steve took over, threading a route through a large letterbox and on up the mixed ridge. Several times he was forced out onto the frighteningly exposed east side to climb short mixed pitches between easier snow gullies on the main ridge. Stances were good; belays were not. The summit (6340m) was several hundred metres away from the ridge top, where a small cairn was found. Descent was by the same route, the ice slope part abseiled, part down-climbed. The route was only a 500m ascent from camp and we had expected to knock it off and be back in time for an early tea. In fact it was nearly dark on our return, the penalty for lazy starts and complacency. Next day down at Base Camp an excessive quantity of Laphroaig was consumed – maybe more than our fair share – in summit celebration.

Phil and Rick's trip
Phil and Rick completed their ascent of the west face of Karl Marx after finding a route into the Central Nishgar valley. The ubiquitous scree led to the glacier snout, which was reached by precarious boulder-hopping. Rows of ice penitents and boulder-topped ice pinnacles lined the route up the relatively flat and safe glacier amid tremendous views of the west faces of Karl Marx and Pik Tajikistan.

A comfortable camp was placed above a small glacial lake, from where they recce'ed the lower west face of Pik Karl Marx before climbing Pik Sosedniy; at 5894m this provided worthwhile acclimatisation. They ascended via a straightforward snow ridge to an enjoyable icy step, followed by a lower summit and, finally, the true summit. This was an excellent vantage point from which to assess the route up the west face of Karl Marx and take in the immense view to the north. Glaciers dropped dramatically below to a sea of brown hills that stretched into the distance. Beyond them, barely discernible against the horizon, lay Pik Revolution and the mountains at the head of the mighty Fedchenko glacier.

From a camp high on the Central Nishgar glacier an unusual pre-dawn start was made up the lower slopes of Karl Marx. Well-frozen snow allowed steady progress across rock-studded slopes towards a small but unstable sérac band. The sun rose, but Phil and Rick remained in the cold shade, working their way up a steep ramp between lines of huge crevasses. Their breathing became harder but persistent plodding took them above the surrounding summits. At two-thirds height their progress was rudely interrupted by a massive crevasse. Stretching the entire width of the face, its only weakness was a very narrow and precarious snow bridge.

Above the crevasse they met the sun and headed across the upper snowfield towards a large flattening where the west face met the west ridge. As the pair made camp, three tiny dots appeared on a snowy ridge far above them. Hunt, Rickards and Sparrow! Antlike, they reached the summit rocks of Karl Marx, faint flashes of their cameras piercing the intermittent cloud that swirled around them.

The following morning Phil and Rick awoke to dense cloud. However, as the morning progressed, several brief clearings exposed sections of ridge above, so using compass bearings they headed up until eventually they sat on a pile of scree below a steep and overhanging mass of rock. The summit was little more than a rope length above, requiring a delicate traverse on steep snow and ice-covered scree. The wind and snow started up for added effect. Retreat to the flat scree was inviting but one more delicate pitch allowed them to reach the snowy south ridge and within minutes they stood on the top of Karl Marx. It stopped snowing and, for a brief moment, the clouds parted, revealing blue sky, dirty glaciers below and, southwards, a faint line of footprints disappearing down the ridge.

An earlier radio conversation with the other three had suggested it would be easy to traverse the mountain, using the southern approach for descent. Their route description proved invaluable in locating the correct route in the whiteout. A brief clearing revealed the 6200m col far below, so with a fresh compass bearing they dropped out of the cloud. The remainder of the descent, involving the traverse of an unknown icefall, was hard work owing to a heavy layer of fresh snow.

To the west of the Central Nishgar glacier lies Ovalnaya, its beautiful east face rising above the lake camp used earlier. Returning to this valley to collect some stashed food and equipment, Phil and Rick set off the following morning up Ovalnaya's increasingly steep slopes towards the serrated north ridge. This gave a fantastic route, exposed and with numerous short pitches of solid water ice, ending abruptly on the short summit plateau. In descent they followed the ridge in its entirety, weaving around rocky gendarmes to reach the northern secondary summit, and then down steep slopes towards camp.

Derek and Kai's trip

On 17 August, after a day's rest at Base Camp, during which Kai made repeated attempts to repair his punctured Thermarest, Derek and Kai followed the others into the Central Nishgar valley. Usuf, our Pamiri Base Camp manager, had previously ferried tent and rope up The Beast to the sandy camp used by the others. The views to the Hindu Kush in the south and to Karl Marx in the north were impressive. Next day, in glorious sunshine, they continued up the rocky moraine leading to the glacier snout, and on to a snowy plateau at 5215m under the rocky south face of Sosedniy and looking across to Karl Marx's vast western glacier.

Continuing north the following day, they traversed just below the Lazar Pass in the hope of attempting Karl Marx from the north-west. Dangerous

22.   West flank of Pik Karl Marx. (*Derek Buckle*)

3.   Kai Green crossing a snow bridge on the west face of Pik Karl Marx.
(*Derek Buckle*)

séracs on this face prompted a rapid reassessment and alternative thoughts of the west ridge. A snow ramp afforded relatively easy access to the steep (60°) ridge, which was climbed to prominent rocks at 5840m. With no ground suitable for a tent, two narrow bivvi platforms were cut, Sosedniy and Ovalnaya providing a dramatic backdrop. As the night chilled, Kai was again carrying out emergency repairs to his Thermarest after an argument with a ski pole created a substantial tear. His partner, on his Karrimat, was unsympathetic.

With poor weather at dawn, the appeal of continuing on Karl Marx waned. A better alternative presented itself. Early on 20 August, Derek and Kai down-climbed to the east ridge of Sosedniy which provided an easy ascent over snow and scree to a summit cairn at 5928m. Descending by the same route they traversed the upper glacier to camp beneath the west face of Karl Marx at 5586m. More Thermarest repairs were necessary before adjourning. Full marks for persistence, if not for efficiency.

Having seen Phil and Rick climb the west face earlier, Derek and Kai decided to follow suit, tracing an essentially similar route up the steep, heavily crevassed glacier and over the massive bergschrund at three-quarter height by the precarious snow bridge from which another rising traverse to the left gave access to the windswept col where camp was established at a height of 6388m.

After a cold, blustery night, morning was little better with poor visibility and light snow and wind. Conditions were uncomfortable but not impossible, so they continued, hoping that they would be able to follow their upward tracks on the return. Being unable to see the vast drop below made the final delicate pitches less nerve-racking but it was nevertheless a relief to reach the summit at 6736m, even though there was no view. Returning the same way the wind had removed their tracks so it was with some relief that they saw the tent appearing out of the gloom. Next day, in fortunately clear weather, they descended their route of ascent. Back on the glacier, camp was made below Ovalnaya at 5361m where they met up with Rick and Phil. This was their only contact with others above Base Camp. Truly empty mountains.

From this camp the east face of Ovalnaya looked inviting, Phil and Rick having expounded its virtues. With excellent weather on 24 August there could be no excuses. Phil and Rick returned to Base Camp while Derek and Kai set off early and repeated the east face route.

The Far East Nishgar glacier

Tim, Steve and Alex, having cunningly manoeuvred to be in front for Karl Marx, found time for a final foray. Reascending The Beast, we camped at the boulder plateau at 4800m and next day continued on scree, 'up the down escalator', alongside the steep icefall of the Far East Nishgar glacier. From below, it seemed that Pik Tajikistan (6585m) would be possible up

24. Alex Rickards and Steve Hunt camping below the Far East Nishgar glacier. (*Tim Sparrow*)

25. Alex Rickards and Steve Hunt descending the south ridge of Nikoladsye South. (*Tim Sparrow*)

easy snow, but the reality of a major wall was hidden from view. We camped on a plateau beneath this and reflected through the evening, as we watched thunderstorms beyond the Hindu Kush in Pakistan, that the only outside evidence we had seen of the human race for three weeks were the satellites overhead.

Next morning, we ascended a small icefall and followed the true left side of the glacier to an attractive peak of about 6250m, to the south of Nikoladsye, which we called, unsurprisingly, Nikoladsye South. Near the summit we exhumed a cairn to find a wrapped chocolate bar and a note which indicated that the peak had been visited in 1958 by a team of Soviet climbers. We added our own names, left some sweets, but eschewed the 48-year-old chocolate. The marble of the south ridge was so soft we kept crampons on. Back in base camp next day, with the donkeys due that evening, the legendary cooking of Chef Wickens produced a feast out of scraps.

The return to Dushanbe was not without incident, involving collapsing donkeys, punctures and breakdowns, all part of the game for our drivers, it seemed. Due to visa extension problems, we had a few days to spare in Dushanbe so we escaped the heat to the Fann mountains just to the north. However, instead of some potentially exciting rock climbing on a recommended peak, we were duped into fitting a three-day trip into two. This allowed only an unpleasant slog up a scree couloir to a col, only to find that we had no time to summit, just time to hurtle straight back down the couloir and race back to the road to meet our lift back to town. Still, it was a beautiful valley and the hospitality of a local shepherd was memorable.

The Shakdara mountains of the Pamir left a deep impression on us all. Wild and empty, the southern valleys offer ample opportunity for middle grade exploratory mountaineering in a remote setting. The Tajik people and those of the Wakhan in particular were hospitable and welcoming and the Wakhi are privileged to live in such a dramatic valley. As Phil commented on leaving the enclosed valleys of the high mountains and seeing once more the vastness of the Wakhan: 'I do love the mountains, but I think I like the spaces between them even more.'

Summary: An account of the Alpine Club expedition to the Shakdara range, south-west Pamirs, Tajikistan, in August 2006, led by Phil Wickens. Four glacier valleys were explored and successful ascents made of seven mountains, all first British ascents.

From the West Nishgar valley, **Litovskiy North** (5905m) was climbed by Derek Buckle and Kai Green. **Great Game Peak** (5635m) was climbed by Tim Sparrow, Steve Hunt and Alex Rickards. From the Central Nishgar valley, **Pik Karl Marx** (6736m, GPS reading), **Pik Ovalnaya** (5780m) and **Pik Sosedniy** (5894m) were climbed by Buckle, Green, Phil Wickens and Rick Allen. From the East Nishgar valley, **Karl Marx** and **Nikoladsye** (6340m) were climbed by Sparrow, Hunt and Rickards. The same trio also climbed **Nikoladsye South** (6250m) from the Far East Nishgar valley.

26.   On the summit of Pik Karl Marx. *From left clockwise*: Alex Rickards,
      Steve Hunt and Tim Sparrow. (*Tim Sparrow*)

ACKNOWLEDGEMENTS

The expedition members would like to express their gratitude to the British Mountaineering Council, the Mount Everest Foundation, and also to the Alpine Climbing Fund (sponsored by First Ascent) for financial assistance.

MALCOLM BASS

Haizi Shan -
A lot to be grateful for

It was late evening as we turned off the metalled road onto a bumpy, rutted track. All through the afternoon we had been travelling across the high, rolling, Tagong grasslands, their ochre colours accentuated by warm autumnal light. As the afternoon had turned to evening the grasslands had given way to larch and birch forests, and now we were following a winding river valley up through patches of trees interspersed with grassy meadows. The jeep was comfortable, our driver appeared quite sane, and we were neither exhausted, famished, nor prostrate in the heat. All in all it really didn't feel much like a 'Greater Ranges' trip.

There was some weak evidence that we were engaged in something that might interest the readers of this journal. I had a fairly severe gastric complaint, always suggestive of impending glacial terrain, and we had actually spotted a snowy mountain. Indeed we had spotted our intended mountain, Haizi Shan, standing in splendid isolation over the rolling dun hills. But that had been many miles and many hours ago and since then it felt like we'd been driving away from the mountain. More definitive and up to date proof was required.

Then suddenly, as the road swung round, away from a low larch covered ridge, there it was; the long, north flank of Haizi Shan, hovering ethereally above the darkening valley. It seemed to be glowing, catching the last of the sun in that strange way north faces do, so that all its spurs and ribs and séracs stood out.

Pat Deavoll and I had decided, from the comfort of our respective New Zealand and North Yorkshire homes, that we would attempt a direct line up the north face. Haizi Shan had been attempted many times; mostly it seemed by the long, undulating north-east ridge over the north summit. In 2004 an Alpine Club team had made a strong attempt on this line, with Geoff Cohen and Dick Isherwood reaching about 5800m before turning back late in the day with about five pitches of corniced ridge between them and the summit. Another strong attempt was made in 2005 on the steep, rocky, west-south-west ridge by John Otto, Chen Cheng, Su Rongqin, and Ma Yihua. They reached about 5600m during five days of snowed-up rock climbing bedevilled by constant wind. Bad weather was reported to have been a feature of many of the previous trips: Haizi Shan is an isolated peak and sits in the Daxue Shan range at the very eastern edge of the

Himalaya, making it rather a weather magnet. A direct, and hopefully short, line had seemed worth trying as an alternative to the time consuming north-east ridge. But now we were here beneath the mountain it looked imposingly steep.

27. The north face of Haizi Shan. (*Malcolm Bass*)

Life at base camp was idyllic. The weather was good; Lenny (Chen Zheng Lin), cooked superb Sichuan food, and the woods around camp were full of colours, berries and flowers. A small river ran nearby, reportedly containing fish, but while there were good hatches of aquatic flies, I wasn't able to elicit any reaction to my limited range of trout flies. Local people from semi nomadic yak herding families visited us most days; and on one day so did armed police, bandits having stolen six yaks from a local family at gunpoint. A base camp with trees? Berries? Fishing? People? What kind of expedition was this turning into?

Over the next eight days we found a way up from the base camp valley (the Tai Zhan valley) to the basin beneath the north face, and spent a few days below the face (at around 4500m) acclimatising and face watching. The route up into the basin followed a 400m-snow gully through the steep lower cliffs. This route was rather fraught as it drained the whole basin and the north face above. We narrowly escaped obliteration when a sérac fell on the north face 10 minutes after we'd descended the gully. A bit of random death potential tipped the scales back in favour of this being proper

28. The last pitch before the west ridge. (*Malcolm Bass*)

Left
29. Pat Deavoll on
the west ridge.
(*Malcolm Bass*)

expeditionary alpinism, but the good news was that from the upper basin the angle of the face looked more amenable, and we could trace an objectively safe line. We dropped back to the Tai Zhan valley for a bath in the hot springs then returned to base camp for a brief rest before our attempt. The night before we were due to go back up it snowed, the only really bad weather of the trip. It kept on snowing throughout the next day, but then obligingly stopped. We allowed a day for the face to clear, then went back up into the basin and camped about 200m below the face.

The most prominent feature on the north face is an arête or nose dropping from just west of the main summit. Gully systems drop to the foot of the face from either side of this nose. We decided that we'd climb a rib between these two gullies, then drop into the right-hand gully and follow it to the west ridge near the summit. On the next day we climbed 800m onto and then up the rib as planned. Snow conditions varied from firm to knee deep. The climbing was straightforward, we took turns breaking trail and didn't rope up. There was a shallow couloir on the rib and we mostly stayed in this, finding snow conditions better here. At 5200m we moved back onto the rib proper and hacked out a tent platform. This was a fine, safe bivvi site, with a good view over the more sérac threatened face to the east. The early part of the evening was worrying as thunderstorms played over the surrounding lower hills, and the odd shower of graupel blew in on gusty winds, but the weather passed around and below us, and the night was quiet. With just over 600m to go the next day we left the tent pitched and set off into the darkness with light sacks. We made a rising traverse into the right-hand couloir, which we reached as the light came. Snow conditions in the couloir were good, and again we were able to climb unroped, until we encountered loose snow over granite slabs at about 5500m. We roped up here as it got a bit scratchy, and climbed two belayed pitches. The best of these was a fine groove in the gully wall that skirted some particularly blank slabs in the gully bed at about Scottish IV. We stopped belaying above here and trailed the ropes, leaving the gully and moving left above the nose. The cornice at the top of the face took a while to break through, and I asked Pat for a body belay as I became convinced that having surmounted it I'd fall straight down the south face. The views from the west ridge were superb, all the better for being seen intermittently through veils of cloud. The ridge was corniced and spectacular, dropping steeply for over 1000m on either side; we stayed roped up and focused.

Pat reached the summit as Haizi was having a Scottish moment, enveloped in thick cloud so we'd had no idea that we were nearly there. As I followed her up the final step the clouds cleared, and we were treated to a glorious vista of mountains and endless rolling grasslands. The final section of the north-east ridge looked like a corniced roller coaster track, and we were glad to be returning the way we had come.

From our hole in the cornice we abseiled a few rope lengths on ice threads and nuts down the upper half of the couloir. The warm autumnal light, the

30. The west ridge of Haizi Shan from the top of the north face route. (*Malcolm Bass*)

31. Malcolm Bass on the west ridge approaching the summit. (*Pat Deavoll*)

leitmotif of the trip, bathed the basin below the face as the couloir sank into darkness. We climbed steadily down towards the glow.

It was fully dark by the time we reached the tent. We bundled inside, fired up the stove for the first of an endless round of brews, and scratted through our pockets and rucksacks for the remaining few edibles. We talked of our gratitude, for the weather, for the line, for the snow conditions, for Lenny and An Ping down at base camp, and for each other's contribution to our partnership. Unknown to us, more memorable moments were yet to come: a superb day spent descending to base camp, the party reunited, Great Wall red wine and mournful Tibetan songs of longing around the fire, the lake of prayer flags. But that night, with the summit, safety, and sleep, we had all we needed.

Summary: The first ascent of Haizi Shan (in Tibetan, Yala or Zhara), 5833m, Daxue Shan range, Western Sichuan. Malcolm Bass and Pat Deavoll via the 1100m north face (IV,3 in Damilano system). October 2007.

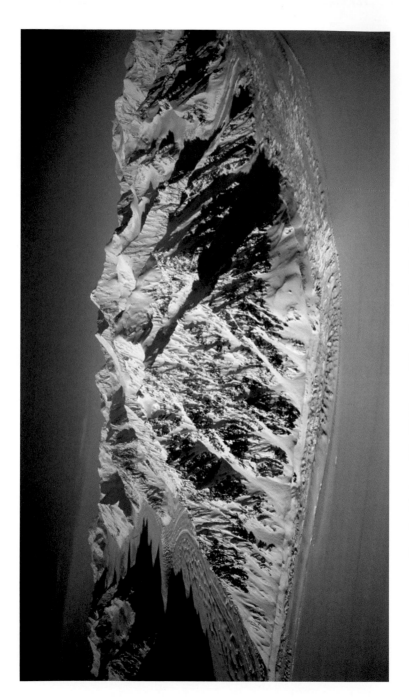

32.   Aerial view of the Walsh massif from the south. (*Graham Rowbotham*)

PAUL KNOTT

The Ascent of South Walsh

On 28 May 2006 Graham Rowbotham and I reached the pointed summit of South Walsh (4223m). This was the highest unclimbed peak both in the St Elias range and, it has been claimed, in North America.

As so often happens in the mountains, the clarity of our objective was matched by the uncertainty of the endeavour. We arrived at the 70km-long Kluane Lake to find it completely frozen over. Above it a thick layer of cloud obscured the mountains. Until the weather changed, we were stuck at the rutted gravel airstrip. There was a sombre mood among the 15 climbers already waiting to fly in, all to Mt Logan. They began to give up, and when the weather cleared four days later we were practically at the front of the queue.

In fact, we flew first. Our pilot Andy Williams dropped us on the upper Donjek glacier directly opposite the striking pointed summit of South Walsh. We stood admiring the imposing faces and ridges of the massif, up to 1650m above us. We quickly wrote off the idea of attempting a face route as there was a generous plastering of fresh snow. Our best hope of climbing South Walsh looked to be the south-west ridge, but even this was blocked in its upper part by rimed-up rock towers and huge cornices. Early next morning the sluggish display on my watch read –19°C in the tent wall. This set the pattern for the rest of the trip, with most nights being only marginally warmer – possibly reflecting the prevailing La Niña.

We acclimatised by making the first ascent of the c3745m snow summit 'Jekden South' west of our base camp. Looking across at South Walsh we convinced ourselves we could see at least one climbable line, making use of the upper south face. Rather than reverse the route, we also decided to traverse over Mt Walsh (4507m). This would be committing, involving around 8km of potentially unfriendly high-altitude ridge, but would bag us the first traverse of the mountain and take us to a known descent.

Early on 20 May my efforts at starting the stove were rewarded by flames in the tent porch (the worn o-rings had failed in the cold). Subsequently we faced the bitter morning wind without the aid of a decent cup of tea. At the base of the ridge we stashed our snowshoes, hoping that wind-crust would render them unnecessary on the high traverse. On the lower ridge was a series of rock towers which we quickly discovered were composed of a shattered quartz-veined limestone. We turned them, using the equally rotten snow on either side. Beyond the towers, a protracted snow-wade took us to a fine campsite with a view of the upper face.

33. *Left:*
The west face of
South Walsh.
(*Paul Knott*)

34. Base camp and the Walsh massif. (*Paul Knott*)

The night was accompanied by the familiar sound of wind-blown snow hitting the tent, and although a morning lull tempted us to continue we faced strengthening wind as we traversed the steeper cornices above the camp. We paused at a broader section, listening to a frightening wind roar over the main plateau accompanied by a flying saucer of wave cloud. Fearful of being blown off the summit ridge, we pitched the tent to await developments. This took much digging in before we felt secure. Heavy snow during the night sealed our fate, and we painstakingly retraced our filled-in steps.

This aborted attempt was followed by five days of classic St Elias festering. The tent became sauna-like as the sun beat on its faded flysheet, yet the cold northerly wind blew drifts of snow into the porch. Ominous cloud billowed at the Walsh-Steele col and lenticulars formed over Mt Walsh. Inside the tent, I remember indulging shamelessly on pancakes and maple syrup in between chapters of Shackleton's *South*. The wind finally dropped and the storm clouds began to dissipate late on 26 May.

Lured by the continuing calm, at 3am we set off. Three hours later we almost turned back as we reassessed the greyness of the clouds and the direction of the wind. By the time we reached our first camp there was a more ominous thickening of the cloud, obscuring the sun and flattening the light. It was exasperating, but not surprising, when there followed more snowfall and a significant drop in pressure. We could not cook or melt snow as spindrift would pour in through the slightest gap in the tent door. Still, the deprivation seemed unimportant as we would probably be descending.

To our surprise, the morning dawned clear. We made double brews, cleared the ice from our gear and continued up the steepening ridge. As we reached our previous high point the weather still held, so we continued up the snow arête on the basis that we may as well reconnoitre the route. Some time later we moved onto the south face to get around the rime-encrusted rock towers above, and our reconnoitre finally turned into a climb.

On the face we relied on a thin covering of sugary snow over the rotten rock. There were no belays of any kind and not even a body-weight placement for a pick, shaft, or stake. Our only security was the compressed snow beneath our feet. In our search for a viable route we moved progressively further onto the face. We began with a descending traverse, having failed to cross a buttress due to thin snow. Above a line of towers we moved right again for deeper snow and ascended towards a twisting exit couloir. Unable to reach this, we traversed right once more over a snow-covered buttress. When yet again our ascent was blocked, we continued the traverse until we were below a huge triangular cornice.

The afternoon sun now shone directly onto the face. Luckily, the low temperature protected the snow from its effects. This was fortunate since the final slopes below the cornice were steeper and consisted of unstable deposits from the swirling wind. The climbing became insecure. It was too

35.   Graham Rowbotham traversing into the couloir on the south face. (*Paul Knott*)

steep to rely on pushing down and I struggled to find axe placements I could pull on. I kicked footholds well into the hollow slope, but this meant my upper body was pushed out by the snow above. I cut a vertical trench, ignoring the numerous exclamations from below, and headed directly for the cornice, thinking there was a ledge below it. After many delicate moves, it was with great relief that I pulled onto the ledge and found solid ice. I sank two fat ice screws and soon we were enjoying this haven under the giant cornice. In all we had spent five hours on the face. Lured by the summit, we eschewed our new shelter and made the short traverse to the summit ridge.

36. On the corniced section of the south-west ridge with the
upper south face behind. (*Paul Knott*)

37. Passing towers on the south face. (*Paul Knott*)

38.   Graham Rowbotham on the summit of South Walsh with
Mt Lucania in the haze behind. (*Paul Knott*)

Buffeted by a gale on the summit, we descended to the plateau connecting the massif. Crossing the plateau was an excruciating wade through deep snow. Finding no relief from what had become a relentless maelstrom, we wearily dug in the tent and collapsed inside. There we stayed, listening in horror to the waves of snow spraying against the fabric. Again the deluge prevented us from using the stove. I felt a distinct sense of exposure and commitment.

During the night we found our already cramped tent compressed by a foot of deposited snow. The snow also iced up the stove pump. Feeling drained, we continued our traverse, over (unclimbed) Pt 4227m and along towards the main summit of Mt Walsh. Fortunately, it was firm underfoot as the snow had been blown off the ridge. Below the final slopes we took advantage of a sheltered, sunny bivvi-schrund to revive the stove and hence our dehydrated bodies. The summit vista was unusually hazy due to the snow and dust blown by the high winds. After the obligatory photos we headed down the long west ridge – the route of the 1941 first ascent and by no means a walk. Late in the afternoon we descended into a sheltered bowl, where the benevolent evening sun provided much-needed relief.

In the morning, as we ploughed through deep snow in the heavily crevassed bowl, I was conscious that we had by no means completed our adventure. Despite careful route-finding, we had a couple of close calls with hollow snow-bridges and were happy to reach the relative safety of the Walsh-Steele col. This still left us with what could have been a post-holing nightmare to reach our snowshoes by South Walsh. Again, our worst fears were not realised as there was a reasonable wind-crust on the glacier.

When Andy came to pick us up, his neighbour Donjek Upton was at the controls. We learned that, in the stormy weather, we had so far been the only team to reach a summit. As we drove south the next day, I observed with pleasure the advancing spring and the strengthening sun.

Summary: Paul Knott and Graham Rowbotham made the first ascent of South Walsh (4223m) in the St Elias range, Alaska, 27-30 May 2006, and the first full traverse of Mt Walsh (4507m).

Acknowledgements: Support for this trip is gratefully acknowledged from the British Mountaineering Council and UK Sport.

DAVE WYNNE-JONES

Celestial Touring

Ski-mountaineering in the Tien Shan

The Tien Shan mountains of Kyrgyzstan sweep west in an arc from their highest peaks, Khan Tengri and Pobeda, along the border with China. Lying to the south of Lake Ysyk-kol is the Ak-Shirak range, identified as a potential ski-mountaineering area as long ago as 1998 by Chris Watkins, an Eagle Ski Club member. In April 2003, I was part of an ESC expedition that attempted to traverse the range but access to the Kara-Say valley by road proved impossible owing to avalanches that had blocked the 4000m Suek pass. The expedition then turned to explore the western flanks of the range from the north, eventually reaching the Kara-Say valley via the Ak-Bel pass but without any hope of penetrating the range further than the snout of the Kara-Say glacier. However, the feasibility of traversing the range by that approach and the potential for ski-mountaineering were confirmed.

In 2006 I led a team of AC and ESC members on another attempt, this time in May so that the Suek pass would be passable: it was, just. Unfortunately the driver then managed to get our vehicle well and truly stuck in thawing ice at a river crossing below the pass. The five-hour delay meant that we were dropped off at 9pm at the Kara-Say river bridge instead of an expected 10-15km up the valley. In pitch darkness we were in no position to argue.

By daylight the level gravels of the river flood plain stretched far away from us to where distant peaks shone whitely. Skis and sledges lay forlorn by the roadside. The drivers had assured us that no vehicle track led up the Kara-Say valley. We were looking at one now. There was no option but to break camp and follow it.

Headaches brought on by a height gain of 2000m in 12 hours of driving were compounded by the need to make double carries of all our kit. The patient and strong, led by Lizzy Hawker, preferred it on their backs, whilst the rest of us towed lightly loaded pulks along one or the other of twin gravel tyre tracks. The first day ended at a roaring tributary torrent, only crossable barefoot when the night freeze had reduced the flow next morning: an absolutely perishing triple wade! The next day we lunched by a derelict building, evidence of another abandoned Soviet enterprise, and recognized by Mike from his 2003 sortie. By evening we were camped on a level shelf above frozen river ice that would finally support our weight and was not under water.

39. Kara-Say valley. Anna Seale crosses the meltwater torrent on the ebb.
     (*Mike Sharp*)

The towed pulks had already sustained some runner damage but as we slid out onto snow-dusted ice our spirits rose, at first. The ice was at least a metre thick in places but elsewhere gravel banks had reduced its depth to nothing at all. The river could drain through this gravel so there were stretches where fingers of ice reached into gravel shallows, then disappeared in the glacial outwash. Depending upon the size of these stony wastes, either we carried skis and rucksacks over them, then came back in pairs to carry loaded pulks, or repacked for yet another double-carry. It was tough going.

During the second day on the river our way was blocked by a steep moraine ridge across which we had to carry the pulks to reach a series of frozen glacial lakes linked by meltwater and ice channels. With only two incidents of ice collapse and some impromptu ski-wading, we reached the snout of the Kara-Say glacier and camped high and dry on a moraine bank. This must have been somewhere near the camp made by John Turk in July 2000.

40. Camp Day 3 in the stony waste of the river valley nearing the junction of two glacial valleys ahead. (*John Goodwin*)

41. Heading up the left fork to the Kara-Say glacier. (*Mike Sharp*)

The glacier ahead looked complex so we decided to carry half loads on a scouting mission. It was overcast as we set out and the flat light meant that we stumbled on the brink of taking 5-10m falls off unseen edges of ice cliffs. There were several false trails and it was a slow business finding a way through. Finally we reached about 4200m and cached our loads. A correlation of map and GPS data revealed that the glacier had retreated 2km since 1972 so spot heights and contours were going to be dubious owing to volume shrinkage. Skiing back to camp in improving visibility allowed us to straighten out our route and place wands at waypoints.

The evocative name of the Mer de Glace resonates with all who ski it, but this sea of ice had more and bigger waves than any of us had seen anywhere from Alaska to Antarctica. Navigating successfully to a high camp, we found ourselves above the waves on a shelving glacier giving access to the peaks to the north. At 4200m, this 'climbing camp' lay on the flank of an icefall sheltered in the crook of a ridge coming down from Kyrgyzia. At 4954m, Kyrgyzia is the highest peak in the north-west half of the range and its ascent was one of our main objectives.

Two days passed making a first ascent of Pik Chasovoi 4765m (Sentinel) in near whiteout conditions, then scouting the route to Kyrgyzia Pass in a bitter wind that was tearing huge streamers of spindrift off the summit ridges. The south-west face of Kyrgyzia looked to be as climbable as I had judged it to be on seeing it from a distant peak in 2003. Our ski descent to camp was so good that Alastair Cairns and I went back up to ski a steep line between séracs and the bounding rock wall of the ridge.

That night temperatures dropped to -18° in the tents and next morning we reclimbed the route to the pass under a hard blue sky. We skinned into a snow bay between the west ridge and the south spur of Kyrgyzia, then up the flank of the south spur. Emerging onto the spur it still looked skinnable but a warning 'whump' vibrated under my skis giving notice that the snow was not as stable as it appeared. Leaving our skis, we cramponed directly up the spur to the corniced summit. GPS readings gave the height as 4954m and there were panoramic views of the rest of the range. Carefully descending the summit slopes, we skied one by one exactly down the track back to the snow bowl, then enjoyed another lovely ski back to camp.

Alastair's precious drams of whisky went straight to our heads via stomachs that were only too used to short rations, our celebratory laughter complementing those moments of stillness, savouring the privilege of this empty snowscape. There was something hugely satisfying about being the only people in these mountains, climbing peaks no-one had climbed before, skiing slopes no-one had skied before, with good snow, magnificent alpine scenery and acres of unclimbed peaks still to harvest.

Next day, following the route we'd taken to Pik Chasovoi, we continued north towards its further neighbour, climbing up onto a broad ridge that became a glacier shelf dropping from the east face of our chosen peak.

There was a broad col at the base of the corniced north-east ridge that fell precipitously away to the north-west, but between the north-east and a north-north-east ridge rose a narrow face. Steep and icy enough for harscheisen, it was nonetheless skinnable until the two ridges drew together and there was no longer room to zigzag. Most of the party had left skis at the col, choosing to follow the north-east ridge on foot to the right of the cornice break line, the whole team being reunited at the point where the ridges joined. Avoiding the cornice, we were forced to crampon onto the upper edge of the steep and exposed north face to reach an airy summit. Pik Karga (4831m) was named after the ravens that shadowed our ascent.

Having skied from the col down the broad ridge and with time in hand, we were tempted by a handsome summit to the east that we christened Point Anna after one of the team. A straightforward climb up snow slopes took us to the bergschrund, where we left our skis and above which a short ice slope led to a pointed rocky top at 4658m. It provided a superb viewpoint high above the main glacier that continued deeply convoluted, a dunescape of snow. We retraced our line of ascent back to camp, enjoying some better skiing than our formation snowplough effort on the descent from Chasavoi. It had been a fine day.

With uninspiring weather, we broke camp next morning and moved to the head of our exit pass at 4500m. The skies cleared by midday and the latter part of the journey was so baking hot that we had little appetite for doing more than get the tents up when we arrived, though the view beyond the pass was absolutely stunning.

The glacier bay to the west of the pass gave access to two more peaks. Next day, skirting the steep north face of 'Pt 4865.9', with its tottering séracs, we gained the col between the two peaks and Derek Buckle found a good line up its steepening north ridge. On the way we were surprised to find tracks that could only have been those of a hare. It seemed to have traversed from one ridge to the other without quite taking in the 4876m summit. It had to be Hare Peak or Pik Koyon in Kyrgyz. Returning to the col, I led off up the south ridge of the other peak that rose in a series of ice bowls to a fine narrow summit ridge. Hunched brooding above the opencast goldmine far below, and given that we were ESC members, it was named Eagles Peak. An occasional faint boom was accompanied by a puff of yellow smoke from the mine workings, the blasting reminding us of another world shaping the landscape far below.

Next day, our final summit lay east of the camp. It was climbed in flurries of snow, first to an easy snow dome, then when it looked as though a nearby rock pinnacle could be higher, out along a mixed ridge to that summit. Derek led the way, scrambling along granite blocks to a kind of turret with twin cannons pointing at the sky. We took turns bridging up between these rocks to a precarious summit. A wrangling banter developed between Derek and Alastair over which top was highest, so I diplomatically christened it Snow Cannon 4720m (at both summits!).

42.   Lizzy Hawker gaining the summit of Pik Karga. (*John Goodwin*)

43.   Dave Wynne-Jones on the summit of Pik Koyon. Behind are Pik Kyrgyzia
      (*left*) and Pik Karga (*right*). (*Mike Sharp*)

We had now been on the traverse for 15 days and it was time to ski out. The unknown glacier system over the pass proved kind to us in providing an easy descent for laden pulks as we glided through stunning scenery to reach the Petrov glacier. Encountering isothermic snow, we roped up, stepping and poling out of trouble to a lunch stop on a medial moraine.

We continued on crusty ice running with meltwater streamlets to the steepening snout of the Petrov glacier. There we were fortunate to find a long ramp that led to just a 2-3 metre near-vertical step down to the snowy banks of a glacial stream. Passing down rucksacks and lowering pulks from an ice screw, the team worked like a well-oiled machine as we climbed down in crampons to gain the moraine. The stream bed led to a beach of fine outwash on the shores of Lake Petrov where we camped. We reckoned we could make it to the transport rendezvous next day so used the satellite 'phone to call in Top-Asia a day early. Our journey was nearly over.

But there was a sting in its tail.

The lake ice would not bear our weight so we were forced to strap skis to our rucksacks and drag our pulks along increasingly chaotic moraine banks. It was a nightmarish effort. When we reached the pumping station, the Kyrgyz workers were impressed enough with our travail to supply us with strong sweet tea.

The Kumtor goldmine ensures that there is good access to this side of the range but dragging the pulks along gravel roads soon removed what was left of the runners. Fortunately Mike Sharp was offered a lift by a passing truck. He managed to contact the mine security force and had no trouble persuading them to escort us off-site in their vehicles. We must have looked pretty wasted as they also donated a pile of sandwich rolls: all meat, to the disgust of the veggies! After a final night camping at the ruined Meteorological Station rendezvous we were picked up by a delighted Rimma, our liaison person, in a 4WD truck.

Safely back in Bishkek despite a clutch breakdown, we sampled the luxury of our modern hotel's swimming pool in temperatures of more than 30° and, like true monomaniacs, spent our contingency day exploring some of the Kyrgyz range with a visit to the Ala Archa gorge.

On returning to the world of mass communications I was hit by a hammer blow, learning of the death of a good friend, Tomas Olsson, whose abseil anchors had failed during an attempt to ski the Norton Couloir on Everest. I think he and I had both had misgivings about the commercial pressures surrounding his attempt, and it is thanks to financial support from the ESC, MEF and BMC that this expedition did not suffer from such pressures.

My thanks also to Derek Buckle, Alastair Cairns, John Goodwin, Lizzy Hawker, Anna Seale and Mike Sharp, for all the fun, good company, and teamwork: an interesting mix of age, experience and youthful enthusiasm.

Summary: A traverse of the Ak-Shirak range from south to north with first ascents of seven peaks exceeding 4600m. 29 April to 21 May 2006.

OSAMU TANABE

Lhotse South Face Winter Ascent
~ The Dream Comes True

A Japanese proverb says that success will come on the third time. The great south face of Lhotse had defeated we members of the Tokai section of the Japanese Alpine Club in December 2001, when we reached 7600m, and again in 2003 when we reached 8250m, though we called it a 'near ascent'. It had been a hard road. When we were defeated in 2003, I felt personally that I would not come back to Lhotse. It would be possible to draw up climbing tactics but the falling rocks were too dangerous. The fact that no accidents took place on the previous two attempts is to be much appreciated. I told myself that we might be proud and satisfied with the safety record of those climbs, but I was very much afraid we could not make a third attempt without fatal accidents. I asked myself 'Can I never climb this face again?' Frustration caused regretful tears and I realised I wanted to climb the south face so very much.

In 2005 I joined an expedition from Gunma Prefecture Mountaineering Federation to Nanga Parbat, teaming up with Noriyuki Kenmochi, who shared my enthusiasm. This triggered the third challenge on Lhotse's south face and soon we had gathered together six strong and experienced climbers. We also increased numbers of climbing Sherpas from 15 to 18. We had organised a powerful team to try and ensure success. (A team of the Gunma Federation succeeded in the first winter ascent of the south-west face of Everest in 1993.)

On 3 September 2006 the team departed from Japan, first to Shisha Pangma for altitude acclimatisation and climbing training. In spite of heavy snow, all the members reached the main summit (8027m) on 9 October. After a rest in Kathmandu we journeyed to the Khumbu and entered base camp at 5200m near the right bank of the Lhotse glacier. There we met a Korean party led by Lee Choongjik. We decided to conduct a joint operation on the south face, and accordingly we shared the work of fixing ropes. Six thousand metres of rope had been carried in, of which 5700m was used.

The south face that I saw after three years' absence was guarded with much snow because of heavy snowfall in the autumn. On 18 November we started climbing and on the 21st camp one (C1) was set up at 5900m on the same spot as in 2003.

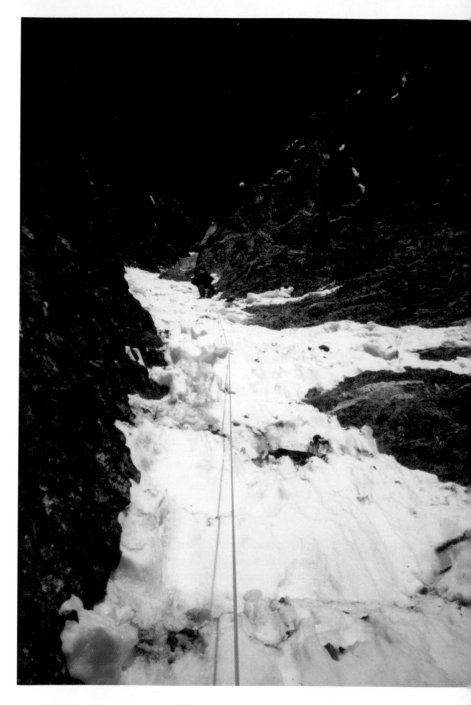

44.   Climbing the upper part of the couloir at 8300m. The yellow rock wall at the top of the couloir was detoured around to the left. (*Osamu Tanabe*)

Thereafter the wind became troublesome. It was not as fierce as in mid-winter but it was strong enough to blow away Atsushi Senda and Toshio Yamamoto and throw them 10 metres, at about 6800m on 28 November. The two climbers did not fall down the face, being protected by the fixed ropes, but it was very difficult to advance. The strong wind caused powder avalanches and falling rocks often beset Sherpas who were ferrying up the loads. A succession of casualties among the Sherpas depleted our resources and reduced our potential. Despite these hardships, on 1 December camp two (C2) was set up at 7100m and on the 6th a provisional camp three (C3) was placed at 7300m. On 7 December, we overcame a difficult pitch on the rock wall above the provisional C3, but the strong wind of the following day stopped our activities for five days. 'Pre-winter' ceases on Christmas Day in a normal year, after which a cold and violent gale of winter starts to blow and makes climbing impossible. At the beginning, therefore, we had judged Christmas to be a time limit. But our climbing speed was so slow that we were much delayed and were forced to extend the time for continuing the ascent. Fortunately the monsoon season lasted longer in 2006 than in a normal year, and consequently winter came later too.

Climbing resumed on 13 December. One of the reasons for the failure in 2003 was considered to be the location of C3, which was set up 150m lower than had been planned. In 2006, the Tanabe party, comprising Takahiro Yamaguchi, Ngawang Tenzi Sherpa and myself, took charge of route paving to C3 and then steadily advanced the route to 8000m. On 21 December, the long awaited C3 was established and the Senda party, comprising Atsushi Senda, Noriyuki Kenmochi and Pema Tsering Sherpa, set off for the summit, collaborating with An Chiyoung of the Korean party. At that moment I estimated that three days of climbing would take us to the summit, and I hoped that the Japan-Korea joint team would finish the first winter ascent of the Lhotse south face.

The Senda party chose a different route to that of 2003. They entered a couloir that went up to the left shoulder of the summit. They gained height step by step but reached only 8200m in three days. With time telling against them, the Senda group ceased climbing and the Tanabe party took over.

On 26 December, the first day after the changeover, the Tanabe party climbed up to the uppermost part of the couloir, 200m from the Senda party's high point. There we found an old fixed rope left on the couloir. It was a big surprise as I thought that nobody had ever climbed the couloir and naturally had never imagined we would have had forerunners. The last part of the couloir was a vertical rock wall of 20m with no cracks that was impossible to break through. The forerunners' footsteps disappeared here. I had believed that the couloir would prove a feasible route to the left shoulder of the summit. But actually it was a dead end.

45. Overall view of the Lhotse south face.
(© *The Chunichi Shimbun Ltd*)

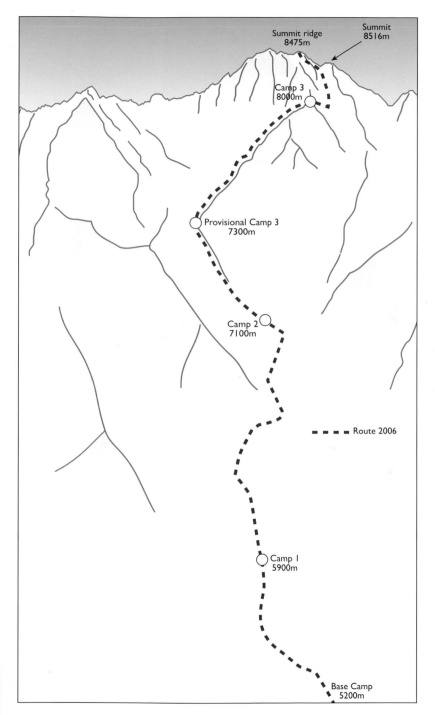

Summit ridge
8475m

Summit
8516m

Camp 3
8000m

Provisional Camp 3
7300m

Camp 2
7100m

Route 2006

Camp 1
5900m

Base Camp
5200m

46. The same view of the Lhotse south face depicted as a diagram showing
the 2006 route and approximate heights of camps. (*Diagram by Gary Haley*)

The only possible line seemed an apparently fragile rock wall on the left side of the couloir. This wall led to the summit ridge but we would have to descend and again ascend the ridge in order to stand on top. That would be exhausting toil, but there remained no alternative option. To be prepared for the next day, after having advanced by a 50m pitch along the left side of the couloir, we returned to C3. On the 27th, Yamaguchi opened a route boldly traversing the fragile wall. We continued to climb, finishing with an extremely difficult push on a snow face that was nearly vertical and made of snow like glass-powder. We found ourselves on the summit ridge at 8475m, with Everest, trailing snow streamers, just in front of our eyes. The time was 15:35. At last we had accomplished the complete winter ascent of the Lhotse south face. It was a moment when I was deeply touched and my dream came true.

There still remained about 200m to the summit in horizontal distance from the point where we stood on the ridge. But we would have to descend and then ascend the ridge if we were to gain the summit. We had no surplus energy to do so and began our return without hesitation.

Now I recollect the hard but enjoyable days inspired by the giant wall. The Lhotse south face was a goddess who warmly kept a close watch and protected us from dangers. During the three expeditions nobody was lost or suffered from frostbite. Not a single finger was lost. We were not merely fortunate, but the goddess blessed us and led us safely to success.

Summary: An account of the first winter ascent of the south face of Lhotse in November and December 2006 by members of the Tokai section of the Japanese Alpine Club, led by Osamu Tanabe. It was Tanabe's third attempt on the face and the summit ridge was gained on 27 December. Expedition members: Noboru Onoe (63) general leader, Osamu Tanabe (45) leader, Atsushi Senda (32) sub-leader, Katsuhito Fujikawa (41), Noriyuki Kenmochi (37), Takahiro Yamaguchi (33), Toshio Yamamoto (32), Goro Takenaka (46) base camp manager.

The 2006 route largely detoured around a rock wall at 8200m that Tomo Cesen reportedly climbed on his claimed solo ascent of 1990. The rope found in the uppermost part of the couloir is believed to date from attempts on the face by Polish teams in 1985, 87 and 89.

Opposite page

47. Everest viewed from the summit ridge of Lhotse at 8475m after the ascent of the south face. (*Osamu Tanabe*)

48. Traversing a fragile rock wall at 8350m to detour around the uppermost part of the couloir to the left. (*Osamu Tanabe*)

SIMON YATES

A Good Day

I recognised the fine spidery writing on the envelope before the stamp and Chamonix postmark. Inside was a letter and a small watercolour. Andy Parkin has often given me paintings. They are thank-yous, I guess, for my work organising our expeditions – unique mementoes of time shared on mountains and in special places together. There was also a map. Looking at it I soon recalled the wind and rain, peaks and glaciers, southern beech forest, shoals of sardines and pods of dolphins that had marked our slow cruise west along the Beagle Channel at the end of our first successful outing to the Cordillera Darwin six years earlier. Throughout the journey Andy had sat on the deck of Celia Bull's yacht, pen in hand, meticulously adding notes to the map. During the trip it gradually developed into a priceless document detailing potential climbing objectives, features and hazards. Then one day in an ice-choked fjord it had been plucked from Andy's hand by a gust of wind and dumped into the water. After turning the boat around I had managed to scoop up the map with a landing net, but the dousing and drying that followed left their mark. It was difficult to make out the tantalising notes – 'waterfalls', 'good pk snowy', 'face mixed' and 'looks good'. It seemed a fitting reminder both of times past and of the adventure to come. So many stories – one small map.

I staggered through the last of the trees and onto the beach. It had been a long day's hike. Beyond the forest a panorama opened up before me. The yacht *Iorana* sat neatly in the small bay of Caleta Eugenio here at the eastern end of Isla Hoste. The water in the bay was almost flat but in the distance the tops of the mountains of Tierra del Fuego were shrouded in cloud, with the snowline below, and out in the open water of the Beagle Channel there were white horses. It was a beautiful view and a magnificent setting. The walk into the mountains had been pleasant enough but it was not where we wanted to be. The wind that had brought us into this place for shelter the previous morning was still blowing, the mountains we were trying to reach still some way to the west. Expeditions always have their ups and downs, sometimes they gain a pace and momentum that you feel will lead to a successful outcome but I was already trying to be philosophical about writing this one off.

Getting to this point had already proved problematical. For months I had struggled to find a yacht to charter. Then the boat I finally secured developed gearbox problems two days before Andy's arrival. The owner kindly arranged a late substitution and now we were on a yacht called *Iorana*. I met the Belgian captain – Marcel de Letter, agreed terms and left him to get on with some shopping. Then Andy's flight arrived, but he did not. Phoning from Rio de Janiero later that day he related a tale of woe caused

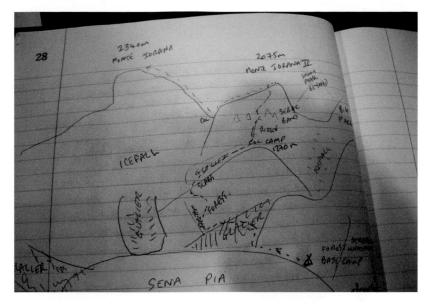

49.   Our 'rescued' route diagram. (*Simon Yates*)

by a delayed flight from Heathrow to Madrid. He hoped to be with us the following morning. The airlines finally delivered Andy, somewhat jaded after days of sleepless travel from his Chamonix home. With just two weeks scheduled for the entire trip, there was no time to relax and in a frantic morning we loaded the boat and prepared to sail. Then we did the whole process again after it was decided there was enough room aboard for my wife Jane and our two young children, Maisy and Lewis, to accompany us. The sail to Puerto Williams was a pleasant interlude but the immigration officials failed to show up that evening in the harbour. Marcel was furious as he had hoped to steal a march on an approaching storm by leaving that night. A lunchtime departure the following day meant we soon hit head winds. Our progress faltered. What could have been a few hours' motoring ended up taking three days.

On the fourth day out of Puerto Williams we woke to silence – the wind had finally dropped. However, once out in the Beagle Channel we met a wall of waves and once again were forced into an anchorage. The following day dawned wet and still. We motored west past the lonely Chilean naval post at Point Yamana and into the north-west fork of the Beagle Channel. Tantalising glimpses of snow and glaciers above the northern shore offered hints of the mountains above.

Our original plan had been to go ashore at Caleta Ola and try one of a number of ice/mixed lines we had seen previously on the south face of Monte Frances. However, two weeks earlier while on the mountain, I had looked at the face and found it bare. Andy suggested looking for a suitable objective in Seña Pia – a long, steep-walled fjord further west.

50. Seña Pia from "Cabbage Daisy" meadow. (*Simon Yates*)

It was a relief to leave the channel later in the day, slip through a gap in a line of rocks – a submerged moraine ridge – and enter the fjord itself. As we crept further along, the rock walls steepened and ice began to appear in the water. The pack-ice gradually became denser towards the head of the fjord, where two huge glaciers spilled down into the water. The cloud base was low, obscuring the mountains above. Andy's map of six years earlier, almost lost at this very spot, now came into its own. There was a 'face mixed' marked above the right-hand glacier and a suitable place nearby for a drop-off. We called it a day and went back to a beautiful anchorage in a tiny bay below a waterfall four miles back down the fjord.

A week had now passed. We still had to find an objective, climb it and make the journey back. Time was going to be tight. To add to our worries Marcel expressed his concern about dropping us off near the head of the fjord. If a lot of ice calved away from the glaciers there was a danger of being stranded. As land-lubbers this was not a scenario Andy and I had considered. The only positive was that the air pressure had now climbed above 1000mb, but during the night it blew hard. A day of torrential rain followed, making a mockery of the rising barometer.

The following morning our luck began to change. The rain had stopped, the cloud was lifting and it was eerily still. We slipped anchor and Marcel motored back to the drop-off. He grounded the yacht on the shore, making unloading a simple matter of passing gear down off the bow of the boat. We stood on the beach with our gear and waved our goodbyes as *Iorana* departed to wait at the anchorage. We had four days before the pick-up.

In a hurried frenzy we set up base camp in the forest and left for a reconnaissance. The glacier nearby was relatively easy to cross, but the moraine on the far side did not extend above an icefall as we had hoped. We tried to go higher on the glacier and found ourselves weaving up through huge unstable séracs. It was soon obvious the dangerous terrain continued for some way above. We opted for another approach.

Back at the base camp we dumped our rucksacks and swapped boots for wellies. A gully/waterfall line up through the cliffs behind the camp offered the only viable alternative way to get above the icefall. It did not look pretty. Bog in the lower section of forest gave way to steep, heavily-wooded slopes. Progress was gained by monkeying up branches and roots. The loose boulders in the stream bed above were little better. Then a waterfall barred the way, the walls on either side coated in dripping moss. I took the plunge and nearly fell on the steepest section as a chock-stone dislodged beneath my feet, leaving me hanging from a loose block by one hand. The ground eased, but pushing through the head-high beech as the tree-line approached was a battle. Finally, I burst out into meadows covered in what I affectionately named cabbage daisies. The sun was now shining, swallows were darting around picking up insects floating above the flowers, and the views of the fjord were stupendous.

Time was getting on so I hurried to get across the meadows, but the terrain proved awkward. Knee-high daisies poked through wet snow and the slope was steep. Snow slipped from the daisy leaves when trodden on and the stems broke off in my hands as I tried to use them for purchase. Staggering progress was regularly interrupted by barely controlled bum-slides until I reached a shoulder and could look down on the glacier. The view was not encouraging. The icefall continued way up the glacier, with a further band of séracs between the glacier and the face. The approach to the face was simply not safe and the face itself was bare of snow and ice.

Retracing my steps I returned to break the news to Andy, having got separated from him in the gully. I met him just above the treeline, looking ragged and dripping wet. 'You cannot be serious,' he said. 'Coming up here with a rucksack on.' It was a fair point. He soon related tales of slips and small falls. His time in the gully had been even worse than mine. I informed him of my discoveries and with the day drawing to a close we set off down.

The descent of the gully was unpleasant, but mercifully quick. Soon we were back in our forest base camp discussing options. Should we try and approach the face and force a way up it, or go for a more modest objective at the head of the fjord? With time pressing, a desire for self-preservation and an urge to make the most of the good weather, we opted for the latter.

The night passed clear and cold. In the morning there was frost in the forest and a skimming of ice on the fjord. The barometer remained absurdly high. After a leisurely start, we packed our rucksacks, re-crossed the glacier and headed off directly up the hillside. Streambed gave way to forest, cabbage daisies and then rock slabs covered in deep snow. The ground was slow going and route-finding difficult but at least we were making progress. Towards the end of the day we reached a glacier and followed it up it to a shoulder below a faint rocky ridge. We chopped out a platform and put up the tent.

The ridge above ran up to another glacier split by a band of séracs. A ramp line through them led into a basin capped by further séracs below the summit. It all looked reasonable and the weather was holding. We went to sleep confident, anticipating a special day to follow.

In the morning there was some work. The glacier had several nasty crevasse bridges to cross. Then there was a terrifying moment as the sérac band boomed and fractured vertically with one of my axe placements, and I shouted up to Andy for advice as to which side of the fracture line I should climb (the fracture had widened to about a centimetre by the time we descended). Above, there was some very deep snow in places but the outcome was never in any doubt. With the sun shining and just day-packs on our backs we could enjoy the moment and the ever-expanding views. When we crested the summit ridge of the peak another higher one to the west presented itself to us, so we climbed that as well.

51.   The south faces of Monte Iorana I & II. (*Simon Yates*)

52.   Andy Parkin on the summit of Monte Iorana I. (*Simon Yates*)

53.   Marcel on *Iorana* heading for the pick-up. (*Simon Yates*)

We reached the tent just before nightfall and were back at our base camp by lunchtime the following day. I called by radio for the pick-up and as we ferried bags to the shore we watched *Iorana* slowly advancing up the fjord through the ice. As it approached we could make out figures on deck. As the boat inched ever closer, 'Hello stinky bum,' echoed around the fjord. We laughed at Maisy smiling, waving frantically from the back of the yacht. The magical silence of the previous few days was broken. A different life beckoned.

Sometime during our incredible summit day Andy remarked, 'It might not be hardest mountain I've ever climbed but it's certainly one of the best.' I had to agree. The peaks had no names, so in keeping with our own tradition (Monte Ada = Celia Bull's boat in 2001) we named them after Marcel's yacht – Monte Iorana I & II. Apparently, it means 'good day' in Polynesian. It seemed apt. It had been a good day.

Summary: An account of the first ascents of Monte Iorana I & II (2340m and 2070m) at the head of Seña Pia, Cordillera Darwin, Chilean Tierra del Fuego, February/March 2007.

Acknowledgements: Andy Parkin and Simon Yates would like to thank the UK Sports Council, British Mountaineering Council and Mount Everest Foundation for their financial support of this expedition.

Anniversary

Andy Parkin *Chogolisa*
Acrylic on canvas
From K2 base camp at 5200m, 1996

DOUG SCOTT

Resisting the Appeasers

An' though the rules of the road have been lodged
It's only people's games that you got to dodge
But it's alright, Ma, it's life, and life only

Bob Dylan

A ll over the planet there is a battle raging between maintaining diversity and losing out to encroaching uniformity. Communities everywhere are struggling to maintain their cultural integrity in the face of economic globalisation as great nature itself loses its biodiversity through thoughtlessness or just plain greed. Evidence of this is all over, from the Amazon Basin right up onto the Great Plateau of Tibet and in all the valleys of the Himalaya and mountain ranges everywhere. This phenomena affects everyone including members of the Alpine Club; in fact especially Alpine climbers.

The rules of the road where climbing is concerned have always been, amongst other aspects, that there should be some uncertainty as to the outcome of the climb and that there would be associated risks to overcome. As it was stated in the Tyrol Declaration (2002) 'without danger and uncertainty climbing loses its defining element – adventure'.

The 'people's games' that have to be watched are those that would dumb down climbing from an adventure sport into an activity devoid of uncertainty and hazard when it comes to personal responsibility for protecting one's life.

Such people include Jürg von Känel who in *Die Alpen*, the journal of the Swiss Alpine Club (April 1998), defined and promoted the concept of '*Plaisir* Climbing' with evangelical vigour. 'What people want,' he says (and has helped achieve), 'is bolts at regular distance...and the bolts should be set in a way that virtually excludes the risk of injuries in case of a fall.... they should be easy to clip.... Also for smaller people...' The bolts are usually fixed by abseil on a regular grid pattern and the main justification seems to be that such 'climber friendly' crags attract the great mass of climbers who enjoy 'carefree climbing in nature' – by moving indoor climbing outdoors.

Plaisir crags have proliferated with the active support of the SAC responding to the demands of hut wardens and guides who benefit financially from the consequent increase in business. Despite this, von Känel laments the fact that '*plaisir* climbing... is not getting that much of a voice'. Could it be there is not a lot one can say about it since such climbing is so predictable and unmemorable? We are only fully conscious when out there on a limb, making judgements, being resourceful and creative whilst taking on responsibility for our own lives. This doesn't happen on *plaisir* crags. *Plaisir* crags, in fact, have many of the elements of urban life: repetitive monotony and uniformity, making the crags more or less the same in France, Spain, Switzerland...safe, predictable, and totally unadventurous. It's the same bland pap in the USA, Russia, Britain or wherever.

We have, of course, been here before. In a wake-up call in the 1998 *Alpine Journal*, Ken Wilson warned of the drift to a 'theme park' emasculation of climbing and called on the UIAA to campaign for the outlawing of the power drill. Thank goodness there were no cordless drills back in the 1960s (for there has to be a degree of self-examination here). There is no telling what damage I might have done in my then quest to climb all of the overhangs around the world. I certainly cannot claim, as does Reinhold Messner, that I have never inserted a bolt. It soon struck me as I bolted directly up towards Kilnsey Main Overhang that all I was doing was making my mark via the use of bolts – not as a 'climber'. It was completely unadventurous and also very boring, literally, doing that by hand, and I quickly gave up. When I used too many pegs on two new routes on Gogarth I was soon brought into line through peer pressure – derisive remarks in the pub and scorn poured upon me in the pages of *Mountain Craft* in the summer of 1967.

I should have been listening to that stalwart of 1930s Scottish climbing Jock Nimlin who, writing in the *SMC Journal* in May 1958 (not that long before my affair with the drill), underscored the principle that if one failed in an attempt on a new route one retreated and left an open field for a more determined attempt.

Nimlin went on: 'It is by accepting the hills on their own terms... that climbers find their deepest satisfaction. There is surely an inner conviction that these principles represent an absolute value; and one seems to detect in the half-apologetic, half-defiant claims of the pitonist a sense of transgression... The whole concept of free climbing is based on increasing standards of performance with no foreseeable limits, whereas piton-climbing imposes a definite limit and offers a future strictly related to the development rate of appliances.' How those 'appliances' have spread. Over the last 30 years continental Europe has embraced the bolt on most accessible crags, not always to the extent of the Swiss *plaisir* crags but enough to make traditional protection redundant. This has the knock-on effect of rendering young climbers unable to climb on anything but *plaisir* or sport crags since the art of self-protection has not been mastered. Unless, that is, the bolts go higher. Inexorably, drilling and bolting is spreading to high mountain rock, including the great Alpine classic rock routes – so much so that routes may bear little of their original character. Not only is the risk of falling lessened but route-finding becomes just a matter of following a line of shiny brackets; retreat from a sudden storm, just a matter of using the lower-offs.

AC members who guide in the Alps as well as amateur climbers have kept the Club up to speed on the changes they have witnessed over the last two decades – Pat Littlejohn and Roger Payne in particular. To their consternation, every few months crags in Switzerland that they had adopted for instructing beginners in traditional methods of climbing would suddenly become fitted out with bolts and brackets. In Roger's opinion 'It is true to say that all easily accessible climbing areas that are good for beginners have been retro-bolted.'

> You never understood that it ain't no good
> You shouldn't let other people get your kicks for you
> *Like a Rolling Stone*, Bob Dylan

One man who certainly hasn't understood is Bruno Durrer who, when medical commissioner with the UIAA, stated that 'the absolute freedom of climbing consists of choosing to climb wherever you want and with whatever technical help one considers as necessary... the adrenalin seeking climbers have the freedom of ignoring all fixed belays or bolts'.

In the European Alps, opined Durrer, 'most mountain regions live off tourism and have a vital interest in offering safe routes'. Furthermore, 'most mountain rescuers in the Alps' wanted a 'moderate number of safe belays' on the classic routes. It is as if Durrer has forgotten what climbing is all about in terms of commitment. How can there be commitment if there is protection every metre and a way off already provided? He seems to have no idea or respect for the basic tenets of climbing, implying that climbers wishing resourcefully and creatively to fix their own protection are elitist and/or adrenaline junkies. There are many like him who seem to have lost the plot completely.

As for rescuers, those of the climbing fraternity who go to the help of others in Britain have never sought to dumb down the mountain but have always stressed the need for the climber to lift himself up to meet the demands of the mountain. According to Durrer, rescuers on the continent are pushing for the partial bolting of Alpine routes, ie up in the high mountains. The routes may be made safer, but not the climbers if they are subsequently at a loss when it comes to protecting themselves on anything but prepared rock. Only by mastering the art of self-protection can a climber become a climber in the full sense of the word, and a safe climber. There can only be absolute freedom in this sphere when a climber can fix his own protection to protect his own life and in such a way that the second can remove that protection easily for use again and again.

After its first hundred years the Alpine Club more or less came to terms with the use of artificial aids, namely the peg. It was noted by Jack Longland in the centenary edition of the *AJ* that the AC had generally lost its preeminence to the continentals who were uninhibited in the use of pitons and artificial techniques. Prominent amongst the critics of aid climbing was, of course, Colonel Strutt and his opinions lived on until at least 1955. AC president Sir Edwin Herbert noted in his valedictory address that 'traditions are good things and.... If you look at the things traditionally frowned on by the Club, you will find that they are just those things which make the full realisation of mountain joys impossible – national aggrandisement, self-display, publicity hunting, a neurotic search for danger for the sake of danger, attempts by artificial means to alter the conditions imposed by nature and all the rest. These things are silly and therefore unbecoming.'

In 1957 Arnold Lunn was able to point out in his *Century of Mountaineering* that the peg did not bring exploration and uncertainty to an end, rather it widened the scope of both. A distinction was made between a peg driven into cracks and boring holes into blank rocks, 'so long as one confines oneself to driving pitons into cracks that exist there is still a place for genuine route finding.' Those climbers using pitons were at least credited with having some regard and sensitivity for the nature of the mountainside and they were still bound by the geography of the crag and could not just go anywhere. It was also noted that the peg, unlike the bolt, was more easily removed leaving little trace for future parties. However, as climbing became more popular, cracks were enlarged by the removal and replacement of pegs and scarring became a valid issue. Eventually this problem was addressed by the development of 'clean' climbing gear such as wires, chocks and Friends.

Now, 50 years later, are those of us who question the drill again contributing to impeding the progress of British climbing? The Club does have a tradition of being conservative in its concern for the founding essence of mountaineering. Guideless climbing, the use of crampons and artificial aids were all initially condemned 'by the high priests of Alpine orthodoxy' and these delaying actions of the old guard probably did no harm. Certainly Alpine Club objections to the peg contributed in no small way to the continuing traditional style of climbing in the British Isles so much admired by climbers around the climbing world.

For most Club members progress is personal to them, progressing on to harder, more remote, longer existing climbs in the Alps and then to the greater ranges. (And then, to keep it going despite the merciless passage of time, even up the Breithorn in a storm in celebration of the AC's 150th anniversary.) For the most committed of AC members, new routes were and always will be the goal and in ever more adventurous setting and style. One has only to browse recent *AJ*s to read of our members Fowler, Cave, Parkin, Yates, Littlejohn and others, plus friends like Ian Parnell, Kenton Kool and Nick Bullock pushing the extremes of world alpinism and creating esoteric gems all the way from Tierra del Fuego to Tibet and beyond.

These pacesetters have positively influenced the course of pure alpinism through their actions, far from the madding crowds and regular haunts of men. Later the rest will follow, awestruck at the courage and imagination of the pioneers. So it was with Mummery's route up the Zmutt Ridge of the Matterhorn – to most admirers of that great peak a symbol of natural wonder and for others a symbol of man's striving in the physical world. More than 100 years later we can marvel at this route and the style in which it was done. But the Zmutt's survival has been a close run thing. Only recently stanchions were to be fixed on difficult passages and a hut built at the base of the climb, primarily for the benefit of local guides. Perhaps it was Divine Intervention that caused an avalanche to destroy and remove all trace of the hut, carrying down the stockpiled metal spikes to boot!

Members of the AC have been effective in combating aberrations such as this proposed dumbing down of the Zmutt. Without vigilance, aided by the writers and journalists in our Club, such aberrations would become the norm if climbing were to be left to the profit motive, market forces and misguided civic concern over safety. Our members were able to show the basic contradiction – on the one hand the Swiss advocated the admirable cache 'leave no trace' when it comes to travelling through their mountains and yet they themselves were littering their mountains with ropes and ladders, devaluing the climbs originally put up by the very pioneers that the Swiss acknowledge brought mountain tourism to their towns and villages in the first place. Our president and our *AJ* editor have played no small part in reminding our friends in Zermatt that the finest memorial to the greats of the Golden Age would be to leave the great routes as the Victorians found them.

Thankfully we Brits are not alone in questioning the use of the drill. Over the past two years I have been lucky enough to travel to Norway, Bulgaria, Sweden, Austria, Switzerland and France as well as further afield to Australia and New Zealand. Everywhere I have come across climbers full of admiration for British climbing, yet somewhat incredulous that we not only drew a line on bolts but also more or less held to it. British climbing is so obviously an inspiration to adventurous climbers worldwide and especially in those countries where the bolt predominates. In Bulgaria, climbers there tell me the only way out they can see is to create bolt-free mountain ranges and this process is under way. This is also an answer being talked of in Sweden, Australia, New Zealand and apparently in South Africa where Greg Moseley tells me they have clearly defined areas for sport climbing. The South Africans were not amused when two Swiss arrived and bolted up three of their great classics at Wolfberg; so much so that the South African Mountain Club wrote to continental clubs requesting their members to respect South African rock and only resort to drilling after consultation with the climbers' representatives.

Roger Payne has pointed out that there is still, in fact, plenty of climbable rock in Switzerland, albeit it in the high country, that is still free from fixed equipment. He has drawn members' attention to *Keep Wild! Climbs* (edited by Daniel Sibernagel and Christoph Blum, 2006), a guidebook to climbs untouched by the drill, sponsored by Mountain Wilderness. According to the promotion, 'Clean climbing is the fairest and most honourable way to move in the rocks'... and: 'The climbing guide *Keep Wild! Climbs* of Mountain Wilderness gives a voice to adventure and brings to the mountain world a little originality.'

Roger has been vocal in supporting the idea that the Alpine environment, and climbing in particular, would be well served by a major, symbolic act. Such is the negative impact of mass tourism and the decline in responsible wilderness management, especially in the Mont Blanc range, that an environmental and economic crisis is on the cards. Roger and others are advocating the removal of all fixed ropes and clutter from the Dent du Géant. Re-establishing this magnificent peak as a formidable mountaineering challenge and one of the hardest 4000m summits in the Alps would send an important and symbolic message that the current trend of the urbanisation of the Alps can be reversed.

France, of course, is the home of sport climbing. So it is encouraging to hear from Bernard Amy that young French climbers are asking why it was that their predecessors brought the progress of climbing to a halt. Excessive use of the drill, the young ones complain, has denied them crags where they can familiarise themselves with the 'mobile' protection necessary to push out the frontiers of free climbing.

In Norway, the home of deep ecology, it is somewhat disappointing to find that many classic climbs have been retro-bolted. Apparently this came about after the climbing federation bureaucrats accepted government funding on the understanding that they would increase the number of climbers. To these officials the best way to make crags more user friendly was to have them equipped with bolts and there does not seem to have been any great outcry or direct action taken against this; however, in questioning the retro-bolting, the Norwegians have gone into interesting territory. Nils Faarland tells me they have deepened the question to its essence, 'daring to comment on joy... speaking of a quality of life, which is archetypal... not related to modernity's shallow fun or high sensation seeking'... but rooted in untouched nature and the 'natural rhythms of the planet' rather than nature subsumed into mechanistic systems.

Somewhere here there is a connection between the Norwegian tradition of *Friluftsliv* – of identification with free nature – and with traditional approaches and attitudes to rock climbing. This is why Nils has alerted me to it – to challenge the 'values and lifestyles imposed by modernity'. He says that although *Friluftsliv*, or joyous satisfaction, might result from great effort, as in a climb, it is an experience of tranquillity. This tranquillity is not a passive attitude. It inspires serendipity and the confidence to act in accord with personal values, including when the initiative might be against mainstream thinking. Put simply, finding one's own way, protecting one's own life will engender greater satisfaction 'and deep joy' than a climb marked out by a line of brackets where protection is arranged by others.

On the scale of world events the devaluing of climbing is insignificant, yet to know about one thing thoroughly leads to understanding many other things. In particular, what has happened to our pastime is in many ways symptomatic of the huge changes in the wider world and seemingly beyond the individual. Ever since mankind first bit the fruit of knowledge his potential in the material world has increased at the expense of his mental and spiritual life. He has limited his freedom by dependence on mass technology. The analogy with the introduction of mass bolting in climbing is obvious.

The key thing in all this, as far as the AC is concerned, is to ensure that at least here in Britain we stand firm against the bolt. We must resist the appeasers in climbing, whether they be those who make a living from guiding or instructing and who would benefit from user-friendly crags or older, over-weight amateurs, losing their bottle. Whilst climbing outside Salzburg a few months ago on a 1000ft limestone buttress festooned with bolts and also chipped holes, questions were naturally asked regarding the origins of such. 'It wasn't always like this,' said the old guard in the party, 'it all happened so quickly, soon after bolts and chains were put in for lower-offs then belays and suddenly, with the cordless drill, bolts appeared everywhere, quite beyond our control.'

The conclusion from this is obvious: that to fit out British mountain rock with lower-offs from bolts and chains, as is being proposed for instance at Sergeant Crag Slab in the Lake District, may well be the thin end of a very wide wedge. We must hold true to our own free climbing ethic for only then can we campaign with any credibility against the dumbing down of great routes and training crags in Europe and beyond. And remember, as Thomas Jefferson said: 'The price of freedom is eternal vigilance.'

KEN WILSON

Recent Himalayan History

The pace of activity on the great Himalayan peaks over the last three decades has been so great that keeping up with events and placing them in their true perspective is becoming increasingly difficult. We are now in a period akin to alpinism after the initial first-ascent surge that *AJ* editors like Percy Farrar and Edward Strutt chronicled so well. The columns of guided parties on Mont Blanc and the Matterhorn during the 19th century is now being repeated in the Himalaya and Karakoram by organised commercial groups. These seem to offer one of the few ways for ordinary climber and expert alike to overcome the pricing and access regulation that guards the great peaks. By this route thousands of people have now taken part in 'the Everest quest' together with hundreds on most of the other 8000m peaks. Recent books have sought to document all successful ascents. But now, to coin a phrase, 'It is difficult to see the wood for the trees' for those seeking to analyse the more innovative climbs.

In the following table dealing with the world's four highest massifs, I have attempted to do this. The *American Alpine Journal,* now the main publication of record, and the guidebooks of Jan Kielkowski have also painstakingly recorded events. These have been my main sources, together with *Japanese Alpine News* and the erstwhile *Iwa to Yuki* magazine. Lindsay Griffin's *Mountain Info* column, which has been preserved through the magazines *Mountain, High* and *Climb*, has also been useful but the failure to index it by the latter two publications makes its information harder to access. Apart from expedition accounts, or articles in the relevant journals (not forgetting the *Himalayan Journal*), periodic books have attempted the chronicling task. Mason's *Abode of Snow,* Dyhrenfurth's *To the Third Pole,* and the Swiss *Mountain World* series were fine earlier efforts. *World Atlas of Mountaineering* (Noyce and McMorrin) and *Himalaya Alpine Style* (Fanshawe and Venables) were two other useful sources. More recently, *On Top of the World* (Sale and Cleare) has made a very worthy contribution.

All sports try to identify top performance. In cricket the first class game is chronicled assiduously. The same should apply in climbing. At present Griffin's column and the magazine *Alpinist* are the only English language publications, both unindexed, that are trying to do this. It thus seemed timely for the *AJ* to make an attempt to record, compare and contrast events at high altitude. One hopes that the following (somewhat abbreviated) tabulation will form a basis for more considered analysis.

There may well be omissions, but I hope the key events will be found here. I am grateful to Jonathan Pratt, Andy Collins, Ian Parnell, Doug Scott, Pavle Kozjek, Jim Curran* and others for their help and advice.

---

* In his books *K2 Triumph and Tragedy* (Hodder 1987) and *K2 The Story of the Savage Mountain* (Hodder 1995).

THE HIGHEST PEAKS

NOTABLE ATTEMPTS / ASCENTS / REPEATS / TRENDS / INCIDENTS

Denotes the first ascent of an important new route.
Expedition style: large party using fixed camps/ropes to allow supply by support climbers and hired porters.
Lightweight style: a small team, all aiming to gain the summit, using some fixed camps/ropes.
Alpine style: small team or solo attempting a climb in one push or trying again after a failed push. Also summit solo attempts from an advanced position, often with broken trail, and rigged glacier hazards.
Challenging 'peak' solos with little or no advance preparation by others.

ɔx) No bottled oxygen used (though sometimes taken for emergencies).
Indicates death, mainly on descent.

Bold type indicates important events or performances.
Medium type indicates other noteworthy climbs/performances.
A claim in italics indicates that it is unclear or awaiting further evidence or convincing debriefs.
All entries on satellite peaks of less than 8000m are in medium type.

EVEREST 8848m   1

922-1938	Everest N Ridge	E/s
952	Everest SE Ridge	E/s
953	* Everest SE Ridge	E/s
955	Everest SE Ridge	E/s
960	* (?) Everest N Ridge	E/s
963	* Everest W Ridge / N Couloir	E/s
963-1973	SE Ridge ascents	E/s

922-1938 Everest N Ridge *E/s* Early Exps. of C G Bruce, H Ruttledge. 1922: **Bruce, Finch** to 8320m; 1924: **Norton** (8575m), Somervell (8538m) both (-b/ox); Mallory+, Irvine+ to ?8570m. 1933: **Wyn Harris**, **Wager**, **Smythe**, (-b/ox) to c8575m. Also of note in 1924 was Odell's 3 days of support/search/rescue exertions at above 8000m.

952 Everest SE Ridge *E/s* **Lambert**, **Tenzing** of R Dittert's 8-man Exp (plus a cadre of h/a Sherpas). To 8540m on the SE Ridge after a night in a tent without sleeping bags.

953 * Everest SE Ridge *E/s* **1st ascent: Hillary, Tenzing**, members of J Hunt's Exp. The South Summit was reached a few days earlier by Bourdillon and Evans. Success achieved after 9 full *E/s* attempts and 3 *L/s* bids.

955 Everest SE Ridge *E/s* **2nd ascent: Schmied, Marmet** and (next day) by Reist and Von Günten, of A Eggler's Exp that had earlier made the 1st ascent of Lhotse.

960 * (?) Everest N Ridge *E/s* **Wang Fu-Chou, Gombu, Qu Yin Hua**, members of Shih-Chan-chun's large, well-trained Chinese Exp. For years thought a propaganda-linked claim. Post cold war debriefs by a range of experts placed 4 bivouacking below the 3rd Step and reported cogent accounts of a summit climb thereafter.

963 * Everest W Ridge / N Couloir *E/s* **Hornbein, Unsoeld**, leaders of a small party within N Dyhrenfurth's large US Exp that climbed the peak by the SE Ridge (Whittacker, Gombu). 3 weeks later H and U traversed the summit (up the 'Hornbein Couloir' and down the SE Ridge) to link up with Bishop and Jerstad who had climbed the SE Ridge. All four survived a bivouac, though some with serious frostbite.

963-1973 SE Ridge ascents *E/s* Exps in 1963 (US), 1965 (Indian), 1970, 1973 (Japanese), 1973 (Italian) put 27 climbers on the summit. Several other Exps in the same period.

1963-1973	SE Ridge ascents (continued)	E/s	**Couloir left of the Geneva Spur** (an important variar was climbed by **Ito**, **Sagawa** and **Yoshikawa**, membe of H Matsukata's and H Ohtsuka's 1970 Exp.
1975	Everest SE Ridge	E/s	**J Tabei** (1st fem asc), **Ang Tsering** of Mrs E Hisano's Ex
1975	* (?) Everest N Ridge	E/s	**Phantog** (2nd fem asc), **Norbu, Lotse, Samdrup, Pasang, Tobygal, Khyen** (Tibetans), **Ho Sheng Fu** (Chinese). *Possible 1st ascent of route after 9 previou. attempts – the 1924 bid is thought an unlikely 1st and 1960 is now thought a probable 1st.*
1975	* Everest SW Face	E/s	**Haston, Scott** (with S Summit bivouac); **Boardman Pertemba**, Burke+ (probable solo ascent), members C Bonington's 24-man Exp. After 5 previous attempts, left-hand gully through the rock band proved the key. The bivouac was influential. Repeats in 1988 (1 to top 3 to S summit, all+), 1992 (6), 1993 (6), 1995 (3) all *E/s*.
1978	Everest SE Ridge	E/s	**Messner, Habeler: 1st asc without bottled oxygen (-b/** by members of W Nairz's conventional Exp (using oxyge
1979	* Everest W Ridge Direct	E/s	**Stremfelj, Zaplotnik; Belak, Bozik, Ang Phu+** – members of T Skarje's Exp that crossed the Lho La ar climbed left of the avalanche-threatened W Shoulder fac that devastated the 1974 French Exp. Snow caves we used at key points with much hard climbing higher up.
1980	Everest SW Face	E/s	**1st winter ascent:: Cichy, Wielicki** on A Zawada's 16-man Exp.
1980	Everest N Ridge	E/s	**Kato** of H Wanatabe's 39-strong Exp soloed the peak from the highest camp, having previously climbed the Ridge (with Ishiguro) in 1973.
1980	* Everest N Face, Hornbein Couloir Direct	E/s	**Osaki, Shigehiro** – of a 12-man team led by H Miyash climbing from the E Rongbuk glacier using a slanting le hand start and much fixed rope.
1980	* Everest South Pillar		**Czok, Kukuczka** of A Zawada's Exp. Direct to South Summit from Western Cwm.
1980	* Everest N Face	A/s S/a (-b/ox)	**Messner's 1st solo ascent of peak** using a low trave to the Great Couloir. A complete solo with no other grou present and a risky glacier approach.
1982	* Everest SW Face Central Pillar	E/s	**Balyberdin, Myslovski; Bershov, Turkevich; Ivanov Yefimov, Krishchaty, Vallev; Khomutov, Golodov, Puchkov, Tamm**, members of Y Tamm's Exp. By the rock spur L of SW Face, using rolling seige style as on Lhotse (1990) and Everest (2005).
1983	* Everest Kangshung Face	E/s	**Buhler, Momb, Reichardt; Cassell, Lowe, Reid** of J Morrissey's 14-man Exp.
1984	* Everest S Pillar (-b/ox)	E/s	**Demjan, Psotka+, A Rita**. Left line of face.
1984	* Everest N Face, Great Couloir	E/s	**Mortimer, McCartney-Snape**, with **Henderson** (to 50 below the summit) – of G Bartrum's 5-man Exp by a dir line right and in Great Couloir (-b/ox).
1984	Everest N Face/Great Couloir	E/s	**Erschler** (solo) from a 3-man bid (with limited oxygen) L Whittacker's 10-strong Exp. By Messner's 1980 line N Col gained from the E Rongbuk glacier.
1985	Everest SE Ridge disaster		**Kumar+, Bakshi+, Negi+, Bahuguna+, Rao+** of Brig J Singh's Indian Army Exp. Kumar fell below the S Sumr exhaustion/cold killed the others on the S Col.
1986	Everest N Face, Hornbein Couloir Direct	A/s	**2nd ascent of route. Loretan, Troilet** (supported by Bégh 2-day ascent (-b/ox) by main couloir at night to a snowho Resting/rehydrating in daytime warmth. Solo bids by Marshall (July 86 to 7700m; June 87 to 8000m). 1991 Gyalbu, Norbu (2nd asc). **Cronland (1st solo)** All (-b/
1987	Everest N Face Hornbein Couloir Direct	A/s	**Béghin, Garido** (-b/ox) – a more direct 'attempt' with succession of steep sections up to 70° (a technical cli at altitude).

1988	* Everest S Col (Kangshung side)	L/s	Anderson, Teare, Webster (to col), Venables to summit (-b/ox).
1988-1995	Everest SW Face	E/s	repeats in 1988 (4 climbers, all +) (to Summit or S Summit) 1992 (6), 1993 (6), 1995 (3).
1988-1996	* Everest N Face of NE Shoulder	L/s	3 new lines by American and Japanese teams (1988) and Russians (1996):

* **Blanchard, Twight.** Starting in the centre, finish near the top of N Ridge.
* **Hasegawa, Koshino.** Well right of the previous route, also exiting on N Ridge.
* **Kohanov, Kuznetsov, Semikolenkov, Bakaleinikov, Zakharov** to NE Shoulder.

1990	Everest S Ridge	E/s	**Commercial Exps develop.** Organiser/guides offer supported ascents to paying clients. Of 72 ascents in 1990, 21 (30%) were from such groups and of 117 in the pre-monsoon of 1999 there were 43 (37%).
1991	Everest E Face R/h Rib (Fantasy Ridge)	E/s	Japanese to 6400m, and an Indian/Nepal attempt to 6900m in 2002.
1993	Everest SW Face	E/s	**1st winter asc: Nazuka, Gotoh; Tanabe, Ezuka; Ogata, Hoshino** of K Yagihara's 9-man Exp. A 1992 bid by the same group reached 8350m.
1995	Everest NE Ridge *Integrale* * (Everest's longest route)	E/s	**Nima Dorje, Furuno, Imoto, Pasang Kami, Lhakpa Nuru, Dawa Tsering** – members of T Kansaki's Exp completing the work of Exps in 1982 (Boardman+, Tasker+ A/s to the pinnacles), 1985,and 1988 (Bryce, Taylor to NE Shoulder) and (1990) to 8700m by M Perry's Exp.
1995	Everest N Ridge/NE Ridge	L/s S/a	**A Hargreaves (f) 1st female solo** (self-sufficient ascent – climbing/camping alone above Advanced Base but with many others on the mountain). An earlier SE Ridge solo claim by L Brady may not have reached the summit.
1997	Everest SE Ridge and N Ridge	E/s	J Krakauer's *Into Thin Air* described the hopes/ ambitions of a commercial expedition on which 4 of its 8 members died in a storm.

2001-2007 Sundry 'record' ascents: fastest/youngest/oldest, men/women, first ski descent summit to Khumbu base without removing skis. These 'feat' ascents/descents grew common. Snowboard descents (tragedies) on the N side followed. First helicopters landed on the South Col and the summit (2005) recalling the first Everest flight (1933), balloon crossings (1992) and a paraglider descent (1988).

2005	* Everest North Buttress Direct	E/s	**Mariev, Shabalin, Tukhvatullin; Kuznetsov, Sokolov, Vinogradsky; Bobov, Volodin.** 3 teams summit over 3 days to complete a rigged (mainly rock) route. Steeper terrain on final band turned on left.

K2 / CHOGIRI   8611m   2

The steepness of K2 and lack of suitable porters tended to discourage bottled-oxygen use on the S side.
Notable early bids: 1938 (route-finding problems on Abruzzi resolved); **1939** (going high on difficult ground)

1954	* K2/Chogiri SE Rib (Abruzzi Spur)	E/s	**1st ascent: Lacedelli, Compagnoni,** members of A Desio's 18-man Exp. Controversial because of frost- bite injuries to a porter during the summit bid blamed on Bonatti's alleged summit ambition. He accused the lead climbers of placing their last camp too high to be reached by support climbers in daylight.

1976	K2/Chogiri NE Ridge	E/s	**Chrobak, Wroz** – members of J Kurczab's 19-man Exp reached 8400m on a direct attempt. Powerful, near successful, bid by a strong team.
1977	K2/Chogiri SE Rib (Abruzzi Spur)	E/s	**2nd ascent**: Nakamura, Shigehiro, Takatsuka; Hiroshima, Aman, Onodera, Yamamoto from I Yoshizawa's and T Matsuura's Exp.
1975	K2/Chogiri NW Ridge	E/s	Whittacker, Patterson, Wickwire of J Whittacker's 11-strong Exp reached 6600m on the hard, pinnacled ridge above the Savoia Saddle (bypassed on later attempts).
1978	* K2/Chogiri NE Ridge/Abruzzi	E/s	**Wickwire, Reichardt; Roskelly, Ridgeway.** 2nd new route on peak. Success over 2 days (on the Abruzzi finish) after attempts on the 1976 Polish Route failed (avalanche risk). Wickwire bivouacked (safely) 150m below the top after taking summit photos. Minimal oxygen used by both teams.
1979	K2/Chogiri SE Rib (Abruzzi Spur)	L/s	**Messner, Dacher.** First (-b/ox) ascent of the peak.
1981	* K2/Chogiri W Ridge	E/s	**Sabir, Ohtani** – members of T Matsuura's 17-strong Exp added a 3rd new route on the peak. Attempted by UK teams in 1978 (E/s) and 1980 (L/s). The ridge was avoided by a rising line on its right flank to join the SSW Ridge.
1982	* K2/Chogiri N Ridge	E/s	**Sakashita, Yoshino, Yanagisawa +; Takami, Kawarmura; Shigeno, Kamaru** (a day later), members of I Shinkai and M Konishi's 14-member Exp (-b/ox). The 4th new route on the mountain.
1982	K2/Chogiri SE Rib (Abruzzi Spur)	E/s	Women's Exp led by W Rutkiewicz aborted (7100m) or Halina Kruger's death.
1983	K2/Chogiri N Ridge	L/s	**Da Polenza, Rakoncaj.** First repeat of 1982 route by F Santon's Exp (-b/ox). Martini, Stefani summited 5 days later. All were aided by 1982 fixed rope.
1986	K2/Chogiri SE Ridge	L/s	**W Rutkiewicz** (-b/ox), L Barrard+ (1st female ascents) with M Barrard+ and M Parmentier (-b/ox). The Barrards disappeared on the descent.
1986	K2/Chogiri SE Ridge (Abruzzi Spur)	E/s	Chamoux climbed the route in 23 hrs, aided by ropes and camps in place.
1986	* K2/Chogiri S Ridge	A/s	**Kukuczka, Pietrowski+** (of K Herrligkoffer's Exp) completed a hard, committing climb (-b/ox). On descent to rejoin team members, Pietrowski, dehydrated and unroped, fell on ice when crampons loosened.
1986	K2/Chogiri SSW Ridge ('The Magic Line')	S/a A/s	**Casarotto+** Solo attempt to 8300m near end of the technicalities. Fatally injured in crevasse fall (on known ground) during the descent. A bold attempt.
1986	* K2/Chogiri SSW Ridge ('The Magic Line')	E/s	Wroz+, Piasecki, Bozik of J Majer's Exp completed a hard climb (attempted by 3 earlier groups). Wroz fell from fixed ropes above the Shoulder.
1986	* K2 SSE Ridge (to shoulder only)	S/a	*Cesen, completing line nearly done by D Scott's 1983 Exp. This (with the Abruzzi finish) may be the easiest line to the summit for A/s teams.* * Done E/s in 1994. *Reservations re Cesen's claims apply pending full debrief.*
1986	K2/Chogiri Sundry routes		**13 deaths in 1986.** Intense summit ambition. Many teams tackling too few routes; over-extended groups descending the Abruzzi seeking support from other teams. These factors developed into situations that, when combined with storms that afflict the SE flank, ensnared an assortment of, mostly, very experienced climbers.
1991	* K2/Chogiri NW Face	L/s	**Imamura, Nazuka** members of T Ueki's Exp climbed the Chinese side of the Savoia Saddle to link up with the 1982 Polish route on the north flank of the NW Ridge to join the Japanese route to finish. (-b/ox)

991	* K2/Chogiri NW Face / N Ridge	A/s	**Béghin, Profit** complete the 1982 NW Face line to the N Ridge finish across the avalanche-prone high glacier. (-b/ox)
1993	K2/Chogiri, W Ridge	E/s then L/s	**Mazur, Pratt,** leaders of a 10-man climbing/trekking Exp, complete 2nd ascent of the 1981 Japanese/Pakistani route – a sustained mixed climb.
1994	* K2 SSE Rib/Abruzzi route	L/s	**J Oiarzabal's team: A and F Inurrategui, de Pablo, Gutierrez** (pre-preparation to Camp 2) climbed the peak in 4 days by the line tried in 1981 (Y Seigneur's Exp), pushed A/s to 100m below Shoulder by D Scott's Exp in 1983, *and completed to the Shoulder by Cesen (1986).*
1993-1995	K2 Deaths on the Abruzzi route		Culver+, Joswig+, Bidner+ ('93), Pazkhomenko+, Izagin-Zake+, Kzaldin+ ('94), Escartin+, Oliver+, Hargreaves (f)+, Grant+, Slater+, Angles+ ('95). 13 deaths in 3 seasons, mainly from mishaps on the final summit push.
2001-2003	Political / topographical problems		After July 2001 there was a break in activity because of 9/11 and the wars that followed. In addition, a sérac fall from above the bottleneck created difficulties.
2004	K2/Chogiri SSW Ridge	E/s	**Corominas. 2nd ascent of route.** Soloed from 8300m with support to that point by Cadiach and De la Matta+ (died of appendicitis at Camp 1).
2004	K2 statistics		7 deaths / 48 ascents during the year. 246 ascents / 61 deaths to Jan 2004.

KANGCHENJUNGA MASSIF 8598m   3

Kangchenjunga Main 8598, Central 8496m (the 5th highest peak) and South 8476m

Early Indian listings of peaks referred to Kangchenjunga Central as South and as the 5th highest peak, with Yalung Kang as the 7th. Yet no doctrine has yet taken hold to systematize these figures. Instead, a loose consensus has come to be accepted, based more on the 'look' of a peak than anything more precise. The col depth of Lhotse, for instance, is 588m, while that of Kangchenjunga Central/South is 218m. We can thus anticipate new bouts of mountain pedantry (doubtless under the UIAA's aegis) as climbers in ever larger numbers take on this challenging (and expensive) form of peak-bagging.

1955	* Kangchenjunga SW Face (Yalung)	E/s	**1st ascent: Band, Brown; Hardie, Streather** (on successive days), members of C Evans' Exp that succeeded after seven earlier attempts.
1977	* Kangchenjunga NE Spur/N Ridge	E/s	**2nd ascent: Chand, N Dorje,** completing climb first tried on 1929 and 1931 Exps led by P Bauer.
1978	* Kangchenjunga South and Central	E/s	**Chrobak, Wroz** (South), **Branski, Heinrich, Olech** (Central). 1st ascents by members of P Molteki's Exp. The summits were linked * **Central to Main** (Koroteav, Mozaev, Pastuk, 1989), **South to Central** (Mitan, Wada, 1984).
1979	* Kangchenjunga N Spur/W Ridge	L/s	**Scott, Tasker, Boardman: 3rd ascent,** with **Bettembourg** in support. The avalanche risk of the N Face was avoided by the N Col couloir. A safer way to the ridge by the buttress right of the couloir was done by J Roskelley's 1985 Exp, two other routes on the right having been done in 1980 and 1983.
1980	* Kangchenjunga NW Face Direct	E/s	**Fukada, Kawarura, Ang Phurba, Sakashita, Suzuki.** 4th ascent with 5 others, reaching the top 3 days later. They took a direct way through the Three Terraces, previously tried (with a fatality) in 1930. Technically easier (but more avalanche-threatened) than the 1979 route via the N Col.

1981	Kangchenjunga NW/W Face (N or NW Ridges)		Exps in 1981 (US), 1982 (Italian/German – *L/s* ascent by **Messner, Mutschlechner, A Dorje** by *N **Ridge** to join 1977 Chand/Dorje route.
1983	**Kangchenjunga SW Face**	*S/a*	**Béghin. 1st solo ascent** alone on a long, heavily crevassed route. An earlier solo by Bachler (*E/s*) was a one-day push from the highest camp. **Marshall** (In 1984) shadowed Polish/French Yalung Kang teams lower on the face (reducing glacier risk) to a camp by the Sickle for his final summit bid.
1986	**Kangchenjunga SW Face**	*E/s*	**1st winter ascent. Kucuczka, Wielecki.** Members of A Machnik's Exp.
1987	**Kangchenjunga NE Spur/ N Ridge** *E/s*		2nd ascent of route (-b/ox). Tsering+, Butia+, Dorje+ of Maj Gen Kuketry's 62-man Indian Army Exp failed to return from their ascent. Bhawan Singh, Limbo and Chander Singh+ repeated the climb; the latter fell on descent.
1989	**Kangchenjunga (all 8000m summits)** (inc Yalung Kang from the Yalung glacier)	*E/s*	**Bershov, Bukreev, Vinogradsky, Pogorelov, Turkevich** (W to S); **Elagin, Lunyakov, Khalitov, Balyberdin, Korotaev** (S to W) of E Myslovsky's 32-strong Exp. They linked the summits, each team doing the climb in two days.
1991	**Kangchenjunga SW Ridge**	*A/s*	**Stremfelj, Prezelj** (-b/ox) by a long, technical, demanding route, to S summit but utilizing some fixed rope from earlier Exps, with support via Hogsback Peak teams on the *Original Route* and having a mid-height escape option onto the Great Shelf.
1995	Kangchenjunga SW Face	*E/s*	8000m peak-baggers had mixed success: Loretan and Troilet (not an 8000m aspirant) reached the top by a W Ridge finish, Loretan thus becoming the 3rd 'completer'.They descended safely. The slower Chamoux+ and Royer+, after radio messages, bivouacked and were never seen again. Earlier, Riko+, one of their 3 Sherpa porters, fell from the gangway. The French climbers, intent on the 'feat', failed to assist, prompting the same response (next day) from the Sherpas.
1998	**Kangchenjunga N Spur/W Ridge** *L/s*		**G Harrison. 1st female ascent**, with Pratt, Horvath and Shaw. (Earlier attempts by Bremer Kampf, Frantar+ and Rutkiewicz+ ended tragically.)

YALUNG KANG 8420m
Kangchenjunga W Summit. The 7th highest peak

1973	* **Yalung Kang SW Face**	*E/s*	**1st ascent: Ageta, Matsuda** + of H Higuchi's Exp.
1975	* **Yalung Kang SW Face**	*E/s*	**Dacher, Lackner, Walter**; and six others from S Aeberli's Exp in the following days. Direct from Great Shelf of Yalung glacier.
1980	Yalung Kang SW Face	*E/s*	Saldana+, Medina+ of J Casanova's 9-man Exp disappeared after summiting.
1981	Yalung Kang N Face	*L/s*	Attempt to 8000m by Chandler+ & Bremer Kampf (f).
1984	* **Yalung Kang SW Face** (S Face Direct from the Hump by Yalung valley)	*E/s*	**Cichy, Piasecki** – members of T Karolczak's Exp. Hard mixed climbing on a 1500m buttress (by **Karolczak** and **Wroz**). Summit gained 3 days later.
1985	* **Yalung Kang** (by the E Ridge from the N Face)	*E/s*	**Bergant+** (-b/ox), **Cesen** (+b/ox) of T Skarje's 14-man Exp by a route from the Upper Snowfield of the N Face. Bergant slipped while waiting to abseil during descent. At night, in the crevassed upper snowfield, Cesen avoided a risky descent and a cold bivouac by pacing out a ledge between crevasses. A later search provided no clue as to where Bergant lay. Skarje's *AAJ* report and Cesen's O'Connel interview differ in some respects.

KHUMBHAKARNA (JANNU) 7710m
Important Kangchenjunga satellite peak. **47th in the listings**
(Kangbachen (7903m) and Gimmigela Chuli (7350m), high satellites of lesser difficulty, are not included.)

1962	* Khumbhakarna	E/s	1st ascent: Desmaison, Keller, Gyalzen Michung, Paragot; Betrand, Bouvier, Leroux, Pollet-Villard, Ravier, Terray, Wangdi.
1978	Khumbhakarna	A/s	2nd ascent: Rouse, Carrington, Baxter-Jones, Hall generally by the 1st ascent route to the *vicinity* of the summit.
1976	Khumbhakarna N Face	E/s	Ogawa, Sakashita, Suzuki, plus 9 others over 4 days, to complete the route attempted by a NZ team in 1975.
1982 /1987	Khumbhakarna N Face	L/s	Two exps led by P Béghin attempted the steep mixed 1987 ground right of the Japanese Route, but were forced to finish by that route (Béghin, Décamp).
1982	* Khumbhakarna SW Spur	E/s	Roche, Jurjon, Fillon of H Sigayret's 8-strong Exp, following attempts in 1979, when I Galfy's Exp reached 150m below the summit, and in 1981, when Martis, Chrenka and Spanik of A Blazej's Exp reached 100m below the top, and then Bakos and Galfy reached the summit by a finish up the French Route.
1989	* Khumbhakarna (Jannu) N Face/E Ridge	A/s	S/a Cesen. A sustained/technical ice and rock route up ground tried by French inc L flank of summit headwall. No plausible account of this is available.
1992	* Khumbhakarna East (7468m) E Face	A/s	Pockar, Furlan to 7100m on the SE Ridge. This face has since had several attempts, none getting higher than the Pockar/Furlan bid.
2004	* Khumbhakarna N Face	E/s	Ruchkin, Pavlenko; Totmyanin, Kirievsky, Borisov of A Odintsov's 11-man Exp direct up summit headwall. Their 2003 attempt reached 7200m.

LHOTSE 8516m | 4

Lhotse Middle 8414m   Lhotse Shar 8382m

1954	**Lhotse and Lhotse Shar**	E/s	N Dyhrenfurth's 7-man team probed Lhotse Shar's S Face then, from W Cwm, attempted W Face. Senn, backed by Spohel, gained foot of W Couloir (8109m).
1955	* **Lhotse W Face**	E/s	**1st ascent: Luchsinger, Reiss** of Eggler's 11-man Exp. They climbed the 50° W Couloir. Later, the Exp placed 2 teams on Everest's summit.
1970	* **Lhotse Shar, S Ridge/SW Face**	E/s	**1st ascent: Mayerl, Walter** of S Aeberli's 7-man Exp by a route pushed to 8000m by Iguchi and Matsuura of H Yoshikawa's Exp. In Indian listings this 8400m peak rates the 7th highest in the world (86m col depth). The twin-peaked Lhotse Middle (8410m) has a 66m col depth.
1971	Lhotse S Face	E/s	R Uchida's 13-man Exp gained 7317m.
1974	Lhotse, Lhotse Shar, E Ridge	E/s	Officially attempting Lhotse by the long/serious E Ridge, **Warth, Diemberger** (of a 4-man Exp) climbed * **Shartse II (7503m)** with 5 camps, from Barun glacier.
1975	Lhotse S Face	E/s	An experienced 13-man Exp team led by R Cassin was hit by avalanches while tackling ramp line well to the left (to 7400m) judging the centre too risky.
1977	Lhotse S Face	E/s	A similar line to the Cassin attempt climbed to 7804m by K Makei's Exp but foiled by deep snow.
1977	**Lhotse W Face**	E/s	**2nd ascent: Warth, Von Kanel, Urkein; Zinti, Sturm, Vogler; G Schmatz** (ldr), **S and P Worgotter, Dacher** (-b/ox), **Lutz+**, the latter found dead at the foot of the face after falling on the couloir descent.
1980	**Lhotse S Face / SE Ridge**	A/s S/a	N Jaeger+ after attempting the S Face, transferring to the Lhotse Shar route in a bid to traverse to Everest's S Col. Last seen moving upwards on SE Ridge.

1981	Lhotse S Face (central line)	E/s	**Podgornik, Stremfelj, Zaplotnik** gain 8250m on edge R of summit buttress. **Matijevic, Kenez** reach 8100m on W Ridge above the Lhotse/Nuptse Col (W Cwm full of mist) – members of A Kunaver's 22-man Exp that spent 2 months on this very dangerous face placing 6 camps (several in snow holes) avoiding casualties despite employing full expedition relay tactics.
1981	Lhotse Shar S Ridge / SE Ridge	E/s	Xabier Erro's 4-man team got to 7550m on unclimbed S Ridge. **2nd ascent: Hauser, Bruchez** of J Fauchere's 14-man team. Petten+, Favez+, fell down S Face after failed attempt. Fauchere+ fell on the return trek.
1984	* Lhotse Shar, SW Face	E/s	**Demjan** (supported by three others): **Bozik, Rakoncaj, Stejskal** of I Galfy's 18-man Exp climbed the face (initially rock, then snow/ice, mixed on final spur).
1985	Lhotse S Face, R Dihedral	A/s	Fine, Fauquet to 7200m on rib right of 1981 line quit after seeing Holda+ fall.
1985	Lhotse/Lhotse Shar S Face (r/h line)	E/s	**Dasel, Flut, Hajzer** of J Majer's Exp gained 8200m on the right flank of Lhotse's summit buttress after a Lhotse Shar S Face start. Holda+ fell down Central Couloir while descending (with Kukuczka). Kukuczka, Majer, Falco-Sasal, Fine (of the French team) reached 8050m. The accounts by the *AAJ* and Kukuczka differ on some facts.
1986	Lhotse W Face	E/s then L/s	**Messner**, Kammerlander. Messner was first to climb the fourteen 8000m peaks. **Kukuczka** repeated the feat a year later with a new route on Shishapangma.
1988	Lhotse W Face	E/s then L/s	**First winter ascent: Wielicki** soloed the couloir from a prepared route. A Zawada's Exp reached 8321m in 1974 but permit dates forced them to quit on Dec 31.
1988	Lhotse S Face (with the Lhotse Shar start)	E/s	**Kukuczka+** (with **Pawlowski**) on gaining the summit ridge at c 8350m fell (cornice break?) and broke the rope being used (for belaying or fixing).
1990	Lhotse S Face	A/s S/a	*Cesen claims 4-day solo completion of route taken to 8250m by compatriots in 1981. Cesen articles (Mountain 134, AAJ 1991) and lecture photos/accounts prompted queries about this very advanced claim. The Russians concluded: 'he nearly made it'. Hard climbing later found on summit ridge. Thorough debriefs now needed.*
1990	* Lhotse S Face, R Dihedral The line taken followed the right rib of the Dihedral (see topo in *Mountain* 147)	E/s	**Bershov, Karatayev,** of A Shevchenko's 20-man team, completed the line first tried A/s in 1985 by Fine and Fauquet. 6 camps were placed and much fixed rope used, and left. The final part, from a snow cave (8300m), on rock thinly covered with snow, had sustained difficulties (UIAA V, VI). Ridge crest dangerously corniced. Summit reached at 7pm. Camp regained after 22 hours. Climbers exhausted – shepherded down by support climbers.
1990	Lhotse S Face, Central Couloir	A/s	Profit, Béghin climbed to 7600m where a storm forced a retreat.
2001	* Lhotse Middle, N Face (from the Khumbu, South Col approach)	E/s	**1st ascent of world's highest unclimbed peak (8414m). Timofeev, Bolotov, Kuznetsov, Vinogradsky; Koshlenko, Gilin, Sokolov, Yanochkin, Volodin** of V Kozlov's 11-man group. Climbed by the Kangshung flank of the N Ridge, then across avalanche-prone slopes to climb the snow-plastered final rock tower.
2006	* Lhotse S Face (central line)	E/s	**Tanabe, Yamaguchi, Ngawang Tenzi Sherpa** of N Onoe's 8-man Exp (plus 18 h/a Sherpas) gained the summit ridge at 8475m some 200m horizontally, 41m below summit, a serious traverse (partly climbed by Bershov, Karatayev, 1990). The climbers took the 1981 route up the Central Buttress, then traversed down right to the R Dihedral. Here the 2001 fixed ropes led up to a 20m wall turned on the left by fragile climbing to gain the near-level ridge crest. After their attempts (2001, 2003) they here considered the 'Face' climbed.

GORDON STAINFORTH

The Crux

Great moments or turning points in British climbing history

To mark the 25th anniversary of the Kendal Mountain Film Festival I was asked to try to achieve the near-impossible – to celebrate 150 years of British mountaineering and rock climbing achievement in just 25 classic images – the concept of 'crux' meaning a step forward in climbing history, a pivotal 'moment' or a yardstick climb, and not necessarily the crux of a climb.

Twenty five pictures covering 15 decades from 1860 to the present day – that's only about one and half pictures per decade! How was I to achieve such a compression of history that was not unbalanced and full of gaping holes? Inevitably as a climbing history it was exceptionally potted (and even more so in the selection that follows as, for various reasons, it has only been possible to reproduce 17 of the images). The captions are necessarily an uneasy mixture of essential facts and details about the particular climb, and the broader brushstrokes of history, providing a context for each image. In a protracted selection process, with somewhat nebulous criteria, mountaineering gradually gained weight (in the end, 12 of the pictures exhibited were of mountaineering, and 13 of rock climbing). Nine were of first ascents (plus two 'reconstructions') and four of solos. The whole world arena of the sport was represented, covering the whole of Britain as well as the Alps, Himalaya and other ranges. The scores here were: England 4, Wales 6, Scotland 4, the Alps 4, Himalaya 5, other ranges 2.

The nature of the pictures was very varied too: from superb photos of great artistic merit to technically imperfect shots that capture a unique moment in climbing history. No fewer than five of the rock-climbing pictures were of such crux moments.

The main theme running throughout was that of bold pioneering, and coupled to this, two other things: a very British disdain for cheating and artificial aids, and an imaginative, artistic element, such that many of the climbers depicted here could fairly be described, without exaggeration, as artists as well as visionary climbers.

What the exhibition could not begin to do is explain what this sport – which was inconceivable before an industrial revolution had given people the wealth, leisure and means to pursue it – is all about. The earliest pioneers tried to kid themselves that it had some underlying scientific basis, but by the 1860s, Leslie Stephen declared openly that it was a simply a sport. 'As for ozone,' he added, 'if any existed in the atmosphere, it was a greater fool than I take it for.'

Right

55. A cannonade on the Matterhorn, July 1862
    Edward Whymper/James Mahoney
    Scrambles amongst the Alps, 1900 edition
    (*Freda Raphael Historical Archive*)

All at once I heard a noise aloft, and, on looking up, perceived a stone of at least a foot cube flying straight at my head. I ducked, and scrambled under the lee side of a friendly rock, while the missile went by with a loud buzz. It was the advance guard of a perfect storm of stones, which descended with an infernal clatter down the very edge of the ridge, leaving a trail of dust behind, and a strong smell of sulphur ...

The few earliest mountaineering photographs taken at the very beginning of the sport, in the 'Golden Age' of alpine mountaineering between about 1854 and 1865, in which almost all the major 4000m peaks of the Alps were first climbed, are frankly dull, and necessarily stilted because of the severe limitations of the early photographic medium. So I choose as my first image this dramatic engraving by Edward Whymper.

Everything about the picture (by Whymper, in collaboration with his engraver, James Mahoney) is very advanced for its age, and represents a crux moment in more senses than one. In one sense it is a terrifying moment of suspended animation, the explosive cannonade of heavy boulders frozen in time with great artistic skill, like a high-speed photograph, long before such a thing was possible in photography. But it also represents a new level of daring, with the a whole new breed of adventurer wandering, sometimes unroped, into hitherto undreamt of terrain – impossible for us to imagine now really how daring this was – for this was the mighty Matterhorn, one of the most extraordinary mountains in the world, which all but a handful of lunatics believed to be totally unclimbable. The indomitable Whymper attempted it no less than seven times; indeed just eight days before this incident, he had fallen 200 feet from near this very spot on the Italian ridge and had been lucky to escape with just a few cuts and bruises.

But the real crux was to come three years later, on 14 July 1865, when several of the rival contenders joined forces into an unwieldy team of seven and finally 'conquered' this most coveted of all Alpine summits via the Hörnli ridge. But the hubris was short-lived. The fateful moment came at 2.15pm on the descent when the novice of the party, Hadow, slipped sending the guide Croz flying and, in a moment, the Rev Hudson and Lord Francis Douglas were plucked from their holds, the 'alpine line' between them and 'Old Peter' Taugwalder snapped like cotton, and all four plunged down the north face to their deaths.

'The Taugwalders and I have returned, 'a grim-faced Whymper announced to the Zermatt hotel-keeper on his return, and the Golden Age was at an end.

Right

56. Beatrice Tomasson and her guide, Arcangelo Siorpaes,
in the Cortina Dolomites, 1898.
(*Bâton Wicks Archive*)

One of the more remarkable features of British alpinism at the end of the 19th century was the surprising number of women who, contrary to the prevailing social mores of the day, took up this apparently very masculine new sport. The best known names in the history books are Aubrey le Blond (who made the first ascent of the East Peak of the Bishorn in 1884), Lily Bristow, Elizabeth Jackson and Gertrude Bell; but one lady whose achievements sank into obscurity, partly because of her own modesty it seems and partly because she was never in a climbing club, was Nottinghamshire-born Beatrice Tomasson. Her futuristic first ascent of the huge 650m south face of the highest mountain in the Dolomites, the Marmolada, in 1901 with the guides Michele Bettega and Bartolo Zagonel, undoubtedly ranks as the finest of them all. Given a modern grade of V-, it was one of the hardest routes in the Dolomites for 20 years. (Another notable achievement around this time was the first ascent of the 1000m north-west face of the Civetta by a long and complex route by Rainer, Phillimore and Siorpaes in 1895.)

The portrait photograph of the 'masculine' and 'wiry' Tomasson with the guide Arcangelo Siorpaes in the mountains above Cortina in 1898 is unusual too for her very informal and relaxed pose, with Siorpaes looking understandably proud to be in her company. She was said by her relatives to be an 'extraordinary character, very determined', and was very much the driving force behind the much-coveted Marmolada ascent.

Right

57. *Central Buttress*, Scafell, Easter 1915. George & Ashley Abraham
(*Bâton Wicks Archive*)

This classic image, of the second great iconic climb in British rock climbing after Napes Needle, was taken in 1915, a year after the first ascent, by the Abraham brothers of Keswick, who were the first truly great photographers in British climbing history. It is particularly interesting because it is one of the first known instances of an important first ascent being reconstructed for a climbing photograph.

Immense care has gone into every aspect of the image – with the performers (C F Holland, who had been on the first ascent, R T Chorley and A N Other) traversing in to the top of the Great Flake from the *Keswick Brothers' Climb* on the left (named after the Abrahams, who had made the first ascent of that much easier route) and then waiting for the sun to catch the edge of the Flake, when Holland, wearing a suitably light sweater, was lowered into the crux position. All this would have been much more difficult to coordinate before the age of walkie-talkies, if there had been any breeze at all; and doubly so, in that the Abrahams could only shoot one or two of their precious 8½ by 6½ inch glass-plate frames in their huge 12" square whole-plate Underwood camera, and each frame would take several minutes to set up. All this while the climber was hanging in a strenuous position on what were then the hardest recorded moves in British rock climbing.

Steady progress had been made in Wasdale since the turn of the century, mostly on Scafell Crag, notable achievements being Owen Glynne Jones' very serious *Jones's Route Direct* on Scafell Pinnacle in 1898 and Botterill's eponymous, outstanding slab route in 1903 – the first full-weight Very Severe climb in the country, climbed in nailed boots and with an ice-axe for aid at the crux. But the great central challenge, the apparently impregnable Central Buttress, remained inviolate.

The climbers who at last believed it was possible were Siegfried Herford, an undergraduate from Manchester University, and his friend George Sansom. Then, with an assortment of talented climbing partners who had all trained on the gritstone outcrops of the Peak District (which had been pioneered by J W Puttrell) – such as Stanley Jeffcoat and C F Holland – they made a number of reconnaissances, even traversing in as the climbers have in this photograph to explore the top of the Flake; but it was not until April 1914 that Herford finally succeeded at the crux, using complex 'combined tactics'. 'I'm glad our mothers can't see us in this place!' commented Herford at the top of the Flake before forging on to the top.

Herford and Sansom wanted to repeat the climb later in the year, with an improved start, but were unable to do so 'owing to unforeseen events'. The 'unforeseen events' was the outbreak of the Great War, which claimed the lives of both Herford and Jeffcoat. *'CB'*, the hardest climb in Britain until the 1930s, thus remains Herford's epitaph.

Top right

58. Siegfried Herford and George Mallory at Pen y Pass,
    December 1913
    Geoffrey Winthrop Young
    (*Alpine Club Photo Library*)

This haunting, moody photograph, taken by Geoffrey Winthrop Young sometime between Christmas 1913 and the New Year in 1914 is, in my opinion (and I believe that of many), one of the greatest mountaineering portraits of all time, with the two most talented rock climbers of the day resting briefly outside the Pen y Pass Hotel after a strenuous day of climbing on Lliwedd.

Winthrop Young, himself one of the great British alpinists before the Great War, describes in rhapsodic terms how the three of them had made a double girdle of the great precipice of Lliwedd in snowy conditions:

> ... as some people remember music, I now recall my view either way across the Lliwedd precipices storming up the sky under ghostly downfalls of ice, forward and back to the agile figures in white sweaters, swinging, turning, belaying in a counterpoint of precision and force... It was all too good to leave. Why make an end? We dropped down then re-crossed the face once more... We travelled on return even faster, and in a rhythm which I never remember attaining again on stiff rock...

Yet now that they are back, this carefree spirit seems suddenly to have evaporated, as a few snow flakes swirl about them (one is visible in front of Herford's knee), and they are lost it seems in a troubling moment of dark reflection, as if a shadow of premonition has passed over them and they have a fleeting intimation of a doomed future.

Winthrop Young described the 'strange, aloof' Herford as not only an embodiment of 'a spirit of the hills' but as 'the future, as I liked to think it would continue and develop in him.' But it was not to be, for they were both to die prematurely – Herford in the trenches in 1916 and Mallory on the most famous of all the attempts on Everest, in 1924.

Right

59. The last picture of Mallory and Irvine, Camp IV, Everest,
    6 June 1924
    Noel Odell
    (*Mountain Camera Picture Library*)

Left

60. Edward Norton at 28,100ft on Everest, 4 June 1924
T Howard Somervell. (*Somervell family*)

Another extraordinary shot, and again it is difficult to say quite why. It is scarcely more than a snapshot, taken on roll film, just three days before Mallory and Irvine disappeared, on a very lightweight Kodak Vest Pocket camera by Howard Somervell, who at this point was suffering acute breathing problems – yet it conveys better than any of the other early Everest expedition photos just how alien and otherworldly Everest was to those early explorers. What is particularly interesting too is that it shows the highest recorded point ever reached by a climber without using supplementary oxygen, a record that would be unbroken for more than 50 years.

Once both the Poles had been reached, Everest had already been dubbed 'the Third Pole', but in modern terms the nearest equivalent of these early high altitude climbers venturing into the unknown at more than 28,000 feet would be a moonwalk. Indeed the alien foreground rocks here and the high contrast with a nearly black sky and the intensely lit summit cone are uncannily reminiscent of pictures taken on the moon.

At about 27,000 feet the effects of height 'seemed to assert themselves quite suddenly,' wrote Somervell, forcing them to take 10 or more breaths to every step, and every five or ten minutes to sit down for a minute or two. As Norton said, 'we must have looked a sorry couple'. Somervell's throat soon became nearly completely blocked (later diagnosed as a frozen larynx), 'so finding a suitable ledge on which to sit in the sun and pull myself together, I told Norton to go on. ... I watched him rise, but how slowly, and after an hour I doubt whether he had risen 80ft above my level.'

Once Norton got into the Great Couloir (to the right of the steep outcrop in front of him in the photograph) 'the going got steadily worse; I found myself stepping from tile to tile, as it were, each tile sloping more steeply downwards. It was not exactly difficult going, but it was a dangerous place for a single unroped climber, as one slip would have sent me in all possibility to the bottom of the mountain.' So he ground to a halt, some hundred feet above Somervell (an accurate theodolite reading taken later from below gave the height as 28,126 ft).

On his return, Norton was beginning to suffer from snow blindness, and by the time they stumbled into Camp IV many hours later by torchlight, to be met by Mallory and Odell, he was in extreme pain. The absent-minded Mallory had forgotten his own camera, so Somervell gave him his for his ill-fated summit attempt. Before doing so, he had to change the film, and it is just as well he did or we would never have seen this strange and mysterious photograph.

Left

61. Joe Brown making the first ascent of *The Right Unconquerable*
Stanage, April 1949
Ernest Phillips

This image of the decisive historic moment of extreme commitment as Joe Brown launches into the first strenuous layback moves on the first ascent of *The Right Unconquerable* at Stanage in April 1949 was to inspire a generation.

The notorious 'Unconquerable Cracks' had resisted all attempts ever since first tried (and named) by Eric Byne in 1932. Immediately after the war there had been a noticeable increase in standard with the likes of Peter Harding, who pioneered many classic new routes both in the Peak District and the Llanberis Pass, but the real breakthrough came with a young builder's apprentice, Joe Brown, who was really in a different league from anyone who had come before (next in line, one might say, after Haskett-Smith, Owen Glynne Jones, Herford and Kirkus.)

The Right Unconquerable represents a whole new level of seriousness and relentless difficulty that is balanced by an unprecedented level of confidence. This is a new post-War age, a truly 'Brave New World'. Joe's equipment is no more sophisticated than that of pre-war climbers (he is wearing identical plimsolls and has a hemp rope.) If he had not managed to arrange any protection, and had fallen off the difficult moves at the very top of the climb, he probably would have been killed. This is a question I often asked myself when looking at this famous photograph. Did Joe manage to get on some kind of protection higher up?

In 1995 I tracked down the original photographer, Ernest Phillips, and he showed me the original uncut strip of negative which answered my question with a categorical 'No'. In the previously unpublished final frame (left) the rope hangs clear from his waist without a single runner (carried, as was the old practice, simply to protect the second).

I then asked Joe Brown if he was worried by the very awkward sloping mantelshelf move above the final overhang, which many people still fall off today with the benefit of modern protection. He didn't recall having any trouble with it. 'Mantelshelves were something I was good at. I was a mass of muscle in those days.'

The strip of film also showed Joe climbing *The Left Unconquerable* on sight, immediately before the *Right*, and it now seems likely that was the first ascent too (and that it had not been climbed in the previous year as has traditionally been stated in the guidebooks.)

These two climbs were just a foretaste of what was to come. Shortly afterwards Joe Brown went into National Service leaving the climbing world buzzing with stories and speculation as to what he would do next....

Right
62.. Rusty Baillie starting up *Cenotaph Corner*,
    Dinas Cromlech, Llanberis Pass
    John Cleare

The great open-book corner in the centre of Dinas Cromlech that dominates the Llanberis Pass in Snowdonia was named, like the Unconquerables, long before it was climbed – in this case by Menlove Edwards in the 1930s, with a perfect name that reflected the 'megalithic tomb' of the crag itself.

After the war, several of the experts of the day, including Peter Harding himself, looked at it and declared it to be impossible, at least without the use of a huge number of aid pegs. But Joe Brown made a serious attempt on it as early as Christmas 1948 (when he dropped his peg hammer on his second and had to retreat); and when he returned from National Service at the end of 1950 it was as inevitable as day follows night that the first ascent of this great challenge would eventually fall to him.

By this time Joe had teamed up with the younger Don Whillans, of equal ability though not having perhaps quite the same genius for discovering new routes. Over the space of a few short years from 1951 to '55 they changed the face of British rock climbing. Joe did not go straight back to the *Corner* – it seemed that he was biding his time, waiting for the time to be truly ripe – instead he climbed an amazing 11 new routes on Cloggy and seven in Llanberis Pass that were almost all harder than anything that had ever been climbed before.

One of the Llanberis Pass routes of this time was the superb vertiginous classic, *Cemetery Gates*, far out on the very exposed right wall of *Cenotaph Corner*. The brilliantly apt name was the result of a destination sign that Joe and Don saw on the side of a bus when returning home.

The great crux day in the history of British rock climbing in the 1950s came on 24 August, 1952 when Joe climbed the *Corner* with Doug Belshaw (I have never quite discovered why he didn't do it with Whillans – perhaps it was simply a matter of Don not being in the right place at the right time?) and it immediately replaced *CB* as the most famous climb in Britain, emblematic of what became called, inevitably, 'the Brown era'.

Unfortunately no photographs exist of this crucial first ascent, so I have used one of the superb, never-surpassed black-and-white images of it that John Cleare took in the mid-sixties for his seminal rock-climbing photo-essay (co-authored with Tony Smythe), *Rock Climbers in Action in Snowdonia*. I have chosen the frame in which Rusty Baillie is just making the moves on the 'first crux', with the whole daunting challenge still lying ahead.

Right

63. John Streetly on the first ascent of *Bloody Slab*,
     Clogwyn d'ur Arddu, 10 June 1952
     E A Wrangham
     (*Bâton Wicks Archive*)

One of the truly outstanding ascents of the very early 50s – it was in fact climbed two months before *Cenotaph Corner* – was the astonishing *Bloody Slab* on Cloggy by John Streetly. No other pictures epitomize the era quite so well as the series of images taken by Ted Wrangham, and John Streetly's own account was the most detailed and gripping written so far by a climber. Here are some excerpts:

> ... it is difficult to recall how the next thirty feet were managed at all.... the previous move being apparently impossible to reverse, left no alternative but to go on up. With the difficult move below and the uncertainty of what was still to come, life at this point seemed to depend more on faith than friction. The only way led diagonally upwards across the smooth and exposed slab to the left ... on tiny finger-holds and toe-holds with the occasional use of a clump of grass growing in the thin vertical cracks.... With a seventy-foot lead-out from the last runner – the shaky flake – the situation was critical ...

Streetly's friends were unable to second this first hard part of the climb, so they tied on another rope – the knot can just be made out near the right-hand side of the picture. Then:

> Movement could again be made diagonally upward to the left on very tiny rugosities until another large loose flake was reached.... It proved quite a surprise when a tentative pull removed the whole issue - all twenty odd pounds of it! This presented an awkward problem, more so in view of the fact that I was holding on to it!... The groove from which the flake had come was rounded top and bottom with no trace of the hoped-for hold. Almost desperate examination of the rock, however, revealed a tiny flake ... Using this as a finger-hold a move could be made across to another grassy strip. Proceeding super-carefully up this (a ninety-foot lead-out from the shaky flake runner), it again became possible to move on to the more rugose left edge of the slab which led up to a good grassy ledge... At this point, like all good things, the 200 feet of rope came to an end and the trouble really started.

So Streetly now unroped and climbed solo to the top of the cliff.

Right
64. Layton Kor on the Central Pillar of the *Eiger Direct*,
    5pm, 19 March 1966. Chris Bonington

One of the new developments of the sixties was the interest taken by the media in mountaineering, and nothing perhaps epitomizes this more than the first direct ascent of the Eigerwand in the winter of early 1966. Led by an American, John Harlin II (who was killed during the ascent), it ended up being a multi-national effort involving siege tactics, by some of the top British, American and German alpinists. One of these was Chris Bonington, who had shot to fame with a series of major first ascents and had now been assigned by the *Weekend Telegraph* to take pictures of the Eiger Direct.

This sensational, dizzymaking picture, which appeared in the Sunday colour supplement (and adorned the wall of my bedroom in my teens), shows a crucial 150-foot linking pitch halfway up the wall that Bonington had just led. In the days before modern ice-climbing techniques, this involved cutting steps all the way, which took him five hours. Chris says that, in the context, it was the hardest pitch he's ever led. Then, having expended all that adrenalin, and opened up the way to the top of the Central Pillar, the ever-professional Bonington got out his camera and took this spectacular picture.

On the upper part of the route, the hero of the hour was very much Dougal Haston, who had by now teamed up with the Germans Sigi Hupfauer and Roland Votteler. As Haston told it:

> The next hour was one of the most testing of my climbing career. It was 60-degree water-ice. The steps of the previous rope had been wiped out. I had no axe or hammer. My left crampon was wildly askew on my boot. The right one was loose. Armed with one dagger ice-peg, I moved off the stance. The wind was crashing the snow into my face with such force that it stuck in huge masses on my eyelids, making it impossible to see ahead. My movements were cautious and groping. I would search around for traces of a step, scrape it out, and then make a breath-holding move up on wobbly crampons. The pitch went on and on and I became increasingly aware of the extremeness of the situation. Sigi and Roland were on a very poor belay. There just could not be any question of falling..

Meanwhile, in these appalling conditions, Chris Bonington had climbed the west flank of the mountain ready to take pictures of them arriving at the summit.

Right
65. Rusty Baillie at the crux on the first ascent of the Old Man of Hoy,
    18 July 1966
    Chris Bonington

Four months after his assignment on the Eiger, Chris Bonington was involved in a completely different kind of adventurous first ascent. Tom Patey, 'that indefatigable pioneer of unlikely crags and sea stacks', had been eyeing up Britain's finest sea stack, the 140m-high pinnacle of Orcadian Sandstone, the 'Old Man of Hoy', 10 miles north of the Scottish mainland. In the early summer of 1966 he recruited Rusty Baillie and Bonington for a serious attempt.

After they had chartered a fishing boat to take them across Scapa Flow to the north side of Hoy, the ascent of Britain's most inaccessible summit went without a hitch. When Baillie got to the crux, Chris had the foresight to reverse the first pitch to get this striking photograph. (Several people were surprised by the number of pictures by Bonington that I used in this exhibition, but the fact remains that he has had an almost uncanny gift of getting into the right place at the right time at some of the key moments of late 20th century British climbing history.)

It's a pity that the most outstanding pitch of the climb is so near the bottom,' wrote Bonington, 'but even so, this pitch has an extraordinary feeling of exposure, which is accentuated by the constant movement of the sea below.... A broad impending crack, too wide to get your body right into it, sweeps up in a great rounded bulge. It is in a corner, however, so that the climber can get some help from either wall, and there are the characteristic horizontal, though rounded, ledge-like holds you so often get on sandstone. One of the principal problems is the softness of the rock, which gives it a ball-bearing-like texture, tending to make feet and fingers slide with off-putting ease....

On the first ascent, Baillie used some aid at the crux, but it was freed a year later by Bonington when he was preparing for the spectacular BBC TV live outside broadcast which featured an all-star cast of Brown, Bonington, McNaught-Davis, Crew, Haston and Patey, backed up by Baillie, Cleare, Clough and MacInnes, and was itself a major technical achievement given the size of early colour TV cameras.

Left
66. Ed Drummond and Dave Pearce pioneering *A Dream of White Horses*,
Craig Gogarth, October 1968
Leo Dickinson

'Perhaps the most satisfying of all climbing photographs ever taken,' said
the late Trevor Jones of this wonderfully evocative image by Leo Dickinson,
who is himself another bold adventurer, as well as being an outstanding
award-winning film-maker of documentaries that have involved everything
from skydiving down the north face of the Eiger, diving in some of the
deepest underwater caves in the world, and ballooning over Everest.

The picture not only captures a spectacular moment on a great classic
rock climb in Wen Zawn on Anglesey, but it also happens to be the first
ascent, by Ed Drummond and Dave Pearce. Drummond, as well as being
a very fine rock climber (the second ascent of *Great Wall* on Cloggy and an
enormous number of new routes in the Avon Gorge, North Wales and
Norway) is a very talented writer, with a gift for verbal imagery and poetic
metaphors. It was he, of course, who dreamed up the wonderful name of
the route, so perfectly suited to the very height of the 'flower-power' era
that culminated in the revolutionary year of 1968 (though rumour has it
that Dave Pearce contributed the 'white horses' bit).

The great American Yosemite pioneer, Royal Robbins, was so impressed
by Leo's picture and the name of the route that he immediately had to fly
over to Britain to climb it:

That great sheet of spray leaping from the sea, rearing from excited
waters like a splendid white stallion, and the two figures fastened to the
rock just out of reach of the tormented foam. With its whimsical and
romantic overtones, the name appeals perhaps more to the American
climber than to his British counterpart... A Dream of White Horses –
five words! Turgid with subtle meanings... Although I knew nothing of
the climb, because of that name and that sensational portrait by Dickinson,
it was a route I had to do.

As far as the wave is concerned, Leo Dickinson told me that he 'could see
that wave was going to happen. What I didn't realize was how big it would
be. So a bit of luck was involved as well.' Leo actually has something of a
reputation for his uncanny knack of having his camera out just before some
unexpected event, such as a huge avalanche or a climber falling.

Left
67. Doug Scott on *The Scoop*, Sron Ulladale, June 1969
     Ken Wilson

This great picture taken during the first ascent of the mighty Scoop of Sron
Ulladale in the Outer Hebrides, a 160-metre hunk of primeval rock that
lurches wildly out over Glen Ulladale – full of wind, wuthering heights,
and overwhelming exposure – is not so much iconic as iconoclastic,
belonging as it does to the transitional, revolutionary age of the late '60s
and early '70s in which so many conventions were being swept away.

The 30-hour ascent, made in the month before man first landed on the
moon, was a tour de force of new technology, made possible by the advent
of high-tensile pegs, skyhooks and RURPs (realized ultimate reality pitons).
Spearheading the whole venture was the unconventional, innovative and
visionary Doug Scott, prince of thieves from Nottingham. 'Thieves', because
he, with Guy Lee, Mick Terry, and Geoff Upton, had snatched it from
under the noses of rival teams from Scotland. Not surprising, too, that this
great picture (actually a montage of three frames) was taken by none other
than Ken Wilson, the enthusiastic creator of the great new groundbreaking
magazine, *Mountain*, who was keen to get a 'scoop'. After he'd reached the
top, Doug described it as 'a unique experience in fear and fascination'.

But the new vogue for extreme artificial climbing was very short-lived,
and the sport actually went the other way, with a whole new movement to
'free the [Llanberis] Pass' in the 1970s, and Scott himself evolving to become
one of Britain's greatest all-time mountaineers. The main free climbers at
this time were first, John Syrett, then John Allen and Steve Bancroft, then
Pete Livesey and Ron Fawcett, successors, one might say, to Brown and
Whillans (Livesey being particularly notable for his *Right Wall* of Cenotaph
and *Footless Crow* in Borrowdale, both in 1974).

The Scoop itself was astonishingly freed in 1987 (following a slightly
different line) by the extraordinary team of Johnny Dawes, rapt climbing
genius, and Paul Pritchard, winner of the Boardman-Tasker Award for
mountain literature in both 1997 and 1999. By the late 1980s Sron Ulladale
had itself evolved (thanks to other activists like Mick Fowler and Crispin
Waddy) into the most impressive traditional, free-climbing crag in Britain.

Strange to report, then, that there was another huge development in the
1980s, at the very opposite pole of the sport, in which ultra-safe and super-
hard bolt-protected 'sport climbing' was effectively imported from the
continent to some of our steepest limestone crags, such as Raventor,
Malham, Kilnsey and Pen Twryn. It is true that some of the climbs created
here by the likes of Ben Moon and Jerry Moffatt ranked with the hardest in
the world, but most traditional 'adventure climbers' looked on with indif-
ference or even distaste. Sport climbing was seen by many as an aberration,
and by some as a kind of vandalism. Johnny Dawes commented scathingly
that it was climbing reduced to little more than 'hard physical tasks'.

68. Ian Clough on the South Face of Annapurna, May 1970
Chris Bonington

Chris Bonington's successful South Face of Annapurna expedition in 1970, though it cost the life of his close friend and climber partner, Ian Clough, was a new high point in Himalayan climbing achievement. Here Ian is seen traversing the fixed ropes on the steepest part of the Ice Ridge above Camp 4.

All the other members of the team (Martin Boysen, Mick Burke, Nick Escourt, Tom Frost, and Mike Thomson) had pushed themselves to the very limit, with Frost and Burke eventually finding a way through the difficult Rock Band to establish Camp 5; and emotions ran high when Bonington decided that Whillans and Haston, being the pair now on best form, should go into the lead.

Whillans and Haston sat out a blizzard for two days at Camp 6, then on 27 May, with the monsoon already encroaching below, Whillans decided to abandon the idea of establishing a Camp 7 and go boldly for the top. Haston had been doing all the leading until this final day, when Whillans steamed ahead in an extraordinarily gutsy final push, reaching the top (and the peak of his whole climbing career) at 2.30pm, followed closely by Haston. Despite the daunting physical and technical problems of the climb, Whillans had been quietly confident throughout. Boysen says, 'he kept on telling us, "It'll go. We'll get the job done."'

69.   Dougal Haston arriving at the summit of Everest
      6pm, 24 September 1975. Doug Scott

This is undoubtedly one of the great moments and greatest iconic photographs in British mountaineering history.

One of the biggest outstanding challenges in the early 1970s was to make a direct route up the south-west face of Everest from the Western Cwm.

There had been three previous, unsuccessful expeditions, including a Bonington-led one in 1972. In 1975 Chris's team consisted of Doug Scott, Mick Burke, Dougal Haston, Pete Boardman, Martin Boysen, Nick Estcourt and Tut Braithwaite (the latter two finding the crucial way through the difficult Rock Band).

Doug Scott's photograph has captured the crucial moment at dusk on 24 September in all its dramatic glory, just as they are about to be the first Britons to put their feet on the highest summit in the world. Scott and Haston then had to spend the night in a hastily excavated snow hole on the South Summit without any oxygen or protective equipment, the highest bivouac that had ever been made. Two days later, Pete Boardman and Pertemba also made it to the top.

Although this was one of the last old-style Himalayan expeditions on a grand scale, supported by a huge team of Sherpas – Boardman memorably described it as 'one of the last great Imperial experiences' – it was another huge triumph, though marred, yet again, this time by the death of Mick Burke.

Right

70.   Tasker, Boardman and Renshaw on the NNE ridge of Everest, 5 May 1982. Chris Bonington

Once again I have chosen a picture by Chris Bonington, only this time to illustrate the darker side of the new, purer-than-ever style of high-altitude mountaineering that developed in the late '70s and early '80s. Bonington has not only taken a stupendous shot that conveys the full scale of the challenge involved, but he is once again in the right place at the right time for an important moment in mountaineering history – one eerily reminiscent of Odell's last sighting of Mallory and Irvine. Actually, this was taken 12 days before Boardman and Tasker disappeared on the north-north-east ridge. Although Bonington took some telephoto shots later of small dots on the higher pinnacles that are even more reminiscent of the First and Second Steps on the north ridge, this is the shot that, for me, best sums up the whole tragic enterprise.

Factual details: the picture, taken from Camp 2 on 5 May 1982, shows the three tiny dots of Tasker, Boardman and Renshaw reaching the top of the First Pinnacle, around 8000m. The highest point on the right is the Third Pinnacle, where the NNE ridge joins the north ridge, and the summit of Everest is on the left. Boardman and Tasker were last seen on 17 May. But their names live on forever, not only in their mountaineering achievements, but in the Boardman Tasker Award for Mountain Literature initiated in their memory.

So often is the huge level of achievement counterbalanced by huge loss.
Alex MacIntyre who had gone on to make stupendous alpine-style ascents
of the east face of Dhaulagiri in 1980 and Shishapangma in 1982, only to
die on the south face of Annapurna later in the year; Alison Chadwick,
who made the first woman's ascent of Gasherbrum III in 1975, only to die
on Annapurna in 1978; Alison Hargreaves, who soloed five of the classic
alpine north faces, mostly the first by a woman, and was the first woman to
climb Everest alone and without oxygen in 1995, only to die on K2 later in
the same year; and Ginette Harrison, first woman to climb Kangchenjunga
in 1998, only to die on Dhaulagiri in 2000.

Left
72. Leo Houlding on the crux of *The Passage to Freedom*
     El Capitan, October 1999
     Andrew McGarr

I have chosen my last of this selection of 'crux' photographs, not only because it is an outstanding image of a crux moment, with both Leo Houlding's hands clear of the rock as he flies up towards the camera in a dizzyingly exposed sea of vertical granite, but also because it sums up the underlying spirit of vision and daring that runs through the whole history of British rock climbing and mountaineering, showing conclusively that the sport is still very much alive and well in the new millennium.

Leo Houlding describes the 500-metre route *The Passage to Freedom*, which he climbed with Jose Pereyra, Jason Pickles 'and other monkeys' in 1999, as 'a work in progress'. It currently joins the Nose of El Capitan halfway up, but Leo's dream is one day to make an independent finish. It has the awesome grade of 5.13d, which roughly translates into English grades as: 'E8 6c,6a,6b,6c,7a,7a(A0),6c,6c,6c,6c,6a,6a,6a'!

Having almost onsighted the existing super-route of *El Nino* in 1998, Leo returned to the valley in the autumn of 1999

> ... with a new perception of the wall and a dream to free climb the biggest, steepest, blankest section of El Cap that is the Dawn Wall. Six glorious weeks were spent exploring the oceans of featureless granite trying to find a line. We climbed ground-up in party style, head-pointing pitches after preparation. The Dyno pitch is one of the coolest in the world! 500 feet up, an 8-foot sideways leap is the only passage to freedom.

As a caption from John Cleare's photographic classic *Rock Climbers in Action in Snowdonia* put it:
'*I had this dream, see, and I was falling upwards in a shaft of light.*'

ED DOUGLAS

Soul Traders:
150 Years of Peddling Adventures

'Money,' as Cyndi Lauper once sang, 'changes everything.' And she should know, since she spent the latter part of the 1970s a self-declared bankrupt working in the New York thrift store Screaming Mimi's. *Money Changes Everything* wasn't her tune but somehow the song fitted her like a threadbare satin glove. Talk of love is all very well, it suggests, but should the opportunity come along to hitch your wagon to a more upholstered star then forego love, and grab the cash. Only the young can do poor with any kind of grace.

Cyndi, who became a mega-star and made millions, is on my mind because I recently chanced upon an article about the commercialisation of alpinism written by Steve Dodd, for which I had written a cover line. In the tricksy way sub-editors have, I had chosen the song title *Money Changes Everything* to match the elegiac attitude struck by Dodd as he trawled the Chamonix scene for examples of how commercialisation was throttling the quixotic soul of mountaineering.

The article, published almost 15 years ago, used as its frame the old-school wisdom of the Chamonix guide Philippe Grenier who was distinctly queasy about the direction his compatriots were taking in their zest for media attention. 'I want to keep the soul in climbing,' Grenier told Dodd. 'I think that soul is going away now. I don't think I will be able to do anything against it. It will get worse. I think there are a lot of things coming which are killing the spirit of alpinism.'

Grenier had deep reservations about what some of his contemporaries were doing to garner attention, to create what amounts to a brand name which can be exploited in a fairly predictable round of lectures and product endorsements. He was openly critical of Catherine Destivelle, who had just completed a new route solo on the west face of the Petit Dru in 11 days. 'I admire her. But not at all like I admired Bonatti. I don't think there's any comparison between what she's done and what Bonatti did.'

Dodd also paid close attention to the victims of a growing public and commercial thirst for daredevils that produced seminal films like Christophe Profit's *Trilogie Pour Un Homme Seul* but left French alpinism frothing at the mouth with over-excitement. He cited the tragic death of Bruno Gouvy, who perished attempting to snowboard down the Y couloir on the Aiguille d'Argentière while shooting a commercial, and that of Jean-Marc Boivin, who died while BASE-jumping for a French television documentary.

Gouvy was a wild child who, his friends suggested, would have met a similar fate sooner or later with or without the support of his sponsors, Marlboro cigarettes. Boivin was an altogether shrewder and more accomplished alpinist who once said, 'If you play Russian roulette too often, you end up finding the bullet., Boivin found his bullet leaping off the Angel Falls in Venezuela on 17 February, 1990, aged 38.

Rereading this article, with the benefit of over a decade's hindsight, some of it seems prescient, some of it seems a little too apocalyptic and some of it jumps out at me very much for the first time, like this comment from Ivano Ghiradini. Ghiradini was one of those outsiders, like Christophe Profit, who was never accepted by the intensely jealous and competitive guiding scene in the Chamonix valley. He remains one of the awkward squad, a friend of Serge Gousseault who died climbing the Grandes Jorasses with René Desmaison in 1971 in circumstances that remain controversial.

'Climbers write too much,' he complained in Dodd's piece. 'Every climber who does something writes about it. They're presented as heroes, and I think it's dangerous.' The philosopher Daniel Dennett once said that human beings are libraries' way of making new books. Maybe climbing books and magazines make new climbers?

Twenty years ago, when I was launching a climbing magazine and trying to push my rock-climbing standard in spite of an absence of any observable talent, I assumed that I would continue to write about climbing long after I stopped doing it. As it turns out, the reverse is true. I find myself now just as absorbed and enthused by the strange restlessness that drove me to take up climbing almost three decades ago. The simple act of studying a map can lift my heart. Sometimes, on a frosty morning walking in the Peak District, I'll hear a cock crowing and catch the smell of wood smoke and be transported to the Himalaya.

Whole worlds of landscape and memory can be thrown up from such fragments. When I fall asleep listening to the curlew and the rush of waves on a beach, or to the velvet nothingness of a night in the desert, then each atom in the universe makes perfect sense to me. Writing about it, however, has become a more difficult and questionable activity. More difficult, because I now realise that I wrote about climbing to understand why we do it. It seems to me a fascinating paradox in understanding human nature. Why do something dangerous with no apparent chance of proportionate reward? That's a slippery question to answer.

Motivation for each of us as mountaineers is so different. I want to disappear in nature, to find that state of mind of continuous present that being among mountains engenders so readily. 'Quick now, here, now, always – ,' TS Eliot wrote in *Little Gidding*. 'A condition of complete simplicity / (Costing not less than everything).' Others most certainly do not want to disappear in nature. They want to be aggrandised by nature, to see extreme environments as adding value to themselves by their achievements or suffering. A few take those experiences back to the public and demand – and get – attention, money, position.

I am really not criticising – honestly. Both philosophies are equally human. Household gods insist on prodding me in the ribs, just like everybody else. Like Cyndi, I don't want to spend all my working life in a thrift store, although freelance journalism often feels like it. So how to balance the depth and value of what goes on out there, with all the greed, competition and complexities of life in what claims to be the real world?

That conflict has been familiar to most professional adventurers over the years. Those who are most commercially exploitative spend the least time thinking about this conundrum. Albert Smith, with his shows at the Egyptian Hall in Piccadilly in the 1850s, was arguably the first mountaineering celebrity, playing to packed houses every night and three matinees a week, accruing a substantial fortune on the basis of a mountaineering career that comprised one ascent of Mont Blanc.

Smith's guide was not an Anderegg or a Croz, but Phineas T Barnum, originator of *The Greatest Show on Earth*, and when Barnum was in town, Smith invited him along to the Egyptian Hall. Barnum got quite a shock. Several of the stories the impresario had told Smith over the years had been written into the Mont Blanc show. Afterwards, during dinner at the Garrick Club, Smith introduced Barnum to his friends as his mentor in the business, and acknowledged his debt to the American. 'Of course, as a showman,' Smith told him, 'you know very well that to win popular success, we have to appropriate and adapt to our uses everything of the sort that we can get hold of.' In other words, plagiarise.

Smith was a commercial and popular success without going through the stress of being original, or even a 'proper' climber. That caused resentment. But there was a public appetite for stories of adventure set in spectacular landscapes that predated the growth of photography and Smith filled that need. Romantic notions of the sublime were popularised not in print but in entertainments, and Albert Smith's success was one of the more spectacular results. Why should Smith care if others didn't regard him as a proper mountaineer? He gave people what they wanted.

More than a century and a half later, it seems not much has changed. The ghost of Albert Smith lingers on. The public still have an appetite for spectacular portrayals of adventure in harsh environments and they don't really care too much about the details. Norwegian polar travellers look on bemused as the British media fête a sequence of rugged heroes who turn modest polar journeys into bitter fights for survival, thereafter raking in the cash on the corporate lecture circuit.

The Edwardian polar boys, needing to raise a lot more cash to reach their objectives because their kit list included items like ice-breaking ships, were switched on to the potential of a public profile more quickly than the more fastidious mountaineers. Ernest Shackleton, for example, needed

£60,000 for his trans-Antarctic expedition in 1914, around £4m in today's money. Shackleton was an adroit self-publicist, however, and as a former sub-editor himself, knew how to pitch a story. The *London Mail* caught sight of him hustling for funds in January 1914, as he prepared to head south that summer: 'The mercenary side of a Polar "stunt" is absorbing. Any day you may see Sir Ernest, always alone, taxi-ing from one newspaper office to another. He is trying to arrange the best terms and it is going to be a battle royal.'

The chirpy cynicism of the *London Mail* is heart-warming. Too easily, we fall into the trap that the whole country regarded polar explorers as somehow emblematic of all that was good about Britain and the Empire. But here we see Shackleton rumbled, as he whips up his own personal ambition into a confection of imperial splendour. Film contracts were signed, his usual ghost, Edward Saunders, was hired to write the book for Heinemann, photographer Frank Hurley was brought on board to take the photographs and the *Daily Chronicle* got the newspaper rights. Unhappily for Shackleton, a Bosnian Serb called Gavrilo Princip trumped the story by shooting dead the heir to the throne of the Austro-Hungarian empire.

Grand adventures look foolish against the backdrop of a global crisis. Shackleton offered *Endurance* to the Admiralty but the First Lord, Winston Churchill, waved them off, despite regarding polar exploration as 'a sterile quest'. Leaving a nation consumed by war, however, would dent even the most self-confident adventurer, and Shackleton struggled to offer some justification in his last public utterance before sailing from Buenos Aires. Britain, at the time, was reading news reports from the first Battle of Ypres:

> We are leaving now to carry on our white warfare, and our farewell message to our country is that we will do our best to make good. Our thoughts and prayers will be with our brothers fighting at the front. We hope in our small way to add victories in science and discovery to that certain victory which our nation will achieve in the cause of honour and liberty.

Shackleton's words reek of discomfort. Soon he disappeared from view and Europe faced apocalypse. When first news of the expedition reached London in March, 1916, Churchill wrote to his wife: 'Fancy that ridiculous Shackleton and his South Pole – in the crash of the world.' By the end of the war the great explorer was playing to half-empty houses twice daily at the Philharmonic Hall in Great Portland Street. In an era of sacrifice, Scott's absence held more appeal that Shackleton's survival. When he died, Shackleton left debts of £40,000. Expedition clocks were sold to pay the man who wrote *South*, Edward Saunders. After the Great War interest in polar adventures waned. But stories of adventure are a trope of culture through the ages. And so a new public fascination with Everest and its technological cousin, aviation, grew, fed by the growing communications industry. This irritated old-fashioned amateurs like Arthur Hinks, secretary of the Mount Everest Committee,who regarded journalists as 'sharks and pirates' and ordered climbers on the 1921 reconnaissance not to talk to them.

But alas, cold, hard cash is the unavoidable starting point for the grandest dreams and in an age of mass media and commerce, the dream had become the product. Hinks showed himself to be something of a pirate, holding George Mallory to ransom over the expedition contract, putting his star climber in a financial corner. The first two Everest expeditions made a profit, partly because of media deals signed by the Committee, but it behaved with abject cupidity in its dealings with Mallory, not quite on his uppers but hoping to earn his living from his pen. Why should he not profit himself from his courage and imagination, and not just enrich organizations lurking behind flimsy screens of nationalism and duty?

Those weeks of indecision Mallory faced in late 1923, about whether or not to go to Everest the following year, offer an exquisite illustration of tensions modern climbers can recognise. He was caught on a web of his own devising, the threads of love, responsibility, ambition, position and the strongest strand of all, his passion for Everest. At the back of his mind was the half-articulated conviction that if he could stand on the summit of Everest, frustration and ambition would be extinguished, and replaced by a steadier light.

Even so, Mallory told Ruth he wouldn't go. It took a visit from Geoffrey Winthrop Young to scour doubt from Mallory's mind. Young's timely intervention persuaded them George should think again. They should, he suggested, consider the 'label of Everest' that would be affixed to the Mallory name. That would secure the family's future. Ruth could see the sense in that, of her husband returning to the field of battle, where men win glory.

'It seems rather a momentous step altogether,' George Mallory wrote to Young after his visit, 'with a new job to find when I come back, but it will not be a bad thing to give up the settled ease of this present life. . . I expect I shall have no cause to regret your persuasion.' Nor did he.

How can you not, though, feel affection towards Mallory for turning his back on the sensible, bourgeois option of getting his head down, for going back on the road for a last shot at redemption. A little over 30 years later, you can find Don Whillans fretting over the same conundrum, in the more prosaic setting of a Carlisle building site, needing £150 to go to Masherbrum. At least Don didn't have any kids, but the motivation of hunting out a life less ordinary seems to me of the same cloth.

'The days of struggling in trenches so deep in mud and water that it was impossible to keep the boots on your feet were relieved by the odd letter from Bob [Downes] saying that the expedition plans were working out well. As far as I was concerned, the departure date couldn't come soon enough.' A few months later, Downes was dead, and Whillans found himself lecturing about the climb, his life falling into very different tracks from those followed by many of his contemporaries. The crags proved anything but barren for Whillans, even if the booze and fags dragged him down. Others were more thoughtful. 'Why not spend the rest of my life doing this sort of thing?' Eric Shipton wrote in *Upon That Mountain*, having escaped the drudgery of climbing Everest for a spot of exploration with Lawrence Wager. 'There was no way of life that I liked more, the scope appeared to be unlimited, others had done it, vague plans had already begun to take shape, why not put some of them into practice? It was a disturbing idea, one which caused me much heart searching and many sleepless nights. The most obvious snag, of course, was a lack of private means; but surely such a mundane consideration could not be decisive?'

Shipton, in 1933, made an act of rebellion, a conscious decision to follow his instinct to become a kind of superior hobo, a thinking-man's beatnik. That choice, which was in essence subversive of what might be described as the mountaineering establishment, cost him the leadership of the 1953 Everest expedition. John Hunt was a remarkable man, who left an enduring and admirable legacy, but for me there is something irresistible about how Shipton conducted himself.

His wife, Diana, could describe Shipton as 'ruthless' and with 'a need for greatness'. Others might argue that I shouldn't mythologise. But most of us live by myths, don't we? Better, surely, to pick a rewarding one. 'There are few treasures,' Shipton wrote, 'of more lasting worth than the experience of a way of life that is in itself wholly satisfying. Nothing can alter the fact if for one moment in eternity we have really lived.'

Philippe Grenier's fears for the soul of alpinism were justified – to an extent. Money really does change everything. The mountain world is in the grip of a consumerist frenzy, making Grenier's world seem rather admirable by comparison. Newspapers and television are interested either in disasters or adventurers hunting attention and sponsorship rather than Shipton's moments in eternity. Fame and wealth are determined in mountaineering by your back-story and the competence of your publicist. Stunts like the so-called Seven Summits are meaningless as mountaineering challenges, but their very glibness attracts followers and shifts products. All of this must have an impact on the public's understanding of what we do.

But has it had an impact on, if you'll forgive the term, proper mountaineering? You could argue that the obsession in the Himalaya with peak-bagging, which was pretty much underway when Grenier was voicing his fears, has meant little progress since the halcyon days of the 1980s. Much of it has been driven by a professional desire to fill lecture halls and satisfy sponsors. But I wouldn't force the point. There are too many exceptions to that rule: Mick Fowler, Nick Bullock, Ian Parnell, Steve House, Vince Anderson, Andrew Lindlblade, Athol Whimp – it's quite a list. (And, I should add, among those peak-baggers are some deeply impressive mountaineers.)

Of those men from that list whom I know, all of them can tell at a glance what's meaningful in climbing, and what is not. Media attention and sponsorship deals seem hilarious distractions by comparison. Ultimately, what the media thinks or publishes doesn't matter, not in the long run. And the money? I suppose we could ask Reinhold Messner what he'd like to be remembered for, soloing Everest in 1980, or owning a castle.

We are familiar still with the names of Whymper, Mummery and other giants of the Victorian era but the name Albert Smith means more to cultural historians, because of his innovative presentations, in an era before photography, than it does to modern mountaineers. At the height of his fame, his contemporaries in the Alpine Club, of which he was a founder member, were resentfully dismissive of someone who had to be carried to the summit of Mont Blanc by his guides, making a fortune. He died a millionaire, in today's terms, but aged just 44, from a lung infection. Money doesn't change absolutely everything, does it?

PETER GILLMAN

Climbing Controversies

The word 'scandal' has a curiously dated ring. It smacks of tabloid journalism, of newspaper hypocrisy and manufactured outrage. As a journalist operating in what I like to consider the upscale end of the market, I would use it only sparingly. But now the editor of the *AJ* has asked me to write about Climbing Scandals. The scandals, so-called, that I have reported on took climbing into difficult territory. Climbers have preferred not to wash their dirty linen in public (apologies for the cliché, but then I am a journalist) but on the occasions I am about to describe they felt it was necessary to do so. Once I became involved, I was uneasily aware that my allegiances could be pulled in different directions, given that I was both journalist and climber. I am also uncertain whether, in retrospect, the term 'scandal' could reasonably be applied to all the episodes in question.

The first of these began, as these things so often do, with a call from Ken Wilson. He and several colleagues were troubled by the claims of a climber named Keith McCallum to have put up an impressive series of routes in North Wales. Ken, Pete Crew, and others had inspected McCallum's routes and their initial respect for his achievements had turned rapidly to scepticism. McCallum was the founder of the Apollo Climbing Club, in the Midlands, but when Ken contacted other club members he was dismayed to learn that none had ever met McCallum's three named partners. There were troubling safety implications arising from the doubts over the routes, as anyone attempting to follow McCallum's descriptions, which had been published in the Climbers' Club's *New Climbs*, could find themselves in difficulty. Ken was equally troubled over the potential legal implications of expressing these doubts in public, and the editor of *New Climbs*, Nigel Rogers, had limited himself to warning that climbers who attempted the routes should do so with 'the greatest caution'.

And so Ken called me. I was then a 27-year-old freelance journalist, writing mostly for the *Sunday Times*, which was then, under Harry Evans, building a reputation for investigative journalism. As Ken explained to me, the coded caveat published by Nigel Rogers was the furthest the Climbers' Club was prepared to go in light of Britain's libel laws. Would the *Sunday Times* care to take a look?

It was an offer not to be refused. At the start of my career I had been diffident about writing about climbing, in view of journalism's bleak reputation for inaccuracy and crude misrepresentation when reporting the sport. But by then I felt more confident, having reported the dramas of the *Eiger Direct* attempt for the *Daily Telegraph* and the 1967/78 British attempt on Cerro Torre for the *Sunday Times*. The *Sunday Times* agreed to my proposal to pursue the story, and in short order I found myself in North Wales examining the disputed routes with Pete Crew. One of them, said Crew emphatically, was 'a chop route', and quite implausible. The Holliwell brothers, Les and Laurie, delivered a similar verdict on a route they attempted.

The next move was to confront McCallum himself. So far as I recall, I contacted him by telephone and arranged to meet him in North Wales. The sports editor of the *Sunday Times*, John Lovesey, attended the meeting, conscious of the potential costs, in legal penalties, of getting this wrong. I am not sure what I expected of an encounter in which we were effectively to accuse a man of lying. But what surprised me about McCallum's demeanour was how defiant and truculent he was. As well as insisting that he had climbed the routes as he had described, he declined to provide any details about his seconds, saying he saw no reason why he should. He also attempted to shift the onus to his detractors – the 'next move', he said, was up to them. 'They started the whole bloody business, and it's on their plates and that's the way I'm leaving it.'

After our encounter, Lovesey and I were in no doubt that McCallum, to put it politely, had been telling fibs. We also speculated that he was a fantasist, which helped formulate the headline that appeared above the article in the *Sunday Times*: 'A Walter Mitty on Craig Gogarth'. McCallum disappeared from the climbing world, as he had hinted he would in his final remarks to us: 'I don't get the same pleasure from climbing as I used to,' he said.

Job done, it might be thought. But there were some complex issues involved which preoccupy me even now. Journalism has always struck me as an accidental process. There is no central clearing house by which stories are allocated. For the *Sunday Times* to take up the story resulted from the network of contacts I was developing, and from the fabled persistence of Ken Wilson in seeking to have the doubts over the climbs resolved and publicised.

To some extent, it went against the grain for the climbing world to expose its problems in the national press, which had a reputation for cheapening the values of mountaineering. And who was I, so early in my career, to act as accuser against a fellow climber? What gave me the right to confront him and charge him with lying?

We were able to invoke one public interest argument, namely that climbers attempting to follow McCallum's descriptions could find themselves in serious trouble. But that was only part of it: both Ken and I were also driven by the desire to solve the mystery and, grandiose though it may seem, to establish the truth.

Similar issues were at the core of another burgeoning scandal I was to write about: the disputed ascent of Cerro Torre by Cesare Maestri. I already had certain possessive sentiments about that bewitching mountain, having reported the attempt in 1967/68 by four of Britain's stellar young climbers, Haston, Burke, Boyson and Crew. While trudging along the glacier below

Cerro Torre, I found a long-handled ice-axe that must have been dropped by the Italian team, Maestri included, who had claimed the ascent, in highly dubious circumstances, in 1958. Sadly I lost my trophy as the climbing team purloined it to use in their camp on the Col of Patience, where it was interred under several metres of snow.

I followed the Cerro Torre saga thereafter, in particular the attempt by Eric Jones, Leo Dickinson, Cliff Phillips and Gordon Hibberd in 1972, which ended at the foot of the final headwall. The four climbers had been enraged by Maestri's use of an air-compressor to drive bolts across the upper sections of the route, and utterly sceptical about his claim to have free-climbed to the summit in 1958.

By now on the staff of the *Sunday Times*, I was keen to write about these dramas for its colour magazine. I was again working with Ken Wilson and with Leo Dickinson, who was intent on making a film about the 1971 attempt and the controversy swirling around Maestri. Together with interpreter Alan Heppenstall, an AC member, we arranged to meet Maestri at his apartment in the Dolomite resort of Madonna di Campiglio.

Looking back, the similarities with the encounter with McCallum are striking. To begin with, Maestri appeared the soul of hospitality, greeting us with a smile and offering coffee and schnapps. But then he showed the same truculence and defiance as McCallum, and also attempted to steer our exchanges away from the 1958 climb. For a time we too avoided the key issues – one of the tactics in this kind of interview is to accumulate material on related matters before homing in on the most sensitive issues, so that if the encounter ends abruptly you do not go home empty-handed.

So it proved on this occasion. We never accused Maestri of lying, at least not directly. It was Ken who came closest when he asked Maestri to mark the line of his 1958 ascent on a photograph. 'You must be joking,' Maestri protested, saying he was unable to remember 'after all that time'. Ken pressed the point, asking for more details of the route.

'Are you saying that I didn't get to the summit?' Maestri asked. Before we could answer, he complained that we had left this question to the end of the interview. 'It's rather impolite, I think.' Maestri was scribbling on a note pad and he tore off a sheet and handed to me. It read: 'Tione Brescia Est. Autostrada per Milano.' It was our route home. Interview over.

By then I had been a journalist for all of eight years. I had joined the staff of the *Sunday Times* where my work with the Insight team left me under no illusions that there were classes of people for whom lying, or being economical with the truth, was not a problem. Sometimes the fun lay in trying to work out whether an official statement that looked like a lie had some kind of hidden caveat, so that the person who delivered it could claim that it was not an out-and-out untruth (government denials that CIA's extraordinary rendition flights landed in Britain come to mind.)

But climbers? Having been a climber for about as long as I had a journalist, I was steeped in the belief that this was an activity where truth was paramount. True, McCallum had proved the exception, but he was a small-time figure compared with Maestri. Was it really possible that a climber of such stature would falsely claim to have made one of the epochal ascents of mountaineering, and then sustain his falsehood with such ridiculous bluster and bravado?

The answer, sadly, was 'yes'. It was a pivotal moment for me, when climbers became as other mortals. True, there were precedents, such as Dr Cook's claim to have climbed Mt McKinley. But it is an unsettling experience, to accept someone's hospitality and then witness his attempt to sustain a manifest fiction. It also made me wonder why Maestri had even agreed to meet us in the first place. Perhaps he thought he could bluff his way through the questioning, knowing that it was immensely difficult for us to establish the negative, namely that he had not done what he claimed to have done. But for us, the case against him was overwhelming.

Did any of this matter? There was no public interest argument, as we could assert over the McCallum affair. In this case we were left with the subjective judgment that truth mattered and lies should be rebutted. In addition, the ethics of the mountaineering world provide further validity. If honesty is the paramount value, then those who violate it deserve to be exposed.

It may be stretching the definition of the word 'scandal' to apply it to these two case histories: the word 'hoax' may be more suitable. But I have no doubt that the term applies to the death of a bright young woman named Colette Fleetwood who joined the University of the West of England Fell-Walking Club in 1993. There were reports of the accident in the mountaineering press, but when I enquired further I felt that the circumstances were so appalling that they should be more widely known. I had left the *Sunday Times* soon after the Murdoch takeover some 10 years before and was now a freelance, writing for whoever would take me – in this case, the Saturday edition of the *Daily Telegraph*.

Colette had done no serious hill-walking when she joined the fell-walking club. Her very first outing was an attempt to climb Parsley Fern Gully in Cwm Glas in January 1994. The weather was hideous, with strong winds and driving rain. Colette was totally out of her depth and poorly equipped, wearing flimsy summer boots and lacking ice-axe or crampons. After reaching a snowfield near the top of the route, Colette was blown from her holds and fell to her death.

It looked like one of those old-fashioned accidents, when naval cadets fell to their deaths wearing Wellington boots. This should never have happened in 1994. I had to spell this out in the *Telegraph*; *Alpine Journal* readers will appreciate the point. What emerged was the fatal combination of ignorance and arrogance from the party leader, a 21-year-old science student, and obfuscation and a bid to disclaim any responsibility by the university authorities. At Colette's memorial service, the university vice-chancellor sought out Colette's father to tell him (a) that the university and students union were 'completely separate' and that (b) the accident was 'a matter for the students union'.

When I approached the students union, it refused to answer my questions, while a solicitor acting for the student in charge tried to claim that he had not really been a leader at all – the effect being to save him from any legal claims. Thus Mike Fleetwood's grief at losing his daughter was compounded by his anger at the cowardice of the university, whose principal thought, he believed, was to evade responsibility for Colette's death.

The BMC did not emerge from the incident with much credit either: although the club was affiliated to the BMC, which provided it with public liability insurance, the BMC appeared to feel it had little or no place in helping the club to handle the responsibilities involved in equipping novices venturing into a risk sport. A legal advisor to the BMC told me: 'If someone goes into the mountains unprepared for that risk, they can't be totally surprised if they have an accident.'

I was unable to talk to the party leader; his solicitor told me that he had wanted to try to explain what had gone wrong, but the solicitor had advised against it. My article appeared bearing the headlines: 'Why did my daughter die?' and 'The buck starts here: why no one takes the blame.' Almost 10 years later, there came an intriguing coda, when the party leader wrote to me and said he would like to meet. I travelled to Bristol, where he was working as a civilian in a police forensic department. After nearly a decade, he clearly still wanted to justify his behaviour and his decisions on the fateful day, and also felt he was not to blame for Colette's death. I called Colette's father to tell him what he had said. 'He still hasn't learned anything then,' Mike Fleetwood said.

It is good to report, however, that the BMC has altered its approach in the past 10 years, as well as being more ready to discuss the dilemmas arising from leadership issues in group activities. It now runs impressive two-day 'good practice' seminars for students, which provide guidance in leadership skills. It also argues that students should adopt a philosophy of collective responsibility in keeping with the ethos of the sport.

Not long afterwards another long-running episode moved towards a denouement. I first wrote about the death of Günther Messner in 1970, together with his brother Reinhold's allegations of incompetence against the expedition leader, the controversial Karl Maria Herrligkoffer. Thirty years later the story flared up again, when Reinhold mounted a furious attack on his former team-mates at a book launch in Munich. In the subsequent row, his team-mates retaliated by voicing their long-nurtured doubts over Messner's original account of events. The accusations against Messner were extraordinary: the worst of them being that he had placed his brother at risk through his own ambition, had sent his brother back down the mountain alone, and had then spun a pack of lies to cover all this up. If true, it certainly amounted to a scandal by any definition of the word.

Furnished with a commission from the *Sunday Times Magazine*, I toured Germany, assisted by Jochen Hemmleb, to meet Messner's accusers. There were inconsistencies in their allegations as well as in the range of accounts Messner had advanced over the years. Here I felt I was on shaky territory. Who was I to second-guess the decisions made in extremis by so accomplished a mountaineer? And it was all but impossible to reconcile the conflicting accounts from a series of strong-willed individuals relating to events and decisions above 8000 metres and possibly distorted by emotion and the passage of time.

The article nonetheless floated the allegations and canvassed the range of explanations. Then came the time to talk to Messner. These days, there is both a legal as well as a moral obligation to put allegations to the person under attack. Under what is known as the Reynolds principles, which have become increasingly important in shaping the laws of libel, journalists have to give the accused person ample opportunity to respond to the allegations. They must make them aware of the full scope and context of the allegations, and must record and report their answers fairly and accurately.

I caught up with Messner by phone at the European Parliament (he was then a Green MEP). It was a testing conversation, as the anger Messner felt at his colleagues' accusations had barely subsided. I had to provide the *Sunday Times* lawyers with a transcript of the entire 40-minute conversation, but they concluded that I had played fair to Messner. The subsequent article largely took his side, although I also tried to fathom the explosive anger Messner was subject to more than 30 years after his brother died. In the end Messner scotched most of his critics when he produced a bone, proved by DNA to be his brother's, which certainly disposed of the wilder allegations against him and was most consistent with his account of events.

So no scandal there, and not a hoax either: but certainly a controversy that attracted public attention, because of both the damning nature of the accusations, had they been proved, and Messner's own celebrity.

I observed near the start of this article that journalism was an accidental process. As well as the scandals or hoaxes I have written about, there are other potential stories that I did not pursue. They involved allegations of greed, selfishness, and dishonesty. Sometimes I just had too much else to occupy me. Several times I embarked on my research, but reluctantly concluded that the allegations would simply be too difficult to prove.

There is one controversy I still cherish, for all sorts of reasons: the story of the Yeti footprint, which I wrote about on several occasions. Supposing Eric Shipton did fake the footprint, as has been alleged [and vigorously denied*]? Would that be a scandal? Not in the least. It would rank as a hoax, and, if so, a better hoax there has never been: mischievous, entertaining, harmless and sheer fun.

---

* *Editor's note*: see Michael Ward's *Everest. A Thousand Years of Exploration* (The Ernest Press, 2003), pages 201-202.

ROBERT MACFARLANE

'All one might wish of wisdom'

Earlier this year, the Everest-summiter Bear Grylls presented a television series called *Born Survivor*. The show's premise was simple: each week, Grylls parachuted into a different wild zone – jungle, swamp, mountain, desert. His task was to reach what he called 'civilisation' alive. He was equipped with only a knife, the clothes he stood up in and the parachute he fell down in. Oh, and a cameraman. Because someone else was needed to film Bear surviving alone in these wild places.

The show's ethos was para-military, its dramatic principle a version of SAS-style escape-and-evasion – but with the landscape as the enemy. Grylls specialised in a gratuity of action. When he caught a trout from an alpine lake, he insisted on first chewing out its spine and then eating it raw like a corn-cob – although he had a knife which would have permitted him to kill it quickly and then sushi it into strips. He munched maggots from the rancid corpse of an avalanche-killed chamois ('Bite their heads off first,' he advised the audience back home, poised over their TV dinners). Scant mention was made of the cameraman who followed and filmed Grylls' every move, and who was clearly equipped with GPS, tent, rope, harness, warm gear, and some non-maggoty rations.

The end-point of each episode was Grylls' 'escape' back to safety and humanity. As the twinkling lights of a coastal village or alpine hamlet hove into view, Grylls would reflect movingly on the experience of having survived in such 'hostile' and 'brutal' terrains.

Landscapes, of course, are not 'hostile', or 'brutal'. They are entirely, gradelessly indifferent. A glacier is as devoid of intent as a brick. A mountain is no more rancorous than a blade of grass or a lightbulb. To attribute hostility to a jungle is as absurd as describing a table as 'delighted' or a bicycle as 'philosophical'. But it was important to the conceit of *Born Survivor* that Grylls should have overcome adversity, should have evaded the depredations of these places.

Born Survivor, in its testosterone-soaked silliness, exemplified one of the ways that we have, historically, approached wild landscapes. According to this tradition of thought, wildness is a quality to be vanquished. Wild places offer challenges: they are to be beaten, escaped from, dominated, or otherwise conquered. This heresy runs deep in our thinking about landscape: the belief that degrees of 'wildness' offer a metric system against which to measure one's resilience, the conviction that sustained contact with the wild gives a person exceptional strength and hardihood.

I write 150 years on from the founding of the Alpine Club, and it was during the first decades of the Club and of British alpinism more generally that this heresy infiltrated what we now awkwardly call 'outdoor culture'. Reading through early issues of the *Alpine Journal*, and other mid-Victorian documents of exploration and ascent, certain attitudes towards wild landscape recur. Foremost are those of victory and defeat, struggle and reward. In these texts, nature is figured most usually as a foe, enemy or lover, to be vanquished, conquered, or ravished according to your metaphor. The mountain-world, with all its hazards and asperities, serves as a testing-ground. Crossing the snowfields of the Alps or the Caucasus reveals what you are made of – and whether it is the right stuff. To climb a mountain is to confirm one's strength, to earn an affidavit of pluck and potency – and of manhood.

In 1843, for instance, the glaciologist and explorer James Forbes tellingly described an Alpine journey as 'perhaps the nearest approach to a military campaign with which the ordinary citizen has a chance of meeting'. Four years later, an editorial in *Blackwood's Edinburgh Magazine* concerning the exploration of the Arctic declared that 'the evident design of Providence in placing difficulties before Man is to sharpen his faculties for their mastery'. From the 1860s onwards, a pungently masculine Darwinism began to rise from the pages of the *Alpine Journal*. 'The law of survival of the fittest,' growled A F Mummery approvingly of solo climbing in 1892, 'has full and ample chance of eliminating [a man] should he be, in any way, a careless or incapable mountaineer.' When John Tyndall recollected his first ascent of the Weisshorn he did so in terms of a virginity being taken. 'I pressed the very highest snowflake of the mountain,' he wrote, 'and the prestige of the Weisshorn was forever gone.'

This understanding of the wild place as a realm of test is millennia old. It is present in the Bible, of course – in the Wilderness of the Wanderings episode in *Exodus*, and in the Gospel account of the Forty Days in the Wilderness, when Jesus is tempted by Satan in the Judean desert. It is there, too, in the Old English epic poem *Beowulf* which is filled with what the poet calls *wildéor*, or savage creatures. In the poem, these monstrous dragon-like beings inhabit a landscape of wolf-haunted forests, deep lakes, wind-swept cliffs and treacherous marshes. And it is against these wild places and *wildéor* that the civilisation of Beowulf's tribe, the Geats – with their warm and well-lit mead halls, their hierarchical warrior culture – sets itself: the slaying of the *wildéor* proves the honour of the men.

The Victorian alpinists, then, by no means invented the idea of a wild place as a testing ground. But they did institutionalise it. And the practice of self-proving remains – as Grylls' carnival of testosterone shows – active and popular in our recreational relationship with landscape. Personal risk and exertion are still too often identified as the charismatic aspects of 'wilderness experience' (even as we ensure we remain umbilically connected to our 'civilisation' by mobile phone and GPS). Miles walked, pounds carried, wind-speed survived, metres ascended – a day in the hills is reduced to a set of statistics. We have come to crave synthetic versions of intrepidity. Wildness has become a commodity, 'wild' a high-sell adjective in adventure-tourism brochures. In many ways and for many people, a wild landscape remains something to be vanquished.

There is, though, an alternative tradition of thought concerning wildness and wild places. It also runs deep in our culture, and especially in the literature of mountains and mountaineering, but we allude to it less often, find ourselves less easy with its values and cadences. According to this tradition, wildness is something not to be vanquished, but to be cherished.

The literature and art of this tradition tell of wildness as an energy both exemplary and exquisite, and of wild places as realms of miracle, diversity and abundance. They represent landscape as a medium of renewal, restoration and joy. Encounters with wildness are seen to induce modesty and humility in the traveller, and also exalt him or her spiritually. To borrow George Eliot's beautiful phrase, the wild 'enlarges the range the self has to swim in'.

Three years ago, I started on a series of journeys to some of the remaining wild places of Britain and Ireland. These journeys began in an attempt to answer a geographical question: what wildness was left in our densely-populated and over-tarmac'ed archipelago? But they swiftly and unexpectedly became explorations into the past histories of 'wildness', and into our present and future needs for the wild.

In an attempt to come to know better the wild places I reached, I went to them in all four seasons, at night as well as by day, and in all weathers – blizzard, heat-wave, rainstorm, mist. I swam, climbed and walked through them, and I slept out wherever I could, spending nights wild-camping on cliff-tops and beaches, deep in ancient woods, on tiny skerries, pilgrim islands, mountain summits and ice-filled lochans, under star-filled skies, and near bird colonies. Along the way I bathed in phosphorescent night-seas of the Lleyn Peninsula, climbed frozen waterfalls, and watched a red sun rise over an Arctic England.

During these years, I also read widely in the literature of wildness and wilderness, trying to understand how the different strands of thought concerning this idea had braided and unbraided over time. I became especially interested in the idea of wildness as a force for good – its ancient antecedents, its periods of samizdat suppression.

The idea can be traced back, in a world context, to the Chinese artistic tradition known as *shan-shui* or 'rivers-and-mountains', which originated in the early fifth-century BC, and endured for two thousand years. Its practitioners – T'ao Chi'en, Li Po, Du Fu, Lu Yu – were usually wanderers or self-exiles who lived in the mountain-lands of China, and wrote about the wild world around them. Their art, like that of the early Christian monks, sought to articulate the wondrous processes of the world, its continuous coming-into-being. To this quality of aliveness, the *shan-shui* artists gave the name *zi-ran*, which might be translated as 'self-ablazeness', 'self-thusness', or 'wildness'. Pilgrims and walkers, they explored their mountains in what they called the 'dragon-suns' of summer, and in the long winds of winter and the blossom-storms of late spring. They wrote of the cool mist that settled into valleys at dawn, of bamboo groves into which green light fell, and of how thousands of snowy egrets would take off from lakes like lifting blizzards. They observed the way winter light fell upon drifted snow, and how shadows hung from cold branches, and wrote that such sights moved them to a 'bright clear joy'.

Within a more recent British tradition, cherishings of wildness and wild landscapes can be found in the work of – among dozens of others – Samuel Taylor Coleridge (especially in his letters and journals of 1802 to 1803), Dorothy Wordsworth (whose 'wild eyes' Wordsworth acclaims in 'Tintern Abbey'), John Clare, Richard Jefferies, the Norwich painter John Sell Cotman, the professional walker Stephen Graham, and Nan Shepherd, whose marvellously parochial vision of the Cairngorms, *The Living Mountain*, is a relatively unknown masterpiece of mountain-writing. Many of the early alpinists were also, for all their machismo, sensitive to wildness as a function of beauty. One thinks here of Douglas Freshfield's ecstatic accounts of his first sight of Ushba, or of Mallory's lush descriptions of Everest in 1921 – 'Keats's lone star', 'a giant', 'a fantastic vision'....

Perhaps above all, this account of the wild is apparent in the work of W H Murray, whose books *Mountaineering in Scotland* and *Undiscovered Scotland* record Murray's magnificent, impertinent adventures in the Highlands during the 1930s and 1940s: night-ascents of the Cuillin, a New Year's Eve spent on the polar summit of Ben Nevis, skinny-dipping, a double-traverse of the Cuillin Ridge. There is a gratuity to Murray's actions, of course – why a *double*-traverse of the Cuillin? – but there is, too, lifting off every page, a sense of wildness as a mystical force. The profound elevation of the spirit which occurs in a wild place, the ways of seeing it ignites: for Murray, these were the gifts and worth of landscape – not the jag of adrenaline it can induce, not the proof of manliness it can supply. Over the past three years, I have come to agree with Murray, and with the fine, careful declaration of the American writer Barry Lopez:

> Less violent events are the common experience of most people who travel in wild landscapes: a sublime encounter with perhaps the most essential attribute of wilderness – falling into resonance with a system of unmanaged, non-human-centered relationships – can be as fulfilling as running a huge and difficult rapid, or climbing a hazardous ice-gully [...] Sometimes lingering in a country's unpretentious hills and waters offers all one might wish of wisdom.

DENNIS GRAY

The Rise and Fall
of the Working Class Climber

The working class, come kiss my ass
I've joined the Alpine Club at last!
(To the tune of 'the Red Flag')

Whenever I pick up a copy of the *Alpine Journal* I always turn first to the obituary section. I did this recently with some journals from the late 1940s, which is when I started to climb. One that caught my eye was of a celebrated Knight of the Realm. 'He was a damned good shot, and a first class angler,' declared the obituarist. Another noted that a deceased Baronet, 'kept a fine cellar and was always a generous host to visitors at his estate in Scotland'.

The impression given from these *AJ*s was of an elite, upper-class organisation; a silver spoon group who actually had not done a lot of hardcore climbing but really cut the mustard in government, professional and social circles. I have said before that when I was a young climber, my mainly working-class companions and I looked on the Alpine Club with a jaundiced eye. This was understandable given the advice we received from an old and respected member approached on how to go about the business of becoming an alpinist. When Alfie Beanland reported back on this at our weekly gathering of the Bradford Lads at Tommy's café one Sunday night in Otley we fell about laughing. The sagacious advice was: 1. Make your travel arrangements through Thomas Cook. 2. Keep your ice axe firmly in front of you. 3. Follow the guides because they know the way. We deduced from this that Alpine Club members were geriatric eccentrics who had no understanding of our climbing lives.

There had been strong working-class groups of British climbers in the 1920s and 1930s, notably of course the Creagh Dhu from Glasgow. Other manufacturing cities such as Sheffield, Liverpool, Leeds/Bradford and Manchester spawned similar groups, but poverty, the effects of the Great Depression, and very limited holiday time for those who had jobs, largely prevented them from being able to make a mark in mountaineering abroad. This was unlike the experience of their continental counterparts, for many of the finest alpinists of that period were drawn from the working class. They were equally poor and deprived but were fortunate in having the Alps almost on their doorstep.

The great Innsbruck climber Matthias Auckenthaler was a chimney sweep and would walk long distances to reach the rock faces. And climbers like Anderl Heckmair, Pierre Allain and Riccardo Cassin were also from the working class. Unfortunately, the Alpine Club simply did not realise the revolution that was taking place, dismissing first ascents such as those of the north faces of the Grandes Jorasses, Eiger and Matterhorn as somewhat politically inspired and of no great merit. In fact, as mountaineering history now records, they were outstanding climbs by some of the finest alpinists of their generation. Even today the manner of their achievement inspires respect. Think of the Schmid brothers, Toni and Franz, cycling from Munich because they could not afford to journey to Zermatt by any other means, and then bagging the first ascent of the Matterhorn's north face.

The Alpine Club worthies of the day seem to have had no knowledge of the climbing standards being achieved in the Eastern Alps. They appear to have believed that most of these climbs were done by proceeding from piton to piton, whereas outstanding leaders such as Toni Schmid, Emil Solleder and Auckenthaler limited piton use to a minimum and achieved free rock climbing standards equal to any in the UK, but on a much grander scale. The AC meanwhile was still wrestling with its old demons of guided versus non-guided climbing and the club's role in the development of British climbing – an area in which it had not previously taken a great interest. Progressives like Geoffrey Winthrop Young, Jack Longland and David Cox tried to move things along but it took the massive influx of working-class newcomers to the sport after the war, and the foundation of literally dozens of new clubs, to sweep away precious protective attitudes. Young (AC president 1941-43) used his great prestige to get the other senior clubs to act along with the Alpine Club and some of the new groups to form the British Mountaineering Council in 1944 as the representative body for the sport.

I only met Young once and that was at the front of the Old Dungeon Ghyll Hotel in Langdale in the autumn of 1956. He was sat on a bench enjoying the morning sunshine, impressively dressed in cloak, tweeds and brogues, a fedora crowning his shock of grey hair, a fine moustache gracing aristocratic features. He motioned me over with his walking stick and demanded, 'Are you the young man who made an ascent of *Cenotaph Corner* this summer?'

I nodded and whispered, 'Yes.'

'How many pitons did you place?' he asked.

'None,' I gasped in surprise. 'There were already two in place.'

'Mmm ... what was it like?'

'Very hard,' I confirmed.

'Well done, well done...'

And off I went to meet up with my Rock and Ice friends heading for the crag, feeling as if I had just been approved by the titular head of British climbing.

The new groups emerging from the working class in Britain after the war had one big advantage. They had no baggage of tradition holding them back. Most young people are rebellious and the new climbing clubs, unlike the older senior organisations, were made up mainly of such individuals. That much needed to change was obvious to us, as instanced by my own experience as a 13-year old in 1949.

A small party of us led by an older climber, an ex-serviceman who had fought at Arnhem, was walking back over Black Hill to Holmfirth to catch a bus home one Sunday night, after climbing at Shining Clough. A keeper appeared, shouted at us, lifted his shotgun and fired. I was petrified. So were my other young companions and we sprinted away for our lives. But not our ex-para, he ran at the keeper and hit him, wrestled the gun out of his hands and threw it as far as he could away into the peat bog. Slowly he returned to where we were waiting at a safe distance from the action, amazed by this whole sequence of events. 'I did not lose all those mates at Arnhem to come home and have someone shoot at me on my own bloody midden,' declared our leader between gritted teeth. Such incidents had been happening for many years. Later in life I got to know Benny Rothman who had been to prison for his part in organising the Kinder Scout Mass Trespass of 1932.

Fortunately, not long after our encounter on Black Hill the Access to the Countryside Bill was pushed through Parliament and the first of the national parks, The Peak District, was set up. The effect that this had on the opening up of the gritstone outcrops and the limestone crags of the area cannot be over emphasised. And the groups that most benefited from this were the new working-class climbers who had a field day developing such places as the Froggatt, Curbar and Gardom's edges. Foremost of these new outfits was Manchester's Rock and Ice Club. With members like Joe Brown, Ron Moseley, Don Whillans, Don Cowan, Nat Allen, Joe Smith and Don Roscoe, the club quickly became legendary in British climbing circles. For us they were the equivalent of the Beatles to the popular music scene in the next decade.

Some may be asking what has all this to do with alpine climbing? Well, in 1953 on his very first visit to the Alps and using skills he had developed on gritstone Joe Brown was able to lead, on sight, the crack that was to become the *Fissure Brown* on the west face of the Blaitière. It was the hardest free pitch in the whole of the western Alps. This attempt was cut short by bad weather but Brown returned the following year, accompanied by Don Whillans, to complete the route. First though, they tackled the west face of the Dru. How could it be in 1954 that two young guys with a minimum of alpine experience were able to repeat one of the most difficult climbs in the Alps (a first British ascent) and then go on to the Blaitière and pioneer the hardest free route in the Mont Blanc range? The answer is that they had honed their skills on the outcrops, crags and mountains of the UK, both in winter and summer.

Complementary to these achievements was the setting up of the Alpine Climbing Group, as a result of even the young Oxbridge climbers becoming frustrated by the lack of enthusiasm emanating from the Alpine Club. The ACG held its inaugural meeting in April 1953 at the Pen y Gwryd Hotel in North Wales, and Allen, Cowan and Whillans from The Rock and Ice were all invited. Brown had not even been to the Alps at that point and Whillans had only been once for a short season of two weeks. Tom Bourdillon, who was elected as the first president, was one of several leading ACG members who were also members of the Alpine Club. From the first, the goal of the ACG was to improve British alpine climbing standards by acting as an information highway and bringing together those most active and keen. Most significantly, the only entry qualification was to be a record of high standard alpine ascents.

Whillans recorded that although he had reservations beforehand about attending the ACG event, he was subsequently happy that he did. For the first time he met climbers from a different social milieu, the toffs, who he discovered were activists as keen as he was. Among them was the Cambridge climber Bob Downes with whom Don was to pioneer *Centurion* on Ben Nevis in 1956 and the next year attempt Masherbrum, when sadly Bob succumbed to pulmonary oedema.

As the ACG was coming into being, the grey fathers at the Alpine Club, along with similar types drawn from the Royal Geographical Society, were preoccupied with the 1953 expedition to Mount Everest. Maybe this is why the Club had little puff left to pay attention to the demands of the younger generation. As to the Everest story, I note only that working-class climbers had no part in its execution. And as a piece of mischief, I wonder what might have happened if the Himalayan Committee had invited the Creagh Dhu to take this on? In 1953, their members – Cunningham, MacInnes, Smith, Vigano, Rowney, Noon and company – were a really potent group of mountaineers. Cunningham and MacInnes actually did try to get permission to attempt the mountain in that year and managed to reach the Himalaya despite a serious lack of funds. Cunningham later was at the forefront of developing modern front-point ice climbing techniques. And MacInnes engineered some of the equipment to achieve this breakthrough.

The 1950s proved the heyday of the working-class climber. The march of egalitarianism was under away (at last), living standards improved dramatically, and it became possible for young British climbers to visit the Alps for longer periods. This meant hard work and saving throughout the rest of the year. One of the most impressive performances was that of north-east climber, Eric Rayson, who cycled to Chamonix, ascended the west face of the Dru, and then pedalled home again (shades of the Munich climbers of the 1930s?). During this decade Whillans emerged as the leading British alpinist whilst Brown simultaneously remained at the forefront of UK climbing developments while further afield making first ascents of Kangchenjunga (1955) and the Mustagh Tower (1956). The ACG fulfilled its role of producing guidebook information, and a selected guide to Mont Blanc was published first in a loose-leaf form and then as a case bound book in 1957.

As the decade of the 1950s drew to a close so did the dominance of the British climbing scene by working-class climbers. The sport was becoming ever more democratic, though it took a few more years for the Alpine Club to catch up. This was finally achieved in 1967 with the merging of the AC and the ACG, by which time the latter included most of the keenest UK alpinists. Higher education was expanding and it was from this direction that many of the next wave of outstanding British mountaineers would emerge. The universities of Manchester, Aberdeen, Bangor, Leeds, Edinburgh, Glasgow and Bristol became hotbeds of climbing activity. And the classless student replaced the working-class climber as the pioneering leader of the future.

SIMON RICHARDSON

Scottish Winter Climbing: the last 50 years

Eagle Ridge to *The Hurting*

Step-cutting to dry tooling

The Scottish hills have always had a mountaineering significance out of proportion to their physical scale. I use the word hills deliberately, because in summer most of the Highlands are little more than grassy rolling upland that seem far removed from serious mountaineering. In winter, however, they take on a different character, and the combination of snow, wind and rain coupled with limited daylight creates a serious and challenging climbing environment. If the mountains were 300m lower, or situated a couple of degrees further south, the interplay of altitude and weather would not create the winter climbing conditions the Highlands are so famous for. Conversely, if the mountains were higher and positioned a little further north, they would not be exposed to the continuous cycle of freeze-thaw that gives rise to the almost unique Scottish snow-ice conditions that are such a delight to climb.

The Victorians were first to recognise the value of Scotland as a winter playground, and quickly made ascents of the great structural features such as Tower Ridge (IV,3 1894) on Ben Nevis and the North-East Ridge (III 1895) of Aonach Beag. Even more impressive was Naismith's winter ascent of North-East Buttress (IV,4) in 1896, followed a few years later by Raeburn's ascents of Green Gully (IV,3) in 1906. These climbs set standards that were comparable with the Alps and were not surpassed in Scotland for more than 40 years. The aftermath of the First World War and the mild weather in the 1920s limited winter climbing activity, and it was not until the 1930s that Bill Murray and his colleagues resurrected the Scottish winter game. They did not significantly push the technical envelope, although *Shelf Route* (IV,6 1937) and *Deep-Cut Chimney* (IV,4 1939) in Glen Coe were certainly as difficult as anything climbed before. More importantly, they viewed all summer routes as potential winter targets – a vision that was to prove 50 years ahead of its time.

The First Grade V Routes
We start this retrospective in the 1950s with the first significant technical advance since Raeburn and Naismith. The first Grade V in Scotland was climbed by an 18-year-old Tom Patey in December 1950 with the first winter ascent of *Douglas-Gibson Gully* (V,4) on Lochnagar, partnered by G Leslie.

The ascent of this long-standing problem catapulted both Patey and Lochnagar onto the Scottish scene. Patey was to play a major role in the development of mixed climbing in the 1950s and Lochnagar reigned supreme with a series of long and demanding routes such as *Eagle Ridge* (VI,6 1955) and *Parallel Buttress* (VI,6 1956). Bill Brooker was the other key player, and he partnered Patey on these ascents as well as the remote Mitre Ridge (V,5 1953) on Beinn a'Bhuird, and established the technically difficult *Route 1* (V,6 1956) on the Black Spout Pinnacle on Lochnagar. Further north in the Cairngorms, the Loch Avon Basin saw two important ascents with *Scorpion* (V,5 1953) and *Sticil Face* (V,6 1954). Fifty years on, all these routes are still highly respected and their ascents are greatly prized.

Across in the West a similar breakthrough was happening in Glen Coe. Hamish MacInnes had a breathtaking few days in February 1953 with a youthful Chris Bonington that resulted in first winter ascents of *Agag's Groove* (VII,6) and *Crowberry Ridge Direct* (VII,7). These routes are more equivalent to modern snowed-up rock routes than classic ice or mixed climbs, but their ascent of the classic *Raven's Gully* (V,5) was more traditional in character.

The ice-climbing advance eventually came when East and West met up in 1957 on Ben Nevis for the first ascent of *Zero Gully* (V,4) in the form of the immensely strong team of MacInnes, Patey and Graeme Nicol. *Zero* had been a target for more than 20 years (Bell had nearly climbed it with Allan in the 1930s, but took to the icy rocks of the neighbouring *Slav Route* instead), and was a huge psychological breakthrough. The lower 100m of the gully is a vertical corner choked with ice overhangs. MacInnes and Patey shared leads, with Patey using tension from ice pitons and MacInnes front pointing between ice pegs.

Opposite page top
74.   Mitre Ridge, Garbh Choire, Beinn a'Bhuird. This great 200m-high feature is one of the most impressive rock formations in the Cairngorms, and its 16km approach means that an ascent by any route is a major undertaking. The classic winter line of Mitre Ridge (V,6), which takes a right to left line of weakness crossing the crest, was first climbed in winter by Patey and Brooker in April 1953. The *Cumming-Crofton Route* climbed by Dick Renshaw and Greg Strange in December 1977 takes the hanging corner right of the crest. Simon Richardson and Roger Webb climbed the true line up the crest itself in February 1995 to give *The Cardinal* (VIII,8). (*Simon Richardson*)

Opposite page right
75.   John Ashbridge climbing *Parallel Buttress* (VI,6), Lochnagar. This 280m-long route was first climbed in winter by Tom Patey, Bill Brooker and Jerry Smith in March 1956 and is still very much respected today. Climbed with nailed boots and a single axe it was a remarkable ascent, and years ahead of its time. (*Simon Richardson*)

Whilst mixed climbing was a natural extension of rock climbing, ascending steep ice in the 1950s was a difficult physical exercise that demanded great skill and stamina cutting steps at the limit of one's balance. There was a marked contrast between East and West Coast climbing techniques. For example, when Jimmy Marshall and Patey traversed Observatory Buttress and Orion Face in January 1959, Marshall wore crampons and Patey used nails. Marshall put his crampon technique to good effect when he grabbed the coveted *Parallel Gully B* (V,5 1958) from under the noses of the locals on Lochnagar.

The next big challenge to fall was *Point Five Gully* on the Ben. Again there was huge competition for the line, but much to the upset of the Scots it was climbed by a Glasgow University team spearheaded by ex pat Englishman Ian Clough. Clough applied a clinical approach to this notorious route, and sieged it with fixed ropes over five days. The furore surrounding this event overshadowed the first ascent of the more difficult *Minus Two Gully* (V,5) by Marshall – a step-cutting tour de force. Equally impressive was *Tower Face of the Comb* (VI,6 1959) by Robin Smith and Dick Holt. Unrepeated for more than 25 years, this was a forerunner to the modern mixed routes on the Ben. Equally impressive in its boldness and execution was the *Smith-Holt Route* (V,5 1959) – the first climb to venture onto the Orion Face.

The stage was now set for the famous week in February 1960 when Smith and Marshall teamed up at the CIC Hut on the Ben. They repeated *Point Five Gully* in good style and then went on to add five new routes including *Smith's Route* (V,5), *Observatory Buttress* (V,5), *Pigott's Route* (V,6) and the outstanding *Orion Direct* (V,5). Smith and Marshall both wrote compelling accounts of their climbs that were to inspire successive generations of winter climbers. That week was the pinnacle of the step-cutting era and brought Scottish winter climbing into the greater climbing consciousness. On a wider scale, these standards were comparable with rest of the world, and in the Alps only the *Cornuau-Davaille* (ED1 1955) on the north face of Les Droites could really compare.

After this high point, the remainder of the 1960s was a period of consolidation. Patey devoted his attention to the development of Creag Meagaidh, culminating in his remarkable solo of *The Crab Crawl* (IV,4 1969), a 2400m-long girdle traverse of the cliff. Marshall added the excellent *Vanishing Gully* (V,5 1961) to the Ben and the difficult *Route 2* (VI,6 1962) to Lochnagar. The outstanding ascent of the 1960s, however, was the first winter ascent of *Pinnacle Face* (VI,7) on Lochnagar by Grassick, Light and Nicol. This winter ascent of a difficult VS rock climb was a 12-hour mixed epic on powder-covered icy rock and was the 'swansong of the tricouni tricksters'. It was not repeated until 1974 by a new generation of climbers with a new armoury of tools and techniques.

76.   Approaching the great North-East Corrie of Lochnagar. In the late 1950s Lochnagar held the greatest concentration of difficult mixed routes in Scotland. This tradition has been maintained, and the Tough-Brown Face on Lochnagar is home to some of the most challenging mixed climbs in the country, such as *Diedre of Sorrows* (VIII,8) and *Mort* (IX,9). (*Niall Ritchie*)

The Curved Axe Revolution

By the mid 1960s, routes such as *Point Five* and *Zero* were being climbed in fast times owing to the development of crampons and front point technique. This eliminated the need to cut footholds, but much time was still spent cutting handholds. Patey and MacInnes were exponents of front pointing with the aid of two axes, relying on driving in straight picks for balance, but this proved dangerous as they readily pulled out. John Cunningham experimented with ice daggers that could be driven into the ice above the head allowing the climber to move up very quickly for a couple of moves. Cunningham teamed up with Bill March to climb *The Chancer* (V,6) on Hell's Lum in 1970. This had a short section of vertical ice, but using ice daggers was a stressful and strenuous technique that was too precarious for sustained climbing at high angles.

The technological advance came later that season when Yvon Chouinard visited from the USA. Chouinard had been experimenting with a curved pick tool to allow fast movement across long ice slopes in the High Sierra. He showed his tools to Cunningham at Glenmore Lodge and MacInnes in Glen Coe, and then proved their effectiveness by climbing the difficult *Direct Finish* (VI,6) to Raven's Gully with Doug Tompkins. MacInnes had also been experimenting with dropped pick tools, but without success, but after talking to Chouinard he increased the angle of his pick and made the Terradactyl – the first of the dropped pick tools.

77. *Left*
Albatross (VI,5) on Indicator Wall,
Ben Nevis (climber unknown).
First climbed by Mick Geddes and
Con Higgins in January 1978,
it was typical of the new high-
standard ice routes climbed in the
late 1970s following the onset of
the curved axe revolution. Thirty
years on, *Albatross* remains one of
the most prized thin-face routes on
Ben Nevis. (*Simon Richardson*)

Ben Nevis Rules Supreme

Mike Geddes was the first to apply the curved axe technique to Ben Nevis,
with quick repeats of *Smith's Route* and *Point Five Gully* in March 1971.
Later that month, Terradactyls were used by Hamish MacInnes, Kenny
Spence and Allen Fyffe on a winter ascent of *Astronomy* (VI,5). In April,
Geddes climbed the prominent icefall of *Hadrian's Wall Direct* (V,5) and the
following winter made the long-awaited second ascents of *Minus Two Gully*
and *Orion Direct* with fellow student Al Rouse. They climbed the latter route
with sacks full of their weekend gear so they could rush back down the
Tourist Track and start the long hitch back to Cambridge that night.

Conditions on the Minus Face during the winter of 1972 were excellent,
and several teams used the new tools to good effect. Stevie Docherty and
Norrie Muir added *Left-Hand Route* (VI,6) to Minus Two Buttress, soon to
be joined by a winter ascent of the neighbouring *Right-Hand Route* (VI,6)
by Al Rouse and Rab Carrington. These ascents were only slightly steeper
than the Smith-Marshall masterpieces of *Smith's Route* and *Orion Direct*,
but they were more serious with long run outs on thin ice.

The 1973 season was quiet, but the big event the following year was *Minus
One Gully* (VI,6) by Ken Crocket and Colin Stead. This was the last of the
major Nevis gullies to be climbed in winter and had seen many previous

attempts which had failed below the great chockstone. Doug Lang and Neil Quinn recorded two excellent routes with *Left Edge Route* (V,5) on Observatory Buttress, and the outstanding *Slav Route* (VI,5) which has become one of the great classics on the Orion Face. The pace now began to hot up. In December 1976, Con Higgins and Alan Kimber were quick off the mark with *Astral Highway* (VI,5), a steep left-hand exit above the Basin on Orion Face. The route of the winter, however, was *Minus One Buttress* (VII,6) by Norrie Muir and Arthur Paul. This superlative line has rarely been in condition since and was a cleverly timed ascent with good snow-ice on the final tower. It received a second ascent a few days later but there have been very few complete repeats.

During the 1978 season, modern winter climbing on Ben Nevis came of age. Excellent conditions prompted a high level of activity, which resulted in a series of outstanding thin face routes. In January, Geddes and Higgins ventured onto the steepest part of Indicator Wall with the serious and sustained *Albatross* (VI,5), and the following day Muir and Paul climbed the now classic *Psychedelic Wall* (VI,5) a little to the right. Good conditions persisted throughout February, and competition for the major lines was intense. Geddes and Rouse just beat Gordon Smith to the excellent *Route II* (VI,6), the first winter climb to venture onto the front face of Carn Dearg Buttress. Smith repeated the route with a difficult direct start (VI,6) three days later with Ian Sykes. Spurred on by Geddes' interest in the area of blank icy slabs to the left of Point Five Gully, Smith then succeeded on the serious *Pointless* (VII,6) with Nick Banks after several failed attempts. Geddes returned with Con Higgins at the end of the winter to add a companion route, *Galactic Hitchhiker* (VI,5), one of the finest thin face routes on the mountain.

British climbers, well practised on Ben Nevis ice, applied their skills with great effect in the Alps and elsewhere throughout the 1970s. Perhaps the best example was the *Colton-MacIntyre Route* on the north face of the Grandes Jorasses (ED3, 1976). This very narrow couloir, totally Scottish in character and similar to Minus One Gully in technical difficulty, was undoubtedly the hardest ice climb in the Alps at the time. Another example was the application of Nevis-style thin face climbing to the north face of the Pelerins (ED2) by Rab Carrington and Al Rouse in February 1975.

By 1978, 45 new winter routes had been added to Ben Nevis in the space of eight hectic years. The leading activists were now venturing out of the main gully and corner lines onto thinner ice on the steep faces in between. Their routes were not significantly steeper than anything climbed before but demonstrated what was possible if front-point technique was applied seriously to thin face routes. In March 1979, there was a further leap in technical difficulty. On the steep right flank of Carn Dearg Buttress, Mick Fowler and Victor Saunders took advantage of the excellent icy conditions to climb *The Shield Direct* (VII,7), a stupendous line up a series of soaring chimneys, which combined steep ice with several technical mixed pitches.

Return to Mixed Climbing

Throughout the 1970s, the curved axe revolution concentrated winter activity on climbing ice, mainly on Ben Nevis, but towards the end of the decade the focus began to slowly turn back towards mixed climbing. The *Cumming-Crofton Route* (VI,6) on Beinn a'Bhuird by Greg Strange and Dick Renshaw in 1977 and *Vertigo Wall* on Dubh Loch by Andy Nisbet and Alf Robertson the following season were early examples. Despite a planned bivouac, the latter ascent was flawed with eight points of aid, but nevertheless it was a bold advance onto a route of awe-inspiring steepness. Nisbet returned to the route in 1987 and climbed the route free at VII,7.

The following year Nisbet was again testing the limits with the ascent of *The Link Face* (VII,7), a VS on the Black Spout Pinnacle on Lochnagar. Always innovative, he was wearing 'trampons', an Aberdeen experiment of filed down crampons with nails welded on. They proved to be excellent on snowed-up rock, but hopeless for the thin veneer of ice that covered the route, which meant that John Anderson, his conventionally crampon-shod partner, led the major difficulties.

The winter of 1980 saw a race between rival Edinburgh and Aberdeen teams to pick the major Cairngorm plums. In January, conditions on Creag an Dubh Loch were exceptionally icy. The Edinburgh team of Rab Anderson and Rob Milne were there first, and climbed the long sought after *White Elephant* (VII,6) on the Central Slabs. They were later overheard in a pub talking about the exceptional amount of ice on *Goliath*. Word got back to Nisbet who climbed the route four days later with Neil Morrison. On their way out, they met Anderson with Murray Hamilton walking in to attempt the same route. It didn't go all Nisbet's way that winter, however, as later in the season he was beaten to the prestigious first ascent of *The Citadel* (VII,8) on the Shelter Stone by Hamilton and Kenny Spence.

The Development of Torquing

Anderson believes that Scottish climbing was going through a remarkable transformation during this period: 'During the front point revolution of the 1970s, everyone thought the future lay in ice. After a while it was realised that you could only take ice so far. Gordon Smith hinted at the next step with climbs like *Route II Direct* on The Ben, but the real pioneers of modern mixed climbing were Andy Nisbet in Aberdeen, and Hamilton and Spence from Edinburgh.'

Hard mixed climbing in the early 1980s was a rather different game to now. For example, the crux pitches on *The Citadel* were originally ascended on powder-covered rock wearing thin gloves. In 1981 Nisbet began to experiment with mixed climbing techniques on Carn Etchachan above Loch Avon. It was a poor winter with little snow and ice but the deep cracks of the Northern Cairngorm granite proved ideal for jamming ice axe picks. It was another three years, however, before the term 'torquing' was coined for this technique. 'Colin MacLean made a winter attempt on *The Outlands* on the Tough-Brown Face of Lochnagar with Arthur Paul,' Nisbet told me. 'He came back raving about laybacking up cracks by torquing their axes. People had used axes in cracks before, but this was the first time it had been done move after move. Colin was so excited that he persuaded me to go up and try *Nymph* the next weekend.' The route turned out to be an eye-opener with MacLean leading the crux pitch, a 30m vertical corner, entirely on torques. The technique had been proven and a whole new spectrum of difficulty was now open.

Nisbet and MacLean formed a formidable partnership in the winter of 1985. In January they visited Glen Coe to try one of the great problems of the day – *Unicorn*, the classic summer E1 corner-line in Stob Coire nan Lochan. 'Climbing in Glen Coe felt like going into bandit country,' Nisbet remarked. 'There was a strong rivalry between the Creagh Dhu and Etchachan clubs at the time, and when we arrived at the Kingshouse, Ian Nicolson guessed which route we were going for and said there was no snow on it. We went up anyway, found it covered in hoar frost, and climbed it on our first attempt. On the way home we dived into the Kingshouse, told Nicolson, and then ran out of the bar before we were lynched!'

Whilst the West Coast climbers gnashed their teeth that one of their best winter lines had been poached by Aberdonians, Nisbet and MacLean were already working at their next project – a winter ascent of *The Needle* on the 250m-high Shelter Stone. 'It took two weeks of continuous effort,' Nisbet recalled. 'We worked out the best winter line, waited on weather then climbed the first two pitches as a recce to the winter start. We then sat out more bad weather before climbing the route with a bivouac in mid February.' Although it wasn't realised at the time, *The Needle* (VIII,8) was one of the most difficult winter climbs in the world, with a technical difficulty 10 years in advance of anything achieved in the Alps. Twenty-five years after the celebrated Smith-Marshall week on Ben Nevis, Scottish standards were again leading the world.

Later in 1985, Nisbet started working at Glenmore Lodge where he met Andy Cunningham. Although Cunningham was new to high standard mixed climbing, he was quick to learn, and the two Andys formed one of the most effective partnerships in the history of Scottish mountaineering. Over the next three winters they added over 25 outstanding Grade V routes all over the Cairngorms and Northern Highlands. These included *Salmon Leap* (V,5) on Liathach, the bold *Vishnu* (VII,6) on the East Wall of Coire Mhic Fhearchair and the demanding *Postern Direct* (VII,8) on the Shelter Stone. It was their routes in the Northern Corries however, which were to have a profound influence on the shape of modern mixed climbing. *Fallout Corner* (VI,7) and *The Migrant* (VI,7) in Coire an Lochain are now both recognised as modern classics, and receive many ascents each winter.

Cairngorms pioneer and historian Greg Strange doesn't mince his words when talking about the significance of these routes: 'Above all else, Nisbet should be remembered for his continued push for the recognition of technical mixed climbing. In 1981 when he did his first Carn Etchachan routes, people were concerned that they weren't really winter ascents at all, as they just had a dusting of snow and were climbed on frozen turf. Now of course, it is recognised that these are the ideal conditions to do this type of climbing, and the routes are at their best. Through his development of modern mixed, Nisbet opened up a new form of climbing.'

Exploration and Consolidation

Throughout the 1990s two main themes emerged. Firstly, there was exploration of other venues away from the well-known winter cliffs in the Central Highlands and Cairngorms. The North-West, in particular, attracted an increasing number of pioneering teams who soon realised that there were hundreds of little-known cliffs that came into winter condition far more often than previously thought. More remote crags in the Central Highlands were also thoroughly explored such as the Aonachs and Ben Alder. The crags of Aonach Mor quickly became some of the most popular winter climbs in Scotland with the opening of the Nevis Range ski area in 1990.

Secondly, the confidence created by this exploration gave climbers the impetus to move away from the surety of following a summer route and move on to harder winter-only lines. At best, these take steep, wet and vegetated terrain that invokes shudders in summer but, when frozen, provides winter climbs of the highest quality. Routes such as *Messiah* (VII,7) on the Bridge of Orchy Crags, *Neanderthal* (VII,7) in Glen Coe and *Salmonella* (VII,8) on Aonach Beag are typical of this genre, and have all become modern classics. In the Cairngorms other teams followed Nisbet's lead, and all summer routes at HVS and below became winter targets – very much following Murray's vision from more than 50 years earlier. A key development here was the series of mixed climbs in the Northern Corries. A 'cragging' atmosphere existed most weekends, and routes such as *The Hoarmaster* (V,7) and *Deep Throat* (V,6) introduced many winter climbers to mixed climbing and revealed the huge potential that Nisbet had discovered 10 years earlier.

At first sight, technical standards appear to have remained static throughout this period, and the big Grade VIII routes of the 1980s were not superseded in difficulty. Undoubtedly the 1990s were a time of consolidation when a new generation of climbers was learning the new mixed techniques. There was also little incentive to repeat routes when so much new route potential existed elsewhere. But slowly the Grade VIII routes saw second ascents in good style. The one or two aid and rest points that were accepted on hard climbs in the 1980s as the norm were shunned by a generation influenced by a purer rock-climbing ethic, and by the turn of the century many of the big routes had been repeated and their aid points eliminated.

But, as always, the big influences came from those operating at the cutting edge and pushing the boundaries. Alan Mullin, a young and forceful climber active in the late 1990s, made one of the greatest impacts. Mullin burst into

78. *Left*
No 4 Buttress, Core an Lochain, Northern Corries. This superb buttress is one of the most popular venues in the winter climbing playground of the Northern Corries. The prominent corner is the line of *Savage Slit* (V,6). *Fallout Corner* (VI,7) takes the hanging groove to the right. (*Niall Ritchie*)

the scene with a repeat of *The Needle* on the Shelter Stone and then went on to climb the neighbouring *Steeple* at Grade IX together with a series of other difficult climbs. Unfortunately many of these climbs were flawed because they climbed routes very early in the season in quasi-winter condition, or they required aid, but the effect on the winter scene was electric. Mullin had arrived on the scene with very little climbing experience, and other climbers soon realised that they could push their own standards too. Within a couple of seasons, average standards had jumped a level, and Grade VII, which was previously held to be the preserve of the elite, quickly became accessible to many.

State of the Art

Winter climbing has now become a mainstream sport, its growth fuelled by a number of factors. Information is freely available from the comprehensive guidebooks from the Scottish Mountaineering Club and accurate and detailed magazine reporting. The Internet provides real time data on weather, climbing conditions and avalanche forecasts. The grading system was extended and enlarged in the early 1990s to include a technical grade, and the interplay between this and the overall grade gives a clue as to the overall seriousness of the climb. Access to the North-West is easier via better roads funded by the European Union, and clothing is lighter and more effective. Crampons and axes have improved too, but curiously these hardware advances have favoured pure ice climbing and dry tooling more

79. *Left*
Halvor Hagen climbing
The Hoarmaster (V,6),
Coire an Lochain,
Northern Corries. This
route is typical of the
Northern Corries mixed
routes climbed in the late
1980s and nowadays sees
ascents most weekends.
(*Simon Richardson*)

than the varied nature of Scottish ice and mixed. As dry tooling took off in the late 1990s and mixed climbing standards rocketed across the world, several climbers attempted to create pre-protected climbs of similar levels of high technical difficulty in Scotland. Typically these developments have not caught on, mainly because of a fierce desire to maintain the Scottish ground-up style. This ethic is driven more by practicality than tradition, because the ancient rocks that comprise the Highlands support on-sight climbing and leader placed protection, whilst the younger rocks in the mixed climbing area in the Alps and North America are made of poorer quality rock that typically require bolts to make them climbable.

Dave MacLeod, undoubtedly the finest Scottish climber of the current generation, has shown an abseil inspection approach can result in climbs such as *The Hurting* (XI,11 in 2005) which have a difficulty comparable to the hardest mixed climbs abroad. But for the majority, climbing winter routes ground-up remains the preferred approach. First ascents of Grade VIII climbs are now regularly climbed in fine style, and on-sight standards are almost certainly on a par with the hardest winter climbs anywhere. More importantly perhaps, there is a growing self-confidence that it is the ground-up style that sets Scottish winter climbing apart and makes it unique. At the beginning of the 21st century, Scotland can proudly lay claim to the most ethically pure form of mountaineering in the world, and I am sure it will stay that way for many years to come.

Journeys & Ranges

Andy Parkin *The Dru, Chamonix*
Acrylic on canvas

TAMOTSU NAKAMURA

Further Travels in Eastern Tibet

By foot, horseback and Land Cruiser

When our team from the Hengduan Mountains Club arrived at Lhasa on 22 October 2006, a letter from Jon Miceler of High Asia Exploratory Mountain Travel, based in Connecticut, was on the front desk of the Himalaya Hotel. He left a message for me saying that, 'As you read this letter, I will be with a few friends walking from Xin Tso Lake NE of Basong to the Tonjuk valley and then reach the Yi'ong valley and march up the Yi'ong Tsangpo (2260m) to Niwu (3400m) and from there head northward to Alando or westward to Lhari (4460m) along the main valley.' I had given Jon all my knowledge of the Yi'ong Tsangpo such as logistics, availability of pack animals and porters, footpaths and high passes that can or cannot be crossed.

I was stunned by this news, as our principal objective was to completely retrace the route along the lower Yi'ong Tsangpo from Lake Yi'ong to Niwu, on which no foreigners' footsteps were recorded since F Kingdon-Ward in 1935. To come second is not of interest to me. I must be the first. We immediately changed our plans. We decided to move to Kangri Garpo after exploring unfrequented glaciers and snow peaks in the valley of the Nye Qu Tsangpo, a tributary of the Yi'ong Tsangpo, north-east of Lake Yi'ong Tso.

On 25 October we left Lhasa by four Toyota Land Cruisers, heading for Yi'ong village. With us were Tashi, who has accompanied me in East Tibet since 2002, another guide and two cooks. Three days later we departed Yi'ong village for a six-day trek with a caravan of 16 horses and 16 muleteers. On our return, we leant that Jon Miceler's party had also returned to Yi'ong, a formidably deep gorge having prevented them going further than Bake village. Timber rafts would have had to be made by local villagers to cross the raging rapids flowing through the gorge. That was too dangerous, so Jon gave up the plan. We were fortunate. If Jon's party had not ventured ahead of us we would have encountered the same difficulty.

Through Tibetan jungle – the Nye Qu trek

At Yi'ong village we were kindly lent accommodation belonging to the local government for use as our base for exploration. We gathered information on the Nye Qu Tsangpo from villagers to find a possible access to the glaciers and veiled peaks in the upper valley basin, but their response was negative and discouraging. Trails had not been maintained and bridges were broken down or too dangerous to cross due to deterioration over 30 years, they said.

The trail up to Bayu village (2340m), north of Yi'ong village, was quite comfortable, but struggles soon began with treacherous Tibetan jungle which resembled tropical rain forest. The ground was covered with mosses and prickly bushes blocked the trail, tearing our clothing. The trail was on the right bank of the Nye Qu. In some sections loads had to be carried by muleteers. One horse almost fell down to the river, but was narrowly saved. On the first day, 28 October, we set up Camp 1 at 2500m near the confluence of the main Nye Qu stream and a side valley descending from the Qiaqing glacier, the longest valley-type glacier (35km) in Tibet. No bridge over the Qiaqing side stream was found.

On 29 October we entered the Qiaqing valley and reached the debris-covered snout of the glacier, but we could not see its upper part. No foreigners had visited this glacier since the Chinese Academy of Science made a preliminary approach in 1989.

Meanwhile the muleteers had constructed a 25m-long temporary bridge over the stream, which made it possible for our caravan to continue up the Nye Qu. A view of the north face of holy Hayungarpo (6388m) was most magnificent, soaring 4000m above the riverbed. The third day our march resumed, the muleteers opening the trail though the jungle with Tibetan swords or axes. They were powerful men and worked efficiently. On the precipitous slopes the muleteers had to belay older members of the party across dangerous sections by rope.

Camp 2 was set up at 2520m in a small pasture where plenty of marijuana grew. On 31 October we left camp (minus 4°C at 8am) and reached a crumbling bridge (2660m) over a rushing narrow gorge below the Ruoguo glacier. We were not so brave as to risk walking on the bridge. The muleteers told us that the bridge had been made more than 30 years ago and currently even nomads went no further. Beyond the bridge the trail would become more difficult. No foreigners had visited the valley of the Ruoguo glacier since an American team had recovered the remains of a crashed airplane in early 1990.

According to the muleteers, in the days when the bridge was constructed domestic animals were owned by the village community, not by individuals. Pasturing of the animals was conducted in a big group and the bridge was installed to take the animals to higher grazing. However, after the government allowed individuals to own their own animals, they ceased going to the higher pastures and the bridge has been almost abandoned. Now only a few hunters enter the upper valley.

We were able to see several peaks of more than 6000m – 6400m in the headwaters of the two glaciers of Nalong and Maguolong but had to give up hope of entering this mountain sanctuary. On the return journey Camp 3 was set up at 2580m in the forest where, in the middle of the night, we heard bears growling nearby as if screaming. On 2 November we arrived back at Yi'ong village.

. North face of the holy mountain Hayungarpo (name corrected from Ayagemo to Hayungarpo according to villagers' information), 6388m, north of Lake Yi'ong, Nyainqentanglha East. (*Tamotsu Nakamura*)

. Dawn over the Lhagu glacier and east face of Hamogongga 6260m (*right*) seen from Lhagu village, Kangri Garpo East. (*Tamotsu Nakamura*)

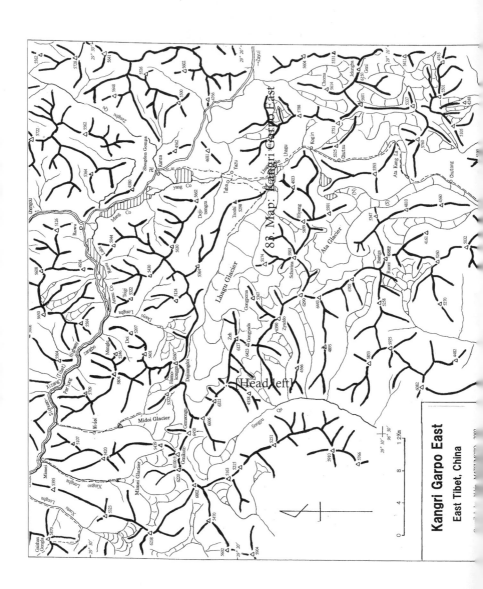

88. Map: Kangri Garpo East

Kangri Garpo East

East Tibet, China

To Kangri Garpo (3-10 November)

My first priority had been to explore the little known Gone Kangri massif, but again we had to change our plan and as a result visited the three notable valleys of Kangri Garpo: the Lhagu, Midoi and Mimei glaciers. We drove from Yi'ong village to Bomi, which has become a modern town, and on the next day entered Lhagu valley from Rawu (3945m). Bomi and Rawu are on the Sichuan-Tibet Highway, easy and comfortable to drive as almost all the sections are paved.

The **Lhagu** (or Laigu) glaciers and Lake Rawu are now tourist spots. Near Lhagu village there was a check post to collect an entrance fee of RMB20 per foreigner. We stayed at a primary school in Lhagu village (4060m) for two nights. Two days of snowfall turned the neighbouring scenery to pure glittering white, which let us know that winter was coming.

The Lhagu glacier has the largest glacier surface area in Tibet, and the surrounding 6000m peaks were breathtakingly beautiful. Though climbers have noticed the potential, so far all the peaks remain untouched. Mick Fowler and others have a keen interest in Gongyada (6423m) and a towering rock peak Dojigtsengza (5662m). On our way back from Lhagu village to Rawu we went up to the Dema La (4800m), a high pass to Zayu giving views of the easternmost part of Kangri Garpo. This too is full of unknown stunning peaks of 5000m-6000m and unique glaciers. We also visited the historic Shugden Gompa.

The **Midoi glacier** valley is being developed for tourism and a vehicle road has been constructed from a junction at 3500m on the Sichuan-Tibet highway southwards to Midoi village. At the village we hired a tractor to reach near the glacier lake. This valley has been explored a couple of times by the Japanese Alpine Club. The glacier, which has icefalls, is magnificent and I saw and heard avalanches of huge hanging ice blocks crashing down toward the glacier lake. The north faces of Gemosongu (6450m) and Hamogongga (6260m) look impressive.

The **Mimei glacier** was surveyed by the Chinese Academy of Science in the 1980s, but I have no report. The glacier is reached from Mimei village (3450m), on south side of the main highway, via a valley running southwards called Xinguo Longba. There was a problem in that no pack animals were available in this valley so we hired 12 villagers from Mimei as porters to ferry our loads up to the glacier end. Xingou Longba, with conifer trees, was wider and more beautiful than Midoi valley. We set up camp at Gongtsa near the snout of the glacier. South, beyond the glacier, were three 6000m peaks, not particularly attractive. Two glaciers join from east and west to form the 2km lower part of the main glacier. Covered with rock debris and crevassed in many places, its length would be about 8km (eastern glacier) and 12km (western glacier) from the snout.

84. Lhagu glacier, Lhagu lake and east face of Gonyada 6423m (*left*) and Zeh 6127m (*right*) viewed from Lhagu village, Kangri Garpo East. (*Tamotsu Nakamura*)

North face of Gemosongu 6450m and Midoi glacier, Kangri Garpo East.
(*Tamotsu Nakamura*)

A bridge over the Parlung Tsangpo near Mimei village, Kangri Garpo East.
(*Tamotsu Nakamura*)

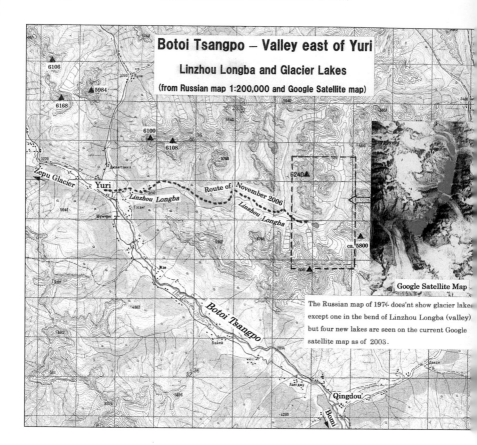

Botoi Tsangpo – Valley east of Yuri

Linzhou Longba and Glacier Lakes

(from Russian map 1:200,000 and Google Satellite map)

Google Satellite Map

The Russian map of 1974 does'nt show glacier lakes except one in the bend of Linzhou Longba (valley) but four new lakes are seen on the current Google satellite map as of 2003.

Return to Nyainqentanglha – Botoi Tsangpo (11-18 November)

I did not hesitate to revisit the mountains above the Botoi Tsangpo north of Bomi. I had explored the Jajong glaciers of Zepu Qu, north of Yuri village (3100m), in the fall of 2002. However the area east of Yuri village has remained unfrequented and a Google map shows the birth of distinct new glacier lakes not indicated on the Russian topo map (1: 200,000) of 1974. This fact much attracted me to enter the valley.

A time lapse of four years has brought a large change in the valley of Botoi Tsango. The road to Qingdou, a centre for timber collection, has been paved and a new wood-processing factory has started operation. The other villages are also developing. As in other remote areas, we found discos in Yuri, motorbikes are superseding horses, and solar batteries, mobile phones and televisions are becoming very popular.

At Yuri we soon organized a caravan with 12 horses and six muleteers. We tried to gather information on the new lakes and approaches but the response of a local government official and villagers was ambiguous. The weather was not stable. Normally stars could be seen at midnight yet cloud covered the sky in the morning. Even when the cloud gradually dispersed, the blue sky did not last long. Sometimes it snowed. On 13 November we left Yuri, marching eastwards with five days' provisions. Half days were good for easy riding. On the first afternoon the trail ascended a steep slope through primeval forest beneath holy Yuri peak (6100m) on the right bank of the valley called Linzhou Longba. Nomads reportedly lived in the upper valley. We set up Camp 1 in a narrow pasture (3585m) with a small gompa. A monk lived alone there.

Next day the trail was through thickly grown rhododendron and conifer trees, a Tibetan jungle of humid and dark forest with mosses under snow. Below the trail a mysterious blue lake encircled with forest appeared. No water inlet or outlet was found. The main stream of the valley flowed far below and could not be seen. Camp 2 was on a wide open pasture (4000m) like a fairyland, at the confluence with a branch valley to the north. An unnamed 6260m peak indicated on the Russian map should have been visible but was hidden in the cloud. Steep rock peaks with hanging glaciers towered on the southern side of the main valley of Linzhou Longba, while 5000-6000m peaks with larger glaciers ranged to the north.

There were several summer huts of nomads and many yaks and zous on the pasture of camp 2. The animals came closer to us wanting salt. Zou (male) and zomo (female) are hybrids of yaks and cows. They have a calmer temperament, live longer, and are more suitable for ploughing than yaks. They are also more expensive than yaks.

On 15 November we made a round trip to the new lakes from camp 2 in a day. The weather had showed signs of improvement but it was snowing in the morning and the temperature at 8am was minus 3°C. The main valley of Linzhou Longba turned northwards before the lakes appeared. We marched up a wide valley to the east and reached a small pass (4250m) at 2pm, where a large glacier and a waterfall of the main stream emerged in front of us, but no lakes were within sight. The lakes were reckoned to be still far beyond the waterfall, but time constraints forced us to return from the pass. Though the lakes did not appear, luckily the cloud gradually lifted. An incredibly shining snow peak with Himalayan fluted ice was unveiled and other beautiful peaks with glaciers came into full view to the east. The peaks seemed to be around 5800m according to the Russian map. The outstanding north face of a 6000m peak (Dojiza) was also in sight to the south. All of us were fascinated by the panorama.

Next day the temperature was down to minus 6°C at 8.30am and the weather was unstable. As we left camp 2 and returned down the valley, bad news came by mobile phone from the drivers who were waiting for us at Yuri village. Two of the three Land Cruisers had been damaged and all the contents, including important personal belongings, had been stolen. They had been stored inside the cars parked in the local government compound. The theft took place during the night of 13 November and villagers came to know about it next day when a primary school teacher saw a boy carrying

88. West face of unnamed shining peak c5800m and glacier in Linzhou Longba (valley) to the east from Yuri village, Botoi Tsangpo, north of Bomi, Nyainqentanglha East. (*Tamotsu Nakamura*)

89. North face of Dojiza 6250m and Juxi glacier, Botoi Tsangpo, north-west of Bomi township, Nyainqentanglha East. (*Tamotsu Nakamura*)

a camera. The teacher questioned the boy and started an investigation. It was revealed that three schoolboys belonging to one family had committed the theft. We were lost for words and worried. Some members of the group discussed how the losses might be compensated by insurance. To our further surprise, however, when we arrived at Yuri village all the items were returned to our guesthouse. Nothing was missing and the drivers did not report the case to the police. Supposedly the teacher managed the case so that it might not become a matter for the police or the public security bureau, considering the future of the schoolboys. The bad news suddenly changed to a good story that enabled us to leave Yuri with no unhappy memories. We were in a hurry to get to Bomi town.

Our wish now was to view the western side of the panorama that we had seen on 15 November and also the north face of Dojiza (6260m) with a prominent glacier called Juxi glacier, south of Qingdou. On 18 November we returned along the Botoi Tsangpo, then drove northeast from Qingdou by a large subsidiary river. Snow and rock peaks of 5500m – 5800m soared on the both sides of the valley. One was like the Matterhorn and another might be compared to a small Ama Dablam. The view of Dojiza from the north was remarkable indeed, as was the west face of two towering peaks (6135m and 5601m) just north of Bomi. It was a wonderful finale to four weeks of exploration.

Summary: Exploration of glacier valleys in the Yi'ong Tsangpo, Botoi Tsangpo and Kangri Garpo areas of eastern Tibet in autumn 2006.

Team: Tamotsu Nakamura (71) leader, Tokyo; Tsuyoshi Nakgai (74) Hiroshima; Eiichiro Kasai (66) Tokyo; Tadao Shintani (62) Tokyo; Hiroshi Onodera (55) Tokyo; Yuuki Tagata (37) Yokohama; Zhang Jiyue (40), President of Sichuan Adventure Travel, Chengdu.

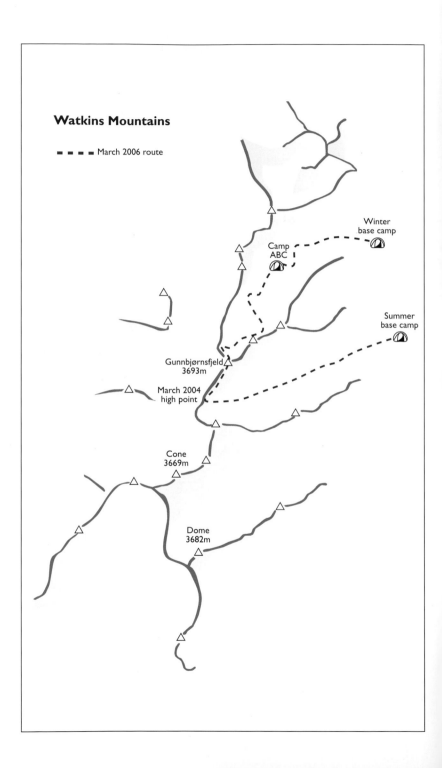

Watkins Mountains

- - - March 2006 route

Winter
base camp

Camp
ABC

Summer
base camp

Gunnbjørnsfjeld
3693m

March 2004
high point

Cone
3669m

Dome
3682m

JOHN STARBUCK

Mad Dogs?

At 3693 metres, Gunnbjørnsfjeld is the highest peak within the Arctic. It has been climbed more than 40 times in summer, but prior to the two expeditions recounted here, had never been attempted in winter. Both were commercial ventures.

The first winter ascent attempt was made in 2004 by a team including the author. Shortly before the expedition was due to depart the UK the team was denied a permit to start before 1 April, thereby effectively prohibiting a pre-equinox ascent. After much dialogue, which employed the skills of a Greenlandic law expert, a permit was eventually granted for a very late start on 15 March.

Members flew by scheduled flights to north-west Iceland from where a chartered ski-equipped aeroplane would carry them to land directly on the glaciers of the Watkins Mountains in East Greenland at about 2100m. As the Greenland coast was crossed, thick cloud was encountered and the small aeroplane had to climb to avoid icing up the wings until it was at its limit of 4400m. At the designated landing site there was no break visible in the cloud to make a descent and a return had to be made to Iceland. Two days passed waiting for better weather before the team was flown in on 19 March, in brilliant sunshine, but leaving just two days to make the ascent attempt.

After establishing a base camp, everyone started up the eastern approach glacier, some with rucksacks, some towing pulks containing safety kit and technical equipment for the climb. Progress was slow in deep, cold snow. At temperatures below minus 30° centigrade, not enough energy can be put into the snow to melt it and allow objects to slide with little friction – the snow has glide properties more akin to sand. When the wind began blasting down the glacier and the temperature plummeted a cache was made at 2870m, before returning to base camp. Two members suffered frost nip, one to a finger and one to the face.

The next and final day of winter, everyone returned to the cache of the previous day. In bitter cold winds, ropes of three were made and the parties continued skiing upwards in deep snow until reaching exposed rocks at the base of the south-west ridge at 3400m. Here, a northerly gale was raging over the ridge adding a very large wind chill factor to the already minus 40°C.

Following page

91. Paul Walker (*left*) and John Starbuck (*right*) ascending the final section of the NE ridge above the steepening during the first summit attempt on Gunnbjørnsfjeld (3693m), 4 March 2006. (*Adrian Pedley*)

A rock band around the summit pyramid requires a single pitch of climbing on the south-west ridge route. This may have been feasible for a pair leading through but just wasn't practicable in such conditions for such a large group. A second cache of gear was hurriedly made before retreating to base camp. Four days of bad weather beset the base camp. As the equinox slipped by, the objective was changed to making the earliest spring ascent. On 26 March, after a record −43°C, some of the group made out for the ridge cache. Progress was intermittent as skins came off skis in the extreme cold. However, strong winds had firmed the snow surface and the first cache was reached quickly. Just before reaching this cache though, the wind began blasting down the glacier once more and the attempt had to be abandoned again. Whilst not achieving the summit, the expedition did succeed, at 3400m on the south-west ridge, in climbing to the highest altitude achieved in the Arctic in winter.

The second attempt was made in March 2006. As before, the ski plane departed from north-west Iceland, this time two weeks earlier. Captain Bjarki made a difficult landing across the glacier slope and the plane slewed sideways in deep powder snow as it came to a stop. As Captain Bjarki tried to taxi towards our intended camp location, the plane slewed further sideways burying a ski into the snow, 'I cannot taxi, you have to unload. I leave engines running,' said Captain Bjarki, coolly. No sooner had we unloaded the aeroplane than Captain Bjarki took off uphill up the glacier in a whirling wake of spindrift, once again leaving us to cope with whatever the Arctic elements would throw at us until his return in three weeks' time. By contrast to 2004, the weather forecast was for a blocking high for the next few days.

Everyone packed food and fuel for six days into pulks and rucksacks. With a view to attempting the north-west ridge instead, the group skied about 5 km up the north-east approach glacier to an advanced base camp location at 2430m on a slight ridge opposite a sérac band, a small depression between offering some protection. After erecting two tents and leaving the food and fuel everyone returned to base camp. Two more tents and everything else for six days was moved up to the ABC the following day.

On 4 March a dawn start was made skiing upwards from ABC. In spite of temperatures below −30°C I found it quite warm skiing in a down suit and I had to unzip everything for cooling. Initially the route climbed gentle slopes until a high steepening in the glacier with a choice of going right or left. We chose the right which had less dead ground and was easier angled but at the top, in the dead ground, was an unseen impassable crevasse which crossed most of the slope necessitating a long traverse left, then back right above it and below a pair of wind sculptured holes which looked just like eyes in a face, looking out down the glacier. Above the eyes, in more dead ground, was another unseen impassable crevasse, again cutting across most of the slope. Again, another long traverse leftwards was needed to find a narrow snow bridge. The route then eased into a bowl below a steep wall.

The easiest line was an ascending traverse left up across the wall on icy névé with occasional snow patches. However it was on the limit for skins to grip and it was a real strain to hold a few centimetres' length of ski edges on the ice. Halfway, John lost his edges, fell into the slope and the steep angle wouldn't allow him to regain his edges whilst staying in balance. I was struggling more than most with narrow half-length skins but managed to get below John to help him, at risk of him sliding and taking both of us down the slope. As John and I battled on up the nightmare traverse, the others pulled steadily ahead.

At the top of the rising traverse were a couple of fallen sérac blocks around which we turned and the ski tracks went easily into another large bowl before climbing out right and back left to a large platform area below the summit pyramid ridge. As we crossed this bowl I realised that I could no longer afford to support John at the rear without putting my own bid for the summit at risk. I baulked at the thought of returning to subject myself to these conditions for a third time and knew I would have to tell him that I must leave him to preserve my chance at the summit. I hated having to do it, but the deed was duly done and he was graciously understanding of my position. I advised John not to attempt to go back on his own but either to stay put and wait for someone's return to go back to ABC with him or to continue on upwards until he met up with the others.

At the platform, the others were changing into crampons whilst Paul and Barry reconnoitred the summit pyramid ridge. A previous summer expedition had reported this ridge to be a walk; the encircling rock band was subsumed on this north-west ridge but nevertheless we thought the last 50 metres of the summit block looked quite steep and exposed. To my surprise and delight John arrived whilst I was fitting my own crampons and presently announced he had forgotten how to put his crampons on. I assumed this was because he had borrowed them to fit his new oversized boots and thought nothing more of it. I fitted them for him but had to remove my gloves at minus 40°C to get the overly short straps to fasten; thankfully there was little wind and I retained the necessary dexterity. I then started up the ridge expecting John to follow shortly behind. I kept stopping and looking back, but the flank of the ridge was convex. Eventually I saw him appear and so I continued upwards.

I soon caught up with the others at the steepening from where the final foreshortened section looked almost vertical. Adrian and Barry had begun carefully picking their way up the final 50 metres. Paul, Doug and Lucy were at the foot, looking up the slope, but not advancing; James and Hugh were resting just below. Paul was advising them that there was neither the daylight remaining nor the quality of snow to deploy a rope for protection and that anyone wanting to continue would have to climb unprotected.

I stepped up a few feet past Doug to judge the angle and the consistency of the snow. It was about Scottish II and the névé was firm, crampons bedded in with a satisfying thud and my axe shaft sank up to the adze –

92   Paul Walker (*left*) and John Starbuck (*right*) approaching the platform during the first summit attempt. Note the long shadows from the low angle of the sun only an hour or so after midday. (*Adrian Pedley*)

93.   John Starbuck approaching the summit of Gunnbjørnsfjeld (3693m) during the first summit attempt. (*Barry Roberts*)

eight out of ten for security. I realised there was never going to be a better opportunity than this; stable high pressure, perfect visibility, almost no wind, no altitude problems and plenty of energy. I wondered whether I would be able to reverse the route but told myself I would just have to reverse down the steps I would be making; after all it was only about 20 metres at this steepest angle. I was reminded of previous times when things looked very steep and had proved to be easier than first seemed.

I looked back at Doug and said it was good stuff, pretty secure. Meanwhile Paul started up and we went up the slope together, Paul preferring two axes into the white névé on the flank on the left, me preferring to balance up the greyish ice on the right, nearer to the exposed ridge crest. It was about twenty steps before the angle eased and we joined Adrian and Barry on the small summit plateau, at about 4pm.

Being so late in the afternoon, we did not stay long. It felt very secure just walking down, facing out. I expected to see the others coming up, but was surprised to see none had come up any further. Doug was very agitated, citing John's tiredness as a vehicle to vent his frustration, saying there could be a problem getting him down the mountain. I felt not a little attacked myself and was confused; Hugh, James and Lucy were not there – why had they not climbed up like the four of us; it had been OK? An intense exchange revealed the reality of the team make-up: for Doug, Lucy, James and Hugh their forte was ski-touring, not mountaineering; John was a piste skier and it transpired that he'd never worn crampons before at all, hence his difficulty at the platform. If they were to climb this last part of the mountain they would need the comfort of a rope. Commonsense then resumed with the realisation that it was more important to put our differences aside and to descend to ABC before darkness beset us.

As we accompanied John to the platform he was swaying about, obviously suffering from tiredness, altitude and probably dehydration. As I removed my crampons at the platform I became conscious of John not preparing himself for the descent. James and Hugh had already set off. Everyone else was busy sorting themselves out so I took John's crampons off for him and packed them into my rucksack along with his axes, harness, gear and thermos. Meanwhile Barry was laying out the para-glider he had carried up to make a first winter flight in the Arctic. As Adrian took pictures, Barry took off on his skis and soared slowly across the bowl, his skis still attached, eventually making a landing at ABC. Paul, John, Adrian and I then started the descent into the upper snow bowl.

Conscious that the light was now flattening rapidly, Paul and Adrian skied ahead trying to discern the faint marks of the uphill track left on the icy névé. Meanwhile I maintained a position just behind John so that I could assist him if necessary. The icy névé had been scoured into hard sastrugi which deflected skis and threatened to break the tips, making the skiing very difficult. In his tired state, John fell many times. Time and again I fought against the sastrugi to precision turn around him and counterbalance him back onto his feet, taking a couple of falls myself. He kept stopping, wanting to rest and I had to encourage him on, knowing the potentially dire consequences if we did not get back to ABC before darkness fell. It took three hours to pick our way down, down across the nightmare traverse and along between the two long crevasses. By comparison, the earlier skiers had got down in just 45 minutes. We reached ABC just as the quarter-phase moon replaced the last light from the sun.

It was a very cold night, probably exacerbated by tiredness and dehydration. Cloud rolled in on the lower glacier, then rose up to envelope ABC and the nearby peaks. Snow fell. I had my sleeping bag hood sealed up and still had to do in-bag exercises to keep warm. I spent the waking hours considering scenarios of how the expedition might develop from this point. I reasoned that ascents of Dome and Cone, the second and third highest peaks in the Arctic, would require each of the remaining nine days to be perfect weather to travel to them and return in the time available. I reckoned this was very unlikely and so resigned myself to assisting with a second summit bid.

For the next four days the weather was poor; food and fuel ran down threatening a need to re-supply from base camp. But, at dawn on 9 March another summit bid was made by all. It was much windier than on the 4th, snow plumes were blowing off ridges. I couldn't keep my feet warm; whereas the others had battery powered boot heaters, I was keen to rely only on my body's own resources. I slackened off my boots, removed volume fillers and socks to increase circulation and was just able to maintain sensations of feeling in my feet if I kept moving.

This time we took the left-hand ramp which steepened at the top to a sunlit col, just below the fallen sérac blocks at the top of the nightmare traverse. I wanted to get to the col for some warmth, but one of John's skins came off and I had to stop to remove it, losing heat in the process and numbing my feet again. I stuffed the skin inside my down suit to warm it whilst John half herringboned, but it was very steep and too slow. I had put on two sets of half-length skins and was only just gripping, it was so steep. Paul and I re-fitted the skin but John still couldn't go any faster and his prospects of making it to the summit were clearly over. We stopped just above the sunlit col. Paul wanted to go on to check on the others. Adrian said he had felt better but decided to carry on. I would like to have gone to the summit twice, but not at the cost of frostbite so I chose to accompany John back down to ABC.

John and I side-stepped down the steepest section, but his skin came off again and so I removed it and put it inside my down suit again. Without quick movement I couldn't regain any sensation of feeling in my feet and began to get concerned. We picked up speed on the shallower ramp and as we passed through beams of sunlight coming between peaks, sensations returned to my feet. Just as we arrived in ABC, there was a fall from the nearby sérac band that fell harmlessly into the intervening depression. We serviced the camp ready for the return of the others. Meanwhile, Barry had put up a fixed rope on a psychological belay but it still left the section above the steepening unprotected. Nevertheless, Doug, Lucy, James and Hugh made it to the summit, but in stronger winds than on the 4th.

The weather for the descent to base camp was not as good as the previous summit day but there was adequate visibility. Pulks were packed after a leisurely start and massively loaded to do the journey in one ferry. Braking and steering such a load down the mixture of sastrugi and deep snow was very demanding on the knees. Then followed a long flat to base camp with lots of herringboning and it was hard to keep the pulks moving against the sand-like friction of the snow.

The following night at base camp I was woken about 11pm by a noise at the back of the tent. Initially I assumed it was someone checking the tent guys before turning in. Then something touched the fabric just behind my head and then moved round to the front of the tent. Simultaneously Paul woke up and asked me what I thought. Then, as we looked at each other, we both had the same thought. Improbable as it was, the most likely cause was a polar bear.

Paul opened the door and saw the bear pass by, heading for the others' tents. As Paul rushed into the kit storage tent to find flares he shouted to alert the others. The bear trashed Doug and Lucy's unoccupied tent and took a bite out of Doug's sleeping bag; luckily they were in with James and Hugh, playing Trivial Pursuit by torchlight. Then the bear returned to Barry and Adrian's tent, tore the porch off the tent and then tore into their front door. They hit it in the face with a saucepan and it moved off. Paul then fired off one of the parachute flares.

By the time John and I had got out of our tent the bear was gone, somewhere out there, invisible in the gloom. People were shouting 'It's over there. No, it's over there' – referring to completely different directions. There was some intermittent moon and star light as clouds passed overhead and it was hard to see anything due to fog lying on the glacier – not being able to see more than a few yards was the worst of it. We placed skis in a stockade formation around base camp and improvised an arsenal of defensive weaponry based on ice axes and burning fuel options, in case the bear returned. An all-night vigil was maintained, the worst periods being total cloud cover and a prolonged hazy dawn during which the very poor visibility would have provided only a few seconds of warning.

Morning eventually broke with good weather to reveal the zigzag tracks of the bear around the camp and there was a hole in my tent next to where my head had been. With only one serviceable tent and pitiful defences we called in the aeroplane early but by 10am haze had reduced visibility. We heard the plane arrive overhead and then recede away; Captain Bjarki had misheard the GPS coordinates and could not see the camp through the low cloud on the glacier. We gave the coordinates again and he returned spectacularly through a notch in a ridge to fly directly over us. We laid out

94.　Looking up the flank of the NE ridge during the second summit attempt, on Gunnbjørnsfjeld (3693m), 9 March 2006. (*Paul Walker*)

95.　Douglas Gurr climbing beside the fixed rope on the NE ridge steepening during the second summit attempt, 9 March 2006. (*Adrian Pedley*)

bags to mark a runway in the flat light and in confusion over right and left over the radio we could see that Captain Bjarki was trying to land on the side of the line of bags where everyone was standing. As Paul shouted into the radio 'Wrong side! Wrong side! Other side! O-t-h-e-r s-i-d-e!' Captain Bjarki twitched the 9-ton aeroplane just feet above the ground and put it down on the other side as everyone struggled to scatter in the deep snow.

Afterwards, Barry said he'd found it harder than his experience on Everest, with no respite from the persistent cold, the temperatures rarely ever rising above −30°C. My own experience tells me that climbing and skiing skills count for little in polar environments compared to the need for highly refined winter camp craft skills, for without these basic essentials one can have little chance of being in good enough physical and psychological condition to utilise those more technical skills. For expeditions in extreme conditions like these, a certain degree of English eccentricity probably does not go amiss either and the saying 'only mad dogs and Englishmen go out in the ....' comes to mind, in a perverse sort of way.

Summary: An account of the first winter ascent of Gunnbjørnsfjeld, 3693m, Greenland, the highest peak in the Arctic. Both visits were commercial expeditions, organised and led by Tangent Expeditions International.

Members of the record setting winter 2004 attempt: Janice Cargill, James Carnegie, Conrad Dickinson, Stephane Manndalert, Glen Morris, John Starbuck (AC), Dagmar Wabnig, Paul Walker (Leader), Chris Weyers.

Members of the successful winter 2006 ascent: John Burness, Douglas Gurr, Hugh MacKay, Lucy Makinson, Adrian Pedley, Barry Roberts, John Starbuck (AC), Paul Walker (Leader), James Wheaton.

EVELIO ECHEVARRÍA

Cordillera Central, Argentina

Five of the seven Andean countries have a 'Cordillera Central' but, curiously, that of Argentina, by far the largest and the highest, is generally the least known of the five. It is commonly called 'the roof of America' since it contains 19 peaks between 6000m and the 6960m of Aconcagua, as well as some 600 or 700 other peaks between 4000m and 6000m. But to the average mountaineer, reasonably well versed in developments in international expeditionary and trekking activity, this particular Cordillera Central could at best evoke two or three names of mountains: Aconcagua, Tupungato and, perhaps, Mercedario. The hundreds of climbers who attempt Aconcagua every year, together with the ordinary trekkers who march along prescribed itineraries, do not seem to notice the world of lesser peaks in the neighbourhood of their destination, for there is no information readily available to draw attention to those other peaks. No monograph of such a vast area has been written and most of the existing information is stored in Argentinian mountaineering journals not readily available abroad. This contribution endeavours to offer a basic monograph, with the stated purpose of drawing attention away from the well-known trio of giants, Aconcagua, Tupungato and Mercedario.

A succinct introduction, which appeared in a British Aconcagua guidebook about the region surrounding the mountain, can be applied to the region as a whole:

> The area ... is quite civilized; transport is good and there is an established structure for mountain access. There are no "nasties" in the region, such as snakes, mosquitoes or wildcats. The people are friendly; food is great and language is not a particular barrier.[1]

The Cordillera Central of Argentina is situated in the central west part of the territory, on the border with Chile and within the political limits of the two provinces of San Juan and Mendoza. It runs north to south for an approximate length of 750kms. The highest point is, of course, Cerro Aconcagua (6960m) in Mendoza province, while the highest point in San Juan province is Cerro Mercedario (6670m, 6770m or 6800m).

Cordones and Cerros

So vast is this world of mountains that in order to gain even a general overview, a step-by-step approach is necessary. First, there are six great rivers born in the high snows: Jáchal, San Juan, Mendoza (or Las Cuevas),

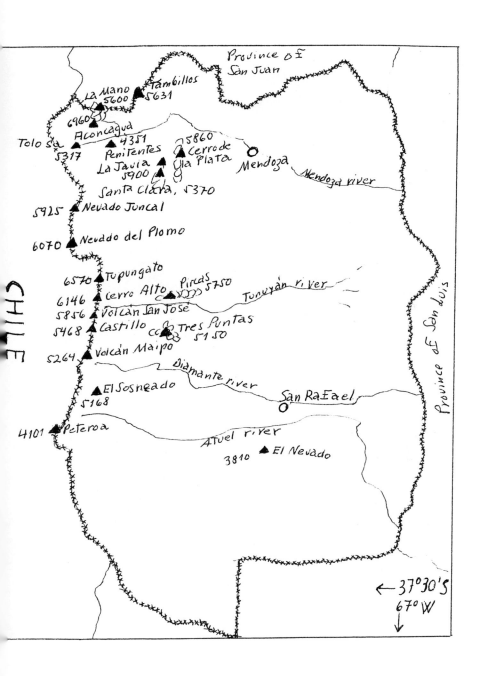

Cordillera Central, Argentina. Province of San Juan. Not to scale.
Approximate location of main peak. (*Sketch map by Evelio Echevarría*)

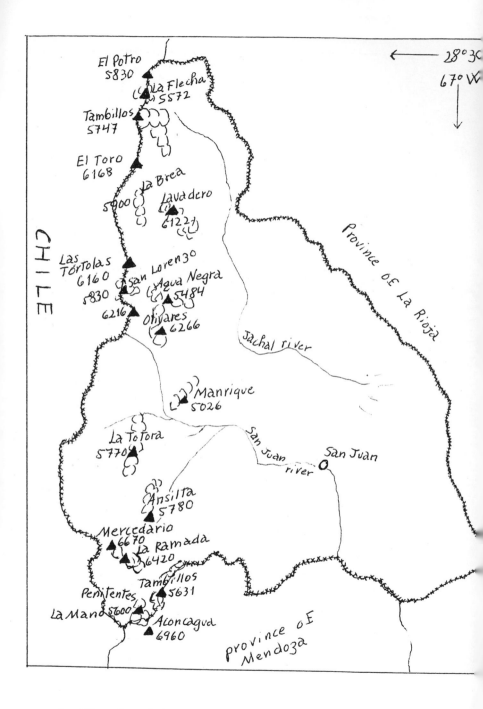

97. Cordillera Central, Argentina. Province of Mendoza.
(*Sketch map by Evelio Echevarría*)

Tunuyán, Diamante and Atuel. Then the *cordónes* (singular: *cordón* and *cordillera*); these are well-defined chains or ridges of peaks. There are 14 such chains in the province of San Juan and eight in Mendoza. Concerning altitude and glaciation, the main San Juan chains are in the south-west portion of this enormous province (90 000 sq.kms). The Cordillera de la Ramada, including Cerro Mercedario, is located there. Other *cordones*, including several 6000m peaks, are near the Agua Negra pass. The chains farther north are not well known and often only the highest point of each has received an ascent.

The even larger province of Mendoza (149 000 sq.kms) shows only eight such chains but they carry heavier glaciation than those of San Juan. The Cordillera del Tigre (c5631m) in the Mendoza or Las Cuevas valley can be seen rising abruptly over the pleasant village of Uspallata (1753m). The Cordón del Plata contains the massif of Cerro de la Plata (5860m) and the resort of Vallecitos, Mendoza's nearest base for rock, ice and snow sports. In the west central district and above the Tunuyán river is the Cordón del Portillo (c5800m), one of the most rugged and heavily glaciated *cordónes* in the Cordillera Central. For a diposition of the *cordónes* and their major points, see sketch map and Appendix A.

As for the mountain peaks themselves, it would prove an onerous task to review even a small proportion of the some 700 that belong to this region. A few of them could be briefly profiled, if only to provide an idea of the bonds between local inhabitants and their mountains. One should, perhaps, begin with the 16 six-thousanders, somewhat lower than Tupungato (6570m), which, curiously, attract fewer local or visiting expeditions than some lesser montains. Nor do the mountaineers of San Juan show a special predilection for any peak other than Mercedario. Mendoza, however, is different: it has its favourite mountains. Cerro de la Plata (5860m), for instance, visible from the streets of Mendoza city itself, is as revered as Aconcagua. Cerro Tolosa (5317m) was much praised by the Europeans in their writings of the last century. It is indeed a fine pyramid especially when seen from the valley around Puente del Inca, the gateway to Aconcagua. The equally visible but smaller Cerro Penitentes (4350m), located a few kilometres south-east of Tolosa, is a serrated mountain showing a steep reddish wall to the travellers who use the highway along the Mendoza valley. In spite of its modest size, it is the depository of more legends than much greater mountains, including Aconcagua itself. And Cerro Penitentes, unlike nearly all the other peaks in the region, can be ascended at any time of the year, even during the southern winter (June to September).

Volcanoes in the area are few and inactive. The main ones, El Toro (6168m) and Las Tórtolas (6160m), are in northern San Juan province. Bleak and remote as they are, they nevertheless received Inca shrines. In Mendoza, on the border with Chile, both Volcán San José (5856m) and Volcán Peteroa (4101m) have weak steam columns rising from their summit craters.

Glaciation is found mostly on the south and south-east side of the major peaks. Glaciers that occupy the upper valleys are in the Mercedario–La Mesa group (Cordillera de la Ramada), in the Cordón de los Penitentes, north of Aconcagua and on the east and southern flanks of the border mountains. From these glaciers flow unfordable rivers, like the Tunuyán and Atuel. In both provinces there are hundreds of peaks of all kinds and all shapes, a good many as yet unnamed. Some may be close at hand, some in the next valley or quite remote. Others may be rejoicing in impregnability behind wicked, impassable brown streams. And, needless to say, countless peaks, tall and small, rise up everywhere, independent of the *cordónes* close to them.

The Past

Unfortunately Aconcagua, or the 'White Sentinel' (not the 'Stone Sentinel' as widely advertised), has always monopolised attention; but some very important mountaineering events, unrelated to the giant, have occurred in this cordillera. In 1883 Dr Paul Güssfeldt, on Volcán Maipo (5264m), made the highest solitary ascent then known. Between 1897 and 1910 the boundary commissions of Chile and Argentina carried out the first scientific survey of their Andean boderlands, erecting a total of 182 two-metre iron benchmarks on mountain passes and even on some summits of this zone. They are still there. In 1897 members of E A FitzGerald's expedition (including the guide Mattias Zurbriggen) climbed Aconcagua (6960m), Tupungato (6570m) and Catedral (5335m) and produced a first-class book covering the entire Mendoza valley (E A FitzGerald, *The Highest Andes*. Methuen, 1899). In 1925 Austrian immigrant Hans Stepanek and one or two companions performed numerous first ascents and even traverses in the Cordón del Plata. In around 1930 the Vela brothers of Mendoza introduced skiing to the Vallecitos area. In 1939 the Club Andinista Mendoza was founded, followed by the Club Andino Mercedario of San Juan in 1945. Since the 1930s national *andinistas* have been participating in the exploration and climbing of their country's central hinterland. They have often invited foreigners to join them since, throughout her history, Argentina has been a country very open to European immigration.

In connection with the history of mountaineering in this region, I would like to mention two Britons who distinguished themselves in its exploration. Stuart Vines, a geologist, was the real source of strength behind the FitzGerald expedition of 1897. It was he who climbed the major peaks; he also contributed magnificent chapters to the leader's book *The Highest Andes*. He must have been one of the strongest mountaineers of his time and yet his name is – and has been – very rarely mentioned. As far as I know, only one photograph of him as a mountaineer exists. His card, recovered in 1906 from the summit of Cerro Catedral, read, 'M.S.R.S. Vines, Fiskerton Rectory, Lincoln'.[2]

98. Cerro Tolosa (5317m) seen from the south. The south face of Aconcagua in the background. (*Evelio Echevarría*)

99. Mendoza: the upper Las Cuevas valley, looking north, with Cerro Piloto (5064m) in the background. (*Evelio Echevarría*)

100. Nigel Gallop in the southern Cordón del Portillo, 1955.
   (*By courtesy of Nigel Gallop, London*)

101. Cordón del Portillo, with the Tres Picos del Amor (5000m), ascended in
   1954. (*By courtesy of Nigel Gallop, London*)

The other Briton was Nigel Gallop, a Londoner, who resided for a time in Argentina in the 1950s. He took advantage of his holidays to climb in Mendoza. His favourite hunting ground was the Cordón del Portillo where, in the early 1950s, he made good first ascents, among which, with two companions, was that of the difficult Torre del Campanario, 5200m, ('Bell Tower'), surely the most difficult peak in the zone. He also pioneered the exploration of the then unclimbed south-east ridge of Aconcagua. I am indebted to him for the constant exchange of much information and many photographs.

The Present

Even for short forays, mountaineering in this region may mean expeditioning. Except for the Aconcagua and Tupungato mountain parks, no permits are necessary. Mountaineering equipment and supplies can be found in trekking company shops and in general stores in Mendoza.

Although access is simple, the valleys are long and the summer sun is strong. Rivers can be impassable on foot for most of the climbing season (December to mid-March). Porterage does not exist but mules and horses, led by the capable local *arrieros* (herdsmen), can be useful for long trips. Transport is not a problem if the Mendoza valley is the destination since it is well serviced by public transport; but in the remaining valleys private transport would need to be arranged.

For exploratory work, ie new peaks and new routes, visitors would need to make their decisions bearing in mind the following points:

• The majority of unclimbed and often unnamed mountains are at the sources of the main river valleys, usually near the border with Chile; for example, peaks at the sources of the Diamante river, south and east of the big lake of Laguna del Diamante.

• Local institutions, such as the Club Andinista Mendoza, can be contacted to obtain maps, sketch-maps, reports of previous expeditions and statistics of ascents in any given valley. Local mountaineering journals and reviews can also be very useful in this respect. However, a fair command of Spanish would be necessary to make use of them.

• Unclimbed faces abound. To mention but two: the impossible-looking east ridge of Cerro Castillo (5468m) and the near-vertical south face of Cerro Santa María (5023m).

Even in very accessible and well-trodden valleys, like Aconcagua's Horcones Inferior, there remains new ground: for instance, the *cerros* at 5450m, 5400m, 5260m and 5274m on the ridge connecting Aconcagua and Cerro Almacenes (5102m). These peaks are unclimbed and look strikingly difficult on account of the downward-leaning rocks, like roof tiles, which cover their walls.

Those who respond to the challenge of this vast and accessible range will have to be flexible enough to adapt themselves to the peculiarities of the region. Relief and landforms are likely to be on a grander scale than those most visitors have previously encountered. Quantity, size and diversity of mountain peaks, severe and solitary valleys and boundless pale-blue skies are the characteristics of the Cordillera Central of Argentina.

Appendix A SUMMIT ARCHAEOLOGY

An Inca mummy, recovered from the summit of El Toro (6168m), is exhibited in an archaeological museum in San Juan city. Another, excavated from the south-west ridge of Aconcagua at 5300m, is kept in a museum of the city of Mendoza. Any archaeological or historical finding becomes automatically the patrimony and property of the two provinces involved. Top experts in this field are Dr Juan Schobinger, Mendoza and Antonio Beorchia, San Juan. Beorchia founded in 1973 in San Juan the Centro de Investigaciones Arqueológicas de Alta (high) Montaña.

Appendix B CORDÓNES AND THEIR KNOWN MAJOR POINTS

In the province of Mendoza:
Cordillera del Tigre (Cerro Tambillos, 5631m)
Cordón del Portillo (Cerro Las Pircas, c. 5750m)
Cordón Bravo or Tres Puntas (Cerro Dos Hermanas, 5150m or 4850m)
Cordón del Plata (Cerro de la Plata, 5860m)
Cordón Chorrillos (Unnamed, c. 5450m)
Cordón de la Jaula (Unnamed, c. 5900m)
Cordón de Santa Clara (Cerro Santa Clara, 5370m)
Cordón de los Indios (Unnamed, 4931m)

In the province of San Juan:
Cordón del Inca (Cerro de la Flecha, 5572m)
Cordillera de la Brea (Unnamed, c. 5900m)
Cordillera de Colangüil (Cerro Lavadero, 6122m)
Cordillera de San Guillermo (Nevado Tambillos, 5747m)
Cordillera de Olivares or Majadita (Cerro Olivares, 6266m)
Cordón de Manrique (Cerro Manrique, 5026m)
Cordillera de la Totora (Cerro de la Totora, 5770m)
Cordillera de San Lorenzo (Cerro San Lorenzo, 5830m)
Cordillera de Ansilta (Cerro de Ansilta, 5780m)
Cordillera de la Ramada (Cerro Mercedario, 6670m, 6770m or 6800m)
Cordón de los Penitentes (Cerro La Mano or La Iglesia, c. 5600m)
Cordillera de la Ortiga (Cerro de la Ortiga, c. 5990m)
Cordillera de Agua Negra (Cerro Agua Negra, 5484m)
Cordón del Espinacito (Unnamed, 4968m)

SELECTED BIBLIOGRAPHY

(Note: Publications exclusively about Aconcagua, Tupungato and Mercedario are not included.)

D Belatalla, *Trekking nella Cordigliera. Cile e Argentina*. Edizioni Calderini, Bologna, 1992.

Antonio Beorchia et al, 'Antecedentes andinísticos de la provincia de San Juan' in *Revista*. Club Andino Mercedario, 6, 77-79, 1971.

John Biggar, *The Andes: a Guide for Climbers*. Big R Publ., 163-177, 186, 1999.

Theodore Crombie, 'Two climbing expeditions in the central Andes' in *Geographical Journal* 107, 325-330, 1946.

Stefan Dazsynski, 'A Polish expedition to the high Andes' in *Geographical Journal* 84, 215-223, 1934.

Evelio Echevarría, 'A survey of Andean ascents' in *American Alpine Journal* 37, 425-452, 1963.

–   'A survey of Andean ascents, 1961-1970' in *American Alpine Journal* 48, 71-106, 1974.

–   'Los Andes centrales de Argentina' in *Pyrenaica* 198, 12-17, 2000.

E A FitzGerald, *The Highest Andes*. Methuen, London, 1899.

Pablo Groeber, *La alta cordillera entre las latitudes 34° y 29°30's*. Imprenta Coni, Buenos Aires, 1952.

Paul Güssfeldt, *Reisen in den Anden von Chile und Argentinien*. Gebr. Paetel, Berlin, 1888.

J Guthman, 'Exploring the central Andes' in *Mountain Craft* 32, 2-4, 1956.

Robert Helbling, 'Beitrage zur topographischen erschliessung des Cordillera de los Andes' in *Jahresbericht*. Academischen Alpenclub Zurich XXIII, 1-77, 1918.

Edward de la Motte, 'Mount Sosneado' in *Alpine Journal* 48, 177-178, 1936.

Fritz Reichert, *Exploración de la alta cordillera de Mendoza*. Biblioteca del Suboficial, Buenos Aires, 1929.

Luis Riso Patrón, *La alta cordilera de los Andes entre las latitudes 30gr. 40min. i 35gr. Sur*. Imprenta Cervantes, Santiago, 1903.

Francesco Santon, *Sulle ali del condor*. Condor Editori, Venice, 1991.

Marcelo Scanu, 'Andinismo en San Juan' in *Pyrenaica 185*, 176-179, 1996.

Walter Schiller, *La alta cordillera de Mendoza y parte de la provincia de San Juan*. Anales de Ministerio de Agricultura, Buenos Aires, 1912.

Seylaz, 'Une expedition peu connue dans le massif de l'Aconcagua il y a 50 ans' in *Les Alpes 28*, 17-22 and 25-29, 1952.

Hans Stepanek, 'Bergfahrten in der Cordillera del Plata' in *Tatigbericht*. Die Naturfreunde Vienna, 23-25, 1925.

Txomín Uriarte et al, 'Expedición al Nevado Las Palas' in *Pyrenaica 196*. 356-363, 1996.

Useful sources of information are Argentinian mountaineering journals: Club Andinista Mendoza, *Nuestras Montañas*; Club Andino Mercedario, *Revista*; Centro Andino Buenos Aires, *Boletín*; Club Andino Bariloche, *Anuario*; Federación Argentina de Montañismo y Afines, *La Montaña* and Centro de Investigaciones Arqueológicas de Alta Montagna, *Revista*.

Maps

Some 15 different hojas (sheets) covering this region at a scale 1:50 000 and 1:250.000 can be obtained from the Instituto Geografico Militar in Buenos Aires. For a complete list of all pertinent maps available see John Biggar, *The Andes: a Guide for Climbers*, 1999. Photocopies of the same maps can be bought at the offices of the Club Andino Mercedario, in San Juan and the Club Andinista Mendoza, in Mendoza.

REFERENCES

1   Jim Ryan, *Aconcagua. Highest Trek in the World*. Cicerone, Milnthorpe, Cumbria, pp19-20, 2004.

2   Fritz Reichert, *Exploración de la alta cordillera de Mendoza*. Biblioteca del Suboficial, Buenos Aires, p73, 1929.

Arts

Andy Parkin *Mont Maudit, Chamonix*
Pastel
From Fourche bivouac hut

ANDY PARKIN

A Night on Les Droites

The story of a new route (by mistake) on the north face of Les Droites, summer 1981. A weak battery in the headlamp, a sense of immortality...and *voila*...

Preparation. Winter and spring, running out to work at Eyam. Climbing ever harder, on-sight solos, running between the cliffs. Head training as much as physical.

The summer and en route for the Alps. Hitch-hiking, a pretty girl stops and I discover Annecy. But that, as they say, is another story.

A few weeks later, one dark and moonless night. Bivouac opposite the dark mass of the mountain. It's the north face of Les Droites. No sleeping bag. Midnight and I'm already cold. When I can't stand it any more I set off. Without a single fallingstone, the silence up on the glacier is total.

The weak light of my headlamp, its battery nearly dead, only
lights a few metres in front of me. My universe becomes tactile to
say the least, with this breakable ice to climb. I let myself be
guided by the climbing, following runnels of ice through which
I can clearly see the granite and the reflections from the quartz
embedded in it.

My idea, at the start, had been to climb the classic route -
La Davaille - and to follow the best line. Since the beginning I
had had my doubts, being unable to see anything at all, was I on
the right route? A worrying thought, without a rope or anything
to descend if necessary.

   During the preceding winter, I'd done the nearby Ginat route and
the climb I was doing didn't resemble the face I'd climbed then.

The climbing continues to be hard and delicate. But I'm starting to relax and the top is in sight. I can definitely get off this thing now.

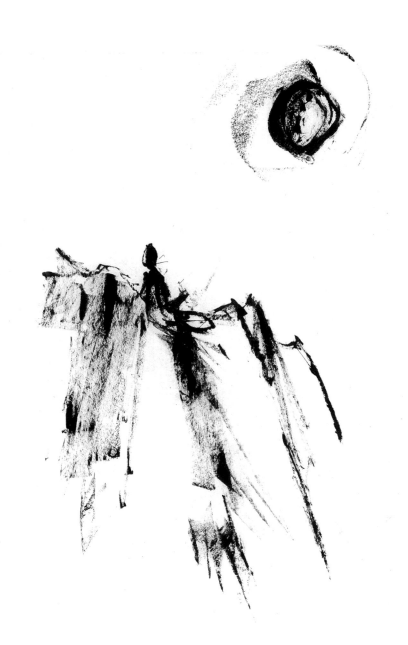

Daybreak. I'm sat on the summit, peaceful and calm. I finally know just where I've been. Too far to the right of the face, right again of the Couzy Spur. I'm on the west summit, not on the east. What have I climbed? Is it new? I'm happy - only 4hrs 30 mins from the bivouac - but am also feeling just a bit of an idiot. I've already nicknamed it the *Faux Couzy*.

TONY RILEY

Preserving our Mountain Art
Digital Technology:
A new imaging landscape

Digital technology has introduced major changes in photographic imaging, some aspects of which are particularly relevant in the context of mountaineering photography. It has also enabled new methods for the digital preservation of visual information in heritage collections, and new levels of accuracy in art reproduction. The changing scientific basis of these topics, from photographic to colour science, should be of interest to all institutions such as the Alpine Club that have photographic and art archives, since funding bodies could increasingly favour digitisation projects that show an awareness of the new scientific guidelines currently in development.

Fig. 1 Digital images now provide greater control over colour.

Mountaineering and photography seem to have strangely aligned histories, maybe by developing over a similar period. Certainly high light levels in mountain regions made them a natural environment for getting the best from the first very slow film emulsions. The unending supply of great pictures in climbing publications is a tribute both to the popularity of photography with climbers, and their documentary and artistic skills. A love of mountains finds natural expression in photography, and few climbing teams are without a camera.

Each advance in camera technology has been rapidly assimilated by climbers, through early roll film formats to 35mm and then the compact cameras. They have been slower to change to digital cameras over the 15 years that consumer models have been available, especially given that digital cameras have been outselling film cameras for the last few years.

There are probably good reasons for the slower uptake of digital cameras in mountaineering, mainly loss of battery power in extreme cold. But digital cameras actually have some advantages in cold conditions, namely fewer moving parts to freeze, less detail-obscuring image noise or 'grain' than film, and the possibility of more accurate colour reproduction.

For the professional cameraman/photographer, film equipment can be degreased and low-viscosity lubricants used to combat freezing. I well remember burying a movie film camera in a snow slope at 25,000ft, rather than carry it back down only to have to haul it up again. I was surprised to find it working a week later.

The purpose of this paper is to draw attention to the advantages of the new science replacing photographic science in digital imaging, rather than trying to compare all digital capture with all film photography. The simplistic answer to this comparison is that some digital images are better quality than some film images, and vice versa.

Fig. 2 Noise in a digital image

However, one advantage of digital cameras used in extreme cold can be a reduction in the 'grainy' texture caused by electrical noise in the image signal. This is easily identifiable in digital images in areas of even tone like skies, and shadow areas. *Fig. 2* shows a close-up from a 3200 ISO exposure, which exaggerates the effect. The improvement at low temperature can be pronounced enough for some scientific digital cameras and professional scanners to incorporate cooling systems to reduce noise in the charge coupled device (CCD) that initiates the image capture sequence.

We accept grainy texture in photographic film images, but the better digital camera images are much closer to reality in the sense of reducing this effect, which can have the same effect as film grain in obscuring fine detail.

Film images are also affected adversely by exposure to heat, but the effect is additive, and something that occurs frequently on expeditions. This can cause both selective and overall colour casts in the colour layers that are designed to work in parallel.

What is the relative colour 'accuracy' of digital and film capture? Film dyes produce a limited range of colour compared to a silicon CCD, given the colour gamut of pixel filters and subsequent data processing. Digital capture also enables more 'accurate' colour than photographic film dye, as we see later in looking at the digital preservation of heritage. Many films also deliberately distort colour rendition and tonal reproduction for aesthetic reasons.

An impeccable scientific experiment[1] in comparative colour accuracy between film and digital sensors, when recording real scenes, placed a custom built IBM system top and a consumer digital SLR second, as having the least colour error. Digital sensors also record a wider range of subject brightness (dynamic range), and produce much lower noisy/grainy images in low light levels, than film. Indeed one method of ISO speed rating for digital cameras is based on the acceptable level of noise in the image.[2]

Fortunately, most photography doesn't have to produce accurate colour, merely a pleasing picture,[3] since pictorial images are rarely compared with the original scene, and perceptual processes can be shown to distort colour memory.[4] The great mountain photographer Ansel Adams recognised very early in his work both the way film distorted tonal distribution and how the picture in his mind differed, compared to the way the actual measured light in the scene was distributed tonally. He sought a way of recording an image that would allow him to print, not the image he 'saw' in front of him, but that image in his mind, 'previsualisation' as he called it. Working predominantly in monochrome to achieve this, he co-invented the Zone System of exposure, that reinterprets film exposure in the light of perceptual behaviour.

Fig. 3 Clearing Winter Storm in Yosemite Valley (Photo © Joseph Holmes)

How would Ansel Adams have worked today? Probably like photographer Joseph Holmes, whose beautiful images[5] also straddle the art/science divide, using colour science and colour management to solve the same problem.

The disadvantage of film's photographic science is that it is based in brightness measurement, not measuring colour separately. Digital photography however is based in colorimetry, which uses the spectral composition of colour, allowing us to separate brightness from colour in the same way that the eye does.

Colorimetry defines colour in terms of its spectral content, plotting it in three-dimensional 'spaces' that take account both of the spectral sensitivity of the cones in the retina, and the subsequent reworking of this retinal response into a different signal set before the information ever reaches the brain. Joseph Holmes works with very high quality scans of large-format film, and has designed the colour spaces used by many discerning photographers. The management of colour refers to the practice of measuring the unique colour characteristics of individual cameras, monitors, scanners and printers with a spectrophotometer, and recording differences in a digital file (or 'profile') that can adjust colour appropriately in image production workflows. Many photographers now use a spectrophotometer to calibrate, profile and monitor their colour workflows.

Colour 'accuracy', however, is crucial when we consider the digital preservation of our heritage collections and art reproduction. Whereas archivists are rightly concerned with the preservation of the original artwork or artefact, even now creating the UK's first low-oxygen storage facility at the British Library, digital preservation is concerned both with capturing and maintaining scientifically accurate image information, for its portability to future technology. Cameras and scanners sense 'raw' image information, but introduce proprietory changes in processing this data, so it is important to record the raw data prior to changes. The individual characteristics of the capture equipment, including lighting, should be measured for image re-evaluation in future technological systems.

How 'accurate' can you get in digitally preserving heritage, and how is it quantified? Colour can be compared to its reproduction, giving units of colour difference on a scale called, among others, delta E.[6] Up to 2 units of difference are considered imperceptible to human colour vision. From 2 to 5/6 is considered acceptable, and more than this is increasingly unacceptable to the average observer. In the colour science lab, accuracies of less than 1 unit have been achieved.

For institutions like the Alpine Club that archive mountaineering heritage, a relevant science-led revolution is taking place in the digital preservation, archiving and reproduction of heritage imagery. Traditionally this has been done either by photography, often using a large-format film transparency that is subsequently scanned, or by scanning direct on a flatbed scanner. But in trying to freeze the visual appearance in time while the original inevitably continues to change, photographic dyes, lighting and individual film scanner and digital camera filters impart their own colour characteristics. These characteristics can be measured and included in the metadata (information about the image data) along with the actual visual information.

In 2005, with Gordon Stainforth, I applied 'digital restoration' to the images compiled by him for The Crux, a photographic exhibition for Kendal Film Festival (*see p89-121*). This presented 25 classic photographs from British moun-taineering and rock climbing from 1860 onwards. A principle of digital restoration is to maintain or even uncover image integrity, meaning to remove artefacts that are added at each image stage as a result of whatever processes it goes through. We rarely had original material to work from, and were dealing with the grain structure produced by the original film or plate chemical processing, noise from the original film scan or print, noise from a scan of that print, and in some cases the screen dot pattern in scans from a book reproduction added to any characteristics of that scanning process. Sometimes a duplicate transparency added its own emulsion characteristics to the original film. Most of the work consisted of grain/ noise reduction with a complicated sharpening process that incorporated some image processing. Although not used for The Crux exhibition, digital restoration can also include Fourier processing. This is the image processing version of the hi-fi filter that removes 'crackle' from audio recordings.

The work enabled us to clarify a third figure and section of rope in the Abrahams brothers' 1915 Scafell Central Buttress picture, that wasn't clear in the scan we had to work from. The most fascinating and difficult picture by far for me was Howard Somervell's picture of Edward Norton at 28,100ft on Everest in 1924 (*see page 102*), and I did slightly lighten the area surrounding the figure to help distinguish it from the background. The area around the ice axe remains particularly puzzling (*Fig.4*).

Fig 4
Edward Norton at 28,100ft on Everest, 4 June 1924. T Howard Somervell. (*Somervell family*)

It helps to be a mountaineer in restoring mountaineering pictures. There comes a point in a close-up examination where it is difficult to tell if certain image detail is actual rock detail against the snow, debris left from film processing chemistry, or system noise looking similar to film grain. Rock against snow has a characteristic feel to how it looks; the bottom line is – if unsure, leave it in.

Colour science isn't new, but digital colour is, and when it was realised that their combination could provide significantly improved digital preservation of the visual information in art and other heritage collections and archives, there was an explosion in the funding made available for research. Art reproduction has become a hot topic in colour science labs worldwide, and perhaps leading the research is the Rochester Institute of Technology's Munsell Color Science Laboratory (MCSL).

Together with the Image Permanence Institute, MCSL recently completed a survey in benchmarking the digital capture of artwork in 52 American museums.[7] The study is remarkable both in defining the problem (current practice being based in photographic science, with different institutions taking their own approach), and the answer (colour science methodology plus an art historian). The report notes the dedication of staff but also many inconsistencies in imaging practice and a lack of understanding of colour science principles. It also gives a recommended best-practice methodology for institutions that are unable to provide scientific skills or facilities. Since the background work culture of these scientists is that of ISO committees in photography and imaging, it seems reasonable to predict an eventual ISO standard for the digital preservation of heritage. The change from photographic to colour science is not yet widely reflected in best practice advice to archivists, and funding bodies could well begin to favour digitis-ation projects from institutions that show an awareness of the scientific lead being given, and that show they are following practical guidelines. It's also possible of course for the applicant to educate the funder.

A major problem in digitizing photographic collections can be the scale of such projects, especially if planned at print resolutions. The Paul Nunn Archive for example, recently donated by his family to The Fell and Rock Climbing Club, contains over 17,000 images. I would propose that for dig-itization, such projects are scaled down into stages. Large collections can be batch processed relatively cheaply direct to low resolution, but scientif-ically more accurate, 'raw' files. This gives a good quality, repurposable, thumbnail image collection that enables cataloguing of the content, per-haps as a basis for selection of the important material for a high resolution digitization funding application. It also enables the selection of individual images for higher resolution scanning for specific purposes. Above all, it makes archives accessible without the cost of a large-scale digitization project, rather than them being hidden away.

The new technology has other advantages for institutions concerned with heritage preservation. It gives electronic accessibility via internet websites where art artefacts are fragile. A state-of-the-art example is the Vatican Library Project,[8] which was able to make previously unseen art available worldwide. Content management system websites now enable easily-managed picture galleries that can hold thousands of images. Also, superb quality short-run art reproductions are available via digital inkjet printing. Because the process is not designed for mass print runs, much better quality inks, pigments, art papers and paper receiver coatings can be used, and a properly produced fine art print can now have a longevity rating (period before discernible fade) in excess of 100 years for colour and 200 years for B/W.

So, should you chuck the film camera away? Well I haven't yet, but it is gathering dust.

The website (www.cumbriapicturelibrary.co.uk) contains further articles on the topics in this paper. Feedback and discussion are welcome – contact tony@cumbriapicturelibrary.co.uk.[9]

REFERENCES

1. R S Berns, *The science of digitizing paintings for color-accurate image archives: A review.* J. Imaging Sci. Technol. 45. 2001
2. ISO 12232, *Photography - Digital still cameras - Determination of exposure index, ISO speed ratings, standard output sensitivity, and recommended exposure index.* 1998
3. R W G Hunt , *The Reproduction of Colour.* Wiley (6th Ed.) 1998
4. M D Fairchild M.D, *Color Appearance Models.* Addison-Wesley, Reading, Massachusetts. 1998
5. Joseph Holmes http://www.josephholmes.com/index.html
6. M Stokes, M D Fairchild, and R S Berns, *Colorimetrically Quantified Tolerances for Pictorial Images.* Proc Tech Assoc Graphic Arts part 2. 1992
7. R S Berns and F S Frey, *Direct Digital Capture of Cultural Heritage – Benchmarking American Museum Practices and Defining Future Needs.* Rochester Institute of Technology. 1992
8. F Mintzer et al, 'Toward on-line, worldwide access to Vatican Library materials' in IBM *Journal of Research and Development, Vol 40, No.2.* 1996
9. T Riley, *An evaluation of the colour fidelity of digital hardcopy in the reproduction of a watercolour artist's work.* BSc Degree Dissertation, Univ. Coll. of St Martins, Lancaster, Dept. of Radiography and Imaging Sciences. Also available as a PDF file from tony@cumbriapicturelibrary.co.uk

TERRY GIFFORD

'The Charged Silence of a Summit'

in Contemporary Mountaineering Poetry

When men got to the summit
Light words forsook them
And their hearts filled with heavy silence

Ted Hughes, *Remains of Elmet*

For the Ninth International Festival of Mountaineering Literature at Bretton Hall College of the University of Leeds in 1995, I commissioned from 14 climbing poets a new poem on the theme of 'The Charged Silence of a Summit'. This invitation produced the eight poems that accompany this paper, five of which were read by the poets who were able to attend the festival. By way of introduction to this group of commissioned poems, which have never been published together before, I would like to discuss the very different insights achieved by each of the poets in approaching this elusive, but commonly experienced, charged sense of a summit.

John Sewell's poem 'The Ascent of Skiddaw from Dead Crags' is about an environment that manifests itself as noise: 'what you thought was a mountain/ turns out to be noise'. This poem is one of a sequence by Sewell about this particular mountain in the Lake District. In this ascent, the mountain is challenging his knowledge of it by what appears to be a physical assault on him. 'What could be the mountain/ comes bodying towards you like soiled quartz./ And your chest's in its path.' Annihilation – his word – is by sensory overload as well as by sensory deprivation (the ascetic's route to the summit): 'You can't hear, can't speak, can't see. You almost can't stand.'

But the regular six-line stanzas are persistent, disciplined steps towards the summit cairn, behind which, as the mist clears, 'what you took for a mountain/ becomes one thought'. That 'thought' is actually the name of a special person which cannot be spoken: 'the silence is too great,/ your voice too weak – zero, less than that'. The emotional charge of coming through this trial is transferred to the absent loved one, the 'weight and pang' of whose name induces the need to 'cry' or 'yell'. Such emotional unity between a loved one and the self across such poignant absence is an expression of the paradox that the moment of self-annihilation can be the moment of self-fulfilment: 'You've never felt so self-effaced/ or so affirmedly alive'. This form of engagement (climbing) with this form of place (a summit) defines self (and the deepest emotions) through self-effacement. One is reminded of Ruskin's humility before the awesome presence of Mont Blanc, which forced him to 'associate' himself 'fraternally with some ants' in order to recover. But more mind-enlarging was Wordsworth's experience of emerging from a moonlit silent mist in his ascent of Snowdon. In the 1850 version of *The Prelude* Wordsworth, the first English rock-climbing poet,[1] abandons the structure of a retrospective 'meditation' upon the experience and suddenly plunges into the physical imagery within this 'spot of time' in order to convey the way the material world connects his mind with a larger one:

> There I beheld the emblem of a mind
> That feeds upon infinity, that broods
> Over the dark abyss, intent to hear
> Its voices issuing forth to silent light
> In one continuous stream.

In this charged emotional state the poet perceives that this enlarged mind 'is the express resemblance' of his own 'when thus moved'. He uses the term 'interchangeable' to suggest the reciprocity of nature and imagination. But more significantly he merges the voices of streams with the silence of moonlight to create the 'one continuous stream' of the mountain landscape's 'silent voice'. The oxymoron is the poetic figure that is necessary to evoke the nature of this reciprocal encounter – mind in the world, the world in the mind. In the breathless silence of a summit gained in John Sewell's poem, the mountain has spoken to give him himself. In his archaic, Wordsworthian phrase, he'd never felt 'so affirmedly alive'.

W H Murray knew this kind of elation which he expressed in a curious allusion to music. After a 'hard fight' on the Tower Ridge of Ben Nevis, he wrote, 'our faculties were in balance yet highly keyed, therefore abnormally alive to the deep peace of the summit. Its grace flowed in upon the mind with a touch soothing and most delicate. We need feel but once the spell of that enchantment to understand Schumann's declaration that the true music is a silence'.[2]

1. *The Prelude*'s vivid detail of climbing to the raven's nest to collect the eggs (for each of which four pence was to be gained from the church warden) is based upon real climbing incidents such as that in 1783 when young Bill Wordsworth (with a young Birkett) was in a group of kids who got cragfast on Yewdale Crags, recorded by T W Thompson in *Wordsworth's Hawkshead*.
2. In *The Guardian* obituary for the musician John Cage he is quoted as saying 'that silence is the mother of music' (22 Feb 1996).

The second poem takes this for granted. Kevin Borman's 'Stac Pollaidh' is about a test of self-judgement and of a lover, who this time is also making the ascent. Using the language of that place, (the 16th century Scottish word for bondage) he admits that he is 'thirled to this place', and has brought his new lover 'these hundreds of miles to confirm/ my suspicion that you would be too'. But the climbing together of the 'good holds [...] hanging above space' leads to the summit where the cairn might symbolise the triangular nature of this experience: writer, lover and this specific place:

> At the cairn we look and look.
> Quinag, Cul Mor, the Summer Isles until
> a dense veil of rain heads in.

This poet uses place names like a mantra. There is no explicit mention of silence in this poem, but one can hear its echo between the quiet concentration of 'we look and look' and the three places which are repeatedly looked at: Quinag, Cul Mor, the Summer Isles. Quinag, Cul Mor, the Summer Isles ... In this mantra of silence, self has been defined this time by place and a partner who is present, in a three-way dynamic. Here is the true music in Schumann's sense. In the silence beyond the test of this summit, the poet's judgement about his partner has been confirmed as he and she 'stare across a thousand lochans'. Borman's poem evaluates the test, by this ascent, of the poet's engagement with both his new lover and the rest of his natural environment, balancing the two in what is also a test of himself. By the end of the poem, it is not so much the handling of the holds above exposure that is important, as her ability to also 'look and look' – 'to stare across a thousand lochans/ Long enough for me to know that I was right'.

The silence of looking and listening after touching 'warm rock', of being 'aware, not wanting to move', is the subject of Bob Cooper's poem of Zen-like stillness about climbing a small crag in Northumberland. As he and his partner stare, 'a car miniatures uphill'. The use of the noun as a verb draws attention (rather too self-consciously, perhaps) to the poet's giving value to small things and his eventual identification with his fellow inhabitants of this summit, the 'watching finches' of the title. But the intensity of focus in the poet's receptiveness is suggested by the line, 'All my life has brought me here'. Bob Cooper is listening to nature in the spirit of Thoreau, who wrote about his climb of the mountain Katahdin, that

> Some part of the beholder, even some vital part, seems to escape through the loose grating of his ribs as he ascends. He is more alone than you can imagine. There is less of substantial thought and fair understanding in him, than in the plains where men inhabit.

The mountain silences the writer because the writer is letting in the mountain. Bob Cooper finds himself concentrating with all his life, reduced to the inarticulateness of the also watching finches. This discipline has been called 'contemplation' or even 'worship' by some poets – Chris Whitby for example. His poem, 'Breaking Silence', complains about noise pollution from the increased number of mountain climbers: 'Now mountains keep their council through the day/ But met at the right hour will whisper still'. The 'old familiar charm' that is whispered is the Biblical/Faustian deal of the summit view. Whitby half-jokingly admits that he would, indeed does, sell his soul for it in his separated punchline: 'Enveloped in the mist, I bend my knee'. Most of us also bend a knee to sit down at a summit and stare in that heightened state like Borman and Cooper. Usually some Faustian compromises have been made to get there.

But Whitby's poem ultimately plays with a cliché that its opening treats almost seriously:

> There was a time you'd climb a mountain top
> And find yourself alone to contemplate
> Whatever promptings God, your inner soul,
> Or nature's trenchant silence might evoke.

'Trenchant' is perhaps a giveaway to the tone here, if 'inner soul' has not registered with the reader as ironic in our post-Lawrencian age. Yet the whole poem's point about wanting, needing, to meet the mountain top at its silent time recognises, underneath the apparent cynicism of its tone, the essentially religious nature of the Devil's or summit's whisper, 'All this I give to you'. That summits do give and that they do whisper has rarely been in doubt.

Ironically, it is the atheist poet David Craig who points out in a book about journeys to the 'great rocks of the world' that 'mountaineer', in Greek, was a common synonym for 'monk'. Writing about the anchorites of the caves of Meteora, he says that this place

> was ideal for the practice of *hezychasm*, which cultivated *hesychia*, the peace of solitude, as a means towards *ataraxia*, freedom from anxiety – paradoxically attained, as rock-climbers do, by breaking through the often intense anxiety of the climb itself. (*Landmarks*)

This is a dangerous business. Anxieties in mountain climbing might well not only be justified, but represent an essential survival instinct. Listening to the mountain and to the inner self, that tuned-in dialogue which guides judgement, is a learned discipline as Andean and Himalayan survivors like Joe Simpson know. Simpson's book *Storms of Silence* opens with his standing on an avalanche-prone slope: 'It was as if everything was holding its breath, waiting to see whether I would pay attention'. The death in 1995 of the experienced British climber Alison Hargreaves on K2 raised questions about her ability to listen to the mountain, read the skies for the storm that blew her off her descent from the summit. I remember her explaining to us at breakfast the morning after the eighth mountaineering literature festival, how she had turned back from the South Col of Everest, despite feeling fit and able to climb it without bottled oxygen, because the intense cold would inevitably result in her losing fingers and toes. She returned and climbed Everest. When she died on K2 her husband reportedly quoted the Tibetan saying, 'It is better to live as a tiger for one day than a thousand years as a sheep.'

The feminist climbing poet Kym Martindale reflected upon this Tibetan saying in relation to the death of Alison Hargreaves in her response to my commission. Her poem is called 'Tigers and Summits'. They are both, she suggests, 'a dangerous faith'; they can be 'lost/ without drama/ while you were looking away', as perhaps we all were in August 1995. Tigers and summits, she writes, 'carry the same tawny light'. This phrase recalls the title of an essay by Gary Snyder, 'Tawney Grammar', in *The Practice of the Wild*: 'The grammar not only of language, but of culture and civilization itself, is of the same order as this mossy little forest creek, this desert cobble.' In order to survive, mountaineers have to understand the way the grammar of their culture 'is of the same order' as the grammar of the performers, their 'clean-limbed ambition', their 'narrowed eyes/ and squared palms', but she knows the electricity she herself really deals in: 'I think of the electricity of arriving,/ the fire in my fist'. This is the risk taken 'for a live, silent moment' of a summit gained. Finally the meditation upon the saying which launched the poem becomes a personal acknowledgement of that enlargement of mind which Wordsworth struggled so often to articulate. Martindale jumps for joy in leaps of lines:

> My mind stretches
> awake
> to summits
> leaping with light.

Alison would have applauded her, I think. So would Aldo Leopold, who in *A Sand County Almanac* proposed the notion of 'Thinking Like a Mountain'. This is, I believe, the same essential discipline that Snyder is referring to in 'Tawney Grammar'. The opposite of this is 'Thinking About a Mountain', as in Coleridge's 'Hymn before Sunrise in the Vale of Chamouni'. The emphasis on silence in this poem is too insistent to carry the conviction of true worship. Indeed, the mountain ultimately becomes a mere idea, an abstraction:

Risest from forth thy sea of silent pines,
How silently!
[...]
Thou dread and silent Mount! I gazed upon thee,
Till thou, still present to the bodily sense,
Didst vanish from my thought; entranced in prayer
I worshipped the Invisible alone.

Coleridge's poem is derided by contemporary critics as either a projection of his Lake District experience upon 'grander external objects' such as Mont Blanc, as David Craig puts it, or as 'a paraphrase and elaboration of a work by the Swiss poetess Frederika Brun' in the words of the Romantic scholar Karl Kroeber. Kym Martindale warns that 'Above the soft meadow,/ the sky crackles'. Those poets confronting mountains unaware of this are either dangerous, or faking it like Coleridge. Martindale's acknowledgement of the potential for both danger and elation in outer and inner electricity qualifies and deepens her claim that 'My mind stretches/ awake'. In his 'Hymn' Coleridge's attempt to stretch his mind by sheer force of rhetoric only succeeded in raising 'the Invisible' to what Shelley called 'vacancy'.

In Shelley's address to Mont Blanc, he also works earnestly towards his climactic poetic thought, but his silence is of a different, observed order, with no abstract 'Invisible' sleight of hand. For Shelley, Mont Blanc is a physical example of the paradoxes of the natural world. It is a 'city of death' that nevertheless 'rolls its perpetual stream'. 'The wilderness has a mysterious tongue/ Which teaches awful doubt', yet 'Thou hast a voice, great Mountain, to repeal/ Large codes of fraud and woe'. The natural energies of destruction could be the very energies of social reconstruction, if only the human mind could 'interpret' or 'deeply feel' them. Once again the oxymoron is required for the interpretation of that voice of the mountain. Shelley shows how Mont Blanc speaks by accumulating combinations of silent winds, silent snow, and 'voiceless lightening' towards the ultimate question:

And what were thou, and earth, and stars, and sea,
If to the mind's imaginings
Silence and solitude were vacancy?

What would be the meaning of a summit if its eloquent silence were not heard, felt, interpreted? It is in itself a mountain, but as soon as poets put pen to parchment about it, it becomes a metaphor. Kym Martindale warns mountaineers who might follow the example of Coleridge that the metaphor can drown out the voice of the mountain, with fatal consequences.

Actually this is exactly what the next poet, Dennis Gray, does in his poem 'A Summit Gained'. As a grizzled and well-travelled climber, he knows a bit about Shelley's 'silence and solitude' of a summit. But his starting point is Gerard Manley Hopkins' notion that 'mind has mountains'.

'A Summit Gained' is a recognition that some inner summits may be impossible to gain and indeed self-annihilating if they were, in present social conditions. 'The hills in my head [that] have still/ not been trod or tried in any way' are a potential, a temptation even, but

> If I could get there I know
> that a silence would reign over me
> with a force of such power
> it will be the end to my life.

This text is open to the criticism of abstraction, of residing finally in an oblivion as abstract as Coleridge's 'Invisible'. But one could argue that the poem is a recognition of limits to the mind's capacity to reach some summits, to grasp some thoughts such as the nature of death, or some aspects of self such as, say, homosexuality in the context of a macho climbing culture. Read in this way 'A Summit Gained' asks: Is our capacity to use summits as metaphors a potentiality, or a delusion?

The answer is both, of course, as David Craig reminds us in his remarkable poem 'The Height of Great Moss'. Craig gives us the silence of the Clearances, the historical reality surrounding many of the summits of the Scottish Highlands. David Craig's poem might be read as a reply to Dennis Gray's. Summits can only become metaphors after we recognise that they are physical and have a history in which we too are implicated. To choose one as the place of one's death, even metaphorically within the discourse of a poem, is to idealise into what Craig calls 'fantasy'. Dying is, Craig says, inevitably 'filth' and 'struggle', not an 'embarkation/ Onto the inland sea'. Ironically, by denying himself this fantasy, the poet honours the familiar place and its complex history in both its geological and human dimensions. Craig denies the spiritual and celebrates the silence of the summit as

> the grizzled head
> Of an old peasant who will not be moved
> Even by civil war,
> Who is bothered not at all
> What politicians and banks are fighting for.

David Craig is reversing Shelley. Rather than evoking energies for social change 'to repeal/ Large codes of fraud and woe', Craig's mountain evokes individual stoicism in the face of change, although the confession of a personal war-time gesture by the young poet, laying 'fenceposts up the summit slope/ In V's for Victory', does introduce a degree of youthful complicity in 'what politicians and banks are fighting for'. The significance of Craig's poem is its resistance to the notion that any mountain summit can represent transcendence from temporal reality, even as an ideal place on which one's temporal reality might end.

Graham Mort might appear to be presenting a different case in writing a poem which ends in the silence of beyond words. His long poem 'Bidean nam Bian' seems to want to articulate all that can be described about an experience of climbing this Scottish mountain on a hot, still summer's day when, having reached the summit, 'Thirst and silence have stilled/ all thoughts but one:/ [...] to fall into the cool stare of the lochans'. The poet asks his partner the English meaning of the mountain's Gaelic name and the answer concludes the poem:

> *Bidian nam Bian* -
> meaning highest; meaning peak
> of the mountains; meaning summit
> which we've hardly begun
> to understand we do not know.

Mort invests the silence of a summit with a meaning that is straining at the limits of human understanding. Perhaps this is the 'silent knowledge' of Gary Snyder's *Cold Mountain Poems*. These are translations of the seventh century Chinese mountain hermit, Han-shan, whose name means Cold Mountain. Snyder says he 'takes his name from where he lived [...] When he talks about Cold Mountain he means himself, his home, his state of mind'. Having reached, with Graham Mort's poem, the limits of what can be articulated about 'the charged silence of a summit', it would be wise to fall silent with Snyder's version of Han-shan's four-line poem:

> Spring-water in the green creek is clear
> Moonlight on Cold Mountain is white
> Silent knowledge – the spirit is enlightened of itself
> Contemplate the void: this world exceeds stillness

The Eight Poems

The Ascent of Skiddaw from Dead Crags

Frictive, clawling, thuggish –
what you thought was a mountain
turns out to be a noise.
A gale with the roar of water,
its pitch strengthening, then fading a little, then strengthening again.
A roar you place your whole head under.

A thousand feet later, the gale
having out-faced sound, scribbles out light.
Layer after wafery layer
of what could be the mountain
comes bodying towards you like soiled quartz.
And your chest's in its path.

Everything quits and runs from itself, or wants to.
The white blast shifts so quickly
when it hits, nothing seemingly stays firm.
You can't hear, can't speak, can't see. You almost can't stand.
This is anti-matter face-on,
as close as you can come to it and survive.

But annihilation misses.
And what you thought was impossible
against all known odds,
becomes suddenly just a few steps more.
You find the cairn
and turn your back on it.

And all at once the roar gives up,
as if it didn't see you anymore
as if there never was a roar, now or ever.
And then a milkiness spills through the mist
which lightens, slides
and lifts away, top to bottom.

And when you look down,
what you took for a mountain
becomes one thought.
Whoever it is you think of
after the struggle, when you're restored to yourself,
you think of them. And you want to cry,

or yell their name,
at the weight and pang of it inside you.
But the silence is too great,
your voice too weak - zero, less than that.
You've never felt so self-effaced
or so affirmedly alive.

John Sewell

Stac Pollaid

For TL
From below, by the road,
it looks improbable, impregnable,
a dragon's spine petrified.
As we gain height
the slope tilts up incrementally,
loose, eroded, awkward under foot.
You are daunted by the
frozen rock profile sawing the sky,
though you don't say so until later.

Then we are there. The blocky ridge, with
air buffeting in from Suilven.
Hunched into a niche,
a Torridonian sandstone windbreak,
we stop for an apple and the view.
I am thirled to this place
and had to bring you
these hundreds of miles to confirm
my suspicion that you would be too.

Aeons.
Then ice scoured the old, old rock.
Water became cold grey lochans.
Peat, slow and acid,
raised itself with infinite patience.

We turned among pillars, working west,
rounding pinnacles from where
winds fall, ravens etch themselves on pale sky,
all Coigach stretches away.

Then we come to exposed moves. They have
good holds but are hanging above space.
You haven't met this kind of thing before
but you size it up and go
like a natural, stepping up and round.

At the cairn we look and look.
Quinag, Cul Mor, the Summer Isles until
a dense veil of rain heads in,
the coast steadily dims and is lost to grey.

No matter. We have had the moment,
long enough for you to put your hands on rock,
To stare across a thousand lochans.
Long enough for me to know that I was right.

Kevin Borman

Watching Finches

Swifts screech, cattle shift.
We climb warm rock then stare
over fields to a sun hanging
slow over Berwick. A car
miniatures uphill, shifts gear,
disappears in conifers.
All my life has brought me here
to gaze at light, untie and coil rope
then sit like the finches around us,
aware, not wanting to move.

Bob Cooper

Breaking Silence

There was a time you'd climb a mountain top
And find yourself alone to contemplate
Whatever promptings God, your inner soul,
Or nature's trenchant silence might evoke.
To do that now, you have to beat the dawn
Or settle for arrival with the dusk
(Having doggedly threaded through the Goretex exodus
to curious looks and snippets of sharp advice).
Now mountains keep their counsel through the day,
But met at the right hour will whisper still
The old familiar charm: 'All this I give
To you, as far as eye can see, and more,
If you will but bow down and worship me.'
Enveloped in the mist, I bend my knee.

Chris Whitby

Tigers and Summits

It is better to live as a tiger for a day than a thousand years as a sheep.

Tigers and summits
carry the same tawny light
and charged silence.

Their symmetry
is the symmetry of focus:
with narrowed eyes
and squared palms,
sinews and heart coiled,
tigers consider
the warning plume;

and summits frame them,
model their passion
and clean-limbed ambition.

Tigers
and summits
fool you,
one minute clear-eyed and whole,
holding you in the eye
of their own storm,
then lost
without drama
while you were looking away.

Tigers,
summits –
a dangerous faith.
Above the soft meadow
the sky crackles;
I think of the electricity of arriving,
the fire in my fist
for a live, silent moment.
My mind stretches
awake
to summits
leaping with light.

Kym Martindale

A Summit Gained

There are mountains of the mind
that never do yield an easy route
Soaring spires of dread delight
their forms inspire us in our dreams

We try to keep these high peaks
just for our own selfish human needs
Safe from those with the fever
to trample them under their feet

The hills in my head have still
not been trod or tried in any way
They offer me a new route
if I can only reach their crest

This I know will be so hard
climbing up steep rock faces all alone
Snow and ice may bar the way
'fore the summit can be attained

If I could get there I know
that a silence would reign over me
with a force of such power
it will be the end to my life

Dennis Gray

The Height of Great Moss

That scalp of hoar is permanent on Cairn Toul
Whether the weather on the Moine Mhór
Is blowing fine or foul.
The blade of the glacier dozing over
Laid bare that stony flay.
Its skull of granite weathered old-man-grey
Before the ptarmigan flew in from Jutland,
Even before the pine.

It is the colour of a silenced brain,
Bloodless and motionless as the coffined dead.
It is the grizzled head
Of an old peasant who will not be moved

Even by civil war,
Who is bothered not at all
What politicians and banks are fighting for.

I have breathed this air before:
On Burrival midway down the western islands,
Little square belvedere above the waters,
Where crofters cleared from Sollas
Wintered along Loch Eport, passed on south,
And left it to its silence;
On Morven in the second year of war
Where I laid fenceposts up the summit slope
In V's for Victory,
Paused to let in the stillness of the moor,
And heard a single Heinkel grunt and snore,
Black as a condor in the summer sky.

The Great Moss lours above them all,
Spreading its blanket for a giant's bed.
Here I will lay my own expiring head
Only in fantasy
When life dissolves in ideal resignation
And dreams of dying as it ought to be -
No filth, no struggle, only embarkation
Onto the inland sea.

                                        David Craig

Bidean nam Bian

Here the road shimmers into the day's
tide of heat, taking the tourists away
to pry at curios of tartan, brooch-pins,
the rusted blood of Highland feuds.

Pipers quarrel in the car park
at Glen Coe, their Strathspeys
and reels strut out, clashing faintly
above birch leaves, the clucking
water in this gully;
its rocks are crampon-scarred
though most snow is gone -
just that pale cravat tucked
into the corrie's throat ahead.

The air is thick here,
trees exhale a chest-tight damp;
granite glimmers, choking the valley
with its unpronounceable history.

Above us, peaks vibrate to struck
notes of summer heat
our tongues swell in mouths that
have nothing to say except curse
the angles of rock, this mad glare
flinching our eyes where the snow slope begins.

We toil up it, touching its illusion
of cold, staring at the sun through the sting
of sweat and sun-cream, staggering its last
groove through an avalanche of light.

Five ravens circle the summit;
their cries fall from throats of bone,
their plumage shines then tilts
into blackness.

The loch's iris of white sand sifts
into its hourglass eye - a prophet's
burned out pupil, blinded to futures
that falter from our mind's certitudes.

A skylark sings briefly
then falls; the sky's blueness
hums in electric gatherings of light,
in crackling gusts of static, in a
vacuuming momentousness that the grass
makes ordinary at our touch.

A breeze laps at us then gutters
into massed horizons where the mountains
stare us down, asking to be named;
the shock of the rock's stored heat
is a hand put suddenly in snow,
an insect zings by, gleaming
in its war-gear.

Thirst and silence have stilled
all thoughts but one:
to reach the ridge below, to fall

into the cold stare of the lochans,
into the corrie's shadow, hugged
close as unspent breath, covetous
as a dark conscience.

Descent is a treachery of skipping
stones and dust, it's a mirage
of cold beers lined at the bar,
buckets of ice, draught darkness,
bubbles rising into white necklets
of foam through which our mouths
would sink to drown this skidding
into unremitting waves of light.

We drink the rock's resolution
into rock, and more rock, and more
until we're plunging over bogland
to gulp our heads at the burn's jacuzzi,
swallowing its snow-melt cold,
its stinging effervescence,
scooping its joy of ice, saying how we'd made it
and never thought we would,
how Christ's climb to Calgary
could not have been harder in such heat.

But the mountain isn't listening.

Our breath hollows out its silence,
our ears balance on their stirrups
of bone, predicting scree's slide
towards another winter.

I'm asking you what it means,
the name on the map. Those
words clumsied as your mouth
translates a mountain
to the English tongue –
Bidean nam Bian –
meaning highest; meaning peak
of the mountains; meaning summit
which we've hardly begun
to understand we do not know.

Graham Mort

History

Andy Parkin *Lhasa detail*
Pastel, 1991

JOHN EDWARDS

The 'Eiger of Africa'

First ascent of the east face of Mawenzi

At an RAF airfield in England in the summer of 1961, I was summoned unexpectedly to the Station Commander's office. 'Congratulations John, you are posted to Kenya.' Whilst the CO emphasised my good fortune and briefed me on the posting, my mind was racing thousands of miles away. The mountains of East Africa! A chance to follow in the footsteps of my great hero, Eric Shipton. A dream come true.

Three weeks after I arrived at RAF Eastleigh (near Nairobi), Paddy O'Connor and I were sitting on Batian, the 5199m summit of Mount Kenya, having climbed the Shipton and Wyn Harris 1929 grade IV route. Gazing south, we were amazed to see the shimmering dome of Kilimanjaro some 200 miles away. Kibo would have to wait, however, as our next ambition was to attempt Shipton and Tilmans' West Ridge route (V) and their classic traverse of Batian and Nelion. Our next leave enabled us to do this magnificent climb. From a bivouac on the Josef glacier, in fine weather and with wonderful views, we reached Batian in eight hours having removed a piton from Shipton's Red Pinnacle en-route. Traversing over Nelion we descended the south-east face in the gathering twilight and in high spirits reached the Lewis glacier as night fell.

In 1943 Shipton wrote: 'I still regard the traverse of the twin peaks of Mount Kenya as one of the most enjoyable climbs I have ever had – a perfect and wholly satisfying episode, shared with an ideal companion.' This was a sentiment Paddy and I heartily endorsed. Having resolved to follow all of Shipton's first ascents on Mount Kenya, we later climbed Point John (IV), Midget Peak (V), Point Pigott (III) and Point Peter (III), and of course had to scramble up Shipton Peak.

On our first visit to Kibo we employed three porters (at five shillings each per day) in order to establish a semi-permanent bivouac at around 5200m between the Ratzel and Rebmann glaciers. During several trips to this base we enjoyed nice routes on the Ratzel, Rebmann, Decken and Kersten glaciers. Remembering that Shipton and Tilman had climbed the lower, but more impressive looking, Mawenzi (5149m), we crossed the saddle separating the two peaks and climbed the west face in four hours by what we later discovered was the Oehler Buttress route. But it was what we saw from the top that astounded us. The precipitous east face plunged seemingly endlessly beneath us, its sheer complexity breathtaking and intimidating as it swept down to two huge gorges below. As we descended, the same thought was in both our minds – what about the east face?

On our return to Nairobi we set about finding out what we could about the face and discovered it had become known as the 'Eiger of Africa' and formed the highest cliffs in Africa. We found a guidebook that described the terrain as 'very difficult and little explored' and noted that just one unsuccessful attempt had been made to climb it, by Arthur Firmin and John Howard in 1954.

Meanwhile, things were hotting up 'in Theatre' and I was deployed on detachments to Kuwait, Southern Rhodesia and Swaziland. Sadly my climbing partner Paddy was posted back to the UK. However, as often happened in the Services, other keen climbers appeared including Harry Archer, Pete McGowan and Tommy Thompson. Together we enjoyed two wonderful expeditions to the Ruwenzoris where we climbed all the peaks and made two first ascents, but perhaps the most memorable highlight was finding the Duke of Abruzzi's ice axe, together with a note dated 1906, on the summit ridge of Mount Stanley (5109m).

The enticement of the east face of Mawenzi was proving irresistible so in August 1964, Harry Archer, Tommy Thompson and myself set off on a recce. Passing the wreckage of the DC3 crash (about which much has been written elsewhere) we set up camp near the south wall of the Great Barranco. Two things struck us immediately. First that it would be very beneficial to descend into the Barranco close to the foot of the east face rather than follow the wall eastwards to find a relatively easy descent into the Barranco floor with the consequence of having to flog back up to the foot of the face. The second, very obvious, point was that the direct descent down 800m plus of vertical crumbling basalt would require extreme care. We realised that our fairly primitive climbing gear needed some improvement, so on return to Nairobi we asked RAF Station Workshops for some help. In quick time they shortened our long ice axes and bent the picks to a steeper angle, made up some two-foot steel stakes, improvised some étriers from aircraft freight restraining tape and fashioned two sling hammocks from aircraft cargo nets. Thus armed, Tommy Thompson (a Cpl PTI) and myself headed off to Mawenzi. To hedge our bets it was decided that I would climb in tricounis and Tommy in Vibram-soled boots.

Helped by three porters we positioned our bivouac at the pre-arranged spot near the south wall of the Great Barranco. The porters then descended to Peter's Hut with instructions to meet us with food and fuel at Mawenzi Hut in three days' time. Soon after dawn on 24 October we set up our first abseil to descend over the lip into the seemingly bottomless floor of the Great Barranco. Using our two ropes (a 120ft Italian hemp and a 120ft Viking nylon) and employing the classic style abseil, it was with some trepidation that I set off down the vertical basalt. However, fortune favoured the brave (or the crazy?) and with Tommy lowering the sacks and adapted kit bag from our pulley block, we made steady progress. Twice I found myself close to the end of the ropes and well out of contact with the rock but with the help of prussik loops and some pendulums managed to

15. Harry Archer and Porter M'Shauri at the cairn built on our recce to indicate the descent point down from south wall into the Great Barranco. East face in the background. (*John Edwards*)

re-position. On several occasions, to avoid overhangs, we traversed precariously across the face to find a better descent line. Natural anchors were more readily available than we had anticipated, the dyke swarms proving particularly helpful, and we only had to hammer in and forsake two of our steel stakes. After about five hours we slid down our final abseil to the floor of the Great Barranco close to the east face where we enjoyed outstanding views.

After refreshments we split the load in the kit bag and started solo climbing up the face about midway between the lip and the Middlerippe (known these days as Downie Ridge) which separates the two Barrancos. As the headwall steepened we roped up and started pitching. Although entering thick cloud, we made good progress for the next two hours or so. Despite the fragile nature of the trachybasalt rock, which we expected, our frugal supply of pitons went in securely and happily came out again. Finding ourselves on a small ledge with enough room to perch together, we paused and were pleased to see the cloud lifting. We were not so pleased, however, when it dawned on us that we were almost directly below Latham or possibly Klute Peak and thus well to the left (S) of our avowed direct line to Mawenzi's summit, Hans Meyer Spitze (HMS). In our enthusiasm to get started we had made an elementary navigational blunder. Debating our position, the options were clear: either we continued our present line which, if successful, would mean we simply finished up on the summit ridge,

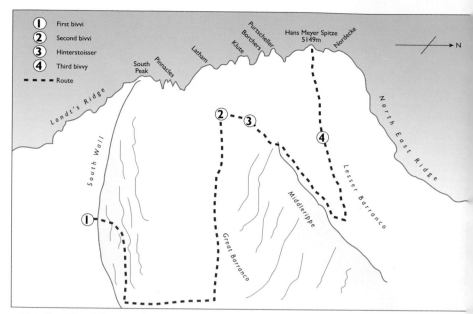

116. Profile of the east face of Mawenzi, Tanzania. (*Sketch map by John Edwards redrawn by Gary Haley*)

or we traversed right and descended down the north side of the Middlerippe to a point on the floor of the Lesser Barranco which we now recognised would position us directly below HMS. It didn't take long to decide to pursue our original ambitions and go for the direct route – a decision made easier by the knowledge that our tour-expiry dates were closing in and this might be our last opportunity.

Throughout the day we had been accompanied by a number of vultures that perched on convenient pinnacles and keenly observed our progress. Did they know something we didn't? As evening approached, they lost interest and swished away, while we used the remaining daylight to begin a delicate traverse towards the point where the Middlerippe joined the east face. It was sensationally exposed. Following the only feasible line, I found myself in a narrow, vertical chimney with no reliable holds but there was a crack at the back. Out came our DIY étriers for my first serious attempt at aid climbing. Our only previous experience had been following Rusty Baillie a few months earlier when trying a new route on Mawenzi's west face. It was dark before I mastered the technique sufficiently well to ascend the 15m chimney where I arrived on a narrow ledge with room for just one.

We decided to bivouac where we were, about 20m apart. However, cooking a meal presented a problem as Tommy had the water and I had the stove and the packets of soup. Our proposed solution was for Tommy to attach our one-gallon water container to the rope and I would pull it up,

7. Mawenzi's east face from south wall with clouds boiling up the Barrancos. (*Tommy Thompson*)

then send down his hot soup. The theory seemed alright but unfortunately in practice it didn't work out. Halfway up the narrow chimney the container became wedged and my desperate tugs on the rope only succeeded in detaching it to send the water plunging into the void. Not to worry; I had a water bottle full of orange squash so made vegetable soup anyway and sent it down to Tommy. He said it was 'great'. The night passed comfortably and we both slept well, secured to the rock in our improvised nets. Next morning dawned cold and cloudy but we had a clear view of the Middlerippe where it met the face about 60m below us and 150m horizontally. We decided to delay breakfast until we could find some snow to melt. The traverse, magnificently exposed and consisting mainly of vertical gullies and ridges, required great care on the crumbling rock but we made steady progress, again accompanied by the vultures, until we came to the best piece of rock we had encountered so far. It was a virtually smooth, bulging slab about 12m high and around 25m in horizontal length. Above it were held tons of scree while below was underhung, making us wonder how the slab stuck there. Our only option was to traverse across the slab. Tommy got a good belay off two pitons and I set off tentatively on the Viking rope with pegs and prussik loops. The tricounis gripped well on the minute footholds and I soon got the first comforting peg firmly in position. Another six metres slightly descending with Tommy giving tension, the second peg went in and we began to feel really confident. It only now remained for me to get around the bulge and we would be off the slab. However I couldn't see around the corner and there was only one vertical crack in which to place a third peg. In it went and I stretched a leg around the corner and found what I thought was a fairly decent foothold. With a 'watch me', I transferred my body weight only to go flying off into space. The first peg came zipping out but even whilst falling I remember thinking, 'It's OK, Tommy has the strength of a gorilla and will hold me.' Happily he did and the other two pegs held, so I found myself dangling free about 10m below the slab.

Prussiking up was tough with the sack on my back but I eventually regained the position of our second peg and set off on the traverse again. When I got back to the corner it was clear that the only way to proceed was to get a peg in as high as possible and to pendulum around to the fairly level platform beyond the slab I had glimpsed during the fall. I had a decent angle piton so by placing a peg in the original crack and attaching an étrier I was able to climb up and peer over the bulge. With huge relief I found a crack in which, at full stretch, I hammered in the angle piton and attached the rope. The rest was easy and having found a secure belay Tommy followed me, recovering all our pegs en route. We relaxed with a pipe and a roll-up for Tommy and joked about our antics on the slab traverse, which we decided to call our 'Hinterstoisser'.

With clouds starting to billow up the Barranco, we continued our traverse using both ropes and shorter leads to mitigate the ever-present threat of a fall. We were really enjoying the challenge of the traverse and the magnificent

118. John Edwards deciding it's time to rope up on Day 1 on the east face. Barranco south wall in the background. (*Tommy Thompson*)

119. John Edwards climbing the basalt rock, Day 1 on Mawenzi's east face. (*Tommy Thompson*)

aspects when just short of the Middlerippe the heavens opened and a heavy rainstorm soaked us through in minutes – our Blacks anoraks and cord breeches proving not to be very waterproof. We now faced the task of descending into the Lesser Barranco. This promised to be very interesting; although not as long as that into the Greater Barranco it was still a few hundred feet of steep insecure rock and we were no longer armed with our steel stakes, the surviving balance of which we had abandoned to save weight. After melting snow and fortifying ourselves with a hot drink, we set off over the edge. The rocks were now slippery from the drenching and being reluctant to abandon any of our precious pitons we were looking to down-climb or find reliable natural anchors for abseiling. Exercising ultra-caution, applying both techniques, and experiencing several exciting moments, we finally arrived in the Lesser Barranco after almost five hours and at a cost of just one piton and two abandoned slings. We were now effectively at the start of our climb for a direct ascent of the east face.

Ahead was a steep, narrow, high-sided couloir slicing straight up the face – a line we judged led direct to our objective, HMS. Due to the lack of reliable maps of this east side of the mountain we were uncertain of the height remaining to the summit, but the geologist D N Sampson has calculated that 'the East Face is precipitous for about 1,200metres'. Before starting, we made soup, noting that the fuel for our small petrol stove was almost exhausted. We roped up and after an awkward start made good progress, avoiding several vertical, loose steps (effectively chimneys) in the centre of the gully by climbing the left-hand wall with nothing much harder than Very Severe. For some reason the vultures appeared disinterested in the couloir and had abandoned us. After about 150m the névé in the ever-steepening couloir had compacted into hard ice, so crampons on and out came our shortened axes for their first airing. This was Tommy's first real experience of hard ice climbing and soon we were confronted by a 30m near-vertical pitch of hard gully ice. This was tricky with the ice chipping away at the lightest touch of the axe and our original Stubai ice screws proving useless. After finishing back down with Tommy on my first two attempts I decided to try cutting 'stoup' steps for both footholds and hand-holds and by keeping close in to the left-hand wall, to use rock pitons for belays. This worked brilliantly once I had learned to attack the ice with less vigour and to accept steps three-inches deep as adequate. An hour later and after a gargantuan struggle for Tommy whose heavier body weight broke off just about every step, we were smiling at the top of the pitch. We found ourselves in a neat little corrie, an ideal bivouac position with plenty of icicles for melting.

The temperature was now dropping rapidly and we were shivering in our wet clothes, so whilst Tommy busied himself with preparing the evening meal I examined the route ahead. The next pitch looked even more difficult than the one we had just tackled but we noticed that the hard ice had shrunk away from the left-hand wall leaving a deep gap three or four inches wide.

120. John Edwards in 1962 holding the Duke of Abruzzi's ice axe, together with a note dated 1906 concealed in a tin, found placed in rocks built as a summit cairn on Mount Stanley, the highest peak in the Ruwenzoris. The items were carefully restored to their original positions. (*Harry Archer*)

121. 'Out of Africa': Leaving Two Tarn Hut to climb Mount Kenya in 1964. *Left to rig* Harry Archer, Pete McGowan, John Edwards, Tommy Thompson. (*Peter Scott*)

We reckoned that with a bit of ingenuity we could use this to our advantage by selecting stones of the right size, of which there were plenty in our scree-filled corrie, hammering them in tight and threading a sling behind them. We were now short of slings so decided to cut off a length from one of the ropes to make some. Thus armed I set off to prepare the first lead for the next morning. The strategy worked well, enabling me to abseil down off a rock piton in the side wall 25m up just as Tommy had supper ready. After a good meal we wrapped ourselves in our Blacks mountain tent and settled down for the night.

Sleep was hard to come by due to the extreme cold so we chatted most of the night, smoked a few pipes and roll-ups and decided to make a pre-dawn start. Whilst making a hot drink the stove finally expired so we had a cold breakfast of compo beans and biscuits, geared up and donned head torches. The first prepared pitch went fine and we began to warm to the task. We estimated that we were now about level with the point where the Middlerippe strikes the east face so only another 500m or so to go. However the difficulties increased as we progressed and we had to resort to more aid climbing, Tommy suffering as I showered him with ice and stones he could hardly avoid on his stances in the narrow couloir. Now climbing in daylight we made quicker progress, overcoming a couple of awkward overhangs and becoming increasingly confident that we could complete this magnificent climb.

Then came what proved to be the crux; a massive cornice-type overhang at the top of an 18m ice pitch. Initially I tried to cut through it but the ice was too hard and thick and what did come down fell straight onto the uncomplaining Tommy. We decided the only way up was to climb the steep wall on the left. After a struggle I managed to get two pegs in, hook in the étriers and I was up and over. Ahead, the twisting ice-choked couloir continued at an unrelentingly steep angle but with the sun now filtering through we made good progress and enjoyed some high-grade ice climbing. After a further two hours or so I climbed over a steep right-handed step and there immediately above was the wonderful steep spire of Hans Meyer Spitze.

Tommy joined me and as we gazed at the summit spire we saw that there were two ways to reach it: one was to scramble up a final rather messy scree gully between Nordecke peak and HMS and the other was to climb direct up to HMS by way of a slab reaching to the very top. I asked Tommy if he fancied it and he was so delighted to be out of the ice couloir that within seconds he was on his way, crampons off, Vibrams gripping well, and on top within minutes. It was a delightful way to finish the climb and as we admired the wonderful views, celebrated with our hip flask and took some photographs, we reflected that the mountain had been very kind to us. Discussing our experiences in the couloir we decided it would be very apt to name it 'Thompson's Horror'.

In anticipation of hot drinks and nourishment waiting for us at Mawenzi Hut we sped down the west face via the Oehler Gully, only to find the hut

122. John Edwards on the summit of Mawenzi (Day 3) – Kibo in the background. (*Tommy Thompson*)

deserted and no supplies. When we finally tracked down our porters at Peter's Hut it transpired that they believed that anyone who plunged down into the Greater Barranco, intent on climbing the east face, was not going to come back. Anyway they were delighted to see us and thankfully had not reported us as missing.

Next day we all walked down together to the Marangu Hotel where we bought the porters a celebratory drink. As we walked away from the mountain I reflected on a great adventure and wondered whether Eric Shipton would have approved – I would love to think so.

Summary: A belated account of the first ascent of the east face of Mawenzi, Tanzania, in October 1964 by John Edwards and Tommy Thompson. The route is around 1200m and graded VI, A2.

Note: The route is understood by John Edwards to be still awaiting a second ascent. For anyone thinking of attempting it but wishing to avoid the Edwards and Thompson 'grand tour' of the east face, it would be possible to make a fairly straightforward descent into the Lesser Barranco, over the NE ridge, from Mawenzi Tarn Hut and thus to the start of the direct route.

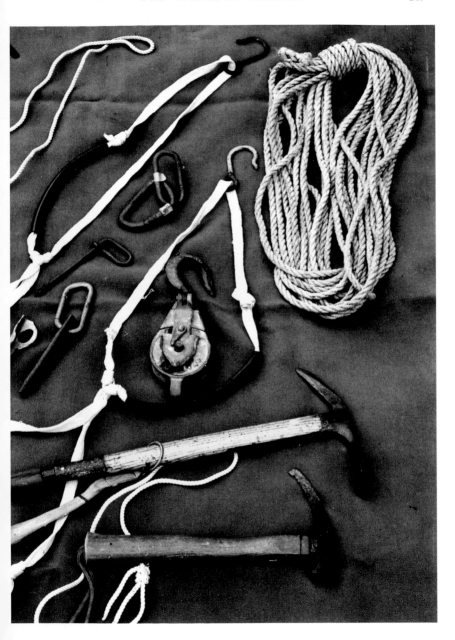

123. Primitive gear used by Edwards and Thompson on the east face climb, including improvised étriers, shortened ice axe with pick bent down, pulley block, original stubai and hemp rope. (*Ben Osborne*)

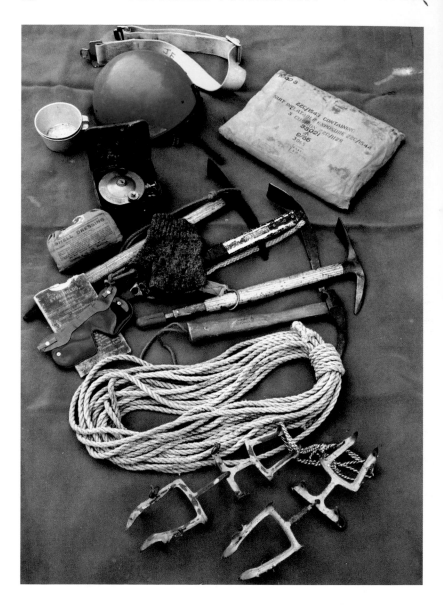

124. Similar to 123. but showing climbing belt, ex WD crampons, small petrol stove and our only emergency gear – a pilot's exposure suit and a single shell dressing. (*Ben Osborne*)

GRAHAM HOYLAND

Testing Mallory's Clothes on Everest

M y arm arched over my head, and the old wooden ice axe bit into the
snow of Everest's north ridge. Splinters of ice showered bright in the
intense glare of the sun. I stepped up and felt the silk underlayers sliding
smoothly beneath my Burberry jacket and plus-fours. Eighty-years-old, and
yet brand new, the clothes were performing perfectly.

I've been to Mount Everest eight times now, and the reason is that I've
been trying to prove something. When I was a 12-year-old boy I met my
great-uncle Howard Somervell, one-time president of the Alpine Club. He
told me an astonishing story of how he had gone to the then-unclimbed
Everest in the 1920s with his friend George Mallory. After a disaster in
1922, when seven of their Sherpas died in an avalanche, they returned to
try to climb the mountain in 1924. Howard Somervell had gone higher
than he ever had before, when something happened in his throat. A piece
of frostbitten larynx sloughed off and blocked his windpipe.

As a doctor he knew that unless he did something rapidly he would
collapse in the snow and die. So as he started to black out he grasped his
hands around his diaphragm and jerked upwards – a self-administered
'Heimlich manœuvre'. Amazingly, the blockage shifted and he breathed
easily again. When he shakily returned to the tents at Camp 4, he met
Mallory coming up for his last attempt.

'Somervell, I've forgotten my camera. Could I borrow yours?' With
Mallory was Sandy Irvine, at 22 the 'experiment' of the 1924 Everest
expedition.

Rather unwisely, as it turned out, great-uncle Somervell handed over his
camera – and Mallory and Irvine walked into history. They disappeared
into clouds near the summit and were never seen alive again. And by that
simple act of passing the camera over to Mallory, my great-uncle gave me a
purpose for life, a quest that has occupied me for more than 30 years. For
he had a hunch that Mallory and Irvine had climbed to the summit.

'If someone could find that camera of mine, and develop the film inside,
he might be able to prove that the mountain was climbed in 1924, before
Hillary and Tenzing in 1953.'

I have had some success in my quest. In 1999 my BBC expedition found
Mallory's body. He was face down at the bottom of a scree slope, having
clearly fallen a long way. He had a broken leg and an injury to his head.
The American climbers the BBC had recruited to do the search removed
all his clothing and possessions, then buried his body in rocks and read
over it the Committal Service that I had brought to the mountain with me.

They also published pictures of the body without informing me or my colleagues, an act which enraged and upset mountaineers all over the world.

The one thing Mallory did not have on him was the camera. This puzzled me. Had he handed it to Sandy Irvine and, if so, why? Could it be to take the one conclusive picture of a successful mountaineer – the photograph of him on the summit? There were other clues. His snow goggles, vital to avoid being blinded by the intense light of high altitudes, were tucked away in a pocket. This suggested to me that they were returning after nightfall – a very likely cause of an accident. I also carefully examined the thin cotton rope that had been tied around his waist. It was so slender that you wouldn't tie your pyjamas with it. It was cleanly snapped, a couple of feet from Mallory's body.

I started to build up a picture of the accident, and it looked very similar to other, more recent, fatal accidents on the mountain: the two climbers reach the summit very late. Mallory passes the camera to Irvine and he quickly snaps a shot of his legendary companion crouched against the wind, with the sun setting fast behind him. They head down the summit ridge and quickly descend into the shadows between the rocks. They are moving as fast as they dare but in their hearts they hug the amazing fact: they've done it! The world's highest mountain is climbed! Their names will resound forever! They will, but not for the reasons that they think.

Mallory's lightly nailed boot skates over a treacherous rock, he nearly recovers himself ... but he falls. And everything changes. His body starts the long sliding fall down the north face, his rope snaps over a sharp edge and he is gone forever.

The one clue I felt that I hadn't examined was the clothing. Many armchair pundits claimed that, as they were wearing only tweeds, Mallory and Irvine could not have survived the cold of the summit, and therefore they couldn't have done it. And yet the clothing recovered from Mallory's body didn't look like tweed. What was it?

Because one of the 1924 group pictures showed the expedition members at base camp wearing casual clothes, it was assumed that this is what they wore to the top. Far from it. In an extraordinary project funded by the Heritage Lottery Fund, two enthusiasts recreated every stitch of Mallory's clothing by using the fragments recovered from the body. With forensic techniques they replicated two suits, one to Mallory's measurements and one to mine. This all cost around £30,000. The plan was to put one suit on exhibition and for me to test the other suit on Everest in spring 2006 to see if the clothing was adequate for a successful summit attempt.

And so I found myself opening the aluminium flight case at advanced base camp and taking out Mallory's new clothes. First impressions were of beautiful natural materials: silk shirts in wonderful muted colours, hand-knitted socks and cardigans, and a jacket and plus-fours made of gabardine. This is a tightly woven cotton fabric, proofed against wind and rain, and in this case a shiny green. There were something like eight layers of material around my waist and yet it all felt warm, light and comfortable. The first thing to report is how extraordinarily comfortable they were. Like most mountaineers I am used to synthetic outdoor clothing: polypropylene underclothes and outer fleeces which are bought pre-sized off the shelf. As a result they never quite fit properly. They are unforgiving in stretch and begin to smell unpleasant if worn for more than a couple of days on a climb. I also find their 'next to skin' feeling is slightly unpleasant: a harsh synthetic sensation.

By contrast the Mallory clothing was made to fit me. This meant that the shirts didn't ride up, exposing my kidneys when I stretched, and the whole ensemble felt of a piece when walking. But, more significantly, the materials are natural, and this makes a huge difference. The first time I noticed this was when I started using the Shetland wool scarf while travelling through Tibet at the beginning of the expedition. By wrapping it around my face at night I was able to breathe warm moist air instead of the cold dry air of the high plateau. The material remained comfortable on the skin whereas a synthetic scarf would not.

When I first put on the clothes I also found they felt warm instead of the slightly clammy feel of the synthetic alternative. Later, when exposed to a cutting wind blowing off the main Rongbuk glacier, I found the true value of the gabardine outer layers. These resisted the wind and allowed the eight layers beneath to trap warmed air between them and my skin.

Any disadvantages? Yes. The buttons would be hard to manage with cold fingers. I think it is significant that Irvine, Mallory's climbing companion, had fitted the recently-invented zip-fasteners to his high-altitude clothing. I guess that the clothes were put on at the beginning of the summit attempt and most buttons were left fastened. Flies? My guess is that these were left undone, as the layers of clothing would interlock. Next is the simple fact that these clothes do not provide the insulation and protection of a full down suit – you would struggle to survive a bivvi near the summit. In my opinion they are warm enough to get you to the summit if you keep moving fast – but not if you have to stop. In 2006 many climbers were waiting in a queue below the ladder up the Second Step, and some of them suffered serious frostbite injuries because they got cold.

I asked Russell Brice, the expedition leader, to put on the clothes that he wears to the summit, and he came out of his tent looking like a polar bear. He had fleece underwear and a huge hooded down suit, several inches thick. As he said: 'The main problem with climbing Everest nowadays is pissing through a six-inch suit with a three-inch penis.'

We climbed up on to the East Rongbuk glacier and did some tests. First I cut some steps with the 1920s ice axe. I immediately found that the layers of silk that I was wearing slid easily against the wool layers, giving me great freedom of movement.

Then I reached up to take a hold on the ice above my head. The patented pivot sleeve of the Burberry jacket allowed me a full reach without dragging the shirt-tails out of the breeches. Before too long I was feeling almost too hot. Not for nothing was this gear developed for polar expeditions.

After extensive testing of this sort I was very confident that Mallory and Irvine could have reached the summit comfortably wearing this clothing. And I am eternally grateful to the Mountain Heritage Trust, Professor Mary Rose and Mike Parsons for dedicating so much care to their project. They have given me more evidence to support my belief that Everest was climbed in 1924.

Having tested the clothing, I have a feeling that I might know what happened to the missing Sandy Irvine. Appalled by the sudden death of his hero, he may have wandered along the route, calling his name. It gets darker. He decides to try to survive the night by squeezing into a crevice among the rocks. As a last thought, perhaps he tucks the camera securely into an inside pocket, thinking that someone one day might discover what they had achieved. Death by cold is a kind friend.

Sandy Irvine maybe hallucinated for a few hours, then slipped away. I'm sure now that his clothes, although good enough for going to the summit, could never have kept him alive during the night. A friend of mine, Mark Whetu, barely survived this ordeal wearing modern clothing. He lost all his toes.

A couple of years ago I interviewed an old Chinese climber in Beijing who claimed that he had seen Sandy's body in 1975, crouched in the crack in the rocks. We searched for three expeditions, but never found him. I am still looking for him – and the camera he may still be carrying.

Further reading: Mike Parsons and Mary B Rose, *Mallory Myths and Mysteries: The Mallory Clothing Replica Project.* Mountain Heritage Trust, p48, 2006, £4.95.

KEV REYNOLDS

Prophets of Pyrénéisme

Gavarnie's backdrop is spectacular. The semi-circular walls of the Cirque rise more than 1300m above the screes to a group of 3000m summits that carry the frontier ridge. Streaked with waterfalls and layered with terraces of snow and ice, throughout the year these walls seduce climbers at the sharp end of the sport with extreme routes and seemingly impossible lines, all in a unique setting that represents the crucible of Pyrénéisme.

So it's fitting that the *mairie* of this little roadhead township should organise a celebration of mountains, using as a focus the 50th anniversary of the first ascent of the north face of the Tour du Marboré – a milestone in local climbing history. My invitation to this gathering came as a surprise, but flattered by it I've taken a few days off, and having caught a cheap flight to Pau and slept in a meadow last night, I now have a couple of hours or so to kill before the celebrations begin. There's just enough time to scamper up the trail beyond the churchyard where the pioneers lie buried, and reaquaint myself with this historic place where my own passion for the Pyrenees began so many years ago.

On the Plateau de Bellevue I perch upon a rock breathless among the flowers and gaze at the Cirque de Gavarnie whose summits wear a pillow of Spanish cloud. From out of that cloud the Grande Cascade pours its misty stream, its message but a distant 'whoomph' carried now and then by a stray breeze. All else is soundless, and on this perfect June Saturday I have the world to myself.

Later today I hope to meet for the first time the Ravier twins, with whom I've been corresponding for a quarter of a century. The Pyrenees is their domain; the Raviers who have dominated climbing activity here these past 50 years, whose routes are a guarantee of quality, and whose grasp of the range's history is all-embracing, their name has become synonymous with Pyrénéisme, and it's a privilege to have known them so long – albeit only by post.

Born in Paris in 1933, Jean and Pierre Ravier spent the war years at their maternal family home in Tuzaguet, a small village in the Pyrenean foothills where in their youth they ran wild and practically terrorised their neighbours. Though it is Bordeaux in which they've lived most of their lives since, Tuzaguet has been and still is their Pyrenean base camp, the springboard from which so many vertical adventures begin. From the village they had their introduction to the mountains with a family outing to the Néouvielle lakes, and a year later (1947) climbed their first modest peak with a free-spirited woman who had a holiday home nearby.

Inspired by Gervasutti's *Scalate nelle Alpi* (translated into French as *Montagnes, ma vie*) and by Robert Ollivier's *Le Pic d'Ossau*, the brothers began to explore on their own, tackling the Dalle d'Allanz on Pic Rouge de Pailla above Gavarnie in 1950, and the following year the iconic Couloir de Gaube on the Vignemale. Pioneered in 1889 by Henri Brulle with the great Gavarnie guide Célestin Passet, the ice-encrusted couloir was not repeated until 1933, and was still seen as a major challenge when the Ravier's swarmed up it at the age of 17. With this audacious ascent they made their mark in impressive style.

That same year the twins became acquainted with Pic du Midi d'Ossau when they made the Petit Pic/Grand Pic traverse, and repeated the 1935 Ollivier/Mailly classic on the north face of the Petit Pic. They also took the Balaïtous by the north-west arête, climbed the neighbouring Pic Pallas, and above Lac d'Oô collected Pic des Spijeoles (by the Grand Dièdre), Pic Quayrat (by the central arête), and Pic Lézat via the Abadie/Arlaud Couloir on the west face.

There was a certain rashness in this early picking off of classic lines, as though dismissive of their stature. If it were not for their meticulous study of the literature, one might charitably suppose they climbed in blissful ignorance and were lucky to survive many of the lines they chose. But it's clear that they understood the serious nature of their selected routes, climbed with a natural affinity for the mountains that showed maturity beyond their years, and possessed full confidence in their own ability. That confidence was not misplaced.

Pic d'Ossau, for example, was to draw them back countless times in the coming decades. This shapely peak of 2885m stands alone a little north of Col du Pourtalet, with an easily recognised profile that's become the symbol of the range. Despite its modest altitude, it has a greater number and richer variety of routes than any other Pyrenean mountain, and over the years it was to become a Ravier speciality.

In February 1952 Jean and Pierre made the first of six attempts to achieve a winter ascent of the Petit Pic's north face which they'd climbed the previous summer, and returned to Pic d'Ossau four more times that year. It was a year of great momentum in which they achieved a winter traverse of the Crête du Diable on the Balaïtous, two ascents of the Grande Aiguille d'Ansabère, three routes on various Vignemale north faces (Pique Longue, Pointe de Chausenque and Petit Vignemale), and made the second ascent of the 1948 *voie Couzy* on the NE face of Pic des Crabioules (3116m).

East of Gavarnie lie the cirques of Estaubé and Troumouse, and backing a section of the vast Cirque de Troumouse, the Barroude Wall took their attention. In that summer of 1952 the wall stood untouched. Long and immensely attractive, it backs a shallow lake and acres of rough pasture-land. Pic Gerbats (2904m) is a significant lump towards the northern end

125. Jean & Pierre Ravier on the south face of the Doigt de Pombie (Pic d'Ossau) 1956. (*Jean & Pierre Ravier collection*)

of the wall, and its 400m high east face became the Ravier's first completely new route, their rope shared with Xavier Defos du Rau, a lawyer from Dax, 10 years their senior, who would become co-author with the brothers of one of the Ollivier guides.

A month after their Pic Gerbats climb, the Raviers made the exciting discovery of the 500m south face of Pic d'Estos in the Vallée du Louron, and created the first ascent of that face in fine style. That same summer, Jean went off to the Alps and made a fast ascent of the south arête of the Aiguille Noire de Peuterey with André Armengaud.

126. The Esparrets Buttress, Mont Perdu, August 1973.
(*Jean & Pierre Ravier collection*)

Still in their teens, the following year they made another winter attempt
on the Petit Pic d'Ossau's north face, but Jean was successful in creating a
first ascent (with Armengaud again) of the SE face of Pointe Jean Santé, a
prominent feature of Pic d'Ossau's Pombie Wall and a route that was quickly

established as a classic. It was one that would be repeated by the brothers several times in the coming years.

They also climbed the north-west arête of Pic d'Astazou above Gavarnie, spent the night in the Tuquerouye bivouac hut and next day made the ascent of Mont Perdu (Monte Perdido), third highest Pyrenean summit, via the north face, after its icefall had collapsed the previous winter.

To a Pyrenean *aficionado* the list of their early climbs is impressive enough. What makes it more so is the realisation that they were serving a mountaineering apprenticeship. Self-taught, with no sophisticated clothing or equipment, and living 200km or so from their mountains, the twins were (and still are) true amateurs who gave no thought to training or physical preparation of any kind. In his recently published biography of the brothers, *60 ans de Pyrénéisme*, Jean-François Labourie makes a comparison with other gifted climbers such as René Desmaison and Reinhold Messner. Desmaison trained almost obsessively at Fontainebleau in all weathers in advance of some of his major climbs, while in his late teens Messner had a list of about 100 summits to climb each season. Both displayed a programme of careful preparation mirrored by some of today's rising stars supported by sponsorship. The Raviers, on the other hand, worked through the week in Bordeaux and had to snatch what time they could at weekends for the long drive south, where their mountains would sometimes be out of condition. But no matter what the condition, winter or summer they'd tackle something, often being forced by a late start to bivouac in what they stood up in, without even the comfort of down jackets.

So they weathered the storms, tackled untried lines or routes that echoed with historic resonance, and exercised a passion that shows no sign of abating even now. Such an apprenticeship gave the foundation for a career that has carried them into their seventies.

The early days were not without their troubles. In November 1953 Jean was starting out on the north face of the curious thumb-like projection of the 2410m Capéran de Sesques set in remote country north of Pic d'Ossau. Though short, at the time of its first ascent in 1935 by François Cazalet and Roger Mailly, the north face was considered the most difficult artificial route in France, and 20 years on its reputation remained high, which is no doubt why Jean was drawn to it. But no sooner had the climb begun when he was hit by a falling rock which crushed his left foot.

Back in Bordeaux the diagnosis was such that amputation was considered, but a family friend, who happened to be a military doctor, intervened and eventually, without surgery, the broken foot was mended. Seven months later, Jean returned to the mountains with brother Pierre and Jacques Teillard, and made the first ascent of the north face of Piton Carré (3198m), which flanks the Couloir de Gaube on the Vignemale. A fortnight later the brothers were joined by Guy Santamaria to make the first ascent of the magnificent north face of the Grande Aiguille d'Ansabère, that great organ-pipe of rock set in a remote cirque approached from Lescun.

Climbing history is peppered with 'last great problems' which, when solved, are quickly relegated to history as new challenges arise. The north face of the Tour du Marboré was one such. First tried in 1945, the problem remained unsolved a decade later when, with Guy Santamaria once more, the Raviers endured poor conditions and a storm-ridden bivouac before making their retreat. Two further attempts also ended in defeat, but with Pierre detained on family business in Bordeaux, Jean teamed up with Claude Dufourmantelle and on 29-30 September 1956 they finally won through, reaching the summit at 3pm.

It's ironic that the foot, damaged four years earlier in the accident on the Capéran de Sesques, had healed sufficiently to enable Jean to create such epic north face routes as that of Piton Carré, Grande Aiguille d'Ansabère and the Tour du Marboré, but was considered serious enough to exempt him from military service in 1957. Pierre, of course, had no such excuse and was passed fit.

The brothers were committed pacifists who had taken part in anti-war protests, and the prospect of being drafted into the army was anathema to the unfortunate Pierre. One day when he should have been on guard duty, he went AWOL to join his brother in Bordeaux – a court martial offence. There followed a total of six months detention in a military prison, a month of which was spent in a tiny cell where, to combat boredom, he undertook exercise which he later claimed was the only time he ever trained. He was then posted to Algeria in a punishment battalion.

While his brother suffered military incarceration, Jean joined forces with fellow Pyrénéiste Marcel Kahn, and three Parisiens, Claude Jaccoux, Noël Blotti, and his partner from the Tour du Marboré, Claude Dufourmantelle. The five crossed into Spain and at the lower end of the Ordesa Canyon, attacked the broad vertical flake of Tozal del Mallo over the two days of 20-21 April 1957, thereby establishing a fresh milestone in Pyrenean climbing history. Four months later, Jean was joined by older sister Lysette to create a new route in the very centre of the Barroude Wall. Then in October the same year, Jean and Claude Dufourmantelle were reunited on a rope with Patrice de Bellefon and Raymond Despiau in making the first ascent of the Grande Aiguille d'Ansabère's east face.

Few climbers anywhere have maintained such a consistent record of high performance, but throughout the second half of the 20th century, Jean and Pierre Ravier were in the vanguard of Pyrenean exploration and endeavour, their routes reading like a tick-list of ambition. And yet, when the substance of their *carnets de course* is analysed, we see that the overall number of climbs in the Pyrenees (including failed attempts and family outings) is surprisingly modest – just 541 in the 50 years from 1950; but of these no less than 208 were first ascents.

By far the majority of their activity has been in the Pyrenees, of course, but Jean also climbed in the Caucasus in 1959 (Shkhara, Koshtan Tau, Dykh Tau and Elbrus); he was with Lionel Terray's Himalayan expedition

127. Pierre (*left*) and Jean Ravier in the family home at Tuzaguet, 2006. (*Jean & Pierre Ravier collection*)

that made the first ascent of Jannu in 1962, and the brothers both took part in two expeditions to the Hoggar Mountains in 1970 and 1972 where they created a clutch of new routes.

Despite inate shyness and modesty, their moral conviction, originality of thought and non-conformity combined in an act outside the mountain environment that has since been replicated by others in many protest actions around the world. Having been part of a strong pacifist movement, one night in 1960 the brothers climbed the twin spires of Bordeaux cathedral and hung a banner between them protesting against the Algerian war.

The reverence with which the Raviers are held among fellow Pyrénéistes goes far beyond respect and admiration for their achievements on rock and snow and ice. Pyrénéisme transcends the physical act of climbing; its defining passion implies an aesthetic and moral attitude towards the whole Pyrenean environment. As the ultimate Pyrénéistes, Jean and Pierre's guiding principle echoes the words of Franz Schrader, the 19th century cartographer and explorer, who wrote: "When the mountain has captured your heart, all comes from her and leads you back to her."

128. Pierre and Jean Ravier with Kev Reynolds at Tuzaguet in June 2006. (*Jean & Pierre Ravier collection*)

Such a romantic expression might sit uncomfortably with the pragmatic alpinist, but the Pyrenees demand affection and a response to favours received. The Raviers have made their response, and over the years have repaid the mountains' favours by devoting time, energy and talent in collaborating with Robert Ollivier in updating his series of guides to the

Pyrenees; to editing *Altitude* (the revue of the Groupe Pyrénéiste de Haute Montagne) from 1965-1970; to producing numerous articles, route notes and sketches of climbs for an assortment of publications; and by maintaining an irreplacable archive of material relating to all things Pyrenean, and generously sharing information with others. Theirs is an attitude of selfless generosity noted by Lionel Terray in his book, *At Grips with Jannu*.

'I doubt whether I have ever known a higher degree of unselfishness than [Jean Ravier] exhibited – almost to the point of saintliness. If one of us was cold, Ravier took off his anorak and gave it to him. When he noticed that rations were short, he suddenly produced a loss of appetite, so as to make his share available to the others. His is a spirit of the most extreme sensitivity and I am sure he finds living in this egoistical and brutal world extremely difficult, but amid the never-failing purity of the peaks he has found a world in which to fulfil himself entirely, and he will remain one of the greatest mountaineers ever nurtured by the Pyrenees.' What is said of one, could equally be said of the other. Jean and Pierre Ravier are twins, after all; joint prophets of Pyrénéisme.

Time has passed and I need to return to Gavarnie before the celebrations begin. That pillow of cloud still obscures the summits as I set off at a jog and take a different route down, leaping streams and dodging the flowers. Soon among trees, I weave among pine and birch and alder on a stony trail that soon has me down to a large open meadow and the track leading to the village. The street is beginning to fill, and at the far end as I go up the slope a large man with a shock of hair and a blue sweatshirt steps in front of me.

'Monsieur Reynolds?' he asks. I nod, for I have no breath to speak. 'The brothers Ravier are waiting for you,' he says. 'Please come with me.'

I want to ask who he is, and how he knows who I am, but he's already walking away, so I follow. Moments later we're at the junction not far from the Maison du Parc. Sweat runs down my face and I need to change my clothes, but there stand the two brothers it's taken me 25 years to meet, and beside them, bless her, is Jean's wife Michèle who speaks English and will translate. Jean and Pierre have no English, I no French, so we simply beam at each other in the street. The Pyrenees has its own language, and the three of us understand it well.

Note: For much of the background to this article I am indebted to Jean-François Labourie and the late Rainier Munsch, whose biography of the Raviers, *60 ans de Pyrénéisme* was published in December 2006 by Éditions Pin à Crochets (see Reviews p358). *Petit Précis de Pyrénéisme* by Joseph Ribas (Éditions Loubatières, 1998) was another source of information, but most of all I am grateful to Jean and Pierre Ravier themselves for a quarter of a century of letters, articles, notes, photographs and books – the bounty of friendship.

C A RUSSELL

One Hundred Years Ago

(with extracts from the *Alpine Journal*)

With the milder weather in Alpine regions has come the avalanche danger, and catastrophes are reported from many districts. A hot sun is loosening the snow on the mountains, which is the heaviest that has fallen for thirty years, and avalanches are falling in all directions.

The hazardous conditions recorded during the early months of 1907 were experienced in many parts of the Alps and very little winter climbing was undertaken. On 20 January Miss Marie Hampson-Simpson accompanied by Gustav Hasler, her future husband, and Fritz Amatter reached the summit of the Schreckhorn and on the same day Gino Carugati and his wife with Joseph and Laurent Petigax completed the first winter ascent and traverse of the north, higher summit of the Aiguilles Marbrées on the frontier ridge near the Col du Géant.

Several weeks later, on 26 March, Professor F F Roget and Marcel Kurz with Maurice Crettez completed the first ski ascent[1] of the Aiguille du Chardonnet. Five days later the same party made the first ascent of the Grand Combin under winter conditions, using ski from the Panossière hut to the foot of the Col du Meiten. Other peaks ascended for the first time with the aid of ski included the Allalinhorn on 1 April, by Alfred Hurter and Max Stahel with Oskar and Othmar Supersaxo.

The winter months were followed by long periods of unsettled weather which continued for much of the climbing season. H V Reade, who arrived in the Bernese Alps on 7 July, recalled that

The year 1907 was one of uncertain weather – one of those seasons when it makes all the difference whether one climbs on Monday, Wednesday, and Friday, or on Tuesday, Thursday, and Saturday, and when one can never foresee a week ahead the condition in which one's peak will be.

As in previous years a number of new routes was completed, an early success in the Graian Alps being recorded by Henri Mettrier who on 17 July with Joseph Antoine and Jules Favre made the first ascent of the steep northwest face of the Dent Parrachée.

On the Italian side of Mont Blanc, also on 17 July, Karl Blodig with Laurent Croux ascended Punta Baretti,[2] on the lower section of the Brouillard ridge, by way of the unclimbed west face. A few days later, on 23 July, Antonio Castelnuovo accompanied by Anselmo Fiorelli made the first ascent of the rock needle now named Punta Castelnuovo, the highest point of Les Dames Anglaises – the group of pinnacles on the Peuterey ridge. Elsewhere in the Mont Blanc range on 10 August Geoffrey Winthrop Young with Josef Knubel made the first recorded complete traverse of the classic ridge between the Aiguille du Midi and the Aiguille du Plan. Young and Knubel then moved to the Pennine Alps where on 21 August, accompanied by C D Robertson and Heinrich Pollinger, they forced a route up the east face of the Zinalrothorn to reach the upper section of the north ridge. In the Bernese Alps on 4 August a successful expedition was undertaken by J P Farrar and H V Reade who made the first ascent of the north ridge of the Gross Grünhorn. To the east in the Dolomites on 16 July Karl Plaichinger and Hans Teifel completed an outstanding new route on the Sassolungo – the Langkofel – by climbing the east tower of the north face.

Following the completion of the first Simplon Tunnel[3] work on another major engineering project continued throughout the year. The construction of the Lötschberg Tunnel[4] under the Bernese Alps from Kandersteg to Goppenstein had been approved to provide a rail link between the Bern region and the Simplon line in the Rhône valley.

During the year several expeditions were undertaken in other mountain ranges. In the Caucasus Dr Vittorio Ronchetti and Dr Ferdinando Colombo visited the Adai Khokh region. After a spell of bad weather they succeeded, on 18 July, in climbing a peak of some 3960m in the Mamison group.

In April Tom Longstaff, with the guides Alexis and Henri Brocherel, returned to Almora in northern India to commence his second expedition to the Himalaya. Longstaff was accompanied on this occasion by A L Mumm and C G Bruce, the climbing party being completed by Mumm's guide Moritz Inderbinen and a number of Gurkhas from Bruce's regiment. Addressing the Alpine Club in the following year Longstaff explained that

Last summer Bruce, Mumm, and I intended to celebrate the jubilee of the Club by attempting the ascent of Everest, or at least by making the first exploration of its unknown glaciers from the Tibetan side. In this scheme we received the most cordial support from the President and Council of the Royal Geographical Society; but in spite of their efforts on our behalf, and of support from India, this expedition was vetoed by the Home Government. I must admit that, great as this disappointment was, it was with a certain feeling of relief that I found my alternative, a campaign in Garhwal, accepted by the others...

After establishing a base in the Dhauli valley an initial exploration of the ridge and glaciers between Dunagiri (7066m) and Changabang (6866m) was completed by Longstaff and Bruce with the two Brocherels and four Gurkhas. Longstaff and Mumm then explored the Trisul glacier and on 12 June after camping at a height of some 5320m Longstaff, the Brocherels and Karbir Burathoki, one of the Gurkhas, reached the summit of Trisul (7120m) – the highest summit attained at that time.[5] After this outstanding achievement and an unsuccessful attempt by Longstaff to reach the Nanda Devi Sanctuary by way of the Rishiganga gorge the party investigated the approaches to Kamet (7756m). Bruce and Mumm then left for the Srinagar district where on 4 September they climbed Haramukh (5142m) near the Sind valley. During August Longstaff completed his examination of the southern and western approaches to Trisul commenced during his previous expedition, making a number of valuable corrections to the existent maps.

Later in the year in the Kangchenjunga region the Norwegians Carl Rubenson and Monrad Aas made a determined attempt to climb Kabru (7315m). On 20 October they reached a height of some 7285m near the north-eastern summit before being forced to retreat by intense cold and a violent wind. Another visitor to this region was Dr Alexander Kellas who in September with European guides made unsuccessful attempts to climb Simvu (6815m) and to reach the Nepal Gap (6300m) on the north ridge of Kangchenjunga (8586m).

In the Southern Alps of New Zealand the Rev H E Newton and Dr Ebenezer Teichelmann accompanied by the guide Alex[6] Graham explored the Franz Josef and Fox glaciers, making the first ascent of Douglas Peak (3087m) on 28 January and, on 4 February, reaching the summit of the unclimbed Torres Peak (3165m). Other peaks ascended for the first time included Mount Haast (3140m) and Mount Lendenfeld (3203m), both climbed on 26 February by Newton and Graham. In the Canadian Rockies in September L M Earle and his party with Eduard Feuz senior and Gottfried Feuz made the first ascent of Mount Douglas (3235m) a conspicuous peak in the Clearwater group at the head of Red Deer River.

In Britain notable new ascents were undertaken in all the principal regions. In Wales during September J M Archer Thomson and E S Reynolds completed *Avalanche Route*, an exposed climb on the East Buttress of Lliwedd. In the Lake District on 7 July H B Lyon, J Stables and A S Thomson opened *'B' Route*, the second of the alphabetical lines on Gimmer Crag. On the Isle of Skye in June A P Abraham and H Harland established *Cioch Direct*, a popular route to the famous rock pinnacle on the face of Sron na Ciche.

Other events of note during the year included the formation of the Ladies' Alpine Club[7] with Mrs Aubrey Le Blond as the first President and celebrations to mark the Jubilee of the Alpine Club:[8] an exhibition of Alpine paintings and drawings by past and present members was held at the Club's premises in Savile Row and the Jubilee Winter Dinner took place on 17 December in the Great Hall of Lincoln's Inn. It seems appropriate to conclude this account with an extract from a speech on that occasion by D W Freshfield, who proposed a toast to the Mountaineering Societies of the World.

9. Members of Tom Longstaff's party on the summit ridge of Trisul,
   12 June 1907. (*T G Longstaff*)

... there is a broad field in the future for mountain societies. They have to do for the mountains of the world what has been done in the last half-century for the Alps.

Will the company which dines here fifty years hence include the conqueror of Mount Everest? Why not? We have raised what I may call 'the man-level' from 16,000 to 24,000ft. There only remain 5,000ft. more to be overcome.

REFERENCES

1. A ski ascent is defined by Sir Arnold Lunn as 'an expedition on which ski were used until the foot of the final rock or ice ridges.'
2. Named by Blodig, whose party had made the first ascent of the north ridge of Mont Brouillard on 11 July 1906, in honour of Martino Baretti who with Jean Joseph Maquignaz had climbed the south ridge of that peak and completed the first ascent of the neighbouring, lower peak on 28 July 1880.
3. The second, parallel tunnel was opened on 4 December 1921.
4. Construction had commenced in October 1906.
5. W W Graham's claim to have reached the summit of Kabru (7315m) in 1883 has never received official recognition.
6. Graham was known to everyone as Alec.
7. The merger of the Ladies' Alpine Club with the Alpine Club was completed on 31 March 1975.
8. The Club had been founded on 22 December 1857.

Area Notes

Andy Parkin *K2 south face*
Pastel on paper, 1996

Area Notes

COMPILED AND EDITED BY PAUL KNOTT

Alps 2006	*Lindsay Griffin*
Russia & Central Asia 2006	*Paul Knott*
Greenland 2006	*Derek Fordham*
Scottish Winters 2006-2007	*Simon Richardson*
Wadi Rum & Jordan	*Tony Howard*
Turkey 2002-2006	*Geoff Hornby*
India 2006	*Harish Kapadia*
Nepal 2006	*Dick Isherwood*
Pakistan 2006	*Lindsay Griffin*
China & Tibet 2006	*John Town*
New Zealand 2006-2007	*Mark Watson*
Bolivia 2006	*Erik Monasterio*
North America 2006	*Ade Miller*

LINDSAY GRIFFIN

The Alps 2006

This selection of significant ascents and new routes progresses, more or less, from west to east across the Alps, and all events took place during 2006 unless otherwise stated.

Mont Blanc Massif

Tony Penning has developed a long love affair with the Italian side of the range, particularly its more remote corners. In 2005 and '06 he added a number of new routes, including two previously unclimbed 'summits'. On the lower SE face of the **Aiguille Noire de Peuterey** he put up *Gollins Gift* in August 2005 with Dave Hope and Nic Mullin. This route lies just around the corner from Penning's previous line, *Luca Gabaglio*, on this part of the face, where a 300m rake ascends to wide cracks. As the three were not carrying big cams, they moved left to avoid the cracks and climbed to the top of the buttress (a further 300m) at E3 5c. Penning returned to the wide cracks in 2006 carrying appropriate gear, and with Gavin Cytlau, Nick Gillett, Mullin and Ali Taylor created the bold *King Fissure* (seven pitches to E4 6a), with Penning leading its leaning off-width and scary wall climbing above. The 2006 team also made the first ascent of the **Castello Rosso** below the crest of the Noire's E ridge. A long approach led to three hard pitches on this 'red tower', with a crux of E4 5c and some eight-metre run-outs on wet rock.

On the rock walls south of the **Aiguille de la Brenva**, Tony Penning and Ali Taylor put up *Spur of the Moment* (four steep pitches to E3 5c).

In 2005 Hope, Mullin and Penning also climbed the E face of **Pta 3095m**, beneath the Dent di Jetoula. *Via Pellin* is 500m and E4 6a; superb climbing but serious. It is believed the right arête of this face was climbed years ago by Walter Bonatti.

On the NE face of **Pta 3019m**, a subsidiary summit of the Aiguille de l'Eveque and home to a number of his own routes, Penning, with Ali Taylor, climbed *The Power of Love* at the end of August 2005. This is a wandering line up the left side of the face to reach a hidden groove, which gives wonderful climbing and a crux of E3 5c.

Deeper into the massif, Matthieu Mauvais, Thomas Mougenot and Patrick Pessi put up the 300m *L'été c'est Chaud, l'hiver c'est mieux* on the Pilier de l'Androsace, **Mont Maudit**. The 300m route, climbed over two days in January, starts with some steep ice and mixed (90°), then has five pitches (6a+ and A1, 6a obl) before joining the *Bertone* for its last two pitches to the summit of the pillar. No gear was left in place.

On the **Dent du Géant** (4013m), Alex Huber made the first free solo ascent of the classic *South Face*. Climbed in 1937, this was the first route in the Western Alps on which pitons and artificial techniques, already known to climbers in the East, were used systematically. Although the face is only 200m and has maximum difficulties of 6b+, it is the problems of altitude, rock quality and the exposed nature of the climbing that make Huber's ascent notable.

The E face of the **Grandes Jorasses** (4208m) saw two new routes. In March, Philippe Batoux and Lionel Daudet climbed a direct route up the middle of the compact face left of *Groucho Marx*. *Little Big Men* was dedicated to two small but recently deceased giants of French mountaineering, Damien Charignon and Jean-Christophe Lafaille. It was climbed in capsule style at ED4, A3, 6a and M6. The pair completed the 750m line to the summit of Pte Walker and then reversed their route. In July the ubiquitous Patrick Gabarrou, together with Christophe Dumarest, climbed the prominent dièdre between the *East Face Pillar* and the *Original* (aka *Gervasutti*) *Route*. Twelve pitches up the left side of the dièdre at 6b+, with two pitches of A1/A2, led to a junction with the *Gervasutti Route* up which the pair finished to the summit of Pte Walker. One bivouac was required above the dièdre.

On the N face there were two notable winter repeats. In early January three young French alpinists, Benoit Drouillat, Pascal Ducroz and Franck Henry, made what is likely to be only the fifth winter and sixth overall ascent of the *Sergé Gousseault Route* (aka *Desmaison*, 1200m, ED3) on the NE flank of the Walker Spur. They followed the original line throughout, which is considered to be harder than some of the lower variations used more recently. High on the route they encountered a pitch of A2, as well as some of the fixed ropes and an old rucksack abandoned by the first ascensionists in 1973. In February, Jean Burgun, Erwan Madoré and the guide Christophe Moulin made a five-day ascent of *Rolling Stone* (1200m ED3). They started from a bivouac at the foot of the spur and made four more on the wall. This may only be the third ascent in winter. At around the same time Stéphane Benoist, Patrice Glairon Rappaz and Paul Robach made the second winter ascent of *Directe de l'Amitié* on the Whymper Spur. Benoist, who has now climbed eight routes on the N face of the Jorasses, mostly in winter, reported that he found the *Directe* to be harder than *Rolling Stone*, the *Sergé Gousseault* or even *No Siesta*. He assessed the technical difficulty at 6a, A3 and M5+/M6, and felt that the original ascent, which was also the first winter ascent, represented arguably the greatest achievement in the Alps at the time.

Russians, Khvostenko, Litvinov, Pugovkin and Tsygankov spent nine days in late winter establishing a nine-pitch variant between *Manitua* and *No Siesta* on the left side of the Croz Spur Monolith. They climbed the route capsule style, finished in a snow storm, and rappelled from the summit.

In March Aymeric Clouet and Christophe Dumarest made probably the first winter and second overall ascent of the *Direttissima* on the N face of

1. The south side of the 4208m Grandes Jorasses. From the summit of Pointe Walker (*right*) the ridge runs west over Whymper, Croz, Hélène, Marguerite and Young to the Col des Grandes Jorasses, before rising again to the Dôme de Rochefort. The large triangular wall facing the camera is the SSE face, aka Tronchey or Phantom Wall, taken by the unrepeated 1985 *Grassi-Luzi-Rossi route*. It is more or less the highest rock wall in the Mont Blanc massif. Bounding it on the right is the Tronchey Ridge and right again, in shadow, the east face, the venue for two new routes in 2006. (*Antonio Giani*)

Pointe Marguerite. They arrived on the summit in bad weather late on the third day and took eight hours to traverse to the Col des Grandes Jorasses. The crux pitch, an overhanging dièdre 50m high, took Clouet four hours to lead and the pair rated the 850m climb at M6 and 'new wave' A2. And in terms of stunts, the Russian, Valeri Rozov, made the first ever BASE jump from the Grandes Jorasses during the summer, when he used the now standard wingsuit to fly from the Croz Spur above the Monolith.

In July, Alex Busca and Marco Farina made the first ascent of the SE face of **Pta 3466m**, a subsidiary summit of the famous Tour des Jorasses. The pair completed two routes on magnificent granite, with superb pitches on the red-coloured headwall; *Il Vecchio Jim* (350m, eight pitches, 7a+, 6c obl) and the slightly easier and less sustained *Horizon Vertical* (350m, nine pitches, 6c+, 6c obl). The summit has now been named **Punta Massimo Farina** after Marco's late brother, a well-known young Italian who died ice climbing in 2005. In September, both routes were repeated in seven hours, Matteo Giglio and partner starting from the valley floor early one day in September. In the same month Busca and Farina returned to add a third route to the face, right of the previous lines. *I-Nery* has 10 pitches up to 6b+ but the difficulties are not sustained, making it the most 'accessible' route on the wall.

Below the Tronchey Wall of the Grandes Jorasses, Gavin Cytlau, Nick Gillett, Nic Mullin, Tony Penning and Ali Taylor made the first ascent of **Pta 2862m.** The team climbed the 450m south buttress in nine pitches at E2 5b/c, having been put up to the job by authoritative Mont Blanc enthusiast, Luca Signorelli. The latter has proposed the summit be named **Punta Giancarlo Grassi.**

On the left side of the N face of the **Aiguille de Talèfre** (3730m), Philippe Collet, Denis Gonzales and Fabian Grimault climbed *L'Odeur aux Males* at III/5 M5 R. The climb slants up left to join the top section of *L'honneur aux Dames* and is 600m in length. It was completed over two days in February.

Shortly before the end of the year Pete Benson and Guy Robertson climbed the previously virgin N face of **Pte 3650m** between the Domino and Triolet at the back of the Argentière glacier basin. Their route was named *Shining Wall* (IV/5, Scottish 6). It is amazing that no one appears to have made serious headway on this c600m face before February 2006, when Valeri Babanov and Fabian Meyer retreated after climbing nine pitches (though still gave their attempt a name: *Orion*, 450m, III/5+ mixed). Benson and Robertson followed a similar line, finding reasonable, if run-out climbing on nice Styrofoam ice, which held the route together until a sketchy loose exit onto the summit ridge. Loose ground prevented them from continuing to the highest point.

And finally, over in the now highly popular Aiguilles Rouges, three new routes were opened above the Combe des Crochues. On Pte Sud of the **Aiguille des Crochues,** *Le Vieux Bouc* was climbed and equipped by Laurant Collignon, Michel Fontes and Nicolas Hanerrau to give a six-pitch 6a+, while Anne-Paul and Eric Favret put up the five-pitch *APO* at 5c. To the right, on an unnamed summit on the ridge leading down to the Tour des Crochues, Andy Parkin and partner put up the four-pitch *Sahara* at 5c+. This face is characterized by a prominent crack in the upper section, which the route avoids on the right.

Valais

In February, Russians, Cherezov, Glazyrin and Prokofiev from the Siberian city of Krasnoyarsk spent 10 days climbing what appears to be the little-known 1983 *Czechoslovak Route* up the left flank of the Matterhorn's N face. In mid-March, Ueli Steck made a remarkable solo ascent of the 1965 *Bonatti route* on the N face. He started up the route a little after 1pm on the

14th, bivouacked at the end of the Traverse of the Angels, and reached the summit at 1pm the following day. He was back in Zermatt that evening and appears not to have unpacked the rope from his rucksack during the trip.

Bernese Oberland

Krasnoyarsk mountaineers, Vladimir Arkhipov, Eugeny Dmitrienko, Piotr Malygin and Dmitry Tsyganov, plugged the 'obvious' gap on the N face of the **Eiger** (3970m) between the *Harlin Route* and Jeff Lowe's *Metanoia*. The four appear not to have taken portaledges, and only used a handful of bolts, negotiating many overhanging rock pitches with the adventurous use of skyhooks and large Birdbeaks. In their 14-day ascent the Russians made seven camps and climbed 52 pitches, enduring continuously bad weather from the Second Icefield to the summit.

In summer, Robert Jasper together with Stefan Eder made the first redpoint ascent of *Yeti*, a 1000m rock route towards the right side of the Eiger's N face and put up in 1998 by Andreas Gianni and Max Ghirondi. Eder and Jasper climbed the route from the foot of the wall in 12 hours during July, freeing the top (crux) pitch at 7c/7c+.

Bregaglia-Masino

On the **Piz Badile** (3308m) Luca Maspes made the first solo ascent of *Ringhio* on the SE face. The route was put up by Aosta guides in 2003 and has 10 pitches with difficulties of 6b+/6c, 6b obl. He had attempted the route a month previously in June, but on the occasion of his successful ascent of this bolt-free route completed the line in a fast time, back roping for only three pitches. He rated the difficulties 6b+ and finished up the last section of *Via Vera*.

On the NW face, left of the smooth pillar known as the Pilastro a Goccia, Domenico Soldarini, Stefano Pizzagalli and Alberto Sanpietro opened *Il Silencio degli Eroi*. This climbs to the top of a subsidiary pillar on the face, now christened Pilastro Dimenticato, in nine sustained pitches (6c+, 6c obl) of classic compact slab climbing. From the top of the pillar a pitch of 5 leads to the crest of the N ridge.

In late August Andrea Barbieri, Marco Farina, Maspes and Mario Scarpa added another route to the SSE face of the **Punta Medaccio** (2350m). *Il Triangolo d'Oro* lies on the lower left section of the face between the four-pitch *Ignota* (6a) and *Aguas y Placas* (6b obl), both bolt-protected slabs. The new route has five sustained pitches of 6a+ to 6b with three points of aid on the fourth pitch.

On one of the smaller buttresses forming the lower part of the huge west pillar of **Piz Balzet** (2869m), the well-known Munich aid climbing team of Gabor Berecz and Thomas Tivadar put up the five-pitch *Joyride*. Four days were spent on overhanging granite and the route rated V 5+ A4. The fourth pitch took Berecz a whole day.

Matteo Foglino and Maspes made the first free ascent of the eight-pitch *Obelix* on the SE face of **Punta Paganini** (2790m) above the Ferro Valley.

Though this route is always attributed to Sonja Brambati and Paolo Vitali, who certainly climbed and equipped it in August 1990 at 6a and A1, it appears it may have been climbed, or partially climbed, a month earlier by Anghileri and friends. Foglino and Maspes climbed the two short aid sections free, with the crux, an excellent corner, going at 6c on natural gear. At the head of the valley, Anna Ceruti, Maspes and Giovanna Novella made the first ascent of the E face of unnamed **Pta 3007m**, a subsidiary top on the long SSW ridge of Pizzo del Ferro Occidentale (3267m). Using natural gear only, the three climbed a succession of cracks and slabs to produce *Ferro e Sungia* (350m, 6a).

On the west pillar of **Pta 2493m**, which lies towards the end of the long ridge running south from the Passo di Val Torrone (2518m) in the Zocca valley, Giuliano Bordoni, Ceruti, Maspes and Giovanni Ongaro created *Tuono* (300m, 6b+/6c) using a mixture of natural and drilled protection. Maspes had got halfway up this route as long ago as 1990 but it took 16 years to finish the job.

Also in the Zocca valley are the steep slabs of **Pta 2987m** on the west side of Piz Torrone Occidentale, home to classics such as the *South Pillar* (Merizzi-Miotti, 1975, 320m, 5–), the most-climbed route in the entire Zocca basin, and the accessible *Melonimaspes Crack* (Maspes/Meloni, 1990, 280m, 5+). During three days in August, Barbieri, Maspes and Fabio Salini opened *Kriminal* (c300m, 6b obl and sustained), which features run-out climbing with no more than three bolts placed per pitch. The route starts to the right of El Diablo and crosses it at the end of the second pitch. At the end of the summer Maspes and Salini added *Zakimort* to the foresummit of Punta Vittoria (3012m), a small peak on the frontier ridge between the Punta Allievi and the Zocca Pass. The five-pitch route is well bolted and has difficulties of 6a+/6b, though a variation first pitch, added later, is 6c.

On **Picco Luigi Amedeo** (2800m: sometimes referred to as the Grand Capucin of the Bregaglia-Masino) Ceruti, Maspes and the very strong Rossano Libera, spent two days creating *Tutto Vero* (400m, 6b+ and A1) up the right side of the SE face. Apart from two bolts placed for belays at the top of pitches one and three, this route was climbed on natural gear. One week later Libera made a completely free ascent at 6c.

Bernina

On the E face of **Sasso Nero** (2921m) overlooking the Scerscen Valley, Maspes soloed *Malenconia* (500m, 6b). The route breaches what was deemed to be the last unclimbed pillar on the face and had already seen off Maspes in 2003. This time he had little difficulty completing the wall in just three hours, only using a backrope on pitch three.

Retiche

East of the Bernina, the Grosina valley holds the S face of the **Cima Viola** (3374m), one of the biggest rock walls in the Central Alps. Reaching the

face involves a three-hour approach from the road up the Grosina Valley
and prior to 2006 there were only three routes, the original put up in 1977
by Cometti, Miotti and Mitta. It has 24 pitches up to 5 and A2. In July,
Bordoni, Libera and Maspes added a direct route up the centre of the face.
Voila Bacia Tutti has 17 pitches, 800m of climbing and difficulties up to
6b+. One bivouac was made and traditional protection used throughout.

A month previously Bordoni and Maspes had made the first ascent of
the S face of **Sasso Maurigno** (3062m) above the northern head of the
Grosina Valley, and just south of the highest and best-known mountain of
this range, Cima di Piazzi (3489m). The pair belayed the first 250m up a
vertical pillar (6a) and then continued unroped for a further 300m of easier
ground to the crest of the SE ridge, up which they scrambled to the summit.
I Fiori di Giada was climbed on natural gear.

Dolomites

Mauro 'Bubu' Bole, partnered by one of Italy's premier female sport
climbers, Jenny Lavarda, made the third free ascent of the *Larcher-Vigiani
Route* (13 pitches, 8a, 7b obl), probably the first true 8a on the S face of the
Marmolada. The *Larcher-Vigiani*, a sportingly-bolted route that lies left of
the classic *Solda Route* on the **Marmolada di Penia** (3343m), was put up in
2000 by Rolando Larcher and Roberto Vigiani. It takes a characteristically
bold line up the Cristina Pillar and the smooth, bulging Lindo Pillar above.
Bole made a 13-hour ascent in September, with no falls and leading every
pitch. The crux is at an altitude of over 3000m.

Three months earlier the 22-year old Austrian Hansjorg Auer made a
rare and very rapid free solo ascent of the classic *Moderne Zeiten* (*Modern
Times*: Mariacher/Iovane, 1982, 800m, 27 pitches, VII+) on the S face of
Marmolada di Rocca (3309m). Wearing just a helmet and chalk bag, Auer
climbed the route in an impressive 2h 40mins. *Modern Times* is one of the
finest routes on the Marmolada and the first ascent, using only pegs and
nuts, redpointing the crux pitch but on-sighting all the others, was an historic
milestone in the evolution of free-climbing big walls in the Dolomites.

In August, guidebook author and established guru of the Marmolada,
Maurizio Giordani, added another major new route to the S face of the
Marmolada d'Ombretta (3230m). Climbed with Massimo Faletti, the
c900m *Colpo di Coda* is an almost free, 28-pitch route at 6c+ with just two
short sections of A2. It follows a line just left of the serious and very much
ahead-of-its-time *Via dell Ideale*. This part of the face often takes drainage
from the summit chimneys and there were two wet sections high on the
overhanging part of the route, where Giordani and Faletti had to resort to aid.

In 2005 Dusan Janak, Pavel Janak and Vasek Satava finished an historic
project when they completed an independent finish to *Fram* on the S face
of the **Ombretta**. The resulting five pitches were on fantastic Buoux-like
rock but only three were climbed completely free; the remaining two,
estimated to be around 8a and 8a+, used rest points. In September 2006

Janak and Satava went back, used *Italia* to reach the Fish cave and then spent two nights there while they completed the route above completely free at 7b, 8a+, 7c+, 8a and 4/5-. Despite fixed gear, the climbing is still quite bold in places.

Mario Prinoth and Bruno Pederiva made an on-sight repeat (redpoint for Pederiva) of *Giallo Dream* on the W face of **Torre Centrale Mezzaluna** in the Val di Fassa, Vallaccia. This 240m, nine-pitch route has a crux of 8a and was first climbed by Rolando Larcher in 1996.

On the **Piz Ciavazes** in the Sella region, Lukasz Muller and Rafat Porebski from Poland repeated *Italia '61* in its new free form. The old mixed free and aid route, climbed free in 2004 by 'Bubu' Bole at 8a and since repeated a couple of times in this fashion, lies towards the left side of the popular S face. The Polish pair recommend some changes: they split the long 7c+ pitch because it involves huge rope drag, and set up a belay directly below the 8a roof, which they say is in a much safer position. Apart from a cleaned strip where the route goes, the roof is very loose and any rockfall would have hit the second at the former, lower, stance.

Just east of the Ciavazes, Roberto Parolari and Nicola Tondini completed a three-year project on the c750m W face of **Sass Pordoi** (2952m). *Il Canto del Magnificat* has 15 pitches to the huge scree terrace (from where it is possible to walk off right from any route on this wall) and then seven relatively sustained pitches up the steep headwall above, where the 7b crux is situated. The route was climbed entirely on natural gear.

On the N face of a subsidiary summit of the **Croda Rossa** (3174m) in the Dolomiti di Bries subgroup close to Cortina d'Ampezzo, Martin Moser and Arnold Senfter put up the jokingly named *Clean e Morto* at VII and A3. The significance of this six-pitch route, completed over five days during the 2006 winter, is that it was climbed totally on nuts and Friends: no bolts or pegs were used and every piece of gear, including belays, was removed from the route. The two Italians hope more Dolomite activists will follow their example of 'clean climbing', a likely scenario given a recent, more widespread interest for adventure climbing in the Dolomites.

On the **Cima Grande de Lavaredo** (2999m), Ines Papert made probably the fourth free ascent of the *Camillotto Pellisier Route* on the N face. This old aid route was free climbed by 'Bubu' Bole in 2003 at 8b, though subsequent Slovenian ascents put the crux at 8a or 8a+. The young German lady spent 10 days on the route before making a redpoint ascent, falling only once when a foothold broke. Papert also felt pitch three, the original 8b crux, was more like 8a+ but found pitch six to be 8a+/8b. Whatever the eventual consensus, it seems Bubu's original ascent really inspired some of Europe's top rock climbers.

Luca Matteraglia and Alessio Roverato made the third ascent of the *South-West Face Direct* on **Monte Pelmo** (3168m), a legendary route put up by Riccardo Bee, Franco Miotto and Giovanni Groaz in 1977 (the second ascent of the 16-pitch route was made from the 15th-17th January 1986 by an Italian-Slovenian team). The two young climbers were most impressed by the efforts of the first ascensionists on this daring line up an imposing 650m wall of friable yellow limestone. They confirmed the grade as VI+ and A3.

In 2005 Maurizio 'Manolo' Zanolla put up *Bisogna Essere Veloci Per Descrivere le Nuvole* (8a) on the S face of an unnamed 2000m summit in the little-frequented **Feltrine** (aka Feltre). The following year he was back to tackle the steep wall to the right. *Solo per Vecchi Guerreri* (*For Old Warriors Only*) is bolt protected, with a crux that Manolo likened to *Bain De Sang* (a 9a sport route), only at 2000m with 300m of air beneath the moves. Although completed in June, Manolo was not able to make the one-day, all-free ascent until August, rating the crux somewhere between 8c and 9a. It didn't wait long for a repeat. The very much in form Mario Prinoth managed a redpoint in September and more importantly confirmed both Manolo's grade assessment and the very high quality climbing.

In the **Alpago-Cavallo** region east of Belluno, Alessandro Bau and Alessio Roverato made the long-awaited second ascent of *Diretta del Gran Diedro* on the N face of **Col Nudo** (2471m: this is actually a summit rather than a col). Put up in 1981 by Miotto and Saviane at VII– and A2, this 700m route has become a mythical line in Dolomite circles and features highly dangerous and badly protected stratified limestone known as 'tegole' (tiles). This repeat is significant for many reasons, not least because Bau and Roverato decided to use newly-built but very old-fashioned equipment, including wooden wedges and 15cm brass chocks for the aid sections.

PAUL KNOTT

Russia & Central Asia 2006-2007

As well as the teams themselves, the following sources have formed the basis of this report: Alpinist news, Alpclub Ural, Extreme portal vvv.ru, Lindsay Griffin, Mountain.ru, Russian Alpine Federation, Russianclimb.com, Sergei Kurgin (sibalp.com), and Stolby.ru.

The above websites contain photo-topos for many of the developed rock walls, for example major Pamir Alai walls, Erydag (Caucasus) and Morcheka (Crimea). Dates in this report refer to 2006 unless stated otherwise.

Caucasus

As has been the case for several years, all the news from this range is from Russian climbers. Some venues such as Erydag have yet to receive reported ascents by non-Russians.

Several new routes were climbed in the Western Caucasus. On **Fisht North (2160m)**, V Afanasev and team climbed the NW rib of the W face at 5A, while on **Dombai Western (4036m)**, from 26-29 June, S A Pugachev's Khabarovsk team climbed the central 'triangle' on the S face at 6A. Earlier, in February 2006, four climbers lost their lives in a major avalanche during an attempted first ascent of a 6B route on **Bolshoi Nakhar (3784m)**. These included the prolific Makhachkala-based climber Konstantin Dorro. A search in May found only some of the bodies.

In the Central Caucasus two significant winter ascents were made in January 2007. A Moscow team including George Kozlov attempted the *Balyberdin route* on **Shkhelda 3rd Western (4280m)**. This 5B winter route has not been repeated since its first ascent in 1984. The team climbed 13 pitches over 4-5 January before retreating due to heavy snowfall. Later, Moscow climbers Sergey Nilov, Sergey Doronin and Yevgeniy Korol made a successful winter ascent of the 6A Myshlyaev route *Rhombus* on **Chatyn-Tau (4368m)**. This route, which has repelled several prior winter attempts, takes a steep couloir and ridge on the N face. The climb took from 18-25 January and was probably the mountain's second winter ascent, the first being in 1984 via Peak Trud. On **Misses-Tau (4427m)**, a team led by A Nikitin climbed a new route on the central E face at 5B.

At the eastern end of the range, in February 2007 a St Petersburg team made an ascent of the *Mirror* (6A) on the left part of the NW face of **Erydag**

(3995m). They found the next-to-last pitch of this route now requires A3 climbing instead of grade 5, after an enormous block fell off in August.

Crimea

From 23-26 June a new route *Rainy Season* (6A F6b A3 340m) was climbed on **Morcheka** by Odessa residents Alexander Lavrinenko and Taras Tsushko. The route name reflects the heavy showers encountered each day during the ascent. The route lies between the *Grishchenko* and *Geniush routes*, coinciding with them for a short middle section. In early June another new route, *DLS* (*Twenty Years Later*) (6B 280m) was climbed immediately right of the *Geniush route* by local climbers Anatoliy Geniush and Alexey Zhilin. They felt the route to be harder than *Machombo* on the same wall. The route is named in celebration of its ascent 20 years after the 1986 *Geniush route*.

Two weeks later Yevgeny Novoseltsev and Shonin made an onsight ascent of the **Shaan-Kaya** route *Samurai*, taking 13 hours. This was probably the second ascent of the route, which the climbers felt to be two grades harder than *Machombo*. Also on **Shaan-Kaya**, in March 2007 Cyril Gostev, Alexander Ruzhkovskiy and Michel Voloshanovskiy climbed a new 200m route in the centre of the face.

Pamir Alai

There has been a healthy level of activity in the Turkestan range, as climbers have gained confidence in the security status of the region. In summer 2006 several parties climbed in the Karavshin area. Mike and Andy Libecki climbed a 21-pitch line on the NW face of **Asan (4230m)** at VI 5.11 A2. They probably climbed a variation finish of *Alperien,* moving to its left above half height. They completed the route in a 50-hour push including a 17-rappel descent down a new section of wall. Also on the NW face of Asan in August, Australian climbers Kent Jensen, David Gliddon, Steve Anderton and Julian Bell freed 20 of the 23 pitches of an existing A3 route up the centre of the wall to make a free route at French 7B. Gliddon and Bell also climbed a new A4 route over eight days. The team retrieved the portaledges left on **Yellow Wall** in 2000 by Tommy Caldwell, John Dickey, Beth Rodden and Jason Smith when they were kidnapped.

A large Polish expedition climbed from the Kara-Su valley in August-September. An early success was the free ascent by Adam and Pawel Pustelnik of a new route on **Ortotyubek (3850m)**, *Amba* (F7c/7c+, 1100m). While most of this route is new, in some places (including in the key 7c/7c+ section on pitches 8-9) the climbers found that it intersects another route (possibly the *Ivanov route*) that is absent from the Yuri Koshelenko topo published in *Desnivel*. The Pustelnik brothers, with Slawek Cyndecki, also made an on-sight ascent of *Perestroika Crack* (F7b, 1000m) on **Pik Slesov**.

Jerzy Stefanski, Artur Magiera and Jan Kuczera made a free ascent of an epic new route on the NW face of **Kotin (4521m)**, *Czarna Wolga (Black Volga)*, on sight with no bolts at F7a, 1700m. Meanwhile Slawek Cyndecki, Pawel Grenda and Marcin Szymelfenig attempted a new route on the SE face of **Pik 4300m** (SE of **Pik 4810m**). They retreated after 22 pitches due to incessant rockfall. Lukasz Depta and Wojciech Kozub made a free ascent of a new route on the W face of a c.4000m tower in the Karasu massif, *Opposite to Asan* (F6a, 800m, on-sight). In addition, the group climbed several existing routes: **Yellow Wall (3800m)** via *Diagonal* (F6a+, 500m) by Stefanski, Kuczera, Kozub and Magiera (partly simul-climbed), **Asan (4230m)** via the *Timofeev route* (6A F7a A3) in alpine style by Stefanski and Kuczera and via the *Alperien route* (American variant) (5B F6c+) by Depta and Kozub.

The Anglo-German party of Daniel Danzer, Jens and Michael Richter, Markus Stofer, Sarah and Tony Whitehouse climbed from the Ak-Su valley in July. They climbed a new route *Russendisko* on **Pik 3700m**, a pyramid immediately west of the **Russian Tower (Pik Slesov, 4240m)**. The route is left centre, and left of existing routes, on the W face and has 10 pitches at 7a, 6c obl. The team also made a free ascent of *Perestroika Crack* (Faivre-Gentet-Givet-Roche 1991) above on the W face of **Pik Slesov.** They made some use of fixed ropes, which facilitated ascents by most members of the party. The first free ascent of this route was by Greg Child and Lynn Hill in 1995.

In the Lyailyak area in July-August 2006, the Ukraine team of V Mogila, A Lavrinenko, T Tsushko and Cheban climbed a new 6A A4 route variant on **Aksu North (5217m)**. This 1700m route takes the centre of the right part of the N face between the 1982 *Troshchinenko route* and the 1988 *Pershin route*. The first 20 pitches of the route are new, after which the remaining 22 pitches coincide with the *Pershin route*. The ascent was awarded second place in the 2006 CIS alpinism championships. The same area attracted the attention of two teams in the winter season. From 27 January to 4 February 2007 a team from Krasnoyarsk region led by Oleg Hvostenko made the second ascent, and first winter ascent, of the 6B 1996 *Pershin-Odintsov route* on the central N face of **Aksu North (5217m)**. The other climbers were E Beljaev, V Gunjkov, I Loginov, D Prokofjev and B Rodikov. Vladimir Arkhipov and Eugeny Dmitrienko from the same group had earlier retreated from an attempt on the 6B *Chaplinsky route*. In the same area in March 2007 a Sverdlovsk region team including Sergey Timofeev and Alexander Korobkov made the ascent of a probable new route right of the *Efimov route* on the central 'bastion' of the N face of **Pik Blok (5239m)**.

There has been one ascent reported in the Fann mountains. S Soldatov's team climbed a new route on **Chimtarga (5489m)**, the highest peak in the range, taking the central W face.

Pamir

The Tajik authorities recently re-named several major Pamir summits. The former **Pik Lenin (7134m)** is now named **Pik Nezavisimosti (Independence Peak)**, while **Pik Revolutsiy (6940m)** is now officially named **Pik Avitsenny**. This follows the earlier re-naming in 1999 of the former **Pik Kommunisma (7495m)** as **Pik Ismail Somoni**

Parties have been returning to the southern Pamir ranges, taking advantage of greater political stability in Tadjikistan. In August, the **Shakdara range** in the SW Pamir was the venue for an Alpine Club expedition organised by Phil Wickens. They approached the area via the Amu Darya (Oxus) river along the Afghan border. The 7-person team climbed from a base in the Nishgar valley, making ascents of **Pik Karl Marx (6736m)**, the highest in the range, and of **Sosedniy (5928m), Litovskiy North (5905m), Ovalnaya (5780m)** and **'Great Game Peak' (5635m)**. (*See 'Top Marx in Pamirs for AC climbers', pp26-39.*) Also in the Shakdara range, a Russian team led by Mikhail Volkov climbed the E ridge (Kustovskiy 1964) of **Pik Engels (6510m)** at 6A. The ascent took from 18-25 August, with a further two days for the descent to base camp.

Further north, climbers from Perm and Orenburg led by Veniamin Reutov and Ugor Zemlyanskiy made an ascent of **Pik Revolutsiy (Avitsenny, 6940m)**, reaching the summit on 11 August. They climbed via an ice rib at the left end of the NE 'Myshlyaev' face. On the summit they found the note from the previous ascent seven years earlier by Lebedev's team. During the expedition the group found two pairs of trainers that they thought must belong to the British climbers who disappeared in this area in 2005 (see *AJ* 111).

On 19 August Nikolai Pimkin made what appears to have been the first ski descent of **Pik Lenin (Independence, 7134m)**, taking the *Arkin route* in the centre of the N face. The less-explored eastern end of the Zaalay range around **Kurumdy (6613m)** received a visit from a 12-person Spanish team including David Taurà. In unsettled and often warm July weather, they made a number of first ascents including that of a 5155m summit they named **Ekishak** (two horns) on the ridge between Golova Orla and Shining Peak. They climbed via the SE face and upper NE ridge at PD+. On **Pik Molly (4748m)**, they climbed a new route via the NW ridge at AD. They also attempted **Zarya Vostoka, Kurumdy West (6545m)** and **Golova Orla (5441m)** but in each case retreated in poor snow conditions. Contrary to the claimed 2001 first ascent described in *AJ* 107, the main summit of **Kurumdy** (though not Kurumdy West) was climbed in 1932 from the south by Krylenko's 1932 expedition. The 2001 party climbed in October for lower temperatures.

Tien Shan

The major news from this range is the successful ascent of two major objectives above the **Inylchek glacier** that have repelled earlier attempts.

Climbers from Krasnoyarsk region including Alexander Mikhalitsin, Vladimir Arkhipov, Vladimir Gunko, Andrey Litvinov, Sergey Cherezov and Alexander Yanushevich made an ascent of the unclimbed NW face of **Pogrebetsky (6487m/6527m)**. The face, claimed to be the last unclimbed high-altitude wall in the former Soviet Union, had repelled three previous attempts in 1984, 1989 and 1991. The mountain had been climbed only by its W ridge/face (Streltsov 1980, 5B). The team reached the summit on 16 August after seven days' climbing at 6A. The descent took almost a further two days, ending with an escape from heavy snowfall that was creating avalanche danger. The lower 1000m of the route is snow and ice, and the upper part a steep 800m rock wall. A new route on **Pik Voennykh (Military) Topografov (6873m)**, also in the upper Inylchek but now lying wholly in China, is described in the report for China/Tibet.

Strangely neglected by European climbers is the Karakol region of the **Terskey Ala-Too**. Here in August on the impressive N face of **Dzhigit (5170m)**, Slovenian climbers Andrej Magajne, Simon Slejko, Andrej Erceg and Dejan Miskovic climbed a 1200m new route *Tretje oko (Third eye)*, ED2 VI/AI6, taking ice strips on the right part of the central wall. The group also climbed new routes *Espresso* (TD+ V/AI5 900m) and *Frappucino* (TD+ V/AI5+ 900m) on the N face of **Pik Karakolski (5280m)**. On an earlier visit in August 2005, Magajena and Slejko had made the first ascent of *Amor Therapeutica* (TD+ V/AI5 700m) on the N face of **Slonienok (4728m)**. Also active on **Dzhigit** in August 2006 was a team from the Tomsk Alpinism Federation which, from 12-15 August, made an ascent of the 6A mixed route *Central North Face* (Slesov 1975). The ascent won them fourth place in the CIS mountaineering championships.

In May Dave Wynne Jones and six others from the UK made a ski traverse of the **Ak-Shirak range** from the Kara-Say glacier to the Petrov glacier. This followed an earlier attempt in 2003 (see *AJ* 109). During the traverse the team reached the summit of **Pik Kyrgyzia (4954m)**, the highest in this part of the range, and made seven first ascents of peaks over 4600m. They accessed the range by vehicle over the Suek pass and on foot up the Kara-Say river, ending the traverse at the Kumtor mine. (*See article 'Celestial Touring', page 54.*)

The SW corner of the **Borkoldoy range** just east of the At-Bashi was visited by UK climbers Dave Molesworth and Mark Weeding. They made ascents of summits 4608m, 4778m, 4661m, 4690m and 4705m, finding large wooden posts and a summit cairn on the latter. The posts were probably placed during earlier border tensions, as there was a Chinese claim to part of this range. The team also climbed from the valley above Akalla village.

Exploratory climbing continued in the **Western Kokshaal-Too**. In September the venue for the 2006 ISM visit to the area was the Navlikin glacier. Characteristically for this range, heavy snowfall made for avalanche-prone slopes. A group led by Pat Littlejohn retreated from **Pik 5611m** but summited on **Argon (4880m)** and made the first traverse of **Macciato**

2. The north-west face of Pik Vektor, in the Mushtuairi valley west of Bielukha, first climbed in 2005 by Vitaly Ivanov and friends via the centre of the face. (*Mark Brits*)

(4656m). Meanwhile, teams led by Vladimir Komissarov and Adrian Nelhams found better conditions on the Malitskovo glacier to make ascents of Piks **Ascha (4717m)**, **Novey (4760m)** and **Berum (4812m)**. They retreated from a forepeak of **Kanashay (4996m)**, the dominant peak of the glacier, due to cornicing. Earlier, in July 2005, French climbers Manu Pellisier, Guillaume Baillarge and François Savary attempted the 700m W face of **Pik 4850m (Sabor)** near Kizil Asker, climbing 11 pitches up to A2 5c, reaching halfway up the face. They retreated in the face of a deluge of snow melt from earlier heavy falls. Following this, Thomas Faucheur, Lionel Albrieux and the above team made an ascent of the N ridge.

Finally, in the popular Kyrgyz range near Bishkek, Russian climbers made three ascents in August of routes on **Korona (5th tower, 4860m)** for the CIS championships. The SW face was climbed by a Tomsk team and a Tatarstan team at 5B. The W rib, also 5B, was climbed by a Moscow team.

Siberia

Previously unreported from July 2005 was an ascent by Colorado-based climbers Roxanna Brock and Heidi Wirtz in the vicinity of **Kupol (2921m)** in the **Eastern Sayan** Mountains. Targeting the only formation in the vicinity not to have been bolted by local climbers (see ascents reported in *AJ* 108), they climbed a new route *Pofigo* (5.11 335m), placing no bolts or pins. The climbing in this range was described in the 2006 *AAJ*.

Visiting parties in the **Altai** have increasingly looked to winter mountaineering activities. Various groups have descended Belukha on skis. There have also been ascents of 300-500m frozen waterfalls in the Ak-Tru area; there are reportedly also falls of 700-800m south-west of Teletskoe Lake. The best climbing season apparently is late February-March. On 16 April 2007 a party of mostly Croatian climbers accompanied by Vitaliy Ivanov made the first ascent of the N face of **Tapduair (3505m)** via 900m of up to 45° ice. Russians Vadim Kabanov and Evgeniy Danilchenko made ski and snowboard descents of this peak from 3200m. Summer activity in 2006 included the May ascent of a modest but accessible new route at 4B, V, 380m on the SE face of **Begemot (c1700m)**. This peak is in the Chuy valley, above the 755km road post on a spur of the Aygulak ridge.

DEREK FORDHAM

Greenland 2006

There was an increase in non-scientific expeditions in 2006 and the
Danish Polar Centre issued 69 permits for 'sporting' expeditions, of
which some 36 were for expeditions on or across the Inland Ice. This year
was, however, no different to previous years and the majority of expeditions
opted for the standard east-west route from the Ammassalik region to
Kangerlussuak, although several attempted longer south-north routes
starting from various points and aiming for Thule or Qaanaaq. In addition,
another double-crossing was made, so perhaps the stranglehold of the trade
route is being slowly broken.

What was very different in 2006 were the largely unpredicted and changing
weather patterns which to some extent affected almost all expeditions other
than those in the very far north. This had a significant impact on the
increased numbers attempting to cross the Inland Ice, where the large
number of failures perhaps suggests that the increased numbers completing
the route are encouraging a false sense of security. As reported by the Finnish
expedition below, it is now becoming increasingly common to meet other
groups on the ice. There was a time when the prospect of 'meeting' people
on the Inland Ice would have been totally unthinkable and would certainly
have been regarded as a major detraction from what is still considered a
major, remote wilderness undertaking. The fact that three of the four groups
met by the Finns were later evacuated adds weight to the idea that some
groups are treating such a wilderness undertaking too lightly and with
insufficient preparation.

The early spring weather proved typically unpredictable and one of the
first groups to start, Eero Oura and Vesa Luomala from Finland, experienced the extremely high katabatic winds, known as the *piteraq*, which in
1997 killed two of their countrymen on the Inland Ice. They completed
their crossing from Isortoq to Kangerlussuak in 34 days, having started on
12 April, and experienced windy, low-pressure weather for almost the whole
trip. The Ammassalik/Tasilaq area of the East Greenland coast is particularly subject to these conditions early in the year and they probably
accounted for the fact that six people starting from the east coast in early
April had to be evacuated by several helicopter missions. The Finns met a
Spanish couple on the west coast who later summoned a rescue by use of a
Personal Locator Beacon, adding to the mounting concern that at least the
trade-route crossing has become too popular. The concern of undue
popularity is supported by the fact that the Finns met two separate
expedition groups in the early part of the crossing, both of which were

evacuated a short while later. They then met a third Danish group at DYE 2, the abandoned early warning station, on the Inland Ice. The above comments on popularity of travel on the Inland Ice are additionally borne out by the Kangerlussuaq Tourism Company's brochure advertising motorised travel from Kangerlussuaq over the Inland Ice to have a 'unique experience' staying in DYE 2.

Among others undertaking the east-west route were the three-strong Grønland Transversale 2006 led by Martin Hülle of Germany who started in Tasilaq on 11 May and ended in Illulissat 34 days later on 13 June having used parawings to significantly help their progress. On 14 May Ben Saunders and his team were flown to the head of the Hahn glacier to test equipment for a future Antarctic expedition. They experienced changeable conditions, from baking sunshine and sludgy snow to complete whiteout and high winds. On 19 July Kai Sundnes and a colleague, both from the Norwegian Army, set off from Tasilaq but due to a gastric ulcer developing after 20 days en route, a helicopter had to be summoned once they were off the Inland Ice. Endre Nakstad and his wife Eva Mari had better conditions when they started later, on 4 August, from Tasilaq, reaching Kangerlussuaq after an uneventful journey on 23 August. They commented on the amount of melt water encountered at altitude and the warm temperatures. Pascal Hemon and Fabrice Baptiste left Tasilaq on 13 June planning to reach Thule in the north-west of Greenland, but they had to divert their journey of 43 days to Illulissat due to lack of wind and heavy snowfall. Also with a south-north traverse in mind, but with kite assistance planned, a four-man French group, led by Frédéric Donzé, left Narsarssuaq in the far south of Greenland on 28 April heading for Qaanaaq. By 23 May, owing to unfavourable winds, they had been forced to divert west to Kangerlussuaq. Even the Arctic Foxes Greenland Quest led by Felicity Ashton, who planned a kite-assisted double crossing of the Inland Ice, encountered winds consistently from the wrong direction. They made the first traverse from Kangerlugssuaq, which they left on 30 April, to a point just south of the Hahn Glacier in 16 days without using their kites. They then set off on the return on 21 May and reached Kangerlussuaq on 4 June having completed a journey of 1120km. They became the first British women's team to cross the Inland Ice.

In the Schweizerland mountains just north of Ammassalik a four-strong team from Cambridge University ferried loads inland to a series of base camps from which they made a number of ascents ranging from F to AD. The peaks ranged from 931m to 1589m and eight of them were first ascents. They experienced poor, wet and rainy weather and found much rubbish, left by an earlier French expedition, which to their credit they removed. Further north an eight-strong party from the Brathay Exploration Group, in weather which was unusually warm, producing poor snow conditions, made five ascents of grades F to D in the area inland from Knud Rasmussen's Land, north-east of the Watkins Mountains.

The Royal Navy Greenland Expedition 2006 was in the Watkins Mountains from 6-27 May. As well as climbing the highest peak in the Arctic, **Gunnbjørnsfjeld (3693m)**, they climbed several of the surrounding highest Arctic peaks in the main Watkins group and around the Upper Woolley glacier. The snow conditions and weather were good for travelling and enabled the party to climb 13 summits, four of them first ascents.

Just north of Scoresbysund a party of three, led by Matt Tinsley, made an interesting journey linking the largely abandoned airfield at Mestersvig to the relatively new airfield at Constable Pynt. The trip of 200km was accomplished in 10 days in mid-July, the major problems being the crossing of rivers high with melt water. Also in the Mestersvig area, three generations of the Laptun family took part in a tour of the area. Otto Laptun, who was first associated with East Greenland as a trapper in the 1930s, his son Hans with his wife and their daughter, explored some of the areas which will have seen much change take place since Otto was first there.

Inland from the Watkins, in an area unvisited since Martin Lindsay's expedition sledged past to the north-west in 1934, the Oxford University Greenland Expedition visited the **Gronau Nunatakker**. The three-man party spent 3-4 weeks in the area during August; climbing on snow and ice they made 12 first ascents graded between F and AD. The team's first climb, a prominent snow and ice pyramid they named Mount Currahee, proved to be the most demanding of the expedition, involving an almost impassable bergschrund, steep ice-climbing and an unplanned bivouac just below the summit. The team made other ascents in an unexplored group to the west of Christian IV's glacier, which they named the **Oxford Nunatakker**. They experienced weather patterns ranging from the high-pressure systems normal for the area to clinging fog and rain. Towards the end of their stay winter was making its advances and the temperature dropped to –20°C with strong winds forcing the group to abandon one route.

Much further north, in Dove Bugt at about latitude 76°N, in late July an enterprising (and presumably wealthy) group from Arcturus Expeditions established themselves by Twin Otter on the south shore of the bay. Prevented by bay ice from using their inflatable boat, they explored the coast and inland through Ravnedalen until it was possible to use the boat when they moved camp to Adolf S Jensen Land where they explored the hills and offshore islands. As one would expect this far north, the weather was of the settled anti-cyclonic pattern to which the rest of Greenland seems to have said farewell in 2006. As one would also expect in such an unvisited area, there was a multitude of wildlife to be observed. At the same time as the above party was enjoying the good weather on the south of Dove Bugt, the Danish 'Nanok' company were once again at work seeking out and repairing the old hunting huts on the north shore. They were frustrated by sea ice but managed to locate some 'new' huts and effect repairs, as did a southern group from the same company who worked on huts further south on Traill and Geographical Society Islands, a little north of Mestersvig.

133. Mikisfjord, East Greenland. The sailing vessel *Dagmar Aaen*, expedition vessel of Arved Fuchs, has been used for Arctic and Antarctic expeditions since 1991. It is a wooden boat, built in 1931. (*Arved Fuchs*)

The icy seas off the north-east Greenland coast attracted the usual number of cruise ships but 2006 saw two ventures of more interest. The first was the three-man Greenland East Coast Kayak Expedition, led by Martin Rickard, which, after considerable delays, started from Scoresbysund, or Ittoqqortoormiit, on 21 July in sea kayaks and made the long crossing of Scoresbysund on the first stage of their projected route to Ammassalik. On the journey down the very steep, rocky Blosseville coast, with each kayak weighing about 140kg, the party had difficulty finding camp-sites on the few beaches available. By the time they reached Kap Beaupre ice, driven by wind, was a increasing problem and at Kap Daussy, after about 280km and many delays, they were forced to turn back rather than try to press on south and risk a rescue. Also starting from Scoresbysund but heading north was the veteran German Arctic traveller Arved Fuchs who set off on 9 August having sailed from Flensburg in the 10-crewed *Dagmar Aaen* with the intention of sailing as far north as possible in what was essentially an unprotected vessel. Having sailed through the fjords of the 'Arctic Riviera' they reached the Sirius Patrol HQ at Daneborg on the 22 August. Further northward progress was frustrated by ice and the boat returned to Scoresbysund on 30 August, and ultimately back to Flensburg.

SIMON RICHARDSON

Scottish Winter 2006-2007

The Scottish winter season started slowly, and poor weather and variable conditions persisted until March. Despite this there were some remarkable routes climbed, with many teams perfectly poised to snatch impressive ascents during the short weather windows. Winter climbing is becoming increasingly popular, and the number of skilled and experienced climbers is increasing year on year. Standards are being pushed, and this year saw the greatest number of new Grade VIIIs ever climbed in a season before. The majority of these were climbed on sight. Style and ethics have become as important as technical difficulty, and climbing routes ground up on the first attempt is of paramount importance. Highlighted below are snapshots of some key ascents that give a flavour of the activity throughout the season. They range from the remote and exploratory to the highly technical, and from serious mixed climbs to fragile ice routes.

Northern Highlands

A high pressure over Scandinavia, sucking cold winds in from the north, is every winter climber's dream. And when it happens in the second week of February after a major snowfall, you know you're in for something special. The Northern Highlands are the place to be in such weather, and this year, as the temperature dropped and conditions came good, several teams raced up to the north-west to put some long sought-after projects into action.

In the flurry of routes climbed during a frantic week, the standout climb was perhaps the easiest. A winter ascent of *Marathon Ridge* (III, 4) on Beinn Lair had been in many climbers' sights for years, but the 18km approach had put off all suitors to date. The 3km-long north face rises up to 400m in height, and is said to be the largest cliff of schist in Britain. Scattered along its length are a mere 20 summer climbs, and the massive approach has kept the number of winter visits to a handful. But it's not just remoteness that keeps the crowds away. The crag is seamed with wet gullies and covered in vegetation, but with a cliff base at only 400m and lying close to the sea, it is rarely in winter condition.

Dave McGimpsey, Dave Bell, Andy Nisbet and Mark Edwards got the conditions spot on when they picked the plum objective of *Marathon Ridge*, which is one of the longest, and most pronounced features on the face. 'The line and location are amazing,' Dave told me afterwards. 'There were some good pitches, especially the wee fissure pitch on the top tower, but there was quite a lot of standard turf-bashing too. We thought it was about III,4 – a low number perhaps, but for all of us it was one of our most memorable winter days out ever.' *Marathon Ridge* is a great example of the new route potential across the Northern Highlands, and mountains such as Beinn Lair will keep future generations happy for a long time to come.

Ben Nevis

Mid February saw one of the highlights of the winter with the first winter ascent of *The Knuckleduster* (VIII, 9) on the front face of Number Three Gully Buttress. This summer HVS was first climbed by Jimmy Marshall and his brother Ronnie in 1966, and had been admired by climbers for several years as a futuristic winter possibility. It came a step nearer to reality when Ian Parnell and Ollie Metherell made the first winter ascent of the nearby *Sioux Wall* (VIII,8) last season. *The Knuckleduster* was clearly going to be a harder proposition, so it was no surprise when it was snapped up by Steve Ashworth and Blair Fyffe on 12 February. Ashworth is well known for his series of very difficult Lake District routes and Fyffe had an excellent season with a string of good new routes from Glen Coe to the North-West. 'It felt good to get the first winter ascent of such an obvious and independent line as this one,' Fyffe wrote afterwards. 'Climbers have finally begun exploiting the massive potential for mixed climbing on Ben Nevis, which traditionally has been an ice venue.' The route was not without its risks. A previous attempt by another team a couple years before resulted in a long fall where the leader broke several bones and was knocked unconscious. They graded the route VIII,9 and Ashworth commented that it was harder than *Unicorn* in Glen Coe.

The season stepped into top gear during the International Winter Meet at the end of February. These bi-annual meets have become established dates on the world mountaineering calendar. This year, 45 international guests from 22 countries teamed up with 30 UK hosts for six days of winter climbing based at Glenmore Lodge. Unfortunately a major thaw set in a few days before the event began, and winter climbing conditions for the first two days were close to non-existent. Apologetic hosts led bewildered guests up wet rock in the Northern Corries and soggy ice on Ben Nevis, but against all the odds, the weather cooled down through the week leading to a superb final day.

Ben Nevis was the venue of choice, and Coire na Ciste saw one of the most impressive displays of mixed climbing ever seen in Scotland. The pace was breathtaking. Steve Ashworth and Nils Nielsen from Norway climbed the 1990s test-piece *Darth Vader* (VII,8), followed by *The Sorcerer* (VII,8), a new line up the front face of the Lost The Place Buttress, before racing up *Thompson's Route* (IV,4) to warm down! Fellow Norwegian Bjorn Artun and Tim Blakemore had a similarly impressive day with *Albatross* (VI,5), one of the most prized routes on Indicator Wall, followed by *Darth Vader*. Nearby, Stuart McAleese and Tomaz Jakofcic from Slovenia climbed *Cornucopia* (VII.9), and Es Tressider and Paul Sab from Germany made an ascent of *Stringfellow* (VI,6).

134. Blair Fyffe on the first winter ascent of *The Knuckleduster* (VIII,9)
on Number Three Gully Buttress, Ben Nevis. (*Steve Ashton*)

Two big ascents took place on Number Three Gully Buttress. Ian Parnell
and Sean Isaac climbed a line based on the summer HVS *Last Stand*, which
takes the blunt arête between *Knuckleduster* and *Sioux Wall*. Parnell has made
this part of Nevis his own after the second ascent of *Arthur* a couple of
seasons ago and first winter ascent of *Sioux Wall* last year. This knowledge
proved vital in putting together the intricate line of *Curly's Arête* (VIII,8).
Just to the right, Freddie Wilkinson and Rok Zalokar made the third ascent
of *Sioux Wall* (VIII,8).

Next door, Viv Scott and Domagoj Bojko from Croatia climbed *Salva
Mea* (VIII,8), the hanging chimney just left of the icicle of *South Sea Bubble*.
The route starts up the lower ramp of *South Sea Bubble* and continues up a
hidden slot to reach the upper snow funnel. Across on *The Comb*, Dave
MacLeod and Hiroyoshi Manome and Katsutaka Yokoyama from Japan
tip-toed up *Isami* (VIII,8), the conspicuous hanging groove to the left of
The Good Groove. This had been stared at longingly by several teams over
the years waiting for the requisite amount of ice, but Macleod solved this
problem by climbing it as a thin mixed climb. Three new Grade VIIIs
climbed the same day in the same corrie is unprecedented in Scotland, and
says everything for the immaculate mixed climbing conditions that day,

and the enthusiasm and skill of the guests and hosts. The Scottish mountains put on such a good show on the final day of the meet, and everyone went home with huge smiles. 'Mixed conditions on the Ben were outstanding,' Ian Parnell enthused afterwards. 'They were perhaps the best I've seen. The BMC winter meet was a superb advert for the chase, both frustrating and rewarding, for the fickle and elusive proper Scottish conditions.'

In late March, a second high-pressure system centred over Scandinavia sucking in cool easterly winds. This is the late season weather scenario that ice climbers drool over, because the clear skies and frosty nights coupled with warm daytime temperatures are perfect for building ice on the higher Ben Nevis routes. Teams were quick to take advantage of the superb ice with ascents of *Sickle, Orion Direct* and *Astral Highway*. It was quickly realised that some of the Ben's most highly prized thin face routes such as *Riders on the Storm* on Indicator Wall and *The Great Glen* on Gardyloo Buttress were in superb condition. The quality of the soft plastic ice was fantastic, with first time placements that gripped axe picks and front points like glue.

The new route action centred on Indicator Wall. Iain Small and Blair Fyffe made an early repeat of the much-prized *Stormy Petrel* (VII,6), taking a more direct variation up a thinly iced groove in the centre of the route. Before setting off, Fyffe tipped off Ian Parnell and Viv Scott that there was a direct start to his route *The Rhyme of the Ancient Mariner* still waiting to be done. Parnell quickly despatched this difficult VII,7 variation that avoided the cunning detour on the original line, and then continued up the original line to make the second ascent. Next day, Andy Benson, Rich Cross and Dave Hollinger repeated Parnell and Scott's direct line and confirmed its superb quality. With three difficult pitches straight up the centre of the wall this is one of the great modern mixed climbs on the mountain. The following day, fresh from his success on *Stormy Petrel*, Iain Small teamed up with me to climb the thin overlapping grooves to the left of *Albatross*. *Arctic Tern* (VII,5) starts just left of *Albatross*, passes the smooth slab of *Fascist Groove* before climbing a spectacular tiered ramp system on centimetre-thick ice before finishing up the upper rib. Eager to capitalise on the exceptional conditions, the route saw two repeats within a week.

On the descent, Small noticed a discontinuous ice smear hanging down the very steep pillar between *Riders of the Storm* and *Albatross*, so a week later, on 1 April, we returned to climb *Ship of Fools* (VIII,7). After the intro-ductory rib, the route takes the very narrow sinuous groove right of *Riders* to bypass the huge roof in the lower section of the pillar. It then continues up the crest of the pillar via difficult mixed to finish up the vertical ice arête left of the exit gully of *Le Nid d'Aigle*. Ian's lead of the crux section pulling through overlapping slabs on discontinuous, hollow, one centimetre-thick ice was one of the finest leads I have ever witnessed. The pitch collapsed as I followed it, and next day a slow thaw started, so this one will have to wait for another exceptional ice build-up to see a repeat.

Cairngorms

The most difficult ascent of the season took place on 2 March when Guy Robertson and Rich Cross made the first winter ascent of *The Scent* (IX,9) in Coire an Dubh Lochain on Beinn a'Bhuird. The pair had tried this summer HVS two weeks previously but failed at the base of the 'awkward ramp' mentioned in the guidebook, and gingerly abseiled off a number of poorly equalised pieces. 'On the second attempt I sorted my ropework out a bit better,' Robertson told me, 'and I simply clipped the poor belay as a runner. As predicted, the ramp was indeed hard – very precarious, blind and rounded seams – and it didn't yield any pro at all for maybe 20 feet or so, when I placed a hook in some turf. I'm not really one for big grades, but this is certainly amongst the most committing bits of climbing I've ever done. In retrospect it was pretty difficult to justify, so it's well protected crack lines for me from now on! It's a bit of a shame about the boldness in some ways as it's genuinely a really nice, cunning line up an impressive buttress in a wonderful setting.'

TONY HOWARD

Wadi Rum & Jordan

NB All grades in this report are French

The weather in Wadi Rum the last two winters ('06 and '07) was unusually wet. In February '06 there was a torrential rainstorm that flooded the Rum valley from the new Visitor Centre south to Khazali. In the parallel Wadi um Ishrin, another unprecedented river carved a small wadi into the heart of the old one. Bedouin were rescued from the floods, which later created vast mud flats; these dried to dust bowls, creating dust storms throughout the spring. The rains continued, on and off until mid April, unusually late for Jordan (though Easter was fine). The north Jordan hills even had snow in March. January 2007 brought snow as far south as Petra and Rum, on one occasion blocking the Petra Highway.

Climbing, however, has continued though visitor numbers are down due to the continuing adverse impact of political problems in Iraq and Israel/ Palestine. Following the developments of spring 2005, dealt with in *AJ* 110, some single pitch climbs of 4 and 5 were added east of Rum on **Seifan Kebir (1256m)** in October '05 by Harry and Lose Adshead. In November Joel Etinger and Gili Tenne attempted the south face of **Jebel Kharazeh (1580m)** opposite the Rest House. The route, named *Ish Hazak* (*Strong Man*), is still uncompleted but so far gives 8 pitches, 6a max, and takes a direct line up the obvious water-polished cracks starting left of *Vanishing Pillar*. Descent is by five abseils.

Behind the Rest House, the rock Mecca of **Jebel Rum's East Dome (1560m)** had yet another quality climb added on the east face, this time by T Sobotka, O Benes and M Rosecku. Named *Rock Empire*, it is bolt protected and is grade 7 and 8 for most its 15 pitches which were climbed over four days. Their verdict: 'A great sport climb on perfect rock – carry 10 quick draws, some slings and 2x60m ropes, also some Friends for the final pitches of *Raid Mit the Camel.*' The route is getting a quality reputation.

Back across the Rum valley again, Rum regular Gilles Rappeneau finally achieved his goal of finding a 'Voie Normale', possibly the long-lost Bedouin route to the summit of **Jebel um Ishrin (1753m).** He was accompanied by Bedouin guide Talal Awad and Robert Mandi on what was a technically easy but long and complex route. Wilf Colonna, a French guide who spends half of each year in Rum, made the second ascent in April 2006 with aspirant Bedouin guide Mohammad Hamdan. The climb, which was another of last November's new routes, is called *Bedu Majnun* (*Crazy Bedouin*). It was graded 4 by Gilles and team who found it necessary to place protection on

135. View west from Jebel um Ejil to Rum village and the east face of
      Jebel Rum. (*Tony Howard*)

the extremely exposed crux pitch. While verifying that ibex almost
certainly go that way (you can see scuff marks on the sandstone), Wilf and
Mohammad said that it was unlikely that any Bedouin hunters would have
climbed solo up and down this pitch. They were not convinced that this is
the lost Bedouin way and Mohammad should know – not only is he the
youngest and best of today's Bedouin climbers, putting up 7b routes, but
both his father, Hammad Hamdan, and his grandfather Sheikh Hamdan,
were well known guides and hunters with their own extremely popular
eponymous routes forming the classic traverse of **Jebel Rum (1754m)**.

There is now talk of continuing the search for the 'Bedouin Way' on **Um
Ishrin** and also on **North Nassrani**, as climbers have discovered ibex
droppings (carried down and confirmed by a Bedouin) on this extremely
difficult summit, and where ibex can go, Bedouin hunters are likely to have
followed. Meanwhile, a new route on the south-east face of **N Nassrani
(1560m)**, *Sandy Silence*, by M Dorfleitner and F Freider is definitely not a
Bedouin way. Its nine pitches on one of Rum's most impressive walls were
climbed on 3 Jan 2006 by a 'long and "spacey" bolted route on good rock
– more demanding than *Guerre Sainte* which is to the left'. (*Muezzin* is to the
right.) All that's needed are 13 quick draws, slings, 2x60m ropes 'and a
good head'!

The Rum bolting debate. Few other than Precht and Brochmeyer seem
able to climb Rum's big faces in traditional style. In spring 2006 they added
yet more routes on the west side of **Jebel Rum**, but no details as yet.
Meanwhile, the number of big-wall bolt routes is increasing although the
use of bolts on the smaller cliffs is increasingly frowned upon, even by the
Bedouin guides, some of whom, without being aware of British ethics, have
suggested that sport climbs with fixed gear should be limited to selected
cliffs. In actual fact, the leaflet on Safety and Environmental Awareness

given to climbers at the Visitor Centre states quite clearly that 'the use of power drills is not permitted in the Protected Area'. I must, however, admit here that we were involved in writing it, though with considerable input from the BMC and based on BMC and UIAA Guidelines. The following UIAA quote is relevant: '...we oppose the trend towards completely eliminating danger from climbing along the lines of the "pleasure" philosophy, thus reducing the sport to its movement aspect. For without danger and uncertainty, climbing loses its defining element – adventure. To climb a route on a minimum of equipment will always be valued more highly than the ascent of a route with perfected infrastructure.'

The UIAA Mountain Code also states: 'Climbers should refrain from increasing the fixed pro on existing routes. When carrying out redevelopment measures, we should strive to preserve the original character of a climb.' It seems a shame therefore that a bolt has been placed to protect the crux of *Rainbow Warrior* (a route first climbed in traditional style in 1986 by Wilf Colonna and myself). A bolt-protected line has also been added on **Jebel um Ejil (1341m)** between *Perverse Frog* and *The Beauty* (both 1985 trad routes by Wilf Colonna and Alan Baker). The climb, *Priez pour Nous* is six pitches mostly 6b, 6c, with a 7b crux; 25 bolts were placed, and shiny ones at that – even visibly glinting in the sun from the Rest House, over a kilometre away. It may be an enjoyable climb but I would suggest the use of bolts here is unsightly and detracts from the ambience of the nearby traditional classics. It has even been mooted by a French regular that some of Rum's traditional Grade 5s should be retro-bolted to attract more visitors; however, if I may reiterate my point of view, Rum was developed as a wilderness adventure playground with few signs of man on the cliffs – let's keep it that way.

Despite being surrounded by political problems, Jordan is struggling manfully to maintain and develop its tourism; climbers and trekkers are still visiting in reasonable numbers. Why not give it a try next autumn or spring? The climbing in Rum is unique, the Bedouin are extremely welcoming, there are canyons and limestone cliffs in the north and the Petra mountains and the Red Sea with its superb snorkelling and diving are both just an hour away.

Some contacts for climbing and trekking guides:

Atieq Auda:	atieq_aouda@yahoo.com
Mohammed Hammad:	mohammed_climber@yahoo.com
Wilfried Colonna:	wilfried@cyberia.jo
	or desert.guides@wanadoo.fr
Guidebooks:	Tony Howard, *Treks and Climbs in Wadi Rum*
	Tony Howard & Di Taylor, *Jordan, Walks, Treks, Caves, Climbs and Canyons*
	Both from Cicerone Press
Tony Howard's website	www.nomadstravel.co.uk for general info

GEOFF HORNBY

Turkey 2002-2006

R ecent mountaineering activity in the southern regions of Turkey have centred around two principal areas, the Ala Dağ just north of Adana and the mountain ranges around Antalya, the Bey and Dedigol Daglari's. At this time, access to the Cilo Dağ remains difficult given its proximity to the Kurdish areas in the north of Iraq.

Ala Dağ
The history of technical mountaineering exploration in the Ala Dağ is quite curious in that it seems to have taken place in waves of exploration usually driven by climbers from single countries. In the 1930s, climbers from the Klagenfurt section of the Austrian Alpine Club were dominant. The British then followed this during the war years, with climbers including AC members Hodgkin, Hurst and Peck. The 1950s saw the return of the Austrians before Royal Air Force mountain rescue teams from Cyprus and British university mountaineering clubs then dominated the 1960s. The 1970s brought Polish, German, Italian and Turkish climbers in the development push and then there followed a 20-year period when the mountains were left predominantly to the local climbing community who added many first winter ascents.

However, in recent years Italian climbers have taken up the challenge, adding a series of long and very hard routes, often using bolted protection. These climbers include Rolando Larcher, Maurizio Oviglia, Helmut Gargitter and Pauli Trenkwalder, all of whom have been putting up long hard routes around the world, including Italy, Jordan and Morocco, over the years. Their style often provides bolt-protected routes but they are extremely hard and run-out in places.

In 2005, Larcher, Oviglia and Michele Paissan put up a hard route on the E face of Demirkazik (3757m), one of the major peaks of the range. The route *Uc Muz* is 650m long and has a crux of 8a with obligatory climbing to 7b.This group then joined forces with local climbers Recep and Zeynep Ince to attempt a repeat of the 1995 French route on the spire of Parmakkaya (2880m). They achieved the repeat, but only after an upgrade from 6c to 7b and with an appreciation of some very run-out climbing. They then added a new route to the E face of the tower with *Mezza Luna Nascente*, 270m 7c with obligatory 7a climbing.

In June 2006 Gargitter and Trenkwalder were on the E face of Parmakkaya, adding *Orient*, a 230m 7b with obligatory 7a climbing. This route lies immediately left of the Italian route of *Mezza Luna Nascente*.

August 2006 saw the following routes added to the Guvercinlik peaks in the Emil valley. On the W face of the Lower Guvercinlik Peak (3000m), Larcher and Oviglia added *Come to Dervish*, a 600m 7b climb with obligatory climbing at 7a. Swiss climbers had attempted this line two years earlier. The climb has six of its 13 pitches graded 7a or harder. Having put the route up over four days with the assistance of local climber Recep Ince, Larcher and Oviglia then returned three days later to free the entire route. This route lies to the left of a line believed to have been climbed by Czech climbers.

Whilst Larcher and Oviglia were creating this extremely hard route, their travelling companions Mauro Florit and Marco Sterni added a further three long routes on the surrounding peaks. They began on the E face of Yeniceri Dagi (3073m), adding *Ocio Muli*, a 210m 6+. They then turned their attention to the Guvercinlik peaks, and on the possibly unclimbed Middle Guvercinlik Peak (3145m) they put up *Italian Classic*, a 600m 6+ on the W face, before turning to the Upper Guvercinlik Peak (3183m) to add *Remembering 1955*, a 500m 6+ on its W face.

Further information can be gained from incerecep@yahoo.com. It would seem that this type of climbing has endless possibilities in this mountain range.

The party of four then finished their trip off with first ascents of a number of short sport routes to 7c in the Kazikli valley.

Dedigol Daglari

This range of peaks has always been a mystery. Basically, you cannot see the main walls from any road despite them being the biggest sweep of limestone in the region between Konya and Antalya. The mystery started when David Lucas published a partial picture of the wall but was unwilling to divulge its location. Susie Sammut and Geoff Hornby then spent three days driving every possible road and track in the region until they found themselves staring at the base of the wall beneath storm clouds.

Following traditional climbing ethics (leaving nothing but abseil tat), Hornby and Sammut opened their account, in 2002, with the first ascent of the *Lightning Pillar* on the W face. This 330m TD 6 (HVS 5b) was named after the incredible weather conditions that this mountain seems to generate. The weather systems boiling up over the coast slam into the wall and create violent lightning storms. In any three-day period one can expect two violent storms and a third day lost to rain. The forest beneath the wall often has burning trees in the dawn following a storm.

During this visit Hornby and Sammut met Antalya activist Ozturk Kayicki who was busy working on a fantastic sport route on the big sweep of slabs. Whilst there, Ozturk with his wife and a friend were caught by a storm and they dropped all metal items before sheltering under three different trees. Two of the trees were then hit by lightning. Be warned!

136. Peter Bishop on the first ascent of *Adam's Rib*. (*Geoff Hornby*)

Hornby and Sammut returned in 2004 with Peter Bishop to add the *Freya Face* up the right edge of the big sweep of slabs and through the head wall above, 800m and TDinf, and then *Adam's Rib* 280m and TDinf, up the beautiful pillar at the right edge of the wall.

The next year Hornby returned with Brian Davison and added a further three routes. On the lower tier at the left end of the wall they put up *Royal Flush*, 175m TDinf, and then immediately left of the big sweep of slabs *Hidden Pillar* 365m and D Sup.

137. South and east faces of Dedigol Daglari, showing route lines of
  Freya Face (left) and *Adam's Rib* (right). (*Geoff Hornby*)

Brian Davison closed his visit with a free solo of *Via Davison* a 300m
grade 4 on the SW face.

Whilst on the hidden pillar they noticed a number of new bolts rising up
the wall to the left and also to the right. Walking along the base of the wall,
further bolt lines were identified and subsequent enquiries have identified
that Michel Piola and friends, often with Ozturk, have made over a dozen
long bolt-protected routes on the wall. Until the local village have agreed
to allow further access, Piola has asked that his routes be left unrecorded.

Access to the Dedigol is invariably going to be made through Antalya
and it has always surprised me that the plethora of limestone walls along
the coast to the west have not received much attention from climbers in the
past. Today, climbers flock to the sport-climbing complex near Geyikbayiri,
north-west of Antalya (see *Climb Magazine* No. 14). This complex is called
JoSiTo's after the names of the three Munich climbers who run the venue.
The mountains of the Bey Daglari are clearly visible to the south.

Bey Daglari

The obvious and stunning peak of Sivridag (Sharp Mountain), the triangular peak immediately west of Antalya, has been the home for some of Antalya's climbing over the years. The 650m-high E face boasts two routes of old known as the *Beginners Route* and the *Experts Route*. The *Beginners* takes a slanting line up a fault on the right side of the face at 3/3+, whilst the *Experts* takes a direct line up the middle left side of the face up steady grade 4/4+ ground.

In 2002 Susie Sammut and Geoff Hornby started by climbing the ridge line up the right edge of the face, which most probably had been climbed before, giving short steps of 4 for almost 1000m of climbing and scrambling. They then climbed a direct line up the face, right of the *Experts Route* and starting from the top of the peg-scarred cracked slab leaning against the base of the wall. *Palestine*, 650m TD 6, was climbed in 2002 with an exit traversing right to the ridge line and then repeated by the same pair in 2004 direct to the summit ridge.

During their 2002 ascent, Hornby and Sammut met with local climbers from Antalya University who were starting up the *Experts route* with full bivouac equipment. These climbers confirmed that their records only showed the existence of the *Experts* and *Beginners* routes.

Hornby and Sammut then climbed *Scimitar*, 205m D Sup 5, climbing the wall directly below the end of the *Beginners*.

In 2005, Hornby returned with Brian Davison to climb the big wall directly west of Gedelme village. The E face of Kandilcik T South was attempted in 2004 by Hornby with Susie Sammut, but after climbing the first and hardest pitch in temperaturesof more than 40°C they abseiled off. Davison and Hornby completed the route in cooler conditions to provide *The Pillar of Alcatus* 755m and TD Sup 6+ (E2). The route was about 250m longer than expected and the easier upper ground proved to be harder, bolder and more taxing. Hornby was thankful that he had not continued in 2004 under those conditions. The descent, too, proved extremely arduous.

The route was named in honour of Alcatus, one of Alexander the Great's generals. Whilst Alcatus and the army marched up through the mountains and beneath the Kandilcik wall, Alexander led his court and bodyguards straight along the coast as a short cut. When, just before Sivridag, they were faced with deep water around a headland, the wind suddenly rose and blew the water away from the cliffs, allowing them a dry passage. Hornby subsequently swam around this headland confirming that the water is about six metres deep – some wind eh!

HARISH KAPADIA

India 2006

Climbing expeditions to the Indian Himalaya appear to be in decline. Overall, there were reduced numbers of teams, both from foreign countries and from India. There was also a reduction in the number of peaks being attempted, especially of challenging peaks and routes. Among the main reasons for this are the unrealistic fee structures and rules imposed by the State governments. Climbing activity was at a much reduced scale in Uttarakhand (formerly Uttaranchal) and nil in the case of Sikkim.

Trekking in the Himalaya has grown by leaps and bounds and more Indians enjoy the range than ever. This has also brought environmental concerns to the fore. However, the impact trekkers can make on the environment is rather negligible compared to the damage caused by the pilgrims, security forces, and even the local population who have now been introduced to packaging from the plains.

Foreign Expeditions

A total of 37 foreign expeditions visited the Indian Himalaya this year. The majority were commercially organised either on easy routine peaks or on popular high mountains. In all, six expeditions climbed Stok Kangri, (officially that is), two went for Dzo Jongo and two for Kang Yissey. The Nun Kun massif was visited by four expeditions; Meru, Shivling and Satopanth received three teams each; whereas Kedar Dome had two teams. Changabang was also visited by two expeditions, of which one ended with the disappearance of two climbers.

There were 16 expeditions to Jammu and Kashmir including one to the East Karakoram. 19 expeditions visited Uttarakhand where the ever-popular Gangotri area drew 13 of these. Six expeditions operated in the Kumaun Himalaya. Two teams visited Himachal Pradesh. The poor weather pattern was the reason for a lower success rate this year. This unpredictability in the weather conditions is becoming a major concern on the Himalayan climbing scene.

Indian Expeditions

Year after year, the number of Indian mountaineers visiting their own mountain ranges is decreasing. The trend of attempting routine peaks such as Kalanag, Rudugaira, Hanuman Tibba, Deo Tibba, Chhamser and Lungser Kangri has been replaced by height, which now seems to be in vogue. Kamet, the third highest mountain, was attempted twice and Satopanth, the seven-thousander in the Gangotri area, had four expeditions, with one attempting Nun. But some climbers also attempted difficult mountains such as Shivling, Dunagiri, Panwali Dwar, Nanda Khat, Manirang and other lesser peaks. 26 expeditions visited Himachal Pradesh, whereas (even after the application of additional peak fees by state government) 20 visited Uttarakhand. Ladakh and its surroundings received six expeditions, all to routine peaks.

An army expedition climbed Junction Peak in the Siachen glacier. It has been climbed twice before (first by the Bullock-Workman team in 1912). However, their attempt on the challenging Singhi Kangri was aborted. Their plans to take on Saltoro Kangri II (7705m), one of the highest unclimbed peaks in the world, could not materialise. Hopefully, this ascent and attempt by the army indicates the opening up of this area in future.

It is interesting to note that except for one major exploration in the Arunachal Pradesh, not a single expedition visited any peaks or areas east of Kumaun. The usually active areas of Sikkim remained unvisited this year. The concentration of mountaineers was restricted to only three Himalayan states, those of Jammu and Kashmir, Himachal Pradesh and Uttarakhand.

ARUNACHAL PRADESH

An Indian team led by Harish Kapadia followed the Bailey-Morshead route to Yonggyap La, the first civil party to follow this trail in the restricted border area. The Dibang valley, in eastern Arunachal Pradesh (formerly NEFA), is deep and thickly wooded. To its north and east lies Tibet (China) and to its west is the Siang (Tsangpo) valley. On the northern border (the McMahon Line) lies the Yonggyap La. This pass, with the adjoining pass Andra La, leads to the Chimdro area of Tibet. The holy mountain Kundu Potrang lies across these passes, almost due north of the Andra La. Pundit explorer Kinthup made a pilgrimage to this mountain during his search for the passage of the Tsangpo into India. Many Tibetan pilgrims visit this place and perform circumambulations now that the Chinese have restored religious freedom. It is also believed that the famous book *Lost Horizon* was based on the imaginary Shangri la located near Kundu Potrang.

F M Bailey and H T Morshead, two British army officers, made a journey to these passes in 1913. After trying unsuccessfully to cross the Andra La, they crossed the Yonggyap La in May in pouring rain. After descending from the la, they had to cross another pass, the Pungpung La, on the fourth day. Many Tibetans, with their supplies running short, have perished after being caught in storms between these two passes. However, Bailey and Morshead continued their trek westwards into Tibet, visiting the Tsangpo falls and Takpa Siri and exiting from the Kameng (Tawang) valley. It was based on their survey and report that the McMahon line was drawn, demarcating the boundaries between India and Tibet (China).

138. A helicopter comes to the rescue. Yonggyap La behind. (*R Wani*)

From Basam, the difficulties of the 2006 trek started and they had to hack a trail through thick jungle on a faint track, with many steep ups and downs. The camps were in small forest clearings and they had to be careful about Dim Dam flies. Mercifully, snakes and leeches were mostly absent as it was autumn. From Chapu the route climbed steeply and there were many difficult stages. Stopping at four other camps, the party reached Pabbow at the foot of the Yonggyap La. In deteriorating weather, they reached the la on 22 November.

As the party returned to the last camp, a fierce freak storm engulfed the area. For the next five days, it snowed without respite with a heavy accumulation of snow prohibiting any movement. It was dangerous and even impossible to find a way through the thick bamboo growth and rickety log bridges. Rations were running low and soon the last of the *chapattis* was eaten. Four porters decided to desert and make a dash back, risking their lives, a sure sign of the grim situation. The party was in contact with the army via wireless. Luckily, on 27 November there was a break in the weather and clouds lifted for six hours. During this opening two Cheetah helicopters of the Indian Air Force rescued the trapped party and brought them back to Anini.

UTTARAKHAND

Kumaun
Nanda Devi East (7434m)
This high peak, a twin of the Nanda Devi peak, can be approached from the eastern side only. This is the route by which it was first climbed. This year an eight-member ladies team from Spain (Rosa Maria Real Soriano) failed due to bad snow conditions and avalanches. They reached the Longstaff col at 6000m and attempted the south ridge (1939 Polish route) where they placed two high camps. This pre-monsoon attempt took place in the months of May-June 2006.

Accident on Changabang (6864m)
The leader of an experienced team from Mexico, Andres Delgado Caldernon, with another member, Alphonso De La Patra, began the attempt on 1 October. It appears that they finished the climb on the west face and returned to base (their route was a minor variation of the Kurtayka route on the west face). They spoke to their family and friends in Mexico via a satellite phone. They were last seen on the col between Changabang and Kalanka by the leader of the Czech expedition attempting Changabang. It is not known what their plans were after the ascent. When they had been missing for several days the alarm was sounded and Indian Air Force helicopters conducted aerial searches. They could neither locate the climbers nor find any trace of them. The Indo-Tibet Border Police team were also unable to make much headway, as it was not known whether the Mexicans had tried to descend into the Northern Sanctuary of Nanda Devi or had taken some other route. Finally, rescue attempts were called off due to bad weather and fresh snow. Search for their remains will resume once summer arrives.

In September-October 2006, seven Czech climbers, led by Tomas Rinn, attempted the north face of Changabang. They reached only 6200m.

Nandakhat (6545m)
A 12-member team from West Bengal (Rajsekhar Ghosh) climbed this difficult peak on 15 September. Arupam Das with Pemba Sherpa and Pasang Sherpa reached the summit. The peak is situated on the northern slopes from the Pindari glacier. It is always tricky to cross the icefall and the glacier at its snout to approach the peak. In 1970, two climbers from a Mumbai-based team were killed in an avalanche in the Pindari glacier. Anup Sah from Nainital, Uttarakhand led the first ascent of this peak in 1974.

Adi Kailash (6150m)
When the pilgrimage to the main peak of Kailash (in Tibet) was stopped, it was this peak in eastern Kumaun that drew the faithful. It is situated at the

head of the Kuthi valley in eastern-most Kumaun. A seven-member British team led by Martin Moran established base camp on 21 September ahead of the Kuthi village. They climbed the peak from its NE ridge after establishing two high camps at 4450m and 5450m respectively. The leader, with Martin Welch, James Gibb, Mike Freeman, Stephan Rink, John Venier and Mangal Singh reached the summit on 30 September.

Panwali Dwar (6663m)

This peak, adjoining Nandakhat peak and on the rim of the Nanda Devi Sanctuary, has a formidable record. It defied several attempts until a Japanese team made the first ascent in 1980. A ten-member team from West Bengal (Debasis Biswas) made a successful ascent on 22 August. Basant Singha Roy, Debasis Biswas, Pasang Sherpa and Pemba Sherpa reached the summit by the route of the first ascent.

Garhwal – Gangotri glacier area
Meru (6660m)

This peak was a happy climbing ground for Australian, Japanese and Czech teams. An Australian team (Glenn Singleman) climbed Meru Central (*aka* Shark's Fin) 6550m, via the west face. After reaching base camp at Tapovan on 3 May 2006, they put up four more camps before reaching the summit. Michael Geoffrey Hill and Malcolm Haskins reached the top on 18 May, followed by Tove Petterson on 20 May. Two members of this team achieved a new world record for altitude base-jumping. For more details: www.baseclimb.com.

A four-member Japanese team established base camp at Tapovan on 1 September and ABC at 4800m, C1 at 5300m as well as two bivouacs at 5800m and 6200m. They climbed via the NE face. The leader with Makoto Kuroda, Okada Yasushi and Hanatani Yasuhiro reached the summit on 26 September. A two-member team, Jan Kreisinger and Marek Holecek, after establishing ABC at 5400m, climbed the NE face in alpine style. On 6 October, both members reached the summit.

Shivling (6543m)

As usual, Shivling had a number of attempts. The eight-member Korean team (Bae Hyo Soon) attempted the NE face by a new route but failed to reach the summit. They reached 6000m and were stopped due to a very steep route, heavy rockfall and some avalanches. The attempt took place in the months of August-September. Spaniards, including Alberto Inurrategui Iriarte (leader), Jon Beloqui Iceta and Eneko Guenechea Sasiain, reached the summit on 11 May. This three-member team climbed the west face after establishing base camp on 26 April and Camp 1 at 5600m. All four members of a team from Poland (Pawel Garwolinski) reached the summit via the west ridge on 18 September after establishing three high camps. An eight-member Indian team led by Debasish Kanji climbed via the west ridge. However, they had to stop 150m short of the summit as the weather turned bad.

Satopanth (7075m)

Italians, British and Indian teams reached the summit between July and September. All ascents were by the normal route, the NE ridge. A Swiss-German team stopped at 6950m. The liaison officer reported garbage and pollution at the base camp of this peak, which is a rather common problem with commercial expeditions on such easy and popular peaks.

Kedar Dome (6830m)

A 12-member French team (leader, Villard Emmanuel) established a base camp at Khada Patthar (4470m). They established three high camps and reached 6470m but gave up the attempt owing to the possibility of avalanches after fresh snowfall. At the same time a two-member British team, Ian Parnell and Tim Emmett, climbed the SE pillar route. They reached the summit on 8 October (*see 'Confounding the Colonel on Kedar Dome', page 17*).

Thalay Sagar (6904m)

A Korean team (Hee Young Park) established base camp at Kedar Tal (4700m) on 1 August. Two high camps at 5100m and 5400m were established on the north face. After one bivvi at 6600m, Sang Bem You reached the summit on 9 September.

Central Garhwal
Kamet (7756m)

An Indian expedition to Kamet (7756m) was organised by A K Bhattacharyya in May-June. The team planned to retrace the footsteps of the first successful team led by Frank Smythe in 1931 and hence the traditional Meade Col route was chosen for the climb, with an intended summit date close to 21 June in line with that of the 1931 ascent. The summit team, comprising four members and six support climbers (Sherpas), reached the summit on 24 June after establishing five camps between the base and summit. All the members of the summit team reached the top, thus representing a satisfying commemorative expedition.

Arwa Tower (6352m)

A four-member Dutch team, led by Michael van Geemen, chose the NW pillar route on this challenging rocky peak. However, as they gained height, bad weather forced them to stop. As there was no hope of improvement, they gave up the climb at 6150m. Their attempt was in May-June.

Arwa Spire (6193m)
It was not the mountain but human factors that defeated this team. The four-member Spanish team (Ruben De Francisco) wasted a week at the roadhead due to non-availability of porters. Finally, once on the mountain, they reached 6000m on the N face before their time and supplies ran out.

HIMACHAL PRADESH

Kullu Pumori (6553m)
This peak is situated in the centre of the Bara Shigri glacier in Lahaul. It is a challenging peak that was first climbed by Bob Pettigrew's British team in 1964. A French-American expedition led by Remy Lecluse was organised in May-June but they were unable to climb the peak due to an early monsoon. However, the main objective of the team was to ski down and that was achieved by various routes. The seven-member team reached up to 6400m. Meanwhile, on 30 August, two members and three high-altitude supporters on an Indian team from Bengal (Samir Sengupta) reached the summit of this peak by the same route.

KR 2 (6194m)
Though their intended peak KR 3 (6157m) was not climbed, an eight-member Belgium team, led by Stijn Vandendriessche, climbed KR 2 on 14 and 19 August. The leader with six members reached the summit via the SE ridge. They had established their base camp at 4800m and Camp 1 at 5600m.

Manirang (6593m)
Manirang was one of the earliest peaks climbed in this part of the Himalaya. Dr and Mrs J de V Graff climbed it in 1952 with the legendary Sherpas Pasang Dawa Lama and Tashi. A 12-member Indian team (led by Kajal Dasgupta) followed the Manali–Kaja–Mane–Yang Lake route towards this high peak on the borders of Kinnaur and Spiti. From there, the team followed the south ridge, climbing the peak via a new route. On 16 July five climbers reached the summit.

EAST KARAKORAM

Plateau Peak (7287m)
Situated in the same basin as the Saser Kangri group, this peak was named as such by J O M Roberts. With strong defences, it has remained one of the few unclimbed 7000m peaks in India. Bad weather interrupted the attempt made by this 15-member Indian-Italian team (M S Gomase and Marco Meazzini) at 5800m. Base camp was established at the snout of the

Phukpoche glacier at 4700m, approached from the Nubra valley to its west. They established Camp 1 at 5400m on the central Phukpoche glacier. From there, slopes leading to the west ridge of the peak were equipped with ropes and dumps of food. The expedition took place in August.

Siachen Glacier

The Indian army organised its own expedition led by Col Ashok Abbey (31 August -7 October) to peaks in the Siachen glacier. The expedition was conducted in four phases. The team commenced moving up the Siachen glacier on 1 September and made base camp at 4900m at the 'Oasis', the junction of the Siachen and Teram Shehr glaciers, on 12 September.

Junction Peak (6350m) A 12-member team climbed this highly avalanche-prone peak via the west face on 18 September from a camp at 5320m. The ascent took eight and a half hours. This peak was first climbed and named by Mrs Fanny Bullock-Workman in 1912 and is a central point on this long glacier.

Singhi Kangri (7202m) This was the second attempt in the history of the mountain – a new route from an unclimbed face was attempted. The Japanese team that made the first ascent in 1976 had crossed the wall dividing the Siachen from the Staghar glacier, where they sited their Camp 2, and climbed along the NW ridge to the summit. The army team established a base camp at 5100m on 16 September on the upper Siachen glacier. After negotiating the difficult west face of the mountain, they established Camp 1 on 21 September at 6325m. This was the crux of the climb. Only one more camp was to be set up prior to attempting the summit of Singhi Kangri and Pt 6850m. After a long wait, a further attempt on the mountain was called off on 29 September owing to inclement weather and dangerous snow conditions.

The **Siachen glacier** was traversed from the snout to Sia la, the western-most tip of the Siachen glacier. **Peak 36 glacier** was traversed. A ground recce of the NE face of Saltoro Kangri 7742m (I), 7705m (II) was also carried out for a future attempt.

Other events

The 70th anniversary of the first ascent of Nanda Devi in 1936 was celebrated at many centres. The new Himalayan Club Centre, the main office of the Himalayan Club, was inaugurated in Mumbai at a central location. It contains a library, displays and the 'Lt Nawang Kapadia Himalayan Collection' under which a large number of Himalayan maps, videos and DVD films and recordings of Oral Histories from leading mountaineers are stored. All these are available for use by anyone from India or abroad at cost.

Henry Osmaston, who passed away this year (obituary page 389), had many admirers in India for his pioneering work in the Indian Himalayan glaciers, especially the Siachen.

Amongst the important publications in India covering the Himalaya were: *India Through Its Birds* (edited by Zafar Futehally), *Birds of Prey of the Indian Subcontinent* (Rishad Naoroji) and *Exploring the Highlands of the Himalaya* (Harish Kapadia). The most noteworthy publication was the *Diaries of Nain Singh Rawat*, the great Pundit explorer, which were recently located at his home in the village of Milam. Though in Hindi, it is a valuable original record.

Finally, a word about a quiet revolution in the Himalaya. Instead of, as a policy, laying telephone wires for landline connections in remote Himalayan villages, mobile towers are being erected in different valleys, giving coverage to a good height. Suddenly these villagers, who had never used or seen a telephone, saw a major shift in their lives and were straight into the mobile age, so much so that most children have not heard of a landline telephone at all. I was asked for my phone number by a girl at a village, which I wrote down for her. 'What is this number?' she asked, 'It looks weird.' She could not understand that it was my landline number in Mumbai. Looking seriously at me she asked, 'Don't you have mobiles in the city? We have plenty here.'

DICK ISHERWOOD

Nepal 2006

I am indebted to Elizabeth Hawley for much of the information in these notes.

The political situation in Nepal appears at the time of writing to be improving, with the Maoist rebels, who have effective control of much of the country, finally agreeing to join the more traditional politicians in an interim government prior to elections and the writing of a new constitution. Whether this will lead to real stability and a return to the good old days when one could wander freely about the outlying parts of this beautiful and engaging country remains to be seen.

On **Everest** yet another record was set with no less than 468 successful ascents in the year, all of them on the two standard routes, with the majority climbing from the north. For the first time in several years there was a successful ascent in the post-monsoon season, by a heavily equipped North American party climbing from the Nepalese side. A strong and very experienced three-man Spanish party (Alberto Inurrategi, Ferran Latorre and Juan Vallejo) made an impressive attempt on the Japanese and Hornbein Couloirs, also post-monsoon, climbing alpine style with no oxygen or Sherpa support, and reaching the top of the Hornbein Couloir at around 8500m before retreating without incident. A team led by Gheorghe Dijmarescu attempted the unclimbed ridge in the middle of the Kangshung face but were unable to get onto it from their starting point on the NE ridge.

Four parties traversed Everest in the spring, using the standard routes, two in either direction. Two of these were solo traverses – Dawa Sherpa, crossing from north to south, claimed a speed record of just over 20 hours, presumably base camp to base camp, for this new competitive activity; while Simone Moro went the other way without a permit for the Tibetan side and had to pay the police $3000 to cross the border back into Nepal.

The total number of ascents of Everest at the end of 2006 stood at 3144, according to the detailed chronicles of Elizabeth Hawley. Even when allowing for repeat ascents by Sherpas and others, the total number of individuals reaching the summit of Everest must by now comfortably exceed the combined memberships of the Alpine Club and Climbers' Club, which perhaps gives food for thought.

There were 11 deaths on Everest during the year, including three Sherpas in the Khumbu Icefall. The most widely publicized incident was the death of the Briton David Sharp at around 8500m on the North Col route; he was attempting a solo ascent, at least of the final section, and, while dying, was passed by at least 30 other people, none of whom offered significant

139. The Stremfelj–Zalokar route on the south face of Janak Chuli (7044m). (*Andrej Stremfelj*)

assistance. There has been extensive commentary on this, including notes by both Stephen Goodwin and Doug Scott in *AJ* 2006, to which there is little to add. It is difficult not to see this behaviour as a consequence of commercial mountaineering, and to be critical of at least the leaders of the various ropes, if not the paying clients, unless they actually failed to see Sharp in the poor evening light. It is, however, worth remembering that there are several instances in the history of climbing of mountaineers, some of them distinguished, abandoning *their own mates* in difficult situations. Not many of us are perfect.

A better example, also widely reported, was set by Dan Mazur, who abandoned his own attempt with two clients to assist a seriously frostbitten and hypothermic Australian down the north ridge. One hopes his reputation as a guide has been enhanced rather than diminished by this display of more traditional values.

Climbing on the Tibetan side of Everest is being complicated by preparations for the carrying of the Olympic torch up there in 2008. Peak fees are being 'temporarily' increased and there is an attempt to ensure that expedition participants have some previous mountaineering experience at or above 8000m (this requirement, applied diligently, could seriously affect the commercial expedition business). Bigger and better ladders can doubtless be expected.

The outstanding climbing achievement of 2006 in Nepal was the first winter ascent of the South Face of Lhotse by a Japanese party, assisted by a Korean team with the same objective whom they met at the base camp. This was the third attempt at a winter ascent of this famous face by parties led by Osamu Tanabe of the JAC. It was a distinctly classical ascent, using 5700m of fixed rope and 18 climbing Sherpas, though apparently no oxygen. (*See 'Lhotse South Face Winter Ascent – The Dream Comes True' on page 59.*)

Elsewhere in Nepal the long and difficult E ridge of **Annapurna I**, starting from Glacier Dome, was traversed for the third time, in alpine style and without oxygen, by a four-man party led by the Polish climber Piotr Pustelnik. Andrej Stremfelj and Rok Zalokar climbed the steep S face of **Janak Chuli** (7044m), north-east of Kangchenjunga, with one bivouac from a base camp at 5715m. The route, which Stremfelj had attempted in 2005, involved 70 degree ice and 5.6 rock. As usual, **Ama Dablam** and **Cho Oyu** had a large number of ascents. Some climbers on Cho Oyu witnessed Chinese border police shooting unarmed Tibetans crossing the Nangpa La into Nepal. Kangchenjunga, Makalu, Dhaulagiri, Lhotse and Manaslu each had several successful ascents, all by the standard routes, and a Kazakh party made a new line on the NE face of **Manaslu**. Jean-Christophe Lafaille disappeared in January 2006 during a solo attempt on **Makalu**, which would apparently have been the first winter ascent of the peak. A Japanese party made the first ascent of **Panbari (6905m)**, near Manaslu, while a French group of four attempted the unclimbed **Ganesh 7 (6550m)** in West Central Nepal but all died in an avalanche. **Merra (6344m)** in NE Nepal was climbed, apparently for the first time, by a Danish party of two.

In the Khumbu area in October, Nick Bullock and Jon Bracey climbed a difficult line on **Machermo**, also known as **Phari Lapcha West (5977m)**. The climb took two days and they abseiled back down the line. In the best traditions of British crag climbing, they named it *Snotty's Gully* in memory of the Americann Sue Nott who perished on Mount Foraker in June 2006. They subsequently abandoned an attempt on the N face of **Khonde** due to poor conditions. (*See article 'Silent Scream' on page 3.*)

A three-man British party led by Alasdair Buchanan made an attempt on the W ridge of **Cholatse (6440m)** but were forced to retreat in poor weather and bad snow conditions.

On a slightly ghoulish note, two expeditions were refused a refund of their $2000 rubbish deposits by the Nepalese Tourist Ministry on the grounds that they had left the bodies of dead team members on their peaks.

Frozen waterfall climbing has re-emerged in Nepal with two fast ascents of *Losar*, a 700m line below **Nupla (5885m)** close to Namche Bazar, by climbers working for the Khumbu Climbing School. This was first climbed by Catherine Destivelle and Erik Decamp over three days in 1994, but now is done in a day. Apparently, if you make your intentions too widely known, you are told you need a permit for such activity, even though you are not going to the top of any mountain.

LINDSAY GRIFFIN

Pakistan 2006

In the West Karakoram, Bruce Normand and Markus Walter made an attempt on 7762m **Batura II**, considered by some to be the highest unclimbed peak in the world. Approaching via the Batokshi Col (5900m) the pair reached 7000m on the S face before being stopped by deep snow. They then moved to the Chapursan valley to the north-west and explored the Yashkuk glacier, making four fine first ascents in quick succession. First they climbed **Nadin Sar** (6211m) via the NE ridge and the following day the outlying **Jehangir Sar** (5800m). After a single night at base, they set off for **Caboom Sar** (6186m), a very attractive peak directly south-east of Pamri. From a camp on the east branch of the Yashkuk they reached the summit via the SE face to the upper, corniced, E ridge. Finally, they set off for the West Yashkuk and climbed Pt 6096m via the E face. They have named this **Mamu Sar** after an old climbing colleague of Walter's, killed on Nanga Parbat in 2004.

After their climbs in Shimshal and Hispar, reported below, Lee Harrison and Peter Thompson visited the Chapursan and from the upper Lugpar Valley made the first ascent of **Ghorhil Sar** (c5800m; altimeter reading). The pair climbed the E ridge at AD+, arriving back on the glacier well after dark. Unable to find their bivouac site, they spent a cold night sitting on some rocks. At dawn they discovered it just a few hundred metres distant.

There is still plenty of opportunity for very modest first ascents throughout the Karakoram, well-exemplified by **Wulio-I-Sar** (aka Chikar Sar: 6050m), which was climbed by Bruno Collard and Mathieu Paley via the S face and E ridge at F. The peak lies above the Braldu river, five days' walk east of Shimshal, and was the first mountain that Paley had ever climbed.

Shimshal Whitehorn (6303m) has been confusing parties recently. In *AJ* 2006 we reported an attempt by the French, who were unaware that it had been climbed in 1999. In fact it was first climbed in 1986 by Paul Allison, Chris Clark, John Burslem, Paul Metcalfe and Dave Robbins. This team approached via the lower Melangutti, climbed an ice face to the W col and then more easily to the NW ridge. The ascent, in fine alpine style, was overshadowed, on the descent, by the death of Robbins. In 2006 the mountain was attempted by two different parties, both believing it to be unclimbed. Ben Cheek, Lee Harrison and Peter Thompson attempted the N ridge on three occasions, following the same line as the French in 2005. On the second attempt Cheek was hit by a rock and the three retreated, leaving just Harrison and Thompson to reach the crest on the third attempt and climb nearby Madhil Sar (c5700m). However, they failed to make much progress up the remaining section of the N ridge.

140. Sunrise from Yazghil Sar (5964m) in the Shimshal region. Left and to
the west are the Yazghil domes (7324m) and Disteghil Sar group
(7885m). On the right is the elegant pyramid of Shimshal Whitehorn
(6303m). The 2006 complete ascent climbed the steep, 750m snow/ice
face in sunlight to the upper col on the east spur, then continued up the
left flank of the NE ridge to the summit. (*Lee Harrison*)

Earlier in the season Alexandra and Mattias Robl, together with Markus
Tannheimer, made perhaps only the second complete ascent to the highest
point of Shimshal Whitehorn. The Germans warmed up with the 5366m
east summit of **Chu Kurrti Dast,** the 5700m west summit, and ascents of
both east (5730m) and west (5685m) summits of **Yeer Gattak** (aka Sunrise
Peak: the west summit has been climbed previously). The three then climbed
the steep c750m north-facing ice wall leading to the high col on the E spur
of Shimshal Whitehorn, at a point where it starts to rise to the junction
with the NE ridge (this short-cuts the line taken in 1999, which started well
to the east and reached the crest of the E spur via the N flank, before
traversing the rounded snow dome before the col). The Germans went some
200m further along the ridge than the 1999 ascensionists and reached a
point that they claim is some 30m higher and therefore the true summit.

Further south in the Hispar a Japanese team tried to make the second
ascent of the S ridge of 7852m **Kungyang Chhish** but failed low on this
difficult route. Next door, Vince Anderson and Steve House made a spirited
attempt on virgin **Kungyang Chhish East** (7400m). Climbing in alpine
style and more or less following the route attempted in 2003 by the Poles,
they made three bivouacs, reached the top of the SW face and then climbed
to 7100m on the S ridge, where they were stopped by a steep rock step that
they could not surmount.

On the opposite side of the Hispar, Kike de Pablo and Iñaki Ruiz Peribañez visited the Garumbar glacier to inspect the awesome NE face of Spantik. Unaware that there had been a previous visit to this valley they made the second ascent of **Uyumrung Sar** (c5900m), first climbed in 1994 by Brian Davison, Bill Church, Tony Parks and Dave Wilkinson via the E ridge. The Spanish also climbed the E ridge but took a more direct finish through the capping séracs.

In between their trips to Shimshal and the Chapursan, Harrison and Thompson walked up the Hispar glacier and from a base camp near the junction with the Yutmaru made the first known ascent of **Haigutum East** (5783m) in the Bal Chhish range. The pair climbed the N face to NE spur with one camp at D. They also made a lightweight attempt on the unclimbed **Khani Basi Sar** (6441m), getting as far as a 5600m col at the start of the knife-edged S ridge.

In the Panmah Muztagh, Jeff Relph and John Walsh failed on the SE ridge of Baintha Brakk (aka The Ogre, 7285m), reaching a creditable height of 6850m. This route has now seen many attempts and remains one of the great prizes of the Karakoram. Back on the Choktoi glacier the two had time to make the first ascent of a 5900m peak they called Choktoi Spire. They climbed a 600m west-facing couloir (50°) and then six pitches of excellent rock on the SE ridge (5.10 and a single tension move of A2). The route was named *Pain is Privilege*, due to Relph having his nose broken by rockfall during the descent.

The N ridge of **Latok I** (7145m) is another unclimbed prize, often attempted and dubbed the Walker Spur of the Karakoram. Two attempts were made last year, one by the Benegas brothers (their third expedition to this objective) and the other by Louis-Philippe Menard and Maxime Turgeon. Neither got very far. Menard and Turgeon also climbed four pitches up the N face, then concentrated on making the second ascent of **HAR Pinnacle** (c5600m) by a new route on the W face (600m, 5.10). They then climbed the N flank of unclimbed Pt 5500m on the E ridge of Latok III. Though they completed the climb to the summit ridge (900m, M7), they missed out the summit. They later climbed a short 5.8 on the ridge directly above base camp. The Benegas brothers had to be content with a short new rock route on **Tony Tower** (six pitches, 5.10).

Doug Chabot, Mark Richey and Steve Swenson made the first ascent of **Latok V** (6190m) climbing from the Baintha Lukpar glacier to a col between Latoks IV and V, and then up the E face to reach the crest of the S ridge. The three Americans then made the second overall but first alpine-style ascent of the S ridge of **Latok II** (7103m), the route followed by a large Italian expedition in 1977 to make the first ascent of this summit. The Americans took five days up and down to make the fourth ascent of the mountain.

On nearby **Latok III** (6949m) Alvaro Novellon and Oscar Perez made the third ascent of the SW ridge, which no doubt influenced its inclusion in the seminal book *Himalayan Alpine Style*. This was also the third ascent of the mountain, and the first in pure alpine style, from the 5300m shoulder at the foot of the ridge. The crux is a very steep rock barrier high on the mountain, giving difficulties of UIAA VI+ and A2.

There was a huge amount of activity on the Trango glacier, which in the last couple of years has become established as perhaps the world's pre-eminent alpine-rock playground. Arriving early in the season, Gabo Cmarik and Dodo Kopold made an incomplete ascent on the E face of **Hainabrakk East Tower** (c5650m). *Dolzag Dihedral* (c750m: VI/6) climbs a couloir on the left side of the face to reach the SE ridge, but the pair were thwarted 300m below the summit by a rock tower they could not cross. They then attempted the unclimbed N face of **Shipton Spire** (5885m) but retreated after 500m. The face is difficult and dangerous but on this occasion it was Cmarik's sunstroke that called a halt to the proceedings. Finally they gained success with a remarkable 54 hour, single push, round trip ascent of the N face of spectacular **Uli Biaho Tower** (6109m). Their c1900m new route, named *Drastissima*, involved hard, thin, ice climbing rated VI/6 (there were four pitches of WI 6 and two of WI 5). This route used the objectively dangerous 800m couloir, originally climbed by the Americans in 1979, to make the first ascent of the tower via the east pillar, then slanted right to climb the 1100m upper N face. The Slovaks made the fourth ascent of the Tower and one of the most impressive technical climbs in the Karakoram during 2006.

On nearby **Cat's Ears Spire** (c5550m) Micah Dash and Eric DeCaria climbed *Super Cat of the Karakoram* (c1000m: 23 pitches: VI 5.11+ R A1) to make only the second ascent of the tower. The route is a variation of the original American line, *Freebird* (VI 5.11d A1), on the SE pillar. There were several parties on the SE face of **Shipton Spire** but the main event was the second ascent, and first to the summit, of the 2001 Italian route, *Women and Chalk*. Young Austrians, Hansjörg Auer, Ambros Sailer and Thomas Scheiber climbed the route capsule style, finishing up *Ship of Fools* to the summit (an extra seven pitches above the original high point). They were unable to climb it all free or on sight, like Bubu Bole, but felt it was perhaps a little overgraded at 8a. Auer and Scheiber went on to make the first ascent of **Little Shipton** (c5400m), the triangular wall to the right (N) of Shipton Spire. Starting on the right of the E face, they reached the bounding ridge and followed this to the summit: *Winds of Change* (550m, 7a+). Other members of this Tyrol party, Matthias Auer and Karl Dung, made the second known ascent of **Trango II** (6327m). The pair climbed the huge snowy couloir on the SW flank that falls from just north of the summit to the Trango glacier close to Shipton Base Camp. At least a good part of this c1700m couloir is known to have been climbed before and is straightforward, though subject to stonefall, until near the top. At two-thirds height the Austrians slanted right through a mixed section to reach the summit (55° and M5). The original ascent was made in 1995 via the SE ridge above Trango Monk.

Slovenians were very active in this region. Andrej Grmovsek and Silvo Karo made the first ascents of **Uli Byapjun** (c4800m) and **Uli Biaho Great Spire** (5594m), which lie SE of Uli Biaho Tower. The first was climbed by the NE ridge at 6b and the second by the NE face to upper S ridge to give *Three Hundred Eggs* (600m, 6b+). The same pair added *Piranski zaliv* (650m but 800m of climbing: 7a obl. R) to the formation close to base camp known as **Base Camp Slabs**. Tina Di Batista, Tanja Grmovsek (Andrej's wife) and Aleksandra Voglar were also part of this team and made the first free ascent of Karakoram Khush on **Garda Peak** (c4700m) at 6b. The route was put up in 2004 by a team of fellow Slovenians that included Batista's partner. The three women also repeated *Oceano Trango* (300m, 6a+) a route on **Base Camp Slabs** put up earlier in the season by the Belgium team of Christophe Bingham, Sanne Bostels, Jasper de Coninck, Stijn Dekeyser, An Laenen and Hans Marien, and climbed subsequently by just about every party visiting the Trango glacier. Later the three women added two further pitches to this climb (5 and easy 6a) to reach the top of the tower, which they christened *Pinocchio* (c4700m).

Poles Maciej Ciesielski, Jakub Radziejowski and Wawrzyniec Zakrzewski added a third route, *Pretty Close* (430m of climbing: 6b), to **Sadu Peak** (c4400m), climbing the bigger SW face to the right of the previous routes. Meanwhile two other members of the expedition, Adam Pieprzycki and Marcin Szczotka, climbed a route up the centre of the SW face of the slabby tower left of Sadu Peak. It is unclear whether this formation has been climbed before, but if not the pair propose the name **Ibex Peak** (c4200m). Their route was named *Escape from the Freedom* (300m of climbing: 6b). The same Poles climbed two routes on the First Tower of the **Severance Ridge** (the SW ridge of Trango II climbed in 2005): Ciesielski, Radziejowski and Zakrzewski climbed the S face to join the original line via *Let's Go Home* (670m of climbing, 7a+ and C1 but only climbed with rest points), while Pieprzycki and Szczotka, unaware that the ridge had been climbed, repeated the original line, making variations to the first three or four pitches (700m of climbing, 7a and A0). Ciesielski, Radziejowski and Zakrzewski made the first ascent of a higher tower to the left (NW) of **Garda Peak**, which they christened **Garden Peak**. They climbed more or less up the centre of the W face to create *PIA* (540m of climbing: 6c+ and A0, the point of aid being a pendulum from a mud-filled crack). All these routes described on the lower rock towers above the glacier will make good warm-ups for more challenging goals in the Trango Group in the years to come.

High above, on 6251m **Trango Tower**, there were a number of significant ascents. Francesco Pellanda, Giovanni Quirici and Christophe Steck made the second ascent of the W pillar (Dedale/Fauquet/Piola/Schaffter, 1987, 1100m, 6c and A4). The Swiss were attempting to free the route and after a lot of work, reached the summit using aid only on pitches 13 (A4), 15 (A3) and 16 (A3). They estimate the 13th pitch would go completely free at around 8a. Grmovsek and Karo made the first one-day, alpine-style ascent of the quasi-classic *Eternal Flame* on the SE face. Starting from the foot of the face at 4am, they were back on the ground by 4am the following day, having climbed the 1000m route at 7b, A2 and M5. This was only the second alpine-style ascent of this climb to the summit (though others have completed it to the summit ridge, above which ice gear is needed). The third was made by Batista, Tanja Grmovsek and Voglar, who took a more leisurely three days, completing the route at 6c, A2 and M5. This was also the first all-female ascent of the Tower. Ales and Nejc Cesen (sons of Tomo Cesen), Matjez Jeran and Matev Kunsi climbed the tower at the same time. They spent three days making a completely free, alpine-style ascent of the neighbouring *Slovenian Route* at 7a+. The Cesen brothers and Jeran then made the second ascent of **Trango Monk** (5850m), the rock spire immediately NW of the Tower. The 450m route is graded 6b, A2 and 70° and was first climbed by other Slovenians in 2004. In addition, the Cesen brothers repeated the original *American Route* (McMahon/Wharton, 2000: 250m: 5.10+) on **Little Trango** (5450m), finding the technical difficulties to be no more than 5.9.

Moving east and a large Spanish team comprising Antonio Bayones, Oscar Cadiach, Ramon Canyellas, Elias Coll, Pilar Rossinyol, Albert Segura and Toti Vales climbed a big new rock route on the **Baltoro Cathedrals** (c5800m), a complex collection of rocky spires rising above the E bank of the lower Dunge glacier opposite the Trango Group. The new route was named *Reflexes Nocturns* (1500m: 7a). Nearby, Anne and John Arran attempted the first ascent of unnamed **Pt 5607m**, a rock peak opposite Lobsang Spire. The pair made two attempts on the NW face, on each occasion climbing 12 pitches up to British E4 6a before retreating about four pitches from the summit in bad weather.

On the opposite side of the Baltoro, a strong Russian team led by Alexander Odintsov made an attempt on the futuristic NE face of **Masherbrum (7855m)** from the Yermanendu glacier. Repeated snowfalls, and the realization that the route was just too dangerous, led to it being abandoned at 5800m. The team returned, leaving this awesome objective for a future generation. A spirited attempt was made on the W face to S ridge of **Gasherbrum IV** (7925m). Oriol Baro and Jordi Corominas first climbed to 6900m on the NW ridge for acclimatization and then climbed the big couloir right of the W face to the col on the S ridge at c7100m. This involves skirting a huge sérac that appears to threaten most of the route. They camped at 7200m but then spent the next two days sitting out bad weather before descending east to the Gasherbrum II Camp 1. From here, Corominas reached the summit of **Gasherbrum II** in a fast single push. Of the many ascents and attempts at the standard routes on the four 8000m peaks that lie above the upper Baltoro, perhaps the most notable was a Japanese ascent of **K2**: Miss Yuka Komatsu, who reached the top aged 23 years and 10 months, became the youngest female to climb the mountain, and Tatsuya Aoki, aged 21 years and 10 months, became the youngest person.

A Spanish team made a rare attempt on **Trinity Peak** (aka Tasa Peak or Tasa Burakha, c6700m). Pep Permañé and Carles Figueras Torrent climbed 1700m in alpine style up the NW ridge, which leads to the c6613m SW summit. About 300m below the top, they were forced to retreat when snow conditions deteriorated badly. The descent involved 25 rappels to the Gondogoro glacier. The route is thought to have been climbed only once before, in 1978, when it was sieged by Japanese. Together with Jordi Bosch and Ramon Estiu, these two then made an attempt on **Chogolisa** (7665m) via the 1100m-high NW face of the SW ridge. They followed a route to the right of that taken in 1986 by the British team that made the traverse of both summits. Bosch and Permañé reached 7400m on the SW ridge, a point where all the difficulties had been overcome, but it was snowing and also late, so they decided not to push on to the summit. At much the same time, a young team from Imperial College climbed a steep, 400m ice line to a col on the NW ridge, above which they made a cache on a flat section of the crest at c6000m. They hoped to return and follow the ridge to the summit, but daily snowfalls of 15cm prevented further attempts.

There seems to be surprisingly little to report from the Charakusa and Nangma valleys. Dani Ascaso, Gorka Díaz and Jonatán Larrañaga from Spain added a fourth route to the **Logmun Tower** or **Roungkhanchan III** (c4700m), climbing the elegant N pillar. They completed the route capsule style, naming it *Inshallah Mi Primo* (850m of climbing, A3 and 6a) and spending 13 days on the climb. During the ascent they found traces of previous passage but estimate that maybe 90% of their climb was new. Common ground is certainly shared with the route climbed in 2001 by Americans Brian McCray and Brenton Warren. Also in the Nangma valley were two teams hoping to make the first ascent of the much coveted N ridge of **Shingu Charpa** (5600m). The Ukrainians Igor Chaplinksy, Andrey Rodiontsev and Orest Verbitsky claimed the first ascent of this 1550m line, climbing at least 58 pitches to the top of the rock and then M5 along the difficult, corniced, summit ridge to the highest point. Later, their publicity stated the route was climbed completely free at 7a or 7a+, and the team was subsequently nominated for the Piolet d'Or. However, it now seems that aid was used, several bolts were placed for rappel anchors, and after the Piolet d'Or, Verbitsky, who did not attend the ceremony, made the announcement that he had stayed at home because the team stopped 100m below the summit and had no moral right to be among the nominees. Kelly Cordes and Josh Wharton later climbed the route (45 pitches to 5.11+ all free), starting from the base of the ridge (on their final attempt the Ukrainians missed the first third by slanting up an easy ramp/gully on the E face) but were stopped 60 vertical metres below and perhaps 150m horizontal from the summit because of inadequate ice gear. Had they known the route to be unclimbed, they would probably have pushed on, but the motivation was not there and they bailed. The N ridge of Shingu Charpa remains unclimbed.

JOHN TOWN

China & Tibet 2006

Qonglai

The rock walls of the Siguniang National Park continued their popularity. Cosmin Andron, from Romania, and Wai Wah Yip, from Hong Kong, made the first ascent of the SW face of the **Fourth Sister of Siguniang Shan** in June 2005. Canadians Katy Holm, Aidan Oloman and Katherine Fraser visited the Changping Goa valley in the same year, making the first ascents of **Chiwen (5250m)** and **Chibu (5466m)**. Cosmin Andron returned with American Bob Keaty to make the first ascent of **Banji North (c5400m)** on 28 January 2006 via the north face. Dates appearing below refer to 2006 unless otherwise stated.

The following October, Americans Ben Clark and Josh Butson also visited the Changping valley, making the first ascent of **'The Falcon' (c5500m)**. Chad Kellogg and Joseph Puryear visited the same area in April 2007 making the first ascent of **'Lara Shan' (c5700m)** via the steeply glaciated W face.

A French Alpine Club expedition made the first ascent of **Siguniang North (5700m)** from the north, reaching the summit on 1 November.

Daxue Shan

After many attempts in recent years, the British/New Zealand team of Malcolm Bass and Pat Deavoll made the first ascent of **Haizi Shan (5833m)** in October via a route on the N face direct to the summit. (*See article 'Haizi Shan ~ A lot to be grateful for', page 40.*)

Shaluli Shan

An American-Canadian party visited the remote Genyen area of Western Sichuan. Dave Anderson and Sarah Hueniken made the first ascent on 20 October of **Shachun (5965m)**, a spectacular granite spire. Molly Loomis and Andy Tyson made the first ascent the next day of **Phurpa (c5600m).**

In the same region, the well-known American climber Charlie Fowler and his companion Christine Boskoff died in an avalanche in November above the Lengu Monastery.

In October 2005, a Japanese team led by Shigeru Akoi visited the Tsonatou Tso area of the Shaluli Shan, north of the Genyen massif and south of the Tibet-Sichuan Highway. In a short visit they made the first ascent of **Peak 5160m** and observed the highest peak (unnamed, 5870m) and the second highest, Xiangqiuqieke (5863m).

Nyainqentanglha East

In April 2007 Mick Fowler returned to the Kajaqiao area with Paul Ramsden to make the first ascent of the striking **Manamcho (6264m)** in an eight-day push. Steve Burns and Ian Cartwright made the first ascent of neighbouring **Point 5935m**.

NyainqentanglhaWest

Christian Hass of Austria, who had made a number of first ascents in 2000 in the southern half of the chain, returned in October 2005. From the valley immediately south-west of the main Nyainqentanglha massif, together with Erich Gatt and Gerhard Grindl, he made the first known ascent of **Pajan Zhari (6221m)** on 1 October via the W ridge. The group also climbed **'Gompa Garpo Ri' (6232m)** which lies directly to the north- west. On 16 October Haas made a solo ascent of **Qungmo Kangri (7048m)** via the first ascent route on the S ridge and of **Qungmo Kangri WSW (6116m)**.

Kun Lun

Between 9 September and 7 October 2005 the Russians Boris Malakhov, Paul Demeshchik, Otto Chkhetiani, Michael Bertov and Sergey Zajko made an impressive unsupported north-east to south-west crossing of the western Kun Lun. They passed near the active Achik Shan volcano and the remote peak of Aksai Chin (7167m) as well as attempting Peak 6903m.

Himalaya

Marko Prezelj and Boris Lorencic made an impressive new route on the north-west pillar of **Chomo Lhari (7350m)** in a six-day round trip. At the same time, Rok Blagus, Tine Cuder, Matej Kladnik and Samo Krmelj climbed a steep couloir on the left side of the N face reaching the summit on 14 October. Team members also made an ascent of **Jangmo Gopsha (6706m)** which lies just to the east.

In the Cho Oyu area, the Catalan Jordi Tosas made a new route on the S face of **Palung Ri (7100m)**, climbing solo.

In April 2007 Slovakians Marek Hudak and Josef Kopold attempted the British route on the S face of **Shishapangma (8013m)**. Kopold reached the summit but Hudak, who had turned back earlier, disappeared on the descent.

Karakoram

A nine-man German-Swiss expedition made the first ascent of **Gasherbrum II East (7772m)** from the rarely visited Chinese side via the East Nakpo glacier. Cedric Hahlen, Hans Mitterer and Ueli Steck reached the summit on 10 July.

Tien Shan
Pik Voennykh (Military) Topografov (6873m)
In common with Pogrebetsky, this now lies wholly in China due to the boundary change highlighted in AJ111. From 10-19 August a Moscow team led by A Dzhuluy made the first ascent of its striking S ridge. In the CIS alpinism championships the ascent was assigned the grade 5B and awarded 3rd place, although the ascensionists report it as more like 6A. The team approached the mountain from Aksu in China.

On 15 August 2005 Isao Fukura, Hiroyuki Katsuki and Koichiro Takahashi of Japan made the first ascent of **Karlik (Harlik Shan) (4886m)**, which lies 70km north-east of the town of Hami.

Pamirs
Muztagh Ata and surrounding summits saw a burst of mostly Russian activity in 2005. **Koskulak (7028m)** received its first ascent on 10 August via the W ridge by Leonid Fishkis, Dmitry Komarov and Alexandr Novik, and its second ascent two days later by seven climbers from the Moscow Aviation Institute. Valery Shamalo and Alexei Gorbalenkov then made the third ascent via the N face from the Kalaxong glacier, a route which is capped by a horrendous sérac wall. This pair then made an ascent of **Muztagh Ata (7546m)** via the unclimbed S ridge, reaching the summit on 24 August. They were followed by Kazuya Hiraide and Kei Taniguchi of Japan who completed the second ascent of the same route on 5 September.

Kalaxong (7277m) is the south peak of Muztagh Ata, which was probably climbed at an early stage via a diversion from the first ascent route on the main peak. Its S ridge was climbed for the first time on 4 September by Dmitry Chijik, Vladimir Kagan and Petr Yudin of Alexandr Lebedev's expedition.

Russian activity continued in 2006 when Ivan Dusharin, Elena Lebedeva, Lev Ioffe (USA) and Alexander Novik made the first ascent of **Kokodak (7210m)** on 10 July.

MARK WATSON

New Zealand 2006-2007

This report covers the period from April 2006 to April 2007. The alpine grades are based on the Mt Cook system, and the rock grades on the Ewbank system.

Darran Mountains
The alpine and rock climbing region of the Darran Mountains (Fiordland) continues to be the area of New Zealand that is generating the most climbing news and new routes of note. In late 2006 the New Zealand Alpine Club published Craig Jefferies' new guidebook to the Darrans. The guidebook's 312 pages capture more than a decade's worth of new route activity since the last edition, as well as revealing the enormous scope for new climbs that this region still provides.

A Hillary Expedition grant from the Government organisation SPARC enabled a group of (mostly young) and highly motivated individuals to make some major first ascents this summer. The 'Rock Solid Progression' team of Derek Thatcher, Mayan Smith-Gobat, Kester Brown, Craig Jefferies and Paul Rogers pooled their talents to make the first free ascent of *Shadowlands* (27) on the remote Sinbad Gully headwall, near Mitre Peak. This sustained 300m route has multiple pitches of hard climbing, including three of 27 and two of 26. Following this, they helicoptered onto the Ngapunatoru ice plateau and rappelled into the isolated 1300m Kaipo Wall, adding the first new route since the 1974 first ascent. The team rapped to a shelf at the base of the upper wall, placing bolt belays, and then Thatcher and Smith-Gobat climbed back out via 11 pitches of varied and often difficult and committing climbing up to grade 25.

At the beginning of their summer Darrans stint, Thatcher and Smith-Gobat teamed up with 2006 CMC/Macpac Mountaineer of the Year Jonathon Clearwater for a quick and inspired first ascent on the NW face of an iconic Darrans mountain – Sabre Peak (2162m). *Tora Tora Tora* (24) takes a direct line up the face right of the *Original Line* and was established on-sight, ground up and with no fixed protection. It is the first new route on the face in over 20 years.

Closer to the Darrans climbing base, Homer Hut, a four-pitch project on the Mate's Little Brother was completed to make the hardest alpine free climb in the Darrans: *Armageddon* (21, 28, 28, 25). This powerful route climbs directly through the *Second Coming* roofs and was redpointed by Derek Thatcher and Stefan Hadfield. The Barrier Face (Gertrude valley) had a new five-pitch line established 200m right of *Joker* by Al Ritchie and

141. Mayan Smith-Gobat on *Shadowlands* (27), Sinbad Gully headwall, Fiordland, during the first free ascent. (*Craig Jefferies*)

Sam Bossard. *Scrabble* (18, 18, 20, 18, 22) was bolted and climbed over several days. Late March saw two new routes added to the NE face of Barrier Knob by Mark Watson and Kristen Foley. *Utu* (25, 22, 24) is the hardest line on Barrier Knob and features intricate slab and face climbing while *Forgotten Silver* (16, 18, 20) climbs a sweep of nicely featured rock. Both routes were bolted and climbed over four days.

New route activity continues at Babylon, with the pace driven by Bruce Dowrick and Jon Sedon. Attention has recently turned to the reportedly Arapiles-like Little Babylon – a very promising cave above Babylon and a number of routes have been added here already. Watch this space.

Queenstown

Winter in the Queenstown region saw the exploration of Cigar Creek in the Eyre Mountains as an ice-climbing venue. A few new routes were established. Rupert Gardiner and Johnny Davison made the first ascents of *Kapa O Panga* (WI5) and the *Cold Light of Day* (WI4+) – the latter reportedly fell off soon after being climbed! Andy Mills and Davison climbed *Balloons and Knives* (WI4), with Mills taking a huge whipper off the top of the route, narrowly missing the ground. A classic 60m moderate was also climbed, *Divine Symmetry* (WI3) and *Hybrid* (WI3+) by Dave Bolger. In great early season conditions Rupert Gardiner and Dave Bolger climbed a new route on the SE face of Double Cone, Remarkables. The route follows mixed terrain and is called *Warthog*. A new route was also done in the South Wye valley, *Bush Lawyer* (WI4), by Adrian Camm and Mal Haskins.

Barron Saddle – Mt Brewster Region

With plums still to be picked, this extensive and remote mountain tract between the Aoraki Mt Cook and Mt Aspiring areas has seen continued activity from a motivated few. Guidebook author Ross Cullen teamed up with Nick Shearer to make the first ascent of the E ridge of Mt Hiwiroa (2281m), a seven-hour scramble. Paul Hersey's name regularly pops up in NZ Climber magazine, and in the past year he and partners have climbed a number of notable first ascents. During winter, with Mat Woods he climbed *The Grr Room* on Peak 2200m, four pitches with a crux of WI4. Also during winter Kester Brown and Jono Clarke climbed a very obvious thin waterfall flow at the head of the North Temple valley, *Temple of Doom* (M6/WI4). New ice routes were also climbed in Bush Stream, off the Aoraki Mt Cook highway.

Hersey's name pops up again, this time with Graham Zimmermann. The pair made a first ascent on the S face of Taiaha Peak. The classic-looking line, *I've Found Cod*, is 500m, 4+/WI3. In February 2007 Hersey and Danny Baille headed into the Ahuriri and climbed a 700m new route on the S face of Mt Huxley. *Hey I Ordered a Cheeseburger* (4 –/16) followed rock most of the way with a mixed section at the top. The same pair also made the first ascent of the E face of Peak 2237m in the west branch of the South Temple valley, a 400-500m rock route with a crux of 14 (3+ overall). On Glen Lyon, at the entrance to the Hopkins valley, Hersey with Mat Woods climbed *Vote For Hillary*, a six-pitch 15. Glen Lyon now has a number of multi-pitch rock routes on its flanks.

Aoraki Mount Cook and Westland

The Aoraki Mt Cook region has been particularly quiet in terms of new-route activity and ascents of the harder routes, suggesting that there are fewer people heading into the mountains for hard climbing, or that they are directing their focus elsewhere. Perhaps it's to the Westland névés as this region is seeing increased activity and busier huts. The popularity is due in part perhaps to the relative ease of access to climbs once based at a hut, and the scope for technical and mixed climbs.

Winter at Aoraki Mt Cook saw an ascent of the E face of Mt Sefton (3151m) by Andrew Rennie, Jon Loeffer and Graham Zimmermann, via the *Direct* route. During August a new mixed route was climbed on the SW face of Conway Peak (2899m). *Life in the Fridge* was climbed by Allan Uren and Johnny Davison and graded 4. Later in the season on Conway Peak (2899m), Allan Uren completed his project *The Vision* with the first ascent of this grade 6+/A1 mixed project. The route had thwarted previous attempts due to marginal climbing and a scarcity of protection. Uren finally succumbed and placed two bolts at the crux on lead – and in the process may have pointed the way for future ascents in the region with bolt protection. In contrast to this style of ascent Uren then climbed a long and sinuous mixed route, named *The Mutant* (6+) on the W face of Mt Lendenfeld (3194m) in December with Julian White and Tim Robinson. Uren said 'the lower five pitches contain some of the most sustained and difficult climbing I've done up there, and some of the most aesthetic.'

Canterbury climber Guy McKinnon has once again been showing his drive for daring solo ascents with his first ascent of the 1400m N face of Hochstetter Dome (2827m) in September. This face was one of New Zealand's largest remaining unclimbed faces. In January 2007 he picked off an oft-looked-at line, an 800m buttress on Mt Whataroa (1988m) – visible from the West Coast highway. It's great to see the adventurous spirit of first ascents in the New Zealand mountains retained with McKinnon's style. Back over the Divide, Daniel Joll and Steven Barratt climbed a new route on Nun's Veil in the Liebig Range (east Tasman Valley). *Curb Your Enthusiasm* (4+) takes a line up the SE buttress.

Canterbury

A couple of new alpine routes were climbed in the Canterbury mountains in the past year. Guy McKinnon, alone again, climbed a new 350m route on the E face of Mt Evans (2620m). Mt Franklin (2145m), in Arthur's Pass National Park was climbed via a new route up the SE face by Don French and James Wright. The eight-pitch route is graded 5–.

142. *The Mutant* (6+) on the west face of Lendenfeld. Allan Uren, Julian White and Tim Robertson, December 2006. (*By courtesy of Adventure Consultants*)

Central North Island

Richard Thomson's new guidebook to Tongariro National Park may have kicked off some fresh enthusiasm, or maybe it was the good early season conditions; either way, some great looking ice and mixed routes were climbed last winter. In the Mangaturuturu Cirque Kester Brown and Jono Clarke climbed *Free Radicals* (WI5), *The Glass Spider* (M4), *Pope's Pillar* (WI5) and *Strung Out* (WI5). On Puggy's Buttress, on the SW face of Matiaho, Clarke climbed *Scratch and Win* (M5).

ERIK MONASTERIO

Bolivia 2006

Thanks are due to the following contributors to these notes: Lindsay Griffin, John Biggar, Nick Flyvbjerg, Juliette Géhard, Arnaud Guillaume, Moira Herring, Alain Mesili, Charlie Netherton and Katsutaka Yokoyama.

Favourable weather conditions arrived early in the 2006 season with a premature end to the austral summer monsoon. As usual, most climbing activity was on the normal routes on Huayna Potosi, Illimani and Condoriri, but it was gratifying to see more trekking and climbing activity in the northern Cordillera Real, which has been quite neglected in recent years. Glacier conditions on the approaches to the western routes of Ancohuma and Illampu were by far the best seen over the past 10 years, as there were few crevasses and penitents, but the overall trend is still for rapid glacial recession. Unseasonably early snowfall arrived later in the season, substantially increasing the avalanche risk. Local guides say the climbing season is moving earlier each year. In 2005 the weather was almost continuously bad throughout September.

The political situation is always important when it comes to planning a trip to Bolivia's Cordillera. The February 2006 democratic elections were unprecedented in terms of voter turnout, and for the first time elected as president an indigenous leader from a non-traditional party. Evo Morales won by a clear majority and formed a government with strong ideological affiliations to Venezuela and Cuba, rejecting US influence. This brought initial stability to the nation and the political demonstrations and strikes that in previous years paralysed the nation were not a problem during the May-September climbing season. Unfortunately political tensions have once again resurfaced and a struggle for autonomy in the Eastern Provinces may well lead to serious unrest in the years to come. Despite the political and social stability during the climbing season, visitor numbers were below those seen in previous years. This may well have been due to the often misleading press coverage given to Morales' government.

CORDILLERA REAL
Southern Real
In June, Japanese climbers Fumitaka Ichimura, Yuki Satoh, Tatsuro Yamada and Katsutaka Yokoyama established four impressive new routes on the S face of **Illimani**, the highest peak of the Cordillera Real. They made a base camp at Mesa Khala (4700m), the site of an old mine, below

the S face. On 14 June Satoh and Yamada climbed one of several obvious ice streaks left of the big central (and sérac-threatened) depression on the S face. This gave eight technical pitches up to WI 4+ to the upper snow slopes left of the séracs. A further 500m led to the straightforward upper SW ridge, by which the pair gained the **South (Main) Summit (6439m)**. The new route, christened *Phajsi Face* (Moon Face in Aymara), has 1200m of height gain and is TD+. The pair descended via the W ridge. On 22nd they added *Inti Face* (Sun Face: TD+) up the parallel ice runnel immediately left. This gave six technical pitches of WI 5 that were steeper and of better quality than those of the previous route. After 600m the pair joined *Phajsi Face* on the upper snow field and rappelled. Yamada notes that they named the two routes after the sun and moon, because like those objects, their spirits rose with the adventures.

On 22 June Ichimura and Yokoyama added *Puerta del Sol* (1200m ED1 WI5R and M5) L of the two previous lines. From c5200m they climbed a relatively straightforward 300m gully to the base of the first large rock wall. This was split by a thin goulotte, which the two climbed in the dark via thin ice pitches to gain the crux headwall. The headwall proved very steep with a thin runnel of ice that petered out, producing run-out climbing with dry tooling up to M5. The pair continued up the slopes above to the summit. They descended the same way, experiencing rockfall low on the descent. Ichimura and Yokoyama also climbed a hard new line on the S face of **Pico Layca Khollu (6159m)** well right of Illimani's main S face. Layca Khollu is the furthest SE of Illimani's summits and was originally named Pico de Paris. The two began climbing on 14 June, negotiating the lower 500m before dawn. This proved mostly straightforward but poorly protected. The headwall above was vertical and appeared quite loose but was split by a beautiful thin ice runnel. The 13th pitch proved the crux at WI5, with thin and fragile ice bulges, giving taxing climbing due to the altitude (above 6000m). The new route was named *Acalanto* (950m; ED1 WI5R). From the summit Ichimura and Yokoyama descended east to gain the glacier that flows south-east (the descent route from the N–S five peaks traverse). They walked down this to 5600m and made four rappels down the west flank to regain their base camp.

Central Real

New Zealand-based climbers Nick Flyvbjerg and Erik Monasterio visited the Chekapa Valley east of the Negruni and north of the Condoriri massifs. These mountains are sometimes referred to as the **Chekapa (Chikapa)** or Lico Group. The pair approached via a six-hour jeep ride along the road to Laguna Jankho Khota and then over the Mollo Pass (5100m) to Mina Fabulosa. Monasterio had climbed in the region 10 years earlier and was staggered by the amount of glacial recession.

On 26 July the pair climbed a new route on **Cerro Choque Santuro (5160m)**. They made a straightforward crossing of the Chekapa Jahuira river and climbed south up the opposite side to the base of the peak. The 350m route started up a rocky vegetated gully on the right side of the N face. Three 60m 5+ pitches led to easier ground on the NW ridge/face and another 5+ pitch on the summit obelisk. It is not clear whether this summit had been reached previously. After this ascent, on 28 July, the pair climbed a central gully on **Cerro Chekapa West (5418m)** to reach the NNW face at c5100m. Above, the climbing, at first grade 4, became increasingly difficult and loose. The pair roped for three final elegant pitches to the summit (6a max). Although these two routes were certainly new, Rudi Knott's 1969 Bavarian expedition made the first ascents of seven summits in this group of peaks. Later, Flyvbjerg and Monasterio followed the main valley south to its head (along a pre-Hispanic stone trail), crossed the c5100m pass west of Cerro Chekapa West and descended to the Palcoco mine and the altiplano.

On 19-20 May, Denis Levaillant and Alain Mesili climbed the east pillar of the south summit of **Chearoco (6127m or 6014m)**. This is possibly the first route on the vast E face of this remote triple-summited massif southeast of Illampu and Ancohuma. The 550m pillar gave difficulties of 5+ on good granite, with sections of mixed at 75° (M5) and some 80° ice. From the top, 150m of narrow ridge, with unconsolidated snow, dramatic cornices and no worthwhile protection, led to the summit. The pair climbed the TD+ route from a camp at 5200m, three hours' walk from the face.

Northern Real

Three new routes were added to the SW face of **Pico Schulze (5943m)**, the fine fluted snow and ice pyramid north-west of Illampu (6368m). In July Catalans Pau Gomez, Faust Punsola and David Sanabria climbed a new route on the right side of the face leading to the 5850m col between Schulze and Huayna Illampu. Starting on 22nd from Laguna Glaciar (5038m) southwest of the mountain, they did not continue to the summit but descended the far side of the col and made their way north down to Aguas Calientes. Their 400m route was rated TD+ WI 5– M5. A little later, a French Alpine Club expedition based themselves at Laguna Glaciar. On 11 August Perrine 'Perrinou' Marceron and Elisabeth Revol with Arnaud Guillaume climbed the couloir immediately left of the 1973 *Original Route* to gain the upper NW ridge. The 11-pitch route lies immediately right of a prominent spur on the left side of the face. It has approximately 550m of height gain and was graded TD– (80° and F4+). Four days later Toni Clarasso with Perrine Marceron and Juliette Géhard climbed the 550m couloir on the left flank of the spur. They found it straightforward apart from unstable snow at its top, and graded it D+.

The French party also put up two routes on Punta 5505m, a subsidiary summit of Schulze. The climbs took two parallel ice smears that flow from the left edge of a large sérac barrier through the rock below. Above the hanging glacier, gentle slopes led to a steeper snow face and the summit.

143. Laguna Glaciar with the locations of *Long Laguna Glaciar* and *Fly the Crack* on Pico Gotico (*centre right*), and of the Flyvbjerg-Monasterio route on Rumi Mallku (*far right*). The snow dome behind is Ancohuma. (*Erik Monasterio*)

The right smear was continuous and more pronounced, and was climbed on 9 August by Guillaume, Marceron and Revol (200m: WI 4+ M4). The left smear led to a shoulder before angling right through rocky terrain to the glacier. This was climbed on the 18th by Clarasso and Perrine Favier (200m: WI 4+ M5 F3c).

Late in the season, on 5 October, Thibaut Tournier and Muriel Zucchini made a rare ascent of the ESE ridge (c750m and probably TD) of **Pico del Norte (6070m)**, first climbed in 1972 by Roger Scull and Dave Steel. In 2004, thinking this ridge to be unclimbed, Mike Brown and Erik Monasterio climbed four pitches before they deemed further progress suicidal due to seriously unstable granite blocks. It seems likely that the more snowy October conditions are better suited to this route.

On 5 August Flyvbjerg and Monasterio made the first ascent of the NW face of **Punta c5982m**, a striking rock peak south-west of Ancohuma above Laguna Glaciar. Starting from a camp at 5500m, the pair climbed unroped up the loose lower walls to reach the start of a compact gully at 5850m. Two steep pitches on sound granite (6a+) led to unstable blocks and the summit. The pair thought they were making the first ascent of the peak but later discovered it had been climbed in May 2006 by a team headed by Bolivian guides José Callisaya and Gonzalo Jaimes. The team had split into two parties and climbed the easy W and NE ridges, meeting on the summit and walking down the S face. As the two ridges look like the outstretched wings of a condor, the peak was christened **Rumi Mallku** (Condor of Stone).

On 7-8 August Flyvbjerg and Monasterio added a third route to the 500m W face of **Pico Gotico (5750m)**. This monolithic rock peak west of Ancohuma was named after the shape of its N and S ridges, which resemble the incomplete arches of Gothic cathedrals. Monasterio had made the first ascent in 1998 via *Long Laguna Glaciar* (6c A2) on the right side of the face and had returned in 2002 to climb *Via del Arco* (6c and A2) on the left side. Flyvbjerg and Monasterio started 100m right of *Long Laguna Glaciar*, creating a more direct start to that route via marginally protected 6b+ climbing over resonant blocks. After discovering two bolt belays, the pair reached the original crux of *Long Laguna Glaciar*. Flyvbjerg led a free ascent at 6c, taking three hours to climb the 50m four-centimetre-wide crack, with two off-width sections, over a succession of roofs. The pitch had three in-situ bolts but also required a comprehensive rack. The upper face appears to have suffered rockfall and four more pitches (6b max), first right then left of the original route, led to the top of the face and a foresummit at 5600m, from which the pair descended (a boulder ridge leads to the main summit). *Fly the Crack* (6c) took 14 hours.

Controversy and confusion has surrounded the attempted second ascent of the *Long Laguna Glaciar* route by Spanish climber Cecilia Buil and the Australian guide, Jeff Sandifort in 2000. The pair terminated their ascent at the top of the crux pitch. In 2001 during a visit to the region, Monasterio received information that his route had been bolted during the attempted repeat. A flurry of email communication between Buil and Monasterio failed to clarify the issue, as Buil steadfastly denied placing bolts on the crux pitch. However, following the recent ascent of Pico Gotico, Monasterio can confirm that a significant breach of climbing ethics did take place: a total of five bolts were found along the route, three of which were at key points of the crux pitch. Sandifort and Buil had information and a topo of the route prior to their attempted ascent, and local porters who provided support to the Buil team confirmed that a drill was taken up the route. For Monasterio, whose country this is, the use of drilled equipment on high mountain terrain is definitely taboo and he champions an ethic that attempts to preserve a traditional spirit of adventure in Bolivia's high mountains (as opposed to low-altitude rock walls). It is regrettable that such practices occur at all, but it is of particular concern that when they do it can take such a long time to clarify the facts.

On 17 August Monasterio and Flyvbjerg attempted the last unclimbed east pillar of Illampu. They encountered bottomless powder snow and a gaping rimaye at 6100m. Avalanche risk on the summit ridge looked to be severe, so the pair diverted their attention to **Aguja Yacuma (6030m)** an elegant pinnacle of graniodiorite at the north end of the Illampu Massif, just above the Mesili-Sanchez col. They climbed a new four-pitch route (6b max) on the ENE face up the main corner to the sharp summit: a three-star classic involving technical face climbing, overhung jam cracks, twin cracks and corner systems. In 2004 Monasterio and Mike Brown had put up *Ojo de la Aguja* (6b) just left on the E face. There is room for other routes on this flank. Two days previously, on 15 August, Perrine Favier, Arnaud Guillaume and Elizabeth Revel approached from the west side via the Huayna Illampu glacier and made a difficult (TD) S–N traverse of the Aguja, descending before reaching the lower rocky crest on which the pinnacle stands. It is not clear whether this traverse has been completed before, though the Aguja has certainly been climbed from the north and north-west.

In late August the New Zealand pair added a second route to the steep slabs of the E face of **PK 24 (Peak 24th September)** aka Punta Badile, but became probably the first party to climb this face in its entirety from the ground up. From a camp at c5000m the two reached the foot of the SE pillar taken by the 1994 Lehmpfuhl/Rauch/Schöffel route, *Don't take the Long Way Home* (c650m, 6b). Here they climbed the gully to the right, which slants up to the mahogany-coloured granite wall that forms the upper section of the E face. Three pitches of 4+ and 5+ led to the big terrace below the wall. From here six pitches of chimneys, cracks and corners at sustained 6a to 6b+ led to the summit ridge. Three long rappels took the team back to the terrace. The route, which took 14 hours to complete, required a full rack and an assortment of pegs.

NORTHERN CORDILLERA APOLOBAMBA

Climbing on equal terms with Bolivian guide, Pedro Quispe, in early September Charlie Netherton attempted an integral traverse of the **Palomani Tranca** Group. They approached this rarely visited area from Paso de Pelechuco with porters, hoping to establish a base camp at Laguna Chucuyo Grande. They were dropped short of this and later discovered that a mining road runs from Apacheta Pampa to a point only an hour from their camp. Above the camp they climbed at III and WI 3 to the snout of the glacier south-west of the group. From here they climbed a loose rocky peak to the left that they felt was the furthest south of the group. Next day, they continued up the glacier to the SE ridge of previously unclimbed **Palomani Sur** (c5500m-5600m), which they traversed at II-III with one rappel. They continued north to the first of three similar-altitude summits of **Palomani Tranca Central**, and beyond as far as a foresummit of Palomani Tranca Main (5638m), before escaping the ridge and heading south-east back to base camp. They rated their outing Alpine D.

CORDILLERA QUIMSA CRUZ

The British party of Alan Dickinson, Sam Hawkins, Moira Herring, Ronan Kavanagh and Tom Stedall made a rare visit to the east side of the southern Cordillera Quimsa Cruz, approaching via Viloco and the c5200m Salvadora Pass to a base camp below Nevado San Lorenzo. After reaching a high bivouac on 16 July at 4800m, Dickinson, Hawkins and Stedall made an ascent of **Pyramidal Peak (5508m GPS)**, the summit marked as San Lorenzo on the Bolivian IGM map, via the W ridge at PD–, finding signs of previous visits. On 22 July, Herring and Kavanagh repeated this ascent intending to continue south-east to the true summit of **San Lorenzo (5560m)**, but were repelled by the steep and extremely loose descent to the first col.

Starting on 16 July, Herring and Kavanagh ascended the narrow Cumbre Ventisquero (glacier) south of their base camp to the col at its head (c5400m). From here they turned left (east) to easy summit 5460m and continued east to dome-shaped top 5550m, struggling through penitentes the size of dinner plates. From the same col, on the 19th, Dickinson and Hawkins climbed the SE flank of **Atoroma (5560m)** on somewhat stable rock at PD. Later Herring and Kavanagh scrambled up peak 5112m immediately west of base camp, and Dickinson and Hawkins climbed **San Lorenzo** (5560m GPS) via the SE glacier (PD-).

In the Northern Quimsa Cruz, previously unreported from 2005, was a new rock route on the north pillar of the **Gross Mauer (c4900m)** in the Taruca Umana Valley. The pillar was climbed by the French guide Emannuel Ratouis with C Aguil and Jean-Claude Razel to give *Un Train Enfer;* 200m and six pitches of magnificent granite at 6b+. They climbed the route with bolts at the belays and one or two per pitch, plus natural gear.

ADE MILLER

North America 2006

The Area Notes for North America would not have been possible without the help of the American Alpine Journal (AAJ) and Kelly Cordes, who provided the original background material upon which these notes are based. These notes cover the highlights and major ascents. For a complete report of all activity in North America, the reader is referred to the current editions of the AAJ and Canadian Alpine Journal.

ALASKA

The very warm conditions that affected the Denali Park during the 2005 season were not repeated this year, as the firn line remained below Kahiltna Base Camp. Fewer climbers visited the park; however, there were still several notable new routes climbed within the park.

Maxime Turgeon from Quebec completed two new routes. On **Denali** he and Louis-Philippe Ménard climbed *The Canadian Direct* (8000', AK 6, 5.9 M6 AI4), an 8000' line on the S face between the *Japanese Direct* (Kimura-Watanabe-Tsuneto-Yamaura-Senda 1977) and the *American Direct* (Eberl-Thompson-Laba-Seidman 1967).

On **Mount Foraker,** Turgeon – this time with Will Mayo – climbed 5200' of new ground to join the *French Ridge* (Agresti-Bouquier-Créton-Galmiche-Thiverge-Landry 1976). This new route, the *McNeill-Nott Memorial* (5200', WI5+ M6R A0), is named for Karen McNeill and Sue Nott who were lost on Foraker in the same season. Barely 20 minutes after Turgeon and Mayo had left the base of the route, a large section of the middle of the face collapsed making a repeat all but impossible.

Masatoshi Kuriaki of Japan completed the first winter ascent of **Mount Foraker** after 39 days on the mountain. With temperatures of minus 50°F, with 20-30 knot winds (resulting in a wind chill of almost minus 100°F), Kuriaki only spent 10 minutes on the summit. Success on Foraker puts him one step closer to his goal of summiting in winter all three of the highest summits in Alaska: he soloed Denali in 1998 and attempted Hunter on several occasions.

Mount Huntingdon was also the scene of significant winter activity as Colin Hayley and Jed Brown made its first winter ascent via the *West Face Couloir* (Nettle-Quirk 1989). The pair also completed the ascent in what is probably a record time of 15 hours camp to camp.

144. The McNeill-Nott Memorial route on Mt Foraker (Turgeon-Mayo 2006).
(*Maxime Turgeon*)

In the Ruth Gorge, Mark Westman and Eamonn Walsh returned to
Mount Grosvenor to establish *The Warrior's Way* (4400', V AI4 M5R A0)
on the E face. The pair spotted the line the previous season but poor weather
prevented an attempt. This time the weather cooperated, thus allowing the
team to make a round-trip ascent in 19½ hours. The pair also made the
third ascent of *The Escalator* (Shaw-Wagner, 2000) on **Mount Johnson**
during the same trip.

The pair returned to the Ruth Gorge later in the same season to **Broken
Tooth** and attempted the E couloir, commonly referred to as the *Root Canal*.
Their attempt was halted on the summit ridge 150ft below the summit by a
gendarme. 'Significant failures' of this type, where all the technical ground
was covered, are common in Alaska and are sometimes treated as new
routes and named. In this case, Westman and Walsh's goal was the summit
and they left the line (1006m, V AI5+R M6) unnamed for the first true
ascensionists.

Also on Broken Tooth, Fumitaka Ichimura, Tatsuro Yamada, Yuki Satoh
and Katsutaka Yokoyama, the 'Giri-Giri Boys' completed *Before the Dawn*
(1000m, AK 5 5.9 WI4+ M6). Their line follows obvious snow and ice
systems in the centre of the N face. The party also made unsuccessful
attempts on the E faces of the **Moose's Tooth** and **Bear Tooth**.

Colin Hayley and Jed Brown climbed a new line on the N face of **Mount Moffit**. *The Entropy Wall* (1500m, VI 5.9 A2, WI4+) takes a line up the centre of the face. This was one of the largest unclimbed faces in North America. The pair also made the first ascent of **Abercrombie Mountain's** *Southwest Face* (1480m, WI4- 5.4), another unclimbed face near Valdez, and Hayley and Brown's third major contribution to Alaskan climbing in 2006.

CANADA

Like the Denali Park, the Kluane National Park and Reserve saw a decline in numbers this year, most parties being focused, as usual, on **Mount Logan**. The most notable ascent was that of **South Walsh** by Graham Rowbotham and Paul Knott. Prior to their climb, this was the highest unclimbed peak in the St Elias range and quite possibly North America. The pair traversed from South Walsh to **Mount Walsh** via **Pt 4227m** (also unclimbed) before descending the W ridge. Rowbotham and Knott also made the first ascent of **Jekden South** (*see 'The Ascent of South Walsh', page 47*).

As usual the focus of Coast Range climbing was the Waddington Range. The ubiquitous Don Serl and Simon Richardson kicked off the proceedings with a new line on the E face of **Remote Mountain** during their visit in mid-May. In July, Benoît Montfort and four other French climbers flew to the Waddington-Combatant col and established two new routes on **Mount Combatant**, one of which featured climbing to 5.11c.

In August Ade Miller and Simeon Warner had a productive trip to the Radiant glacier where they made the first complete ascent of the *Buszowski-Kippan route* (Buszowski-Kippan 1981) to the main summit of **Serra 3**. The pair also climbed a new, narrow couloir line on **Mount Shand**, *The Madness of "King" George* (250m, WI3), and completed the previously tried 200m *Southwest Ridge* on **Unicorn Mountain**. Tom Gray, Seth Hobby, and Ian Wolfe also visited the area and added a new unnamed line (D 5.9 A1) on the S face of **Tellot Spire Number One** between the *Central Dihedral* (Glick-Hironen-Richardson 1998) and the *Fabische-Waters* (Fabische-Waters 1987).

The Bugaboos was the scene of significant activity with new routes being added, as well as some other major lines being freed. On **North Howser Tower** Ulysse Richard and Manuel Quiroga made probably the first free ascent of *Seventh Rifle* (Jones-Rowell-Qamar 1971) at 5.11b. On North Howser's W face, Bean Bowers and Dave Nettle climbed *All Along the Watchtower* (Robinson-Walseth 1981) in 11 hours with Bowers freeing all of the climb. This is probably the first time the route has been done free in a single day. The same pair, accompanied by Chris Swetland, also completed a new free linkup on **South Howser Tower** and **The Minaret**: *Bad Italian Hair*, which starts with a new 5.10 variation to the start of *Bad Hair Day* (Scully-Wirtz 2002) and then joins the *Italian Pillar* (Stedile-DeFrancesco 1987) before finishing on the top of South Howser.

Steve Su and Ari Menitove also added a new route to South Howser: *Serge Overkill* (V 5.11–), which takes a line near the *Catalonian Route* (Cabau-Burgada-Masana-Wenciesko 1983). On **The Minaret**, Bruce Miller and Chris Weidner added *Reinhold Pussycat* (600m, V 5.10+ A2) to the W face. The line had been attempted numerous times by other parties over the years but never finished.

Chris Brazeau and Colin Moorhead added several routes during their trip to the Bugaboos: *Bugaburl* (5.11d) on **Snowpatch Spire**, which takes the obvious corner system right of the *North Summit Direct* (Morand-Sonnenuye 1979); *Divine Intervention* (300m, 5.11) on **Bugaboo Spire;** and – rounding off their visit – a first free ascent of *Cleopatra's Alley* (Knox-Thomas-McCormick 1987) on the E face of **Pigeon Spire.**

While changing conditions in the Rockies have led to some routes becoming dangerous rubble chutes in summer, milder-than-usual winters have made these same lines reasonable winter and spring outings in some cases. Winter alpine activity was somewhat limited, perhaps by the prevalence of excellent roadside ice conditions. Greg Tkaczuk and Eamonn Walsh made the first winter ascent of *Humble Horse* (Marshall-Elzinger 1981) on the N face of **Mount Diadem.**

The outstanding ascent of the season was Chris Brazeau and Jon Walsh's new line on the N face of **Mount Alberta**. This is the first time a Canadian Rockies grade VI route has been climbed in a day and is only the third route on the face. Their route, *Brazeau-Walsh* (1000m, VI M6 5.11), follows the *Lowe-Glidden* (Lowe-Glidden 1972) before breaking out right at the start of the rock headwall. One of George Lowe's other routes, *Lowe-Hannibal* (Lowe-Hannibal *1979*) on the N face of **Mount Geikie**, also saw two ascents, notably by Steve Holeczi and Mike Verwey who both free-climbed the route; previous parties typically resorting to some aid or the second jumaring.

Scott Semple and Raphael Slawinski added a new line to **Mount Andromeda's** NE face. *The Doctor, The Tourist, His Crampon, and Their Banana* (700m, V M7) follows a faint weakness about 100m left of the *Andromeda Strain* (Blanchard-Cheesmond-Friesen 1983) and features more sustained climbing than its neighbour. Will Gadd also finished his project of eight years on **Mount Yamnuska**. To date, *Yamabushi* (300m, 5.13a) is the hardest multi-pitch rock route to be completed in the Canadian Rockies.

Newfoundland has become a more popular winter venue recently, but last autumn Justen Sjong and Chris Weidner visited the area and climbed *Lucifer's Lighthouse* (1300', V 5.12c) on **Blow-Me-Down Wall** above Devil's Bay. They described it as some of the best sea cliff climbing in North America. The trip relied on access to the cliff by boat. They and another party were forced to weather the tail end of Hurricane Florence in a nearby abandoned fishing village rather than at the base of the cliff.

CONTINENTAL UNITED STATES

The 2006-2007 winter season in the North Cascades provided fewer weather windows than usual, resulting in less activity. However, Dave Burdick and John Frieh made the first ascent of the *Northeast Face* (IV WI4+ M3) on **Three Fingers Peak**, a line long admired by local climbers. During the summer of 2006, several notable projects in the Picket Range were completed, including *Haunted Wall* on **Spectre Peak** (2100', IV 5.9+) by Wayne Wallace and Mike Layton. Wallace returned for an epic solo first ascent of *Mongo Ridge* (4,000', VI 5.10–), a mile-long line on **West Fury Peak**.

In Yosemite Ivo Ninov and Nico Favresse established *Lost in Translation* (1200', 5.12b/c R) on **El Capitan**. They climbed the route free from the ground up in a day, something of a first for Yosemite where many projects require a top-down approach with aid over many days. Also on El Capitan, David Turner added *Atlantis* (VI 5.9 A4) in the autumn of 2005, which he established solo over 13 days. Turner returned with Matt Meinzer in spring 2006 and added *House of Cards* (VI 5.9 A4+) to the **Porcelain Wall**, taking 11 days on the wall.

In the Sierra Nevada Dave Nettle, Donald Otten and Nils Davis added *Tradewinds* (IV/V 5.11+) on **Incredible Hulk**, which pieces together other routes to form a direct, free line. Dave Nettle returned to **Balloon Dome** with Brandon Thau to start *The Crucible* (IV 5.11 A1), a project that Thau eventually finished with Chris LaBounty and Neal Harder. The same party of three also freed *Leaning Tower Route - Free Dike Variation* (IV 5.11+).

Pavel Kovar and Misha Logvinov's ascent of **Mount Clarence King's** *Northeast Ridge* (IV+ 5.7) shows that the Sierras, like the North Cascades, still offer a lot of adventure. The route involves more than a mile of ridge traversal before it joins the E ridge to the summit. Also in the Sierras, Jake Whitaker and Renan Ozturk completed a new direct free variation to the *East Face* (V 5.11) of **Day Needle** in the Mt. Whitney cirque. While on **Keeler Needle** Michael Strassman completed the eponymously named *Strassman Route* (2000', ungraded), soloing it over a period of eight days.

In the Zion National Park Mike Anderson and Rob Pizem made the first free ascent of one of Zion's longest routes, *Thunderbird Wall* (16 pitches, VI 5.13- R). This is just one of numerous high-grade lines freed by Anderson over the past couple of years. Cedar Wright and Renan Ozturk were also very active, as they established three new lines, all with onsight and in-a-day ethics. Immediately to the right of *Monkey Finger* they added *The Monkeys Always Send, Dude* (900', 5.11+R C2 or 5.12). Next, on **Mount Kinesava**, they added *Free Lhasa* (1300', 5.11+), a clean variation to *Lhasa* (Anker-Quinn, 1990). They also added *The Birthday Bash* (700', 5.12c), which follows the crack system just right of *Free or Burn*.

Black Canyon of the Gunnison National Park was, as usual, the scene of lots of activity.

Josh Wharton, accompanied by numerous partners, completed several free linkups and ground-up ascents in the canyon. On the wall between *Cheap Shot* and *Dry Hard,* Topher Donahue and Jared Ogden added *The Blacksmiths* (1600', 5.12), which starts up Earl Wiggins' route *Dry Hard* before adding a further six new pitches to reach the canyon rim. Finally Jeremy Collins and Jonny Copp added *Sistine Reality* (IV 5.11+) on the W face of **Gothic Pillar**.

In the Rocky Mountain National Park, Chip Chace and Roger Briggs completed *Endless Summer* (300m, V– 5.12– (5.11R)) on the lower E face of **Longs Peak**. This was the end result of attempts spread over several years.

In the winter of 2007 in Grand Teton National Park, Greg Collins and Hans Johnstone completed the first winter ascent of **Mount Owen's** N ridge. Johnstone, along with Stephen Koch, also added *Squeeze Box* (1000', IV M7 A0) to the N face of **Grand Teton**. Johnstone and Collins, this time accompanied by Bean Bowers, also visited **Mount Moran** and added *South Buttress Prow* (5.12b) to Moran's south buttress. The team rappelled from the top of the technical difficulties, leaving 2500' of 5th-class slabs between them and the summit.

MEXICO

There was a significant amount of activity in Mexico in 2006 with several longer routes established, often by locals rather than visiting climbers. Javier Israel, Odin Pérez Arias and Luis Carlos García Ayala added *Guerrero de Luz* (550m, V 5.12– A0) on the **Neptuno Wall** in La Huasteca National Park. Ayala had spotted the wall the previous season but access issues had prevented a serious attempt. Oriol Anglada and Marisol Monterrubio added *Via Lactea* (270m, 5.12c or 5.12a C2) to the S face of **Peñon Blanco** near Yerbanis in the desert of Durango. Alejandro Rene Gomez Aldama, Jose Manuel Gomez Aldama, Carlos Miguel Hererra Tapia and Calvin A Smith climbed a new line, *Hombres del Pañuelo Rojo* (500m, 5.11 A1) in the **Sumidero Canyon**, part of the Sumidero Canyon National Park.

Mount Everest Foundation
Expedition Reports

SUMMARISED BY BILL RUTHVEN

After the first successful ascent of Everest in 1953 (and initially financed from the surplus funds and subsequent royalties of that trip) the Mount Everest Foundation was set up as a continuing initiative between the Alpine Club and the Royal Geographical Society (with the Institute of British Geographers). Since then it has supported over 1500 British and New Zealand expeditions planning 'exploration of the mountain regions of the earth' with grants totalling some £900,000.

In return for supporting an expedition, all that the MEF asks is a comprehensive report. Once received, copies are lodged in the Alpine Club Library, the Royal Geographical Society, the British Mountaineering Council and the Alan Rouse Memorial Collection in Sheffield Central Library.

The following notes summarise reports from the expeditions supported in 2006, and are divided into geographical areas.

AMERICA – NORTH AND CENTRAL

British Mt Dickey 2006 Paul Ramsden with Andy Kirkpatrick. March-April 2006

There is no doubt that the mountain areas of the world offer some of the best evidence of global climate change. In Autumn 2005 Ramsden had experienced problems climbing in Alaska due to a record hot/dry summer, but on returning a few short months later he faced the coldest winter for 20 years. The aims of this trip to Mt Dickey (2909m) were to make the first ascent of a new route on the steep south face icefall and/or the 'laser line' on its east face. But they were disappointed to find that the icefall no longer existed, having sublimated in the cold conditions. They therefore tried a line on the east face, which led to the leader's most frightening mountain experience ever when he discovered that a 30m pitch of vertical névé that he had just climbed without any protection was no more than a thin crust. Seeking sunnier routes, they therefore investigated the south face of Mt Bradley but were once again thwarted by the conditions.

MEF 06/20

AMERICA – SOUTH AND ANTARCTICA

Huantsan East Face 2006 Nick Bullock with Matt Helliker. June-July 2006
The main aim of this team in visiting the Cordillera Blanca in Peru was to climb the couloir on the east face of Huantsán (6395m). After experiencing several forms of transport including a so-called 'express' bus shared with a herd of sheep, they eventually established their base camp at 4400m in the Quebrada Alhuina. It was clear that due to the unsettled weather the intended route was not in condition so, as an alternative, they decided to attempt the 1000m central NE buttress on the separate peak of Huantsán Sur (5919m) to its left. Despite overhanging séracs and massive ice umbrellas they successfully climbed this over a three-day period, calling the route *Death or Glory* and grading it TD/ED. For more details see: nickbullock2003@yahoo.co.uk MEF 06/04

Welsh South Tower of Paine 2006 Mike (Twid) Turner with Stu McAlease. November-December 2006
These two Patagonian stalwarts hoped to climb a new route on the SE face of the south (and highest) Tower of Paine (2500m), which would also be the first complete British ascent of the Tower. After initially free climbing, they reached a crack on the SE ridge, and then a series of hanging corners, where progress became desperately slow, with some pitches taking three days. After about 800m of vertical climbing they reached easier ground but were then hit by a monster storm with winds well over 200 kph. After five days of this they initiated an epic descent, feeling lucky to get down alive. They named their incomplete route *The good, the bad and the ugly* and graded it A3+, E2.

MEF 06/13

Eastern Blanca Reconnaissance Paul Hudson. July 2006
Originally this leader planned to combine reconnaissance with first ascents in the area of the Cordillera Blanca to the west of Pompey (Hualcán group), but although several other people expressed interest in participating in this trip, all withdrew as the departure date approached. Hudson therefore decided to go alone, limiting his trip to a non-climbing photographic survey. In this he seems to have been successful, having produced a very comprehensive coverage of the mountain ranges in the area.
For more details see: www.therockface.co.uk MEF 06/14

The Huayhuash Hikers Will Parsons with Ian Arnold, Norbert DeMello, Ken Findlay and Paul Hudson. July-August 2006
Although much of the Cordillera Huayhuash range of Peru has become popular in recent years, its southern spur has been largely ignored,

particularly from an eastern approach. The group focused on two main objectives, the first being the east ridge of Quesillo (5600m) on which, despite several attempts, they were unable, without appropriate rock protection gear, to get higher than 5100m. They therefore turned their attention to the NE ridge of Carnicero (5960m) on which they reached 5270m but realised that further progress was beyond their TD ability.　　　MEF 06/16

Huaguruncho 2006 Tony Barton with Andrew Houseman (USA). June 2006

This team chose the Cordillera Oriental of Peru which, as one of the less frequented mountain ranges, they hoped would provide plenty of scope for exploration and virgin peaks/new routes. They only experienced six days of reasonable weather during their time in the area, which naturally limited their activities; these included an attempt on Nevado Huaguruncho Chico, aborted due to unstable snow conditions. Nevertheless, they achieved what was probably the first ascent of Nevado Huaranco Sur (c5150m) by its SE ridge. Unfortunately, the joy of success was spoilt when they discovered on their return that their base camp had been raided and most of their food stolen. This, plus continuing bad weather, hastened the end of the expedition.
MEF 06/17

Kings College London MC Bolivia 2006 Charlie Netherton with Jon Holman plus Pedro Mamani from Bolivia. August-September 2006

When Holman injured his knee during the first warm-up climb of this trip to the less popular northern region of the Cordillera Apolobamba, the leader was fortunately able to recruit a local climber to replace him. Together Netherton and Mamani attempted a traverse of the Palomani Tranca Group from the east, but after climbing Palomani Sur (its first ascent), Palomani Central and a subsidiary summit of Palomani Tranca, they encountered appalling rock on the main summit. Although it might have been possible to continue, deterioration in weather, the illness of both climbers and the prospect of a horrendous scree descent prompted an abandonment at this stage.　　　MEF 06/24

Cambridge Quimsa Cruz 2006 Alan Dickinson with Sam Hawkins, Moira Herring and Tom Stedall from the UK, plus Ronan Kavanagh from Ireland. June-August 2006

Most – if not all – previous expeditions to the Cordillera Quimsa Cruz have approached from the south, but having trekked on the other (ie 'jungle') side in 2003, the leader had a good idea of what to expect, and decided to use that approach. Despite confusing maps, the team was successful in climbing six peaks ranging from 5112m to 5550m but are uncertain how many were by new routes.　　　MEF 06/25

GREENLAND

Brathay Exploration Group Greenland 2006 Paul Williams with Peter Clutton-Brock, Miles Doughty, Anna Griffith, Gavin Henderson, Thomas Moorcroft, Andrew Watson and James Watson. July-August 2006

Although carried out under the auspices of a commercial company, this was actually an independent expedition of present and potential leaders. Their aim was to explore a previously unvisited area of the East Greenland ice cap and also to collect lichens for scientific research. The area was chosen in conjunction with Paul Walker of Tangent Expeditions who arranged for them to be dropped off at an area known as 'camp icefall'. Despite the weather being too 'warm', with temperatures never dropping below –12°C and usually between –6° and +3°C overnight (and up to 19°C during the day) they succeeded in making first ascents of five mountains by routes ranging from Alpine F to D, as well as three others climbed on ski.

MEF 06/03

Cambridge University East Greenland 2006 Mark Reid with James Dynes, Lachan Low and Steve Mounsey. July-September 2006

These young students chose a seldom-visited coastal area of the Schweizerland Alps immediately west of the Knud Rasmussen Glacier and 20km south of the Arctic Circle for their first expedition. Travelling to Greenland by normal commercial flights they chartered a boat to reach their selected area. Despite very variable weather conditions which lost them eight days' climbing time, they were successful in making first ascents of eight peaks of up to 1588m and a repeat of one other peak at grades from F to AD.

MEF 06/19

Oxford University Greenland 2006 Hauke Engel with Chris Abbott and Ben Spencer. August 2006

Using Tangent Expeditions to land them by Twin Otter on a glacier in the Gronau Nunatakker range, these young students undertook a 100km ski traverse (with pulks) of Knud Rasmussen Land to a designated pick-up point. They broke the journey into several sub-sections in order to explore as they progressed. They achieved first ascents of 12 peaks of up to 2700m by snow/ice routes which they graded F to AD.

MEF 06/21

HIMALAYA – INDIA

British Kedar Dome 2006 Ian Parnell with Tim Emmett. September-October 2006

When his original partner withdrew from this project to climb what Parnell suggested could be 'the hardest route in the Himalaya', he was fortunately able to recruit a replacement who, despite an excellent climbing

CV, would be making his first visit to the Greater Ranges. The aim was a new route on the east face of Kedar Dome (6831m), and despite Emmett's lack of altitude experience, in a six-day push they successfully climbed an entirely 'free' on-sight route up the massive SE pillar, descending by the west face.   MEF 06/07

Miyar Nala 2006 Oliver Metherell with Jeremy Frimer from Canada and Michel van der Spek from Holland plus Sarah Hart in support. September 2006
Although the original objectives of this team lay above the Jangpar valley, stomach problems persuaded them to seek an area with (hopefully) safer water. They moved south to the Dali valley from which they made the first ascent of Goya Peak (5230m) via its 600m north ridge (Alpine grade D–, French 5C). They also attempted the first ascent of *Gateway Ridge* leading to the summit ridge of a rock peak (c5650m) near Dali on which they reached 5600m with some simul-climbing but also pitches up to 5.9 (HVS).
                                                                       MEF 06/11

British North Sikkim 2006 Julie Ann Clyma with Roger Payne. October-November 2006
This husband and wife team left home thinking they were to be issued a permit to attempt Gurudongmar (6715m) in North Sikkim, but when they reached New Delhi everything changed. Instead they were issued a permit – the first ever for a foreign expedition – for two peaks in West Sikkim, Koktang (6147m) and Rathong (6679m). They attempted both, but reached neither summit because of bad conditions and/or weather. However, they made first ascents of two minor peaks, Chogyl Peak (5750m) and Frontier Peak (c5650m). At the end of the trip, they received encouraging news about future permits for North Sikkim, and have high hopes of more success in 2007. The leader of this expedition received the MEF Alison Chadwick Memorial Grant for 2006.   MEF 06/28

HIMALAYA – NEPAL

'Khumbu Double Trouble' Jon Bracey with Nick Bullock. October-November 2006
Phari Lapcha (aka Machermo 6017m) is one of 33 mountains recently given 'trekking peak' status by the Nepalese authorities, and although fairly accessible from the Lukla to Gokyo trek, only had one route, *Bonfire of the Vanities*, (ED1) on its north face. Several teams had tried to add to this (including Owen Samuel's 05/21) but this duo was the first to succeed. Their 1000m route, which they called *Snotty's Gully*, (ED, WI5, M5+) landed them on the coffee-table-sized west summit (c5977m) – the first people to reach it. (*See 'Silent Scream', pa*ge 3)   MEF 06/23

2006 Scottish Lobuje East Alasdair Buchanan with Dave Chadwick & Tristan Hamade (September-November 2006)
When his lead climber withdrew from the team, this leader had to re-evaluate his objectives. To acclimatise, Chadwick and Hamade climbed the normal route on Lobuje (4943m) and after a reconnaissance, Buchanan decided to repeat a route on the west rib of Cholatse (6400m). On this he reached 5900m before avalanche hazard and the difficulties of breaking trail made retreat the safest option. MEF 06/31

CHINA AND TIBET

Hong Meigui Zhongdian Draughting Holes 2006 Hilary Greaves from UK with Peter Ljubimov, Artem Oganov and Dmitry Prashin from Russia. 1-25 February 2006
The theory behind this expedition was that with a light snow covering, warm air rising from caves would melt snow around the entrances, thus making them clearly visible. The area of interest was the Zhongdian Plateau in Yunnan Province, which it was hoped might offer a cave with a 2500m depth potential. Unfortunately this was not possible to prove as, on arrival, they were surprised to find there was no snow. Undeterred, the team carried out a reconnaissance of a new area which they found to be speleologically uninteresting, but on revisiting an 'old' area they logged 26 minor entrances, found a significant new cave, and extended a known one. For more details see: www.hongmeigui.net MEF 06/01

Qionglai Shan 2006 Jez Thornley with Ian Gibb and Felix Hoddinott. March-April 2006
Unseasonably heavy snowfall one week before this team arrived in Sichuan Province created high-risk avalanche conditions on the approach to Peak 5609m, one of their prime objectives, so they turned their attention to other peaks. They made the first ascent of Dorsal Peak (5050m) via its NW ridge (PD+), and what they thought was the first ascent of Ding Ding Peak (5202m) via its SW ridge (AD) – until they found signs of an unknown previous visitor on the summit. An attempt on Peak 5260m via its south flank/west ridge had reached c5000m when a sudden deterioration in the weather prompted a rapid retreat.
For more details see: www.fhoddinott.com MEF 06/30

British/American Alps of Tibet 2006 Jim Lowther with Mark Richey & Mark Wilford, both from USA. October-November 2006
Since its 'discovery' by Tom Nakamura, East Nyainqentanghla has become an increasingly popular destination. This trio planned to explore the Lake Basong area (south of Yigong Tsangpo) and make first ascents, in particular of the holy mountain Nenang (6870m). After a very challenging

13-day alpine-style push up the east ridge they had reached within 300m of the summit when further progress was barred by a huge crevasse. Already very extended, they had little option but to retreat.   MEF 06/34

Hong Meigui Cave Exploration Society Liangshan 2006 Duncan Collis with Johan Bengt, Si Flower, David Haskel, Martin Laverty, Fleur Loveridge, Matt Ryan, Lenik anak Saymo, Andy Sewel, Pete Talling, Jon Telling, Yvo Weidmann and Sarah White. July-August 2006
Topographical and geological maps of southern Sichuan show a large area over 3000m in the Da Bing Shan (Big Ice Mountains) west of Leibo. Unfortunately, a few days' reconnaissance by jeep showed that although mainly limestone, it was seamed with insoluble rocks, making the presence of deep caves unlikely. The team therefore moved west to Yanyuan County where they found high karst plateaux between 2400m and 3500m with limestone extending to peaks c4000m, and logged over 80 caves and shafts, with entrances up to 3686m. Finally, a splinter group made a quick trip to Wudu County in Gansu Province where they found an impressive limestone gorge containing a large show cave at 1200m and potential for deep caves. No doubt they will be returning to investigate further.   MEF 06/35

PAKISTAN

Unclimbed Hispar 2006 Peter Thompson with Lee Harrison, also Ben Cheek and Greg Nunn part time. June-August 2006
Although initially just planning to explore the N side of the Hispar glacier, the team decided to extend the itinerary to include visits to the Shimshal and Chapursan valleys. Although they did not attempt their originally specified main objective (Hispar Sar, 6395m), they climbed a number of peaks, including a first ascent in each of the areas visited, viz: Mudhil Sar (5800m) in Shimshal, Haigutum East (5783m) in Hispar and Gharhil Sar (5800m) in Chapursan, each by snow/ice routes of Alpine D. They also discovered that heights of the lower peaks were rather less than marked on the widely used Swiss map of the area.   MEF 06/08

Lobsang Spire 2006 John Arran with Anne Arran. July-August 2006
This husband and wife team visited the Muztagh glacier to explore and search for big-wall climbing potential. Their main objective was the first ascent of the S face of Lobsang Spire (5707m) but the route appeared dangerously loose, and an alternative traversing line proved unsuitable for big-wall technique and did not hold enough snow for an alpine-style ascent. Nevertheless, they reached a height of 5200m. They then turned their attention to an unclimbed/unnamed 5607m peak directly to its south, twice reaching 5450m on the NW face of its West Pillar in 12 pitches from

scrambling up to E4 6a (with about four still to go) before being repulsed
by rain and snow.   MEF 06/26

CENTRAL ASIA AND THE FAR EAST

Eagle Ski Club Ak Shirak Dave Wynne Jones with Derek Buckle, Alistair
Cairns, John Goodwin, Lizzy Hawker, Anna Seale and Mike Sharp. April-
May 2006
  The Ak Shirak range of mountains in Kyrgyzstan is still largely
unexplored, and by going later in the season than previous trips, this team
hoped to make a SW–NE ski traverse without experiencing the problems
of snow-blocked passes. They completed 50km of the route, achieving first
ascents of seven peaks over 4600m in the process, including Kyrgyzia, at
4954m the highest in the north of the range.   MEF 06/09

AC Shakhdara 2006 Phil Wickens with Rick Allen, Derek Buckle, Kai
Green, Steve Hunt, Alex Rickards and Tim Sparrow. August-September
2006
  Although the Shakhdara range of Tajikistan has been popular with
Russian competition climbers (and possibly others from the eastern bloc)
for some time, the area was not visited by western climbers until 2005: this
Alpine Club expedition therefore planned to explore and make first ascents.
Their prime objective was Pik Karl Marx (6736m) which they climbed by
three different routes. They also climbed a number of other peaks between
5600m and 6400m – five by possible new routes, and a total of seven being
first British ascents.   MEF 06/12

MISCELLANEOUS

Twin Gardens Ethiopia 2006 Giovanni Chiodi with Andrew Burns, Laura
Evenstar and Brigid LeFevre. July-August 2006
  This was a multi-discipline scientific expedition to the Bale Mountains
of Ethiopia by a tri-national team based in the University of Aberdeen.
The mountains lie to the east of the Great Rift valley and rise to 4000m.
Although the area has no natural boundaries, it has been a National Park
since the seventies, but has never been well managed: although it was once
a major highland forest, rapid population growth has brought massive
deforestation with all its attendant problems. Data collection for two main
projects was successfully completed – forest glades and honey gathering
(a major source of local income) – which should help the team to put
together a new management plan with conservation of natural resources as
one of its main aims.   MEF 06/33

Reviews

COMPILED BY GEOFFREY TEMPLEMAN

Brotherhood of the Rope
The Biography of Charles Houston
Bernadette McDonald
Bâton Wicks, 2007, pp250, £16.99

One of my most prized possessions is sitting on the bookcase in front of me. It is a silver tankard, engraved with the unmistakeable silhouette of K2 and bears the famous inscription: 'We went to the mountain as strangers and returned as brothers – K2 1953.' Charles Houston sent it to me after his last visit to England in 2004. In the bookcase is another precious memento – a rare first edition of *Five Miles High*, the account of the first serious attempt on K2 in 1938. It follows, therefore, that as a reviewer of this biography of one of the Grand Old Men of American mountaineering, I could be accused of lacking objectivity. I plead guilty.

Since I first met Charlie in 1991 he has become a close and valued friend, and I read the book with a warm feeling of recognition; that it gets right to the heart of a complex, talented and ultimately fulfilled man after a lifetime of incredible highs and lows.

Bernadette McDonald has delved deeply into Charles Houston's astonishingly varied life. Born into a family of East Coast privilege he was easily able to gain admission to Harvard and use his contacts to explore many fields, as doctor, research scientist, mountaineer, Peace Corps worker – almost every chapter reveals another of Houston's multi-talented ventures. It is not, however, a hagiography. Bernadette does not shirk from pointing out Houston's failings, both personal and professional. Prone to deep depressions, he felt that many of his projects either came to nothing (for example, he was one of the first to attempt to construct an artificial heart before transplants were invented) or that he didn't always get the credit he deserved. He described himself as a 'nearly' man – in medicine, science and of course mountaineering... 'Mount Crillon I missed, Nanda Nevi I missed, K2 I missed twice, and Everest I didn't really try.' His books and films were 'good, sometimes quite good, but never really what they could and should have been'.

There seems little doubt that at times Charlie could be hard to work with, abrasive, critical and tactless. But what shines through this book is that adversity is there to be challenged. Almost despite (or possibly because of) the relentless self-criticism, here is a portrait of a man whose life has been far more than the sum of its parts.

When he came to the International Mountain Literature Festival at Bretton Hall, I introduced him as a man who had probably saved the lives of some of the audience, and if he hadn't already, he probably would do so in the future. For this is Houston's major contribution: Mountain Medicine, in particular his studies of pulmonary and cerebral oedema. I hadn't realised just how much and how long Charlie had experimented in this field, dating back to his wartime service in the Navy where he was one of the first to test, in controlled conditions, pilots' ability to adjust to altitude. Since then, of course, Houston has been at the forefront of most high-altitude research: an interest that seems to have been rekindled by the death on K2 of Art Gilkey in 1953.

Inevitably, I found the mountaineering chapters dealt with all too familiar ground, which is not to say they are any less interesting. Like the Tommy Cooper line, 'I'm only laughing because I know what's coming next.' I know the K2 stories all too well, though a small surprise was the admission by Charlie that Art Gilkey may well have killed himself on the epic attempt to lower him down the Abruzzi Ridge; a selfless sacrifice to save the rest of the hard-pressed rescuers; a question that can never be answered. (By the way, a heart-rending 45min DVD of the two K2 expeditions is tucked into the back-cover of the book.)

But what Bernadette has very well pointed out is that Charlie Houston's contribution to Himalayan history is almost unparalleled both in style and humanity. Even Reinhold Messner describes his expeditions as 'an inspiration for a lifetime'.

Now nearly 94, Charlie has the mind of a man half his age. As ever his critical faculties are still finely honed. These days it is directed at widely different targets: the Bush administration and the folly of Iraq, the dubious ethics (or lack of them) in modern Himalayan climbing and the evils of a materialistic society that he feels has corrupted climbing. Money he says 'is a great big ball of wax that sticks to everything'.

As an honorary member of both the Alpine Club and the Climbers' Club (not the *Welsh* Climbers' Club Bernadette!) 'The Brits' as Charlie calls us, will always hold Charlie as a special friend. The book will enhance what is already a formidable reputation and it is surely well deserved. Charlie has always 'walked to the beat of a different drum'. *The Brotherhood of the Rope* has gone a long way to explain and evaluate Houston's reputation as a man of absolute integrity and honesty.

A story that perhaps sums up his life came with an invitation by a friend to give the graduation address at a Rocky Mountain School.

'Why me?'

'You're ideal Charlie; you've had an interesting and varied life, and tried all sorts of activities. But, most important, you've failed in all of them. I think the graduating class would be inspired by your philosophy.'

Stunned, deflated and bruised, Charlie turned him down... but his words echoed in his head. 'You keep coming back, you keep trying again and you never give up.'

A week later he rang back and said 'yes'.

History will judge Charlie Houston's individual achievements, and perhaps give him more credit than he gives himself. But in his heart of hearts, Charlie must know that in the biggest test of all, he has passed with flying colours.

Jim Curran

Khangchendzonga: Sacred Summit
Pema Wangchuk and Mita Zulca
Little Kingdom Pvt Ltd, at Hillside Press Pvt Ltd, Kathmandu, 2007, pp 375, npq

There is something exciting and rather special about the arrival of a book from India – the slightly exotic smell and texture of the packaging – carrying with it the sense of a long journey made around the world. *Khangchendzonga: Sacred Summit* came to me from Sikkim, in the very shadow of the mountain itself. Written and privately published by Pema Wangchuk, Editor of *NOW!* an English daily newspaper published in Gangtok, in collaboration with award winning filmmaker Mita Zulca, this substantial and profusely illustrated book is a significant and welcome addition to our existing literature on the Himalayan peak Kangchenjunga (8586m), third highest mountain in the world. What makes this book different, however, is the perspective of its main author Pema Wangchuk. He is part-Sikkimese, people for whom the mountain is both a powerful spiritual and political symbol. Kangchenjunga is, of course, a source of national pride in the rest of India too, being, after all, India's highest mountain, situated at the north-eastern border of the sub-continent – an obvious but often overlooked fact when authors of a western perspective come to write about it. Over the years, the Indian Government has commemorated Kangchenjunga in a number of ways: with a stamp featuring a painting by Nicholas Roerich (issued in 1988) and currently the mountain appears on the reverse of the 100-rupee note. It was seeing Kangchenjunga featured on India's currency that first gave Wangchuk the idea of writing a book about the mountain. As he puts it: in the small state of Sikkim (an independent country until 1975) – the relationship between people and mountain 'transcends to a different level'. Wangchuk goes on to explain that although the accepted international spelling is 'Kangchenjunga'...this book spells it 'Khangchendzonga' because that is how Sikkim pronounces it locally and has decided to spell it.

It follows, therefore, that the early part of *Khangchendzonga: Sacred Summit* deals with the significance of the mountain to the communities of Buddhist, Lepcha and Limboo people that comprise part of the diverse population of Sikkim. Although a vague sense of the mountain as a sacred space, and its main peak as the abode of a god, pervades the European canon of Kangchenjunga literature from Victorian times to the present day, a clear and comprehensive explanation of its differing religious and ritual significance to the various Sikkimese communities has hitherto only been found in dispersed and fragmentary form, much of it within the realm of academic anthropology. To my knowledge, Wangchuk and Zulca are the first authors to present all this to the general reader in a single book. They explain it all admirably in three chapters that deal in turn with the customs and religious beliefs of Lepcha, Limboo (a religious and culturally distinct group originating in an area of eastern Nepal) and Buddhist Sikkimese. It becomes clear that a certain amount of political manoeuvring and appropriation has occurred over time. It was Buddhism that later adopted Kangchenjunga as *dZonga* – the principle guardian deity of Sikkim – in an attempt either to subsume or annex the older Lepcha *Mun* faith. Today, many of the old stories of Lepcha folklore have been lost whilst Lepcha religious practices hang on precariously in the remote village of Nung within the Lepcha reserve of Dzongu in North Sikkim. There, until recently, a solitary, aged *Khangchendzonga Bongthing* (shaman or priest) offered prayers and made annual sacrifice to the mountain from an ancient open-air altar. Recently, in 2006, these ceremonies were revived by young members of the local Lepcha community – indicative of a widespread resurgence in cultural identity that happily now seems to be spreading throughout Sikkim.

The chapter on Buddhism contains interesting images of the overgrown ruins of what is believed to be the first monastery to be constructed in Sikkim and also some curious 19th century photographs of monks wearing the relics of Lhatsun Chenpo – Sikkim's patron 'saint' and instigator of the annual *Pang Lhabsol* ritual of thanksgiving to Kangchenjunga. This celebration with its *Pangtoed Chaam* dance is currently being revived at Ralang monastery (Karma Kagyu school) in Ravangla in South Sikkim amidst some criticism from purists over variations in the costumes and some rituals. Their arguments may seem esoteric to the western reader, but Wangchuk concludes: in Sikkim even a child knows that Kangchenjunga is to be worshipped ... it inspires awe effortlessly.

This book gives a brief account of how Kangchenjunga was 'discovered' by westerners and how it came to lose 'the battle of the heights' before moving on to a chapter on early explorers. Amongst the most interesting parts of this section is that on Pundits: native explorers and surveyors, recruited and trained by the government of British India to map the areas of the Himalaya beyond their control. Tales of specially marked logs being floated down rivers and of a boarding school opened in Darjeeling by the British as a front for grooming Pundits from an early age all sound like something out of a novel by Rudyard Kipling. It comes as no surprise, therefore, to learn that the school's headmaster was the famous Pundit Sarat Chandra Das – a major player in the *Great Game* and inspiration for Hurree Chunder Mookerjee in Kipling's *Kim*.

It would be wrong to suggest that this is primarily a book for the climbing enthusiast, although Wangchuk and Zulca devote an interesting chapter to Himalayan pioneer Alexander Kellas before navigating their way through the early climbing history of Kangchenjunga in a compact 50 pages. However, they manage to bring the climbing stories to life with some well-researched photographs of Crowley, Tombazi and others in Sikkim and press cuttings of the period. One of these newspaper articles, published in the *New York Times* in 1930, at a time when there had been a number of tragic and unsuccessful attempts on the mountain, reports Buddhist priests maintaining that there were in fact 'five easy paths' to the top of Kangchenjunga, each of them accessible by a stone gate with a key, hidden nearby.

In 2005 there were celebrations at the Alpine Club to mark the 50th anniversary of the first ascents of Kangchenjunga by Band, Brown, Hardie and Streather in a compact expedition team of nine men, launched by the Alpine Club and led by Sir Charles Evans. Arguably, the second most important achievement of this expedition, after conquering the mountain in May 1955, was to leave the sacred summit unviolated, as a mark of respect to the Sikkimese people. This decision has become a historic moment in mountaineering history and Wangchuk and Zulca assert that it has made Kangchenjunga 'the most special mountain in the Himalaya'. Undoubtedly, it continues to be of utmost importance to the Sikkimese: when in September 2005 George Band and Norman Hardie were invited by the state government of Sikkim to a special function to mark the 50th anniversary of the expedition, it was to give thanks for the resolution to 'leave the last six feet un-done' rather than to commemorate the climbing of the mountain. 'It was an emotional moment', writes Wangchuk, and the event is com-memorated in this book with many photographs of the felicitations featuring George Band, Norman Hardie and Col Narinder 'Bull' Kumar, who led the Indian Army expedition to climb the north-east route in 1977 that placed the Indian Tricolour six feet below the summit.

Khangchendzonga: Sacred Summit is a comprehensive book that gives a new perspective both to some of the established climbing stories and to recent mountaineering history. An interesting chapter is *Lady Killer*, which brings together the exploits of women mountaineers and their attempts on Kangchenjunga. Austrian born Gerlinde Kaltenbrunner, who climbed Kangchenjunga in May 2006, followed Ginette Harrison and became only the second woman to succeed in doing so. *Lady Killers* contains some of the most tragic stories in the whole book. *'Tigers' on the Mountain* traces the role of the Sherpas in the climbing expeditions to Kangchenjunga and gives special credit to the key role of Chettan, who accompanied all three early Everest expeditions and was one of the porters selected by Paul Bauer for the 1929 German expedition to Kangchenjunga. He returned to the mountain again in 1930 on the Dyhrenfurth expedition and met his death in an avalanche accident. Frank Smythe wrote of losing 'a valued friend … one whom members of several Himalayan expeditions will mourn'.

Chettan's obituary, written by Tom Longstaff for the *Himalayan Journal*, is reproduced here in full. Further chapters on the art and literature of Kangchenjunga discuss not only well-known works by Edward Lear and Nicholas Roerich but also Hiroshi Yoshida, a Japanese artist who was active in the 1930s, creating woodblock prints that are testimony to the deep beauty that the artist perceived in mountain subjects. There is even a photograph – first reproduced in *National Geographic* magazine – of Sikkimese ruler Chogyal Sir Tashi Namgyal painting a canvas of Khangchendzonga – the sky full of painted symbols that express his inward vision. *'K' and the Written Word*, brings together Mark Twain, Cale Young Rice, the Trappist monk Thomas Merton and many others besides. This chapter is something of a potpourri and I would have welcomed a much more comprehensive bibliography to support it. However, an important inclusion is Satyajit Ray's 1962 film *Kanchenjunga,* where the illusive mountain is used in an oblique and symbolic way to reflect on family and personal relationships amongst a group of Bengalis on holiday in Darjeeling. Even Arthur Ransome's classic *Swallows and Amazons* gets a mention because the Lakeland fell Coniston Old Man is imaginatively dubbed Kangchenjunga by the children in the story. Inclusions of this kind – also perhaps Raymond Benson's *A High Time to Kill* (1996) which sees James Bond grappling for a microdot on the icy slopes of Kangchenjunga, may seem peripheral but they serve to demonstrate the deep roots that the mountain has in our (western) cultural history and collective imagination. Arguably, though, the most fascinating parts of this book are those that reveal Sikkim's very deep and special relationship with Kangchenjunga. These make *Khangchendzonga: Sacred Summit* essential reading for anyone contemplating a visit to Sikkim. The book is available directly from Pema Wangchuk (pamdorjee@gmail.com) or from *Les Alpes Livres* (www.les-alpes-livres.com).

Simon Pierse

The Climbing Essays
Jim Perrin
The In Pinn, 2006, pp320, £18

Jim Perrin has said that this is the nearest thing we shall get autobiography from him. To this end he has added a series of brief autobiographical sketches to this collection of climbing-related articles for magazines and journals, the earliest of which, from the 1970s, were written for the *Climbers' Club Journal*. So there is an invitation to read this book as the whole story, from the unhappy, attention-seeking angst of those early pieces to the mellow, often mawkish, prose of the later monthly magazine columns. But Perrin's future biographer will find that, for all the elegant manipulation of the prose here, the author perhaps gives away more than he realises.

From the beginning, Perrin's writing could capture the search, the momentum, the intensity of reading rock and being alert to the physicality of place. 'Fictive Heroes', written for *Crags* in 1981, does this with a coolness of focus that becomes the survival mechanism for a climber whose partner must be left for dead at the bottom of a sea cliff. After many days the narrator is still, he says, 'Climbing. Climbing up the walls of my mind. Trying to get out.' The titles of those early essays, 'Hubris' (1971), 'A Valediction' (1973) and the drug-heightened confusion of 'Street Illegal' (1977) anticipate the preoccupation with Primo Levi in 'Eating Bear Meat' (1992) and 'In Dreams Begins Responsibility' (1993). The appeal of Perrin's climbing writing has always derived from his willingness to partially reveal the way his highs are inextricably linked to his lows, as when, alluding to Primo Levi, he empathises with 'a man who desires to survive the concentration camp of his own nature'.

Perrin is always on the side of 'adventure' rather than 'sport', of 'dreams' rather than 'responsibilities' and of subversion rather than the establishment. In a public interview with Ed Douglas at the last Boardman Tasker Award Perrin characterised his approach as one of playful subversion, which he feared may have upset a few people. 'Well, I'm sure you'll be forgiven', suggested Ed Douglas generously. So here is Jim Perrin in 'Trains, Cafes, Conversations' (1981) regretting that 'our clubs are not the same': 'We are not entrained together in humour, good fellowship, and joint purpose'. If this does not seem to be entirely right, that's the point: provocation. Like threatening to take your own club to court because they had not asked permission to republish 'Street Illegal' in their *Centenary Journal* and had omitted the pompous 'Note' (included here) that the original editor had foolishly demanded. This 'good fellowship' cost the Climbers' Club £3000 and I, as voluntary editor of that celebratory journal, really appreciated the humour and joint purpose of our then club member. 'I am not hubristic,' writes Perrin, and Robert Macfarlane in his Introduction abandons a natural caution to write, 'But with Jim it is true'. Indeed, the most amusing line in this book is Macfarlane's suggestion that 'what has distinguished him perhaps above all is his immense lack of ego'. If one takes the text at face value a generous reader could reasonably come to this conclusion, such are the seductions of Perrin's style.

Robert Macfarlane draws attention to the biblical rhythms, inversions and 'how revelation can be a function of syntax' in Perrin's style, citing Hazlitt, Johnson and Menlove Edwards as clear influences. In my review of Perrin's first collection of these essays, *On and Off The Rocks*, I used the word 'elegant' to represent his argument as well as his style, and I still think this is true for the best of the work here. But with time, it seems to me now that these mannerisms will come to be seen as rather arch and affected. Quite the opposite of Menlove Edwards' struggle to find a plain language adequate to his insights. 'And I, I wanted the heights ...' – where's the lack of ego in this affectation? However, 'It was so beautiful, I was lost', is a stunned, and in its turn stunning, effect. The call of the golden plover is, indeed, 'of all the sounds of nature, most perfectly of its place'. His truest insights are often his simplest.

On the other hand there are the crass attempts to embarrass, such as the long footnote about a teenage Gill Kent's apparent desire to seduce him. And what is one to make of the references to the physical abuse of women that recur in Perrin's work? These jar with the reader, as does his pride in his son's nearly getting expelled from primary school. The recent double tragedies of his son's suicide and his wife's death are dealt with in this book with a directness that does not flinch from the pain and are part of the whole picture of the climbing life.

Re-reading the range of essays collected here one cannot help but feel a deep ambivalence, which, for a playfully subversive writer, is presumably the necessary, the essential response. As Dr Johnson might have said, complexity demands caution.

Terry Gifford

Safety, Risk & Adventure in Outdoor Activities
Bob Barton
Paul Chapman, 2007, pp 189, £19.99

This book is not aimed at the individual recreational mountaineer or adventurer. It is a practical handbook for teachers, leaders and instructors who provide outdoor adventure activities for others, especially for groups of children and young people.

Following a number of high-profile tragic accidents such as at Lyme Bay, Stainforth Beck, Glenridding Beck and Manchester Hole, there has been much media concern in recent years about the safety of school trips. The reality is that such activities are very safe. On average there have been three deaths of pupils per year on school trips, most of which are due to road traffic accidents. In contrast, every year over 30,000 people die from obesity and unfitness and over 100 under-19s commit suicide. The proven benefits to health and mental health of involvement in positive outdoor activities mean that it is vital we do not allow the moral panic around the rare accidents to reduce opportunities and to frighten teachers and others into lack of involvement.

Much work has been done to identify and spread good practice in the management of risk in outdoor activities, while still maintaining the essential elements of challenge and adventure. Bob Barton's book goes a long way towards describing best practice.

Bob, an AC member, has vast experience in the management of adventure activities provision. He is a UIAGM mountain guide, Director of the European Avalanche School, former Principal of Outward Bound Eskdale, and advises Outward Bound and the Duke of Edinburgh's Award on safety.

The book is very clearly written and presented, and it demystifies the process of risk assessment and risk management – so much so that it all seems like common sense (which of course it is, but informed by years of experience and clarity of thought).

The author rightly rejects a simple mechanistic view of risk management and focuses instead on the human factors involved. While recognising the importance of technical skills, he emphasises the importance of leadership qualities such as judgement empathy and issues such as fatigue. He analyses the cultural aspects of risk management within organisations and identifies key aspects of an effective safety culture. He also describes psychological traps for leaders, including: failing to see the whole picture; trying to please other people; perceived time pressure; being blinded by the prize; false assumptions; the myth of instructor invulnerability.

There is a brief overview of child protection, protection of leaders against false allegations, and the importance of attention to the health and safety of leaders themselves. A welcome emphasis is given to the process of authorisation of prospective leaders to lead activities.

Bob Barton's book should become an essential text for instructors, outdoor centre managers and outdoor education advisors.

Steve Lenartowicz

The Artists of the Alpine Club: A Biographical Dictionary
Peter Mallalieu
The Alpine Club and The Ernest Press, 2007, pp 219, £20

Peter Mallalieu is to be applauded for having produced an impressive volume that brings together the range of artists whose work is in the Alpine Club's considerable art collection, or who have been associated with the Club. It therefore documents not only an historically and internationally important art collection but also reflects the admirable way that from its earliest days the Club has opened its doors not only to those actively climbing in the Alps and Greater Ranges, but also to those whose literary, scientific or artistic endeavours have furthered an understanding of the mountain scene. Under this rubric the Club has offered membership to artists as varied as John Ruskin and Hamish Fulton; major figures deeply and intimately engaged with exploring the meaning and value of mountains and mountain activity, but not climbers or mountaineers per se. And it is this inclusivity that has in turn produced an extraordinary collection reflecting the variety of the visual culture of mountains and mountaineering.

Peter has selected 100 artists and provides a brief biography and (in most cases) illustrates at least one work by each. Being a biographical dictionary, his text focuses on the facts and dates of his subjects' lives, although he also includes some wonderful and evocative little character sketches. For example, I'm intrigued to know more of J F Cheetham (1835-1916), who in 1859 travelled from Simla to Srinigar via Leh, fuelled by breakfasts of opium pills that gave him 'wonderful powers of endurance'. I like the sound of Arthur Cust (1842-1911), who was 'devoted to sketching in watercolour and pencil, and never liked to leave a peak or pass without a record. As a consequence, he was often benighted....' How different from today, when one merely points a camera, takes a picture and then moves on.

Of course, the advent of photography has changed everything (of which more later). To make paintings in a high mountain environment is a challenge of a different order to that of taking striking photographs. Consider Gabriel Loppé (1825-1913) whose *View from Mont Blanc Summit, sunrise*, 1869 is one of the highlights of the collection. He endured long painting sessions on the summit of Mont Blanc and apparently climbed the mountain 40 times. 'Several times he concentrated for so long that, as Freshfield recalled, his turn-ups became frozen and had to be freed using an ice axe.'

The book then, is a valuable resource for researchers and those with a general interest in the subject. But what of the art? Here we are on curious ground. A number of those whose biographies are recorded here are important artists in their own right; for example Loppé or Edward Theodore Compton (1849-1921). These professional painters would hold their own in any gathering of landscape artists of the 19th century. However, also represented are climbers who made sketches or paintings on their mountain journeys, amateur artists whose images gain currency through their association with important ascents. Some of their work is of questionable artistic value, but undoubtedly of historic importance. For example, many of Howard Somervell's (1880-1975) works are technically unsophisticated. However, the paintings made on the 1922 Everest expedition in particular have a wonderful evocative power and resonance, which is perhaps in part due to the context in which they were made, with which we are so familiar.

This unique mixture of professionals and amateurs is the most beguiling aspect of the AC collection and is well represented in Peter's book. There are many delights. George Baxter's (1804-1867) fantastic early aquatints of Mont Blanc are more akin to the kind of landscapes Jules Verne imagined on the moon than to anything one might find in the Alps. Arthur Croft's (1828-1902) *Monte Rosa, Lyskamm, Castor and Pollux*, 1871, is an extraordinary painting, in which hallucinatory precision creates a kind of surrealism. It is a phenomenon I have noticed in real life – the crystal clarity of the air in the high mountains, the piercing light which renders the world strange, everything present and seemingly close to – and Croft's painting captures it perfectly, in a way no photograph could. At the other end of the spectrum William Mathews' (1828-1901) sketch of the Pelvoux group is not much more than hasty notation, but incredibly evocative nonetheless.

Peter devotes 12 pages to John Ruskin (1819-1900), and illustrates seven works by him. They are all wonderful and one – *Grutli, Uri Rostock from Lake Lucerne* – is unquestionably a masterpiece. One could make a fascinating study of Ruskin's strange relationship with mountaineering yet whatever his misgivings about the morals of actually climbing mountains he was a great painter of their forms.

And while topography is the dominant mode it is good to see other kinds of artistic responses to mountains being developed and included here, for example in the work of Julian Cooper (born 1947), John Dugger (born 1948) and Hamish Fulton (born 1946). In this respect the collection is moving and developing with the times.

This then is certainly an important book. It is well designed and on the whole the quality of reproductions is very good. I regret that there is no listing of works in the collection by each artist but this is a small and very particular complaint. What I feel is problematic – and unremarked upon here – is the status of photography, which is not included. Undoubtedly most of the iconic mountain images of the last 60 years are photographic and the AC has important holdings. Perhaps these will be included in volume two?

Peter Mallalieu has been an exemplary curator of the Alpine Club collection and has made an important contribution to the literature of mountaineering history and culture. This book makes apparent the breadth, richness and importance of the Alpine Club's collection (as well as its quirkiness) and makes me think that it would be wonderful to see a major exhibition, carefully selected, at an important venue such as Tate Britain or the Royal Academy. It would be wonderful if such treasures and the fascinating artistic heritage of the Club could be seen and enjoyed by a very wide audience.

Ben Tufnell

'Art at the Rockface: The Fascination of Stone'
Exhibition at Norwich Castle Museum & Art Gallery and
Millennium Galleries Sheffield 2006
Catalogue edited by Andrew Moore and Nigel Larkin
Philip Wilson Publishers, 2006, npq

A new house for me means a new local crag, and the discovery that to start one route at Harborough Rocks there is a step up from a fossil, half polished away, but half still staring back from the Pleistocene in the dolomitic limestone. The older you get, the more you find to appreciate in the rock itself. This remarkably rich exhibition reveals the range of artists' uses of rock, from subject matter in Ruskin's intense study *In The Pass of Killiecrankie* (1857), to material in which the gods found their mythic forms in Thomas Banks' sculpture titled *Falling Titan* (1786), to raw beautiful matter to be celebrated in the modern settings of the rings made by Desmond Clen-Murphy (1963), to the found forms developed into bas-relief like the Ibis made by the inhabitants of Creswell Caves in Derbyshire, not far from Harborough Rocks, 12,000 years ago.

Throughout the exhibition are invitations to feel flint, granite, gritstone, as though we city dwellers (and indoor wall-climbers) need reminding of our tactile relationship with the earth and our lost bed-rock knowledge. Also placed throughout the exhibition are jars of pigment beside the rocks from which they are made, a reminder that for 77,000 years the earth has been a palette, a canvas and a mysterious subject that it has been important to try to get to know. That is the implicit project in all the varied forms of artworks in this exhibition.

What can we learn of our relationship with stone from Neolithic cup marks found in Scotland or the concentric rings in twinkling Northumberland sandstone? The stone seems to give as much as the marks themselves to the mystery of their meaning. What can we learn from land in David Bomberg's search for 'the spirit in the mass' when painting the fiery reds and yellows of Spanish stone in *Ronda, Summer* (1954)? What cosmic understanding is suggested by Emily Young's placing a light behind a six foot diameter disc of chalcedony in *Solar Disc 1* (2005)? What irony, given the current acceleration in the collapse of the Matterhorn, might we find in Ruskin's 1849 attempt to paint its 'calm' and 'the absence of all aspect of convulsion'. Why does Henry Moore's *Mother and Child* (1936) in Ancaster stone still have something to teach us from its association with pebble, egg, persistence and amelioration? Is a *Standing Stone* (2006) of golden Kinder grit actually added to when Gary Breeze carves in it the words 'A Stone stood up to free the Soul'? And what are we forced to confront by AC member Julian Cooper's huge canvas *Eiger Face* (2005) in which the recognisable places our climbing culture has named are washed over with a thin film that leaves us facing, as if for the first time, raw energies at work in ice and rock?

How amazing that this exhibition conceives of itself as 'groundbreaking'.

Terry Gifford

'The Mountaineer and the Artist'

The Alpine Club of Canada Centennial Exhibition, Whyte Museum of the Canadian Rockies, 2006

A century ago the founders of the Canadian Alpine Club had an amazingly broad and ambitious sense of what an alpine club might do beyond simply climb the peaks. Their first three objectives were: the promotion of scientific study and exploration of the Canadian alpine and glacial regions, the cultivation of art in relationship to mountain scenery, and the education of Canadians to an appreciation of their mountain heritage.

This is not about what a club can do for its members, but about what an alpine club might contribute to a national culture. All the verbs are boldly proactive: to promote, cultivate and educate. And in 1906 it was possible to see science, exploration, heritage and art as closely related activities, although not necessarily undertaken by the same individuals. Although this exhibition, which pairs a mountaineer with an artist, was funded by the ACC's Centennial Committee, the ACC's Vice-President for Mountain Culture chairs a committee that funds the annual journal, special publications, and photography and painting workshops. I mention these details in the belief that there might be something to learn from other models.

Artists were matched with mountaineers taking into account proximity to each other, hiking abilities and appropriateness of the artist's medium to the location of special significance chosen by the mountaineer that they visited together. So the resulting 13 art works in paints, pencil, ceramics, glass, stone, wood and textiles form the exhibition. The catalogue, which has a page from each participant, is greatly enhanced by the offer from Craig Richards to make portraits of the pairs. Then unexpectedly (does this only happen in Canada?) Joseph Potts offered to make video interviews with the artists in their studios, so a DVD is also on sale alongside the splendid catalogue (at www.AlpineClubofCanada.ca).

The viewer of the exhibition might find the results rather variable in quality, but the range of media and the range in age of the mountaineers are particularly striking. So are some of the images. Among my favourites were Brent Laycock's freely painted atmospherics of Barry Blanchard's Yamnuska, the amazingly varied effects achieved by Barbara West's embroidery portrait of an elderly Marjorie Hind with pack and ice axe at Lake O'Hara, the clever combination of Ed Bamiling's photography echoed by his ceramics catching facets of Chic Scott's Mount Assiniboine, the exquisitely made rope wound around a lump of quartz represented in glass by Susan Gottselig after visiting Jim Tarrant's Mount Sir Donald. Most striking, moving and superbly crafted was a small cabinet in the shape of Mount Lorette by Mary Lynne McCutcheon that is in two irregular halves sliding along a shelf supported by ice axes. It represents the relationship of Richard and Louise Guy who met 68 years ago, but it might also represent the creativity released by the pairings of this brilliantly conceived exhibition.

Terry Gifford

The Boys of Everest
Clint Willis
Robson Books, 2006, pp535, £16.99

The knife-edges of extremes sharpen understanding of the human condition. Clint Willis's lengthy foray into the world of high-altitude mountaineering takes both protagonist and reader to the alluring intersection of fear and desire. It is an attempt to 'leave behind the tether of a single mind...and deviate into the minds and bodies of others.' Willis's choice of this quotation from Virginia Woolf encapsulates his task as he sets out to produce both a chronological account of British post-war mountaineering achievement and an imaginative exploration of climbers' thoughts and feelings.

Although Willis's writing is informed by what was clearly lengthy and meticulous research, his forays into existentialism sometimes form an uncomfortable alliance with the minute detail and painstaking chronology of the climbs that form the body of the book. It is too obviously Willis's voice that re-creates these moments and this authorial intrusion unpicks the sense of character instilled earlier in the narrative. The moments before Mick Burke's death on Everest in 1975 are described in jarringly poetic terms: 'And this mist is merely a curtain; he can lift it to peek at infinity, and what a joy it is – what fun – to know that this invisible blue is the blue of God.' This of a man earlier described as 'steady and cheerful...the kind who could be trusted to speak his mind...'

Elsewhere and often the rhythms of the prose work well, to produce memorable and evocative snapshots of mountain scenery: 'the mountains looked...like black velvet cut-outs against the starlit sky' or illuminating comments on a climber's state of mind, as here capturing perfectly the relative inexperience of the 23-year old Bonington on the Bonatti Pillar: 'He was again aware of the exposure; it gave him to understand that he was stuck in a universe that operated by implacable laws, that circumstances and outcomes did not reflect his wishes, that he was alone and mortal.'

Proposing improvements to the text of an experienced writer can be frustrating, but *The Boys of Everest* would have benefited from a stronger editorial hand. Although the minutiae of the technical aspects of climbing are invariably fascinating to the committed climber, the armchair adventurer does not enjoy such relentless and often unintelligible detail. Willis's scrupulous pitch-by-pitch record of every ascent erodes the reader's tolerance and a more careful balance between informing and educating might have been achieved with judicious editing.

Willis combines introspection and analysis with a wider anthropological view, chronicling the history of British climbing from 1958 to 1985 and setting it in the context of changing social attitudes and class. These parameters bound Chris Bonington's climbing career up to and including his ascent of Everest and the careers of two generations of mountaineers who accompanied him on seminal climbs. Willis has done his research well and has listened carefully to both survivors and the family and friends of those who perished and the result is an informative and often gripping panorama of achievement and endurance. Death is ceaselessly interesting to us: all these climbs contain the elements of tragedy and the inevitable examination of the motives of those who attempt such high-risk activities.

On the subject of motivation the book is less successful. There can, of course, be no definitive answers and the usual suspects are aired again: once away from the world climbers feel their own humanity more intensely;

after such remote and challenging experiences the 'real' world seems less meaningful, less important, a place to be escaped from; challenge defines personality...

Willis offers us no personal perspective here other than his desire to 'work through my own sense of not having taken certain chances, done certain things that I was, on one level, drawn to do'. This blurring of personal and universal detracts from the incisiveness of the narrative, leaving readers to come to their own conclusions without sufficient and substantial debate. Willis, an outsider to the world of British climbing, leaves us, too, on the edge of an often impenetrable but compelling world – anxious to know more but not always certain how to proceed.

Val Randall

Jean & Pierre Ravier: 60 ans de Pyrénéisme
Jean-François Labourie & Rainier Munsch
Éditions Pin à Crochets, Pau, 2006, pp370, £67

Had they concentrated their efforts on the Alps, instead of the Pyrenees, Jean and Pierre Ravier would be better-known across the climbing world, for their achievements throughout the second half of the 20th century kept them in the top rank of French mountaineers. But for 60 years their passion has been for that less-glamorous southern range, whose summits have always been overshadowed by those of the Alpine chain.

With refreshing modesty and a catalogue of top-grade climbs, the Ravier twins earned the respect and admiration of all with an interest in their mountains, and in *60 ans de Pyrénéisme* their devotion to the range is given due prominence.

It's a book of two halves. In the first part, Jean-François Labourie relates the brothers' biography from their birth in Paris in 1933, through childhood in a foothill village, to discovery of mountains and their meteoric rise to become the greatest climbers ever to concentrate on the Pyrenees.

The early years make for interesting reading, but as climbing dominated their teens, it's not long before the story becomes a series of vertical highlights. In this Labourie is fortunate to have a vast archive of information to draw on, for in their *carnets de course* Jean and Pierre kept detailed notes of every climb and expedition made in 60 years of activity.

This biographical half of the book is written in unconventional style, being broken into sub-chapters that read like magazine articles or short stories. The family business in Bordeaux, for example. Opened in 1930 as an auto-spairs retailer by their father, when the brothers took charge it became an unofficial annexe of the CAF's South-West Section, where customers would come as much to discuss mountains as to collect spare parts for their cars. Bosses and employees worked for more or less the same salary, and in winter the premises also provided a refuge for the city's down-and-outs.

Though Jean was passed unfit for military service through a foot injury sustained four years earlier, it did nothing to diminish his climbing abilities, for in addition to a rash of new routes in the Pyrenees, he went to the Caucasus in 1959, and in 1962 was a member of Lionel Terray's team that made the first ascent of Jannu in the Himalaya.

But the most moving story concerns the accident in 2001 on l'Arbizon, which they were climbing with younger brother Paul when the arête they were on collapsed, killing Paul instantly. Though they'd taken part in rescues in the past, in six decades of top-grade climbing, this was the first fatality on their rope.

The second half of the book is a retelling and evaluation of their major climbs by Rainier Munsch – another high-performance climber who sadly died in an accident on the Pène Médaa above Gourette just a few months before the book was published.

After a brief run-down of the brothers' mountaineering career and their influence on today's Pyrénéistes, he journeys across the range from one massif to the next, looking at the most important *voies Ravier* created in each one. This is fascinating stuff, for we not only have Munsch's assessment of their climbs, but quotations from the *carnets de course* written at the time and, in several cases, a contemporary article on specific climbs produced by either Jean or Pierre. For the uninitiated, this part of the book serves as an invaluable lesson in what to climb and where.

60 ans de Pyrénéisme is handsomely produced by Éditions Pin à Crochets in Pau. Sturdily bound, and weighing almost 1800 grams, it's illustrated with some 450 photographs.

Now, if only there were a publisher out there who would produce an English-language edition....

Kev Reynolds

High Infatuation
A Climber's Guide to Love and Gravity
Steph Davis
The Mountaineers Books, 2006, US$16.95

Within the Alpine Club we all, to a greater or lesser degree, share something of an infatuation with the high places of our world. So, I think all of us will find nuggets of truth and wisdom within the pages of this new book by Steph Davis.

Davis is one of the most accomplished North American women climbers and has an impressive list of achievements including first ascents in Pakistan, Patagonia, Baffin Island and Krygyzstan. She was the first American woman to summit Fitz Roy in Patagonia, and has set high standards in big-wall, solo, free and alpine style climbing. Her role as an ambassador for Patagonia, a company that is setting the standard for environmental responsibility, reflects her enthusiasm for the natural environment. It is, however, her honesty and sheer love of climbing that shines through this collection of essays.

Some of the essays are presented here for the first time, while others have been previously published in a range of magazines. As such they are not a coherent collection, and some are better written than others. However, they all present an enjoyable insight into a climb or an adventure, and there are some real gems where Steph shares her feelings and thoughts about climbing and life. In some of these pieces she reveals her soul, her motivations and the inner conflicts. It is easy to empathise; the joy and wonder of mountain and climbing adventures must always be balanced with the costs and sacrifices.

The essays are accompanied by a very stimulating collection of quotes that give us an insight into the philosophy with which Steph lives both her climbing and her life. Throughout the book Steph's perseverance, enthusiasm and joy are a source of inspiration and encouragement.

Lizzy Hawker

Himalaya: Personal Stories of Grandeur, Challenge, and Hope
Edited by Richard C Blum, Erica Stone, and Broughton Coburn
National Geographic Society
and the American Himalayan Foundation, 2006, pp 255, US$35

From time to time one runs across a book that sparkles like a precious stone, which draws the eye and captures the mind. *Himalaya: Personal Stories of Grandeur, Challenge, and Hope* is just such a book. The essays in this collection cover a variety of mountain related topics with their focus on the Himalaya, yet the messages transcend any specific geographical setting and apply to and call for reverence, respect and protection of all earth's wild places.

The forward by His Holiness The Dalai Lama invests a religio-cultural history of the peoples of the Himalaya with this insight: 'I am very wary of idealizing old ways of living, because there is much that is commendable in the modern world. However, the clear challenge that faces us, whether we live in the developed or developing world, is to discover how we can enjoy the same degree of harmony and tranquility that we find in traditional communities, while benefiting fully from modern material developments.' This passage pretty much sets the theme for this anthology, which helps point the way for sustainability in a global sense. All the essays are strong and insightful. The reader is treated to many divergent points of view covering a variety of topics that work to pull the reader to an active participation with the writer and the text. One can not help but be inspired by the accounts of great mountaineer/explorers like Charles Houston, Jim Whittaker, Brent Bishop, Conrad Anker, Maurice Herzog and most certainly Sir Edmund Hillary. The voices of Himalayan natives like Chokyi Nyima

Rinpoche, Lodi Gyaltsen Gyari, Norbu Tenzing, and Ang Rita Sherpa offer the western world an understanding of what it is to exist on a daily basis at the foot of the world's highest and most dangerous landscape. While life may be difficult for people who are born and raised in the Himalaya, another strength to this collection is to have their native perspective juxtaposed with insights of western visitors, many of whom have chosen to spend a good part of their lives in and around the Himalaya like Broughton Coburn, Peter Hillary, George Schaller, and Stan Armington. It is through their writing and photographs that the peace and harmony, as well as the difficulty and sorrow, of this isolated part of the world is presented to many who will never actually see it first hand.

The epilogue is, fittingly, by Sir Edmund Hillary who has dedicated his life to making life better for the peoples of the Himalaya through the building of schools and clinics. While reaching the top of the world was a milestone in his life, it is not the 'high point'. 'I have been fortunate enough to be involved in many exciting adventures,' writes Sir Edmund. 'But when I look back over my life, I have little doubt that the most worthwhile things I have done have not been standing on the summits of mountains or at the North and South Poles, great experiences though they were. My most important projects have been the building and maintaining of schools and medical clinics for my good friends in the Himalaya...These are things I will always remember.'

To everyone who opens *Himalaya: Personal Stories of Grandeur, Challenge, and Hope* it is a call to action, for personal involvement in worthy causes that will lead to making the world a place of harmony and peace.

Mikel Vause

The Mountaineer's Pontiff
William Lowell Putnam
Authorhouse, 2006, pp485

Mountaineers may sense a spiritual benefit from being among mountains but only one true mountaineer was ever ordained Pope. History records numerous men of the cloth who have lifted their eyes to the hills and recognised an eternity beyond, a few early Popes pottered among the Alps, but none had a record to equal that of Ambrogio Damiano Achille Ratti, the poet, scholar and alpinist who became Pope Pius XI.

He led the Roman Catholic Church in the critical years leading to the Second World War when religious faith came under siege from the growing fascism of Germany and Italy with the dark shadow of communism looming in the east. Steering such an ancient, unwieldy and controversial vessel as the Roman Catholic Church through the prevailing dangerous political waters of Europe took courage and tactical skill, qualities Achille Ratti had doubtless honed among the ice slopes and summits of the Alps.

But *The Mountaineer's Pontiff,* by William Lowell Putnam, covers a wider canvas than the story of one man and delves into the fascinatingly dark and troubled history of Holy Roman Church, from the medieval era when banishment, imprisonment, poison and even strangulation were thought to have been among Papal resorts, to more contemporary times when the Church stood accused of maintaining a lofty silence on such temporal issues as the Holocaust.

Pius XI was elected Pope in 1922 and held the office until his death in 1939 at the age of 81, long after the time when his love of being among mountains could be turned into a passion for climbing them. Born at Desio in northern Italy in 1857, Achille Ratti entered the priesthood when he was aged 22 and his career as mountaineer ran in parallel with his scholarly progress through the archives of the Church, as assistant director and then director of the Ambrosian Library and later Prefect of the Vatican Library. A sturdy, reddish-haired man of middling height, his climbing gear consisted of high gaiters, reaching to his knickerbockers, and a coat of military cut, but always with the usual clerical collar. He wore the biretta and never failed to carry his cassock in his knapsack along with his prayer-book from which he would occasionally read a few sentences when resting.

His most spectacular achievement was in 1889 when with one companion and two Courmayeur guides he completed an early ascent of the Marinelli route on Monte Rosa followed by the first traverse of the mountain by an Italian party, during which they were twice benighted and obliged to shiver on a ledge. Two days later Ratti set off from Zermatt without his companions and climbed the Matterhorn on which he was once again forced to spend the night in the open. As the *Tablet* reported at the time: 'Msgr Ratti has a special weakness as an alpine climber. He loves to pass the night in the open in the midst of the great rocks.'

The following year he climbed Mont Blanc, adding to a long series of notable climbs, a record which would still, more than a century later, as Putnam says, reflect a vigorous and determined spirit. The following year Ratti was back in Courmayeur and made a swift ascent of Mont Blanc in perfect conditions.

The Great War, advancing years and the press of clerical duties combined to curtail his climbing activities. He railed against the growth of Nazism which he saw emerging from the humiliation Germany suffered after the Treaty of Versailles. He thundered, in the Delphic manner of Popes, against the fascism of Hitler and Mussolini. Hitler attempted unsuccessfully to ban his encyclical to the faithful in Germany, composed in the German vernacular and making clear the Papacy's attitude towards the 'master race' philosophy. Gestapo agents snatched the document from the hands of priests as it was read from their pulpits on Passion Sunday.

Pope Pius XI emerges from this portrait a gentle, scholarly man who in his time was a formidable mountaineer with always the influence and authority of the Roman Catholic Church looming powerfully in his experience. His climbing record won him an invitation to become an honorary member of the Alpine Club which he courteously declined 'for reasons of policy', but his legacy remains in the climbing club and the huts in Wales and the Lake District that bear his name.

Ronnie Faux

Wasdale Climbing Book
A History of Early Climbing in the Lake District
Michael Cocker
The Ernest Press, 2006, pp 240, OP

The climbing of a new route is usually a thrill, that moment when the crux is done, when the route is in the bag, that secret line, that plum of a route, that load of choss to have a second ascent by the next guidebook writer! Pressure off, memories for the future. What about a name? And how should it be recorded? Nowadays, new routes can be recorded on the internet. However, traditional new route books are still in use in places such as Pete's Eats in Llanberis and Amandiers Hotel in Tafraoute, Morocco.

In the past there were new route books at the Lamplighter Café and Packhorse Inn, both in Keswick. But the grandfather of them all was the Wasdale Climbing Book. This was kept at the Wasdale Hotel and detailed a golden age of climbing in the Lake District, starting in 1863 through to 1919, and then a second volume covering 1920 to 1939. Many early members of the Alpine Club visited Wasdale Head during this period to use up their surplus energies and then set their pens to record their activities. An article about the Napes Pinnacle (Napes Needle), in 1890 in the *Pall Mall Budget* raised the national profile of Wasdale. There are also many routes recorded by early members of the Fell and Rock Climbing Club, formed in 1906.

Many important climbs were recorded in the Wasdale book, including *The Needle* (1886), *Eagle's Nest Ridge Direct* (1892), *Botterill's Slab* (1903) and *Central Buttress* (1914) as well as the exploits of the likes of J W Robinson, Geoffrey Hastings, Haskett Smith, the Pilkingtons and Hopkinsons, Archer Thomson, Norman Collie, Cecil Slingsby, Godfrey Solly, George Mallory, O G Jones and so many more.

What a place the hotel must have been to reflect on the activities on the crags, and no doubt the conversations ranged widely over other topics.

In 1922 the secretary of the FRCC arranged for a typed copy of the original volume to be made and kept in the club library. Now, to coincide with the centenary of the FRCC, a facsimile edition has been produced. It has been painstakingly put together by Mike Cocker as writer and editor together with an eminent group of helpers and published in a volume that is a credit to the specialist skills of Peter Hodgkiss at The Ernest Press. (Unfortunately the book is now out of print and will not be reissued.)

Following a foreword by Lord Chorley (who seems to be related to most of the main players), an introduction tells the story of the original Wasdale Climbing Book. This leads into a very detailed but concise history of climbing around Wasdale Head from 1800 to 1920 that sets the stage for the record of the action in the original book. The centrepiece of Cocker's book is the reproduction of the pages, showing the original scripts on buff-coloured paper.

Reading the descriptions of those early climbs you almost feel you are reading the original in the hotel all those years ago. Guidebooks still describe these same climbs, however seeing the original detail adds a new awareness of the time and the first encounters with the route. Next comes a commentary on each of the routes detailed, giving a flavour of the background to the climbs, and finally there is a list of first ascents and various appendices.

The *Wasdale Climbing Book* opens a window on a world when climbing was young. After a day having done *Napes Needle* and *Eagle's Nest Direct* my son Michael (16) was enthralled to see the original detail of the *Direct* written up by Solly. For those interested in the formative years of British rock climbing this finely produced volume is a must.

Ron Kenyon

The Avalanche Handbook
David McClung and Peter Schaerer
The Mountaineers Books, pp344, US$19.95

January 2007 saw the death of Ed LaChapelle, the grand old man of avalanche research in the USA. LaChapelle once rejected the tag of expert with the rejoinder that 'the experts are all dead'. Maybe that means we can now call LaChapelle an expert too, though the implication of his riposte was that to really qualify as an expert on avalanches one had to have been interred in one. And that was not his fate. In fact for the skier, snow addict and mountaineer that he was, LaChapelle could hardly have scripted a better departure. Aged 80, he died of a heart attack while skiing knee-high powder snow with his partner Meg Hunt and friends at Monarch Mountain, Colorado.

In his final months, LaChapelle also had the satisfaction of seeing publication of this third edition of *The Avalanche Handbook*, which in various guises has been a hefty bible on avalanches and snow safety for more than half a century. LaChapelle authored the important 1961 update and wrote the foreword to this latest edition, which embodies much of his earlier work on evaluating snow slope stability (or instability.)

That anyone who skis away from the piste should know this stuff goes without saying. As David McClung – joint author, with Peter Schaerer, of this latest edition – observes, most avalanche victims in North America and Europe triggered the slides that caused their own deaths. 'Clearly their perceptions about the state of instability did not match reality.' McClung is leader of the avalanche research group at the University of British Columbia where for 15 years he has taught about the human factor in natural hazards, an area he feels has had insufficient attention in avalanche forecasting. He corrects this omission in a completely new chapter on forecasting, including fascinating work on risk propensity and personality traits. Depending on age, family, skill, confidence and so on, we set our risk thermostats at different levels.

There is a suggestion here that the wearing of avalanche transceivers might lead ski-tourers to take risks on potentially unstable slopes that, without the reassurance of the transceiver, they would steer clear of. This picks up on the studies of the Canadian psychologist Gerald Wilde who coined the term *risk homeostasis*, meaning that when safety devices are used, people modify their behaviour to maintain the same level of risk as before.

'For example,' say the authors, 'avalanche transceivers provide a greater level of safety, pushing people toward more thrilling experiences than without. The same applies to mountaineering: climbing with and without a rope implies different human behaviour. The concept from the perspective of human perception is then that the reward is greater when a safety device is used, with no apparent increase in the level of risk.'

However McClung and Schaerer draw back from the extension of this logic to any suggestion that safety devices don't have much effect on saving lives. And I for one will not be casting aside the avalanche transceiver.

With hundreds of photographs and diagrams, up-dated sections on the character and effects of avalanches, snow formation, on current search and rescue techniques, forecasting and decision-making, this third edition further enhances the authority of the *The Avalanche Handbook*. When he wrote the foreword to the 1993 edition (also a McClung Schaerer production), LaChapelle wondered whether he would be around to see the next one. He was, just, and rightly judged it a 'worthy successor' to the long tradition.

Stephen Goodwin

An Afterclap of Fate
Charles Lind
The Ernest Press, 2006, pp 126, £15

Subtitled *Mallory on Everest*, this book was the surprise winner of the Boardman Tasker Award in 2006, and the focus is indeed upon the perennially fascinating George Mallory, intensely so. Lind takes us on an excursion into Mallory's mind as the great climber makes his fateful last attempt on Everest in the company of Sandy Irvine. In doing so Lind advances a thoroughly researched interpretation of the most recent evidence to construct a persuasive scenario for the pair's last day on the mountain seen through Mallory's eyes.

But the book is much more than just another piece of Mallory myth-making. For a start there is its challenging structure written in spaced paragraphs, or perhaps that should be stanzas, divided into 38 sections. The story seems to share characteristics of the novel and one might expect a treatment drawing on the tradition of the 'stream of consciousness' explored by Joyce and Woolf. In many places one feels the authentic rhythm of reflective thought:

> This is what one hungers for... what the spirit needs, in the face of modern life, is the sense of freedom...and that is the essence of the mountains... the natural solace of the hills coming with their inspirational air and the promise of the heights. And the quickening joy you experience in the feeling of something vast and infinitely serene... that mysteriously uplifts the heart and mind...and sometimes quietly leads you to an open, very tranquil space...beyond the borders of within and without.

Elsewhere – 'I'm lowering myself down now to Sandy' – there is a literalness that owes more to the need to ravel out events than any debt to Mallory's thinking. Lind has described the work as a prose-poem, and as such it dramatises Mallory's situation in a way that reminds one more of Browning's 'dramatis personae' delivering their monologues or the strange shifting narrators of Eliot's *Wasteland*, emblematic of states of mind...which brings me to the Notes.

There are 71 pages of prose-poem and 40 pages of notes; quite an apparatus! So what is going on here? Lind gives us a clue when quoting Wittgenstein in the introduction to the five-page glossary that follows the notes: " 'The limits of my language mean the limits of my world.' Sometimes it is necessary to push at those limits." And in his acceptance speech at the Boardman Tasker Awards ceremony he referred to the notes as filling gaps in the knowledge of many modern readers. Undoubtedly he is right. Few people today have a familiarity with Winthrop Young, Whymper, Mummery, or for that matter, Milton, Shelley and Blake who stride with equal presence through Lind's notes and Mallory's mind.

I would suggest that what we have in the structure of the book is a Brechtian type of alienation device that forces us to recognise the essential otherness of George Mallory.

There is a disturbing modern tendency to see others as reflections of ourselves, to select the most sympathetic characteristics and ignore those others that we struggle to understand, to recast historical figures as naive moderns, whereas in reality they have an idiosyncratic context that would repay recognition and reflection. It is the reverse of empathy; a kind of sympathetic fallacy that assumes 'everyone thinks like me'. No wonder it has been described as a culture of narcissism.

And it's there in the climbing world. When an ambitious couple declared their intention to race my team for the summit of an unclimbed peak, we decided not to jeopardise our safety by adding the pressure of competition to what would be a difficult enough climb, so pulled out. They simply could not understand why we didn't want to share our base camp with them.

That's where *An Afterclap of Fate* succeeds, and where it will fail for those most determinedly tied to their blinkered views, because the book asserts Mallory's values in language that challenges and extends one's thinking in its interpretation of his experiences. And those are values that challenge the public face of the climbing world today with its assiduous self-promotion and scrambling after sponsorship. Instead, Mallory thinks of 'annihilating self'.

Cherry-Garrard, after meeting Mallory, described him as 'burning with a kind of fire, an ardent impatient soul, winding himself up to a passion the higher he got'. And in his acknowledged masterpiece on Scott's last expedition, *The Worst Journey in the World*, Cherry-Garrard refers repeatedly to the unselfishness of men like Wilson and Bowers as the core of their strength.

Lind quotes Winthrop Young's warning against 'the fatal crowd infection of judging results above the spirit and manner of the doing'. *An Afterclap of Fate* is a timely reminder of such values that is well worth reading and rereading for its imaginative voyage into another mind, another era.

Dave Wynne-Jones

Reconnecting with John Muir. Essays in post-pastoral practice
Terry Gifford
The University of Georgia Press, 2006, pp201, US$ 39.95

Terry Gifford is John Muir's doughty champion. The two omnibus editions of Muir's work that Terry edited in the 1990s[*] brought together the books, letters and other writings of the great naturalist-mountaineer and founder of the national park movement in the US. Now, with *Reconnecting with John Muir*, he uses Muir as an exemplar of integrated, environmental conscious knowing and writing. The key, and often quoted lesson that makes Muir sound every bit the 21st century holistic Greenie, is of course: 'When we try to pick out anything by itself, we find it hitched to everything else in the universe.'

The sub-title, *Essays in post-pastoral practice*, signals that this is an academic book addressed primarily to Terry's fellow professionals in literary studies and eco-criticism. But that does not mean that his observations will necessarily be lost on the less cerebral of us, his fellow climbers and members of the Alpine Club. Indeed, if that were so Terry would have failed in his aim

* John Muir: *The Eight Wilderness-Discovery Books*, 1992, Diadem (Bâton Wicks) and *John Muir, His Life and Letters and Other Writings*, 1996, Bâton Wicks.

of creating an accessible narrative that weaves together critical writing, teaching environmental awareness, and mountaineering and its literature – all suffused with the philosophy of Muir.

It is a bold project, the more so for interspersing the chapters with his own poems, each one addressed to John Muir as Terry visits the 'noble landscapes' that Muir eulogised and helped conserve. Terry is practising what he preaches, through Muir, and hitching everything to everything else, breaking down our modern tendency to compartmentalise.

Muir used the term 'mountaineer' in a broader sense than it has come to be understood today, and there may still be those of a narrower, hardcore mentality who would not think of him as mountaineer at all. He most certainly was, though the notion of mountaineering as a 'sport' never appeared in his vocabulary.

As Terry puts it, 'For Muir the exhilaration of reading rock in order to climb it, or reading the skies to make crucial judgements, of taking in what a summit has to offer are not the activities of a sport, but of a deeper reconnection with nature...' So it must have been on his first ascents of Mount Ritter and Cathedral Peak; Terry noting in an aside born of following in his subject's footsteps, that Muir could not have avoided using a hand jam as he climbed to the Cathedral's topmost spire.

Terry is pushing at boundaries and the adventurous approach of this book may well surprise those steeped in more conventional forms of literary criticism. Poetry and the 'self-expanding act of climbing' are recruited in support of academic argument, all marshalled in the wider ecological cause. He wants us to rediscover what it meant to John Muir to be 'hopelessly and forever a mountaineer'.

Stephen Goodwin

Hostile Habitats
Scotland's Mountain Environment
Editors Nick Kempe & Mark Wrightham
Scottish Mountaineering Trust, 2006, pp 257, £16

A stonechat most likely. A bright morning and this little black-capped chap is proclaiming his territory with a ratchet call from a stem of marsh grass as I head up Mousthwaite Comb, bound for Sharp Edge. Or one day last winter, walking up by the Dee on the Mar Lodge estate and wondering at the past lives of the settlements that today are just a ground plan of old stone and turf walls. It was too windy to go higher and even the birds and beasts were keeping a low profile, save for a water vole busy foraging beneath the sheltering supports of White Bridge.

A lot of our time in the mountains is spent not in narrow focus for the next handhold or axe placement but on long approaches or ambling returns across moorland or through forest. I've never set out to look for an eagle, but over the years I've seen dozens. One might set out as a climber but if you've any sense

/

of curiosity at all you become an amateur naturalist along the way, and the usefulness of a rudimentary grasp of geology goes without saying.

Hostile Habitats (the choice of title is about my only complaint) is a multi-subject reference book that informs and enriches one's observations in the Scottish hills with sound scholarship on climate, geology, vegetation, wild life and the traces and impact of human beings. It is not likely you would take it on the hill in your rucksack, but if you're heading for the Highlands it is worth having along in the car to mull over in the evening.

After that day on the Dee, I read up on the former sheiling settlements, relics of transhumance when cattle and other livestock were moved to higher pastures in the summer. Other important activities were carried out at the sheilings, such as cheese making and weaving, and there is the reminder of another on the Mar Lodge estate with the remains of an illicit whisky still discreetly set amongst the ruins. I love this kind of detail, filling out the picture of the land I've travelled through.

And yes, the noisy bird was a stonechat. There is a well-illustrated section on mountain birds, with others on invertebrates, mammals, vegetation and so on. The fact this particular stonechat wasn't in Scotland at all but in the English Lake District makes a small point about the versatility of the book, mountain environments thankfully extend well south of Hadrian's Wall.

Each of the nine in-depth chapters is written by a different specialist but in an easily accessible style. The joint editors are Nick Kempe, a former president of the MCofS and a board member of Scottish Natural Heritage (SNH) from 2003 to 2006, and Mark Wrightham, an upland vegetation ecologist with SNH. This is an inspired piece of publishing by the Scottish Mountaineering Trust – but I wish they'd chosen a title that didn't sound more appropriate to central Carlisle on a Saturday night.

Stephen Goodwin

Scottish Hill Names
Their origin and meaning
Peter Drummond
Scottish Mountaineering Trust, 2007, pp240, £15

The excellent Scottish Mountaineering Trust publishers seem intent on turning us into Renaissance mountaineers, well rounded in not just the climbs and trails of the Scottish hills but in their natural and cultural history. Close on the heels of *Hostile Habitats* comes this completely revised edition of *Scottish Hill Names*, a mine of serendipitous inquiry if ever there was one. The product of years of painstaking work by Peter Drummond, it is both an informative work of reference and, for those with any sense of curiosity, an enriching enhancement to the day's outing.

Let's take a well-known hill – Buachaille Eite (Etive) Mòr, the big herdsman at the junctions of Glens Coe and Etive. How often have you heard it referred to as the great shepherd? But as Drummond points out in a chapter on the characters immortalised in hill names – cobblers, witches, warriors and so on - only in the Biblical sense of a shepherd watching over the glens is this likely to be true. 'Given Gaeldom's reaction to the hated Clearances that introduced the cheviot sheep – "Woe to thee O land, for the Great Sheep is coming." – shepherd seems less likely than herdsman.'

Most of the hill names in Scotland are in one of four languages, the oldest being Cumbric, spoken by the Britons, and then Old Norse, mainly in the islands, followed by Scots, related to English, and finally the dominant Gaelic. But apart from in the Western Isles, where Gaelic is still in daily use, these are languages which are either dead or on life-support systems. Hence the case for this fascinating book.

It had never struck me before, but although mountain names in the Alps sound 'foreign' to me, and hence their meaning is often puzzling, they are in the everyday tongue of the locals, so no 'Hill Names' book is necessary. Scotland, as ever, is in an incomprehensibility class of its own. However, while grasping the origin of a name becomes a pleasure with Drummond's guidance, it will take a lot of tent-bound days and practice before I can do other than mangle the pronunciation.   *SG*

Northern Highlands South
SMC Climbers' Guide
Andy Nisbet and Noel Williams
Scottish Mountaineering Trust, 2007, pp396, £23

If there is any time left after studying your chosen mountain's wildlife and the origins of its name (see above), why not try a bit of climbing? And as this offering drives home, there is just so much to do. The third of three volumes to the Northern Highlands, it details the area from glorious Torridon south to Applecross, Glen Carron, Glen Shiel and Knoydart. The sandstone crags of Torridon and the coast around Diabaig have seen much new activity since the area was incorporated in the 1993 guide, while winters have produced new routes across the board. And if this makes it sound a little busy for what once was regarded as a virtual wilderness destination, Knoydart remains as remote as ever, perfect for the committed optimist.
                                        SG

A History of the Association of British Members of the
Swiss Alpine Club
James Bogle
Hatcham Press, 2005, pp (4)+98, npq

James Bogle has done an excellent job of writing a history of the ABMSAC in its first almost-century – 'almost' because that event doesn't occur until

2009. James has obviously decided to get in first. Original overtures made to the SAC in 1908 for the formation of a London Section were refused, as their statutes did not allow sections outside Switzerland. However, persistence paid off, and the next year an Association was agreed to (subtle difference) under the presidency of Clinton Dent.

The club went from strength to strength over the years, and in 1912 achieved the second of their original objectives – to build a hut in Switzerland. On 17 August the inauguration of the Britannia Hut took place on the Kleine Allalinhorn, in the presence of a great crowd. An al fresco lunch was served, one of the first to eat being the young Noel Odell. History repeated itself 63 years later when another opening ceremony took place, that of the George Starkey Hut in Patterdale.

The Association has changed over the years, from a social and dining club for gentlemen climbers who were members of the SAC, to today's club of about 250 climbers and hillwalkers whose activities take them all over the world, including two or three meets in the Alps each year. We wish them success in the future. *GT*

And Nobody Woke up the Dead
The Life & Times of Mabel Barker – Climber & Educational Pioneer
Jan Levi
The Ernest Press, 2006, pp264, £16

This is an intriguing story of a quite remarkable woman who deserves our attention and our respect.

> But is it mere fantasy to feel that something of us remains in Staffa and Iona, as in all places of the earth that one has loved and touched and slept upon? At least it is true that something of them goes with us, entering into our very being and forming part of us through life; so that whether we ever return to them or not, we shall never say farewell to the waves beating on the Herds-man, the cry of the sea-birds, and the songs of the people of the Isles.

I'm sure that each and every one of us can identify with the feelings Mabel expresses in the paragraph I have quoted above, though not all of us can hope to capture it in words so eloquently. Once we have made the mountains and wild places our own, they are always part of us.

Jan Levi has won a number of awards for her short stories, including the International Festival of Mountaineering Literature Writing Competition. She is also a founding member of the group *Women, Words and Mountains*. Having now turned her hand to biography she has penned a very well researched and engaging account of the life of Mabel Barker, a pioneer amongst British women climbers. Threaded through the book are numerous excerpts from Mabel's diaries, together with many historical photographs. These writings give an intriguing insight into her personal thoughts and feelings, and amongst them are some delightful passages.

Born in the 1880s, Mabel lived during an era when women were not generally expected to hold a passion for the hills. Despite this, Mabel managed to become a highly talented rock climber who held her own amongst the best of the day. Amongst her numerous and varied achievements were the first female traverse of the Cuillin Ridge and the first female lead of the Great Flake on Central Buttress. To Mabel climbing was the physical expression of her love of nature and the outdoors which included cycling, fell-walking and all manner of wild camping.

Her chosen profession was that of teacher. This suited her desire to share her love and knowledge of the environment. Between the First and Second World Wars (during both of which she volunteered her services) she founded a school at Friar's Row in Caldbeck. It was here that she was able to put into practice the thoughts and ideas that she had developed, making nature and the environment the central part of her young pupils' lives.

Mabel lived her life to the full, a pioneering woman in both her work and her play, and we can learn much from both her climbing and educational adventures. She provides an inspiration to us all, having had the courage to stand up for her convictions and to fight for what she believed in. We must thank Jan Levi for opening our eyes to the fascinating life of an incredible woman.

Lizzy Hawker

The Eiger Obsession
Facing the Mountain That Killed My Father
John Harlin III
Simon & Schuster, 2007, pp 285, US$26

A key to this absorbing tale lies in that curious Americanism that John Harlin attaches to his own name – the Roman figure III. It is a story of a man overly conscious of his father's shadow, haunted by the belief – quite erroneous – that he isn't big enough to fill his father's boots. Appending the 'III' surely only underlines the fact that one is part of a dynasty and invites comparisons.

John Harlin II needs little introduction to this readership. The 'blond god' fell to his death in 1966 when a fixed rope broke during the first ascent of the Eiger Direct. Harlin II, founder of the International School of Mountaineering at Leysin, had become obsessed with forcing a *dirrettisima* up the north face and the route, completed by Dougal Haston and four Germans, bears his name.

There is a perceptive quote from Ted Wilson, Harlin II's friend and Leysin colleague, in which he refers to a 'certain Hemingway type fatalism' persisting in the mountaineering world of the 1960s and its effect on Harlin, Gary Hemming and many others. 'Like Hemingway, they lived large, took life by storm, and were willing to die young if necessary. They truly were a committed generation,' Wilson wrote.

Young Johnny was nine at the time of the accident, and within the family they referred to Dad being 'away on expedition'. In *The Eiger Obsession*, Harlin III is frank about the toll on their lives, dreams of Dad showing up, silent, at dinner, and the tantrums of Harlin II's daughter Andrea, eight at the time, who turned the anger of loss on her mother.

The emotional story, coupled with Harlin III's own suppressed ambitions as an alpinist, make this as close to being a 'page turner' as any climbing-related book I've read since *Touching the Void*. Tragedy aside, thank goodness, I suppose the fact that Harlin juggles mountaineering and family with editing the *American Alpine Journal*, gives me added identity with the author, but his turmoil over the potential destructiveness of climbing is common enough.

That Harlin III is in turn drawn to the north face of the Eiger comes as no surprise. The actual manner, however, was not initially of his choosing. John had hoped to climb the face away from the limelight and only tell his Eiger widow mother about it afterwards. In fact, in 2005, he climbs for the movie cameras – following the Heckmair route with Robert and Daniela Jasper.

The result, and the spur for this fascinating autobiography, is *The Alps*, a MacGillvray Freeman film for IMAX theatres – perhaps the only format that can do the *Nordwand* a degree of boot-shaking justice. (AC president Stephen Venables had a hand in the script, suggesting to the film's Swiss backers that the Harlin story would make a good vehicle for conveying the beauty and drama of the Alps to potential tourists.) The film is certainly a visual treat, but it is no substitute for the real life story told here by John Harlin – no Roman numeral necessary.

Stephen Goodwin

El Macizo del San Lorenzo
Silvia Metzeltin Buscaini
Fondazione Giovanni Angelini, Belluno, 2005, 80pp, npq

Compressed into the 80 pages of this work is an efficient biography of Patagonia's second major massif. Besides its straightforward and descriptive text, readers will find 24 black & white and four colour illustrations, 10 detailed photo-diagrams of routes on major peaks, nine maps and two line-drawings. 41 named peaks and passes are included in this survey. The orography of the massif of Cerro San Lorenzo (3706m) is surveyed first. Following are sections on history, geology, glaciology and mountaineering. The history of the San Lorenzo district is told by describing actual climbs.

It begins with the discovery of Cerro San Lorenzo by Chilean surveyors (1896-1898) and we are brought to 2004, the year of the first winter ascent of San Lorenzo. Pages 33 to 54 are devoted to the mountain itself. The other six main chains or ridges are reviewed next. To summarize, instead of the usual book on a Patagonian vertical wall, we have here a whole area rich in rock and ice peaks, briefly but effectively portrayed. And no other author-climber would have been better qualified for the task than AC member Silvia Metzeltin Buscaini, herself the winner of 68 Patagonian summits, among which are the three culminating points of San Lorenzo.

Evelio Echevarría

Travels in Far-Off Places
Michael Clarke
Classic Day Publishing, 2006, ppx+210, npq

Michael Clarke's book is a mini-autobiography, with the broad details of his life summarized in the first seven pages, and the remaining 19 chapters devoted to the bulk of his travels between 1968 and 2001. As might be expected, his early years saw the most successes, from summiting Trisul in 1975, Nanda Devi in '78 and Denali in '83, to a near miss on Gasherbrum II in '82. The rest of the book covers travels ranging from Peru to Bhutan, Africa to Tierra del Fuego, and Tibet to New Zealand and Antarctica. Sadly, his more strenuous ventures came to an end with a heart attack in 1999, but he still manages to get about quite a bit, and this book is a fitting tribute to a life of travel. *GT*

Guide to the Rwenzori. Mountains of the Moon
Henry Osmaston
The Rwenzori Trust, 2006, pp288, npq

The first edition of this guide appeared in 1972, written by Henry Osmaston and David Pasteur, but conditions in the country since that time meant that the Rwenzori received few visitors, and there was little call for a revised edition. The fact that the situation in the area has now improved markedly, plus the fact that climatic conditions have changed the face of many mountains, made a second edition desirable. Sadly, David Pasteur died in 2005, but Henry Osmaston did a magnificent job in producing this nearly-300-page revision, complete with numerous black & white and colour photographs and diagrams. He was for many years a District Forest Officer in the region, and last visited the Rwenzori Mountains National Park, of which he was an honorary warden, in 2005. Shortly after delivering a copy of his guide to the AC Library, it was learnt that Henry had died suddenly (obituary, page 389). *GT*

Exploring the Highlands of Himalaya
Harish Kapadia
Indus, 2006, pp248, Rs 650

The review of M S Kohli's book (above) mentions that it is his twentieth book. Indian mountaineer authors are certainly prolific, as this is Harish's fifteenth book. Such industry is remarkable. The present work is split into nine main chapters, one for each area of the Indian Himalaya, stretching from Arunachal Pradesh in the far east of the country to the Siachen glacier. Each chapter has a general description of the area and its mountaineering history, mini-biographies of some of the explorers of the area, and extracts from relevant books. The remaining chapters give useful general information on the Indian Himalaya, covering the rules for climbing and trekking, geology, rivers, pilgrimages and the recent wars in the area. It forms a good, well-illustrated guide to the whole Indian Himalaya. *GT*

The Alps. A Cultural History
Andrew Beattie
Signal Books, 2006, ppxiv+246, pb. £12.00

The first thing that confronts you when you open this volume in the 'Landscapes of the Imagination' series, is a small colour photo of Julie Andrews dancing across a Swiss hillside in true *Sound of Music* fashion, which doesn't exactly encourage you to delve deeper. This would be a pity as you would miss a good general introduction to the Alps. The book is in four parts: 'Landscape', which is self-explanatory, 'History', covering everything from the Romans to the Nazis, 'Imagination', ranging from Rousseau and Mary Shelley through to the afore-mentioned *Sound of Music*, and 'Visitors', which covers Thomas Cook and the coming of the mountaineers. The background information in this book is well set out and likely to contain something you didn't know. *GT*

The Last Blue Mountain
Ralph Barker
Rippng Yarns, 2006, pp216, pb, £15.95

Ripping Yarns has been doing the climbing public a service by reprinting classics of mountaineering literature. *The Last Blue Mountain* is considerably more recent than the others and, they say, will be the last in the series. It is a facsimile reprint of the original 1959 edition and tells the well-known story of the ill-fated 1957 expedition to Haramosh in the Karakoram range, from which two members failed to return. *GT*

Into the Untravelled Himalaya. Travels, Treks and Climbs
Harish Kapadia
Pp256, Rs 400

Touching Upon the Himalaya. Excursions and Enquiries
Bill Aitken
Pp 168, Rs 150

Adventure Travels in the Himalaya
John Angelo Jackson
Pp 256, Rs 400

Indus Pub. Co, New Delhi, 2004/5

These three paperbacks, between them, cover almost every aspect of travelling and climbing in the Himalaya.

The book by our Honorary Member Harish Kapadia describes travels in Tibet, explorations in Arunachal Pradesh, journeying in Bhutan, the history of Kangchenjunga and of Nanda Devi, treks in Himachal Pradesh and East Karakoram and, finally, thoughts on mountaineering and war around the Siachen glacier.

Bill Aitken is a Scottish-born naturalised Indian who was Hon Librarian of the Himalayan Club for many years and has written articles for the *AJ*. *Touching Upon the Himalaya* is a collection of his articles first published in the 2004 volume of the *Himalayan Journal* which celebrated 60 years of the Club's existence. These range from 'Gorging in Zanskar' to 'An Enquiry into the Real Name of Mount Everest'.

The late John Jackson was principally known for taking part in the successful Kangchenjunga expedition in 1955, and later as director of Plas y Brenin from 1960 to 1976. But, as this book shows, much of his life was spent travelling, often with his wife Eileen, in the Himalaya, and it covers a period of 60 years of his adventures.

Kapadia's and Jackson's books have excellent photos, and all three books are enhanced by sketches by Geeta Kapadia.   *GT*

Mountain Area Research and Management
Integrated Approaches
Edited by Martin F Price
Earthscan, 2007, pp272, £49.95

In this academic work, our member Martin Price, professor of mountain studies at the University of the Highlands and Islands, has brought together scientists and practitioners from six continents intent on improving our understanding and informed management of mountain areas. Its publication comes shortly before the AC's 'Summits of Learning' seminar in December 2007 that Martin has organised and at which Professor Bruno Messerli, our new honorary member and an important contributor to this book, is due to take part.

No one who climbs or ski-tours in glaciated regions will need much convincing that climate change is particularly apparent in the high mountains. Even so, the statistics given here from research in US national parks are staggering. Take Glacier National Park in Montana: only 27 glaciers remain of the original 150 that existed when the park was founded in 1910; the park area covered by ice and permanent snow has shrunk from 99sq km to just 17sq km in 1998. That this will have consequences for vegetation, wildlife and human beings downstream should be self-evident. And global warming is only one of the forces of change at work in the mountains, though perhaps the most pervasive – deforestation, tourism, migration, war…it's a long list.

Integrated Approaches is, in a way, the scientist's equivalent of Terry Gifford's *Reconnecting with John Muir*. The message is strikingly similar – Muir's dictum that everything in the universe is hitched to everything else, and in Price's case that research and management must be all embracing. Thus scientist, farmer, forester, economist, shaman and politician must all be involved, understanding change and devising sustainable policies specific to the particular mountain community.

Note: More detail on the contents of the book and its case studies can be found at www.earthscan.co.uk   *SG*

Kilimanjaro & East Africa
A Climbing and Trekking Guide (2nd Edition)
Cameron M Burns
The Mountaineers Books, 2006, pp240, US$19.95

An updated and expanded edition of Burns's 1998 guide. New content includes a chapter on the three highest summits of the Rwenzoris, Uganda. Altogether more than 50 routes from summit walk-ups to serious technical climbs (though not the 1964 Edwards Thompson route up the east face of Mawenzi, the first ascent of which features, belatedly, in this *AJ*). Packed with useful info' on how to plan a safe and, all being well, successful trip; website listings, glossary of several languages. I was particularly taken by the pages of endnotes in which Burns passes on informal tips gained from his East African journeys, including his valid doubts about the efficacy of Diamox on Kili'.   *SG*

Meetings with Mountain
Stephen Venables
Cassell, 2006, pp192, £25

There has been a number of books collecting together various mountaineering escapades but this latest large-format one by Stephen Venables is a particularly good, well-illustrated example. Thirty-five adventures are included, ranging from Gertrude Bell on the Finsteraarhorn in 1902, to the Arrans on Autana in 2002 and John Harlin III on the Eiger in 2005. All the continents are covered, with exploits both well-known and not so well-known. Amongst the former would have to be Everest '53, and amongst the latter the expedition to Mt Huiten on the Mongolian border, made in 1992 by Lindsay Griffin, Julian Freeman-Attwood and Ed Webster, which so nearly ended in tragedy. Also included is that lovely shot of Lindsay chatting to a Bactrian camel. *GT*

Fontainebleau. Bouldering "Off-Piste" at Grade 6 and above
Jo and Françoise Montchaussee & Jacky Godoffe
Bâton Wicks, 2006, pp288, £18.99

Following Bâton Wicks' earlier guide *Fontainebleau Climbs*, this new guide is a boulderer's dream. More than 3000 individual problems at the harder grades, 6a-8b, are illustrated with colour photos, general location maps and detailed boulder layouts. *GT*

Walks and Scrambles in Norway
Anthony Dyer, John Baddeley and Ian H Robertson
Ripping Yarns.com, 2006, ppviii+304, £24.95

Ripping Yarns has moved on from reprinting classic mountaineering books in paperback format to the present major hardback guide to the mountains of Norway. More than 180 colour photos illustrate 53 routes in mountain groups stretching from Telemark in the south to the Lofoten Islands and Lyngen Peninsula in the north. This is an essential guide for anyone considering walking or climbing in the Norwegian mountains. *GT*

One More Step
M S Kohli
Penguin Viking, 2005, ppxii+322, Rs 495

Manmohan Singh Kohli has written a considerable number of books, starting with *Last of the Annapurnas* in 1962 , proceeding to *Nine Atop Everest* in 1969 and culminating in the present volume, his twentieth. He had four books published in 2003 alone. This is all the more remarkable when you consider what else he has packed into his 75 years. He has, in effect, had four careers – in the Indian Navy, in Air-India, in the Indo-Tibetan Border Police and in adventure tourism.

M S Kohli is best known for his leadership of the 1965 Indian Everest expedition which, after two early attempts, succeeded in putting nine members on top, but here his story starts with his childhood flight from Haripur, which is now in Pakistan, to Amritsar in India in 1947 at the time of partition, during which he witnessed horrific scenes of killing. Other expeditions described in the book include Annapurna III, the 'Ocean to Sky' Ganges trip with Sir Edmund Hillary, and the notorious attempt to place surveillance equipment on top of Nanda Devi. In all of this, Kohli, as the blurb says, 'conveys an amazing zest for life'. *GT*

Climb Every Mountain
A Journey to the Earth's most spectacular High Altitute Locations
Colin Monteath
Frances Lincoln, 2006, pp232, £25

Colin Monteath is one of New Zealand's best-known photographers, running a photographic library with his wife Betty and supplying mountain and polar-related material to publishers around the world. He has spent 26 seasons working in Antarctica for the New Zealand government, and for 35 years has been an active mountaineer in all parts of the world.

You would expect, then, a superbly illustrated book, and this large-format volume does not disappoint. As well as New Zealand it covers Greenland, Tibet, the Karakoram, Bhutan, Mongolia, South Georgia, Alaska, Nepal and Patagonia. This is a book that would grace the coffee table of any lover of the outdoors. *GT*

Holding On. A Story of Love and Survival
Jo Gambi
Portrait, 2006, ppxvi+302, £17.99

This is an account of how two people – Jo and Rob Gambi – climbed all 'Seven Summits' – eight, actually, because they included both Kosciuusko and Carstenz – and trekked to the South and North Poles. Now they can boast that Rob is the first Australian to do this and that they are the first married couple ditto, that Jo is the woman with the fastest time to do the seven summits and the only English woman alive to have climbed Everest's north ridge, and so on. What makes it even more remarkable is that, after they married in 1996, Rob was diagnosed with cancer for the second time. After 18 months of illness and treatment, they set out and achieved all their objectives, and even fitted in some other climbs, such as Cho Oyu and Ama Dablam for good measure. A stirring tale. *GT*

In Memoriam

COMPILED BY GEOFFREY TEMPLEMAN

The Alpine Club Obituary	Year of Election
Keith John Miller	1975
Joy, Lady Hunt	Hon 2000
Henry Arthur Osmaston	1961
David Vernon Nicholls	1982
Gillian Elizabeth Nisbet	1991
John Stuart Whyte (d.2005)	1973
Robert Edward Hemphill	1953
Roy Campbell Tudor Hughes	2003
John Cameron Oberlin	1953
John Kenneth King	1957
Stanley Lewis Sheldon Thomas	1963
Malcolm Neil Herbert Milne	1995
Bradford Washburn	1939
	Hon 1956
Martin Albert Walker (d.2005)	1971
Barry Norman	1993
Henry David Archer	1973
Ken S Vickers	1967
Lt Col Charles Geoffrey Wylie	1947
	Hon 2004
Rick B Eastwood	2004

Sadly, there is quite a long In Memoriam list this year – 16 members, many of whom are remembered in the tributes that follow. As you will see, two of those members died in 2005. The announcements were, unfortunately, missed at the time, as was that of William Kenneth Jamieson Pearon who, so far as I can ascertain, died in 2003. As usual, I will be pleased to receive tributes for any of those not included here. Obituaries for Charles Wylie and Rick Eastwood will appear in the 2008 volume.

Geoffrey Templeman

Henry Bradford (Brad) Washburn 1910 - 2007

In 2000, the year he turned 90, the cartographer, mountaineer and photographer Bradford Washburn told the *Boston Globe* he'd be happy if his obituary were just one sentence: 'He built the Museum of Science.' Until he arrived in 1939 at the age of just 29, what was then the New England Museum of Natural History in Boston's Back Bay was more or less a collection of decaying stuffed animals, described by one patron as 'a grandmother's attic, a hodgepodge of ill-cared and often repulsive exhibits'. By the time he left in 1980, Washburn had completely rebuilt what became the Boston Museum of Science, making it one of the foremost institutions of its kind.

Washburn was already famous in 1939, thanks to his precocious talents as a mountaineer and photographer. Born in Cambridge, Mass, his father was dean of an Episcopal theological college, while his mother, Edith, was an enthusiastic photographer who gave Washburn his first camera, a Box Brownie, at 13. By then, he was already a keen outdoorsman and had climbed Mount Washington in New Hampshire's White Mountains aged 11. His experiences there led to his first publication, a climbers' guidebook, illustrated with his own photographs, at the age of 16.

That summer his parents took him to the Alps where he climbed the Matterhorn, Mont Blanc and Monte Rosa. The cold mountain air, he claimed, was a wonderful cure for the misery of hay fever. The young polymath climbed with some of the best guides of the day, but Washburn's natural humility made him more avid student than arrogant tyro. By the age of 19, with the guides Georges Charlet, Alfred Couttet and André Dévouassoux, Washburn had taken part in the first ascent of a major new climb on the north face of the Aiguille Verte above Chamonix. By then, George P Putnam had already published Washburn's account of his first alpine season, the first of a trilogy about his youthful exploits, *Among the Alps with Bradford*. Typically, Washburn had hired an aircraft to get aerial shots of the mountains he climbed.

By the time he went to Harvard, Washburn was an American climbing legend. He had been elected to the elite Groupe de Haute Montagne in 1929 for his climb on the Verte, and soon after to the Explorers' Club in New York. Fees from lectures at venues like Carnegie Hall, as well as his books, helped him through college, where he became part of a group of five Harvard climbers who more or less defined American mountaineering in the middle part of the 20th century. These were men who 'influenced as much by how they comported themselves throughout their lives as they did with their prodigious accomplishments,' according to writer Christian Beckwith.

Bob Bates was one of them, and in 1937 he and Washburn shared one of the great mountain adventures, the first ascent of Mount Lucania in the Yukon, at a little over 17,000ft then the highest unclimbed peak in North America. While not Himalayan in altitude, Lucania was far more remote,

Bradford Washburn 1910-2007

making survival, let alone success, a tough challenge. But the exigencies of their epic adventure were modestly told and quickly forgotten, until the publication of a compelling account, written by David Roberts, almost 70 years later.

For three decades, Washburn was a leading exploratory mountaineer, ranging over the peaks of Alaska and building a formidable resource of photographs, maps and experience that produced sumptuous books. Washburn's depth of knowledge allowed him to debunk the claims of Frederick Cook to have made the first ascent of Denali, or Mount McKinley, a mountain Washburn climbed himself more than once, the first man to do so.

But despite all his first ascents and expeditions, Washburn saw himself as 'a photographer who climbs, not a climber who photographs. I've had a pretty good record of taking a picture of something that hasn't been climbed, indicating the route that I would do and watching it get climbed right away.' This is true, as all Alaskan mountaineers acknowledge, but it typically under-sells Washburn's talent, which at its best matched that of his friend of 40 years, Ansel Adams.

Strapped into the back of a light aircraft hopping and yawing in the mountain winds, Washburn would throw back the side door and manœuvre his 53lb Fairchild K-6 camera into position in freezing temperatures. The results were sumptuous but calmly restrained landscapes, which belied the adventure of their creation but captured Washburn's rapture. But despite appearing at an exhibition at New York's Museum of Modern Art in 1963, Washburn's library of 15,000 negatives were largely unprinted when Tony Decanaes began exhibiting his work at his Panopticon Gallery in 1990 and were unknown outside the climbing community.

Washburn's reputation in the 1930s as a flier and photographer brought an invitation from Amelia Earhart to be her navigator as she attempted to fly around the world. He told her to put a radio beacon on a remote Pacific Island to safeguard the dangerously remote region but Earhart disagreed and turned him down. She disappeared somewhere in the South Pacific. 'An excellent pilot,' Washburn concluded, 'but pathologically self-confident.'

Washburn too was self-confident, and endlessly enthusiastic. Some found him too single-minded, but he needed to be when he took over the museum in Boston. He raised millions of dollars and built new premises in the Charles River Basin, aiming squarely at delighting and educating America's youth, not to make them scientists, he said, but to enrich and broaden whatever else they chose to do. He brought under one roof for the first time natural history, physical, applied and medical science and a planetarium stuffed full with hands-on exhibits that reflected his own desire to engage with new ideas.

Early in his career as director, he cajoled a young graduate at Harvard's biology department called Barbara Polk to join him as his secretary. 'I didn't want to go work in that stuffy old place with a crazy mountain climber,' the future Mrs Washburn said after 60 years of marriage to the 'crazy' Washburn. Barbara would become a determined explorer herself, the first woman to climb Denali, and shared in Brad's later adventures, including several important mapping expeditions to Everest and the Grand Canyon. They had three children, a son and two daughters.

Washburn, who became an honorary member of the AC in 1956, was awarded degrees and medals by universities and societies all over the world, and yet still preserved an aura of courtly modesty. Having tea at the Royal Geographical Society during one of his visits to London, I confessed to him that I was frightened of flying in big jets. He gripped my arm. 'Me too!' I wondered how he coped. 'Well, for a while I took temazepam.

But then I just got bored of being scared.' Typically, Washburn left instructions there was to be no service to celebrate his life. 'He didn't want any fuss,' Barbara said.

Ed Douglas

Joy Hunt 1913-2006

Joy Mowbray-Green was born and brought up in Wimbledon. She attended St Paul's School for Girls and excelled at all sports – tennis, netball, hockey and gymnastics – rather than academically, but tennis became her first love. She went on to play for the Middlesex county team and also at Wimbledon. It was while competing in the top tennis circuit at Eastbourne in 1936 that she met John Hunt, a handsome young officer in the King's Royal Rifle Corps. John's widowed mother was living in Eastbourne and he was home on leave from India, possibly also looking for a potential wife. They were married on 3 September. She was just 23 and John three years older. He was already a member of the Alpine Club with six alpine seasons behind him, and had climbed to over 24,000ft in the Himalaya. In contrast, Joy had never seen a mountain or been abroad, and indeed never further than her aunt's cottage in Devon for summer holidays.

So it was quite an adventure for her to spend her honeymoon rock climbing in the Lake District and, only five weeks after being married, to board an ocean liner taking them to India. Her letters home bubbled with excitement about her new experiences:

'John and I get up and bathe before breakfast every morning. After that we run round the deck six times to work up an appetite. We have already earned a reputation for being mad as no one else thinks of running!'

Their first home was in Rangoon, in Burma. It was there she discovered her life-long love of gardening amongst the tropical trees and flowers: gorgeous bougainvillea, sweet-smelling frangipani, and jacaranda with vivid blue blossoms. 'It is such fun gardening,' she wrote, 'I simply love the garden and wander round it bulging with pride.' John was no ordinary conforming officer and in Joy he had found the ideal companion. Rather than playing polo or taking part in other traditional army pursuits, they would go bird watching and chasing butterflies.

In autumn 1937 John was able to secure leave for another Himalayan expedition. He and Joy joined up with Reggie Cooke to explore the eastern side of Kangchenjunga, setting up a base camp beside the Zemu glacier. Joy exchanged her butterfly net for an ice axe and felt very adventurous. They shared their first big climb on Sugar Loaf, 21,300ft, where, with startling suddenness the entire slope which they had just climbed broke away in a wind-slab avalanche and went thundering down to the glacier with terrifying speed, or rather, according to Joy's diary: 'I was too astonished to be terrified'. John later recalled it was one of his most providential escapes in 50 years of climbing. But the wind and cold were unbearable and they turned back less than 300ft from the top. 'Joy has done amazingly well', he wrote in his diary that night. As a natural athlete, she had taken to climbing like the proverbial duck to water. Her balance, co-ordination and fitness developed by tennis made her a more gifted rock climber than John, who relied on his huge hands, brute strength and determination, rather than delicate footwork. She went on to become a talented climber and mountaineer in her own right.

In 1938 when Neville Chamberlain returned from Munich promising 'Peace in our time', John and Joy were in Darjeeling awaiting the imminent arrival of their first child, Sally. Two days after she was born, John walked at great speed to Tiger Hill to view Everest 80 miles away, in the clear morning air. It was as good a place as any to offer a prayer of thankfulness for the safe arrival of their firstborn, and for the promise of peace.

While bringing up their four daughters, Joy continued to accompany John whenever possible on mountain adventures. John's decision, made soon after leading the successful 1953 Everest expedition, to leave the army after 28 years' service and embark on the totally uncharted waters of the Duke of Edinburgh Award scheme must have been a major issue for the family. For Joy it meant a slightly more stable life, but it also offered her the opportunity to travel far and wide across the world and do what she loved best. Mountains and climbing and adventurous travel in the company of friends became her passion. Together with John, she travelled and explored the world, from the Himalaya to the Sinai desert and Jordan, from Borneo to South America and Canada, from climbing and skiing in the Alps to walks and climbs in Devon, Wales, the Lake District and Scotland. She took part, also with their daughters Sue and Jennie, in the Endeavour Training expeditions to East Greenland, the Pindus mountains in Greece, and to the Polish Tatra. In addition, there were sentimental journeys on the 20th and 25th Everest anniversaries, involving ambitious treks between Darjeeling and Solu Khumbu.

In his autobiography *Life is Meeting,* John Hunt recalls one climb they did together with John Hartog in the Dauphiné in July 1950 – the traverse of Mont Pelvoux by the Arête de la Momie. They had bivvied, as planned, some way up the ridge and resumed climbing at first light, the weather worsening as they began a long horizontal traverse across a steep rib of rock.

> Hartog was leading and had continued beyond the end of the level part to the main ridge, fifty feet higher. Joy followed him, stopping at a ledge before reaching the leader, because of shortage of rope; it was my turn. I asked jestingly whether there was any difficulty in making the next move, round a bulge of rock, and started across. Suddenly, the ledge on which I was standing broke away and I was falling down the appalling steepness between the Momie and Violettes ridges. There was about forty feet of rope between Joy and myself, most of it in coils in my left hand; I remember anticipating anxiously the moment when all the slack rope

would have run out, and doubting whether Joy was secure enough to withstand the violence of the tug when the rope tightened; indeed, I fully expected her to join me in a long and rapid descent to the glacier. Thinking thus, it was a considerable relief when, a moment later, I found myself sprawling in the steep snow of the couloir, unharmed except for rope burns on my fingers... On climbing up to Joy I found to my astonishment that she was not belayed at the time of the fall, but had been hugging a solid block of rock for dear life. It was a magnificent effort on her part.

Joy's energy, enthusiasm and stamina were legendary. On the occasion of the 40th Everest anniversary trek, from Kathmandu to Khumbu, John, then 83 years old, was happy to fly with daughter Prue directly to Lukla. But Joy, a mere 80 years, insisted on joining the trekking group for the week's walk-in from Jiri to Lukla. She was so anxious not to hold anyone up that she invariably finished in front and was certainly the first of us to arrive in Lukla.

Joy was not a natural joiner of clubs, apart from being secretary and treasurer of her local tennis club at Peppard, and devoting much time to social work with the WRVS in Henley. Although most warm and kind-hearted, she was quite a private person, modest, even rather shy, and happy to remain in John's shadow. Despite her love of mountains, she never actually belonged to the Ladies Alpine Club nor the Alpine Club until after John died in 1998, when she was offered, and accepted, honorary membership in 2000. That same year, at the age of 87, while visiting her grandchildren in Australia, she had to be restrained from climbing Ayres Rock, but managed to persuade the staff at the iconic Sydney Opera House to allow her to climb to the apex of the topmost shell! She donned a climbing harness, and with grandson Bruce filming the ascent, scaled a vertical ladder, exiting through a trap door to the two-foot square platform on top, just like a mountain summit. Spreading her arms skywards, and with her silver hair streaming in the wind, she released a wild whoop of joy! That simple sense of excitement and sheer exhilaration lasted throughout her life

George Band

John Stuart Whyte CBE, MSc (ENG) 1923 - 2006

John Whyte always treasured his membership of the Alpine Club to which he was elected in 1973. He was also a member of the ABMSAC (1948) and was their Vice President from 1975 to 1977 and President from 1988 to 1990. In addition he was a member of the SAC (Monte Rosa Section, 1948) and the Rucksack Club (1964).

In his professional life, John enjoyed a distinguished career in telecommunications. He gained his Bachelor and Masters degrees in Engineering from the University of London and spent the first years of his career at the Post Office Research Centre at Dollis Hill where during the Second World War he worked on disguised radio transmitters and was involved in the development of the Gee bomber navigation equipment. His early involvement with digital techniques led to his appointment to lead a classified Anglo-American defence project, the success of which resulted in a personal commendation by President John Kennedy at the time of the Cuban missile crisis. John was awarded the CBE in 1976 for services to telecommunications. He was a Chartered Engineer and was elected a Fellow of the Royal Academy of Engineering in 1980 and a Fellow of the Institution of Electrical Engineers also in 1980. He was appointed to the National Electronics Council in 1977 by Earl Mountbatten and was invited to join its Executive Committee by the Duke of Kent, becoming deputy chairman.

John retired from BT as Engineer-in-Chief and Managing Director (Major Systems) in 1983 when he joined Plessey Telecommunications International, finally retiring from professional life in 1988.

Despite his busy professional life, John always found time to pursue his great love of the mountains. He enjoyed the grand occasion such as when, as President of the ABMSAC, he attended the celebrations in Zermatt in 1990 to mark the 125th anniversary of the first ascent of the Matterhorn. Together with Lord Hunt, the Earl of Limerick, Tony Streather, Stephen Venables and other distinguished guests, he marched through the streets of Zermatt in a grand procession with the British delegation leading the way. During the commemorative service held in St Peter's, the English chapel, John presented the chapel with a handsome new visitors' book from the ABMSAC.

Although we had climbed together in the Alps on several occasions, it was on our 1979 British Hinku Expedition that I got to know John really well. Our objectives were to attempt the first ascent of Gonglha – just to the south of Kusum Kanguru – and to undertake some scientific work on behalf of the Natural History Department of the British Museum. However on arrival, one of our four-man team in Kathmandu, Mike Cheney, informed us that the permit for Gonglha had been withheld but that he had obtained permission for us to climb Kwande, in the Lumding Himal,which, if successful, would be a second ascent and first British ascent. We proceeded with the first part of our original plan by visiting the Hinku valley and climbing Mera Central and North and nearby Naulekh. It was while carrying a bivvi to the Mera La that we came across large animal footprints in the snow, our Sherpas immediately proclaiming them to be made by the yeti. John was hugely excited by this find, taking many photographs and having much fun on return to the UK with television appearances and magazine articles, including a Basil Boothroyd article in *Punch* and a piece in Arthur C Clarke's book *Mysterious World*. After trekking west for three days to the Lumding for a crack at Kwande, John was feeling rather weary after three weeks' strenuous activity – he was 56 years old – and opted for a more gentle trip to Namche Bazar, the Thyangboche monastery and some nice views of Everest. John Brooks elected to accompany him, leaving Dr John Allen and myself to attempt Kwande. The problem now was porters and rupees – the Kwande team having insufficient of either to reach and stock a base camp for the climb. Without hesitation and although it might well endanger his own plans, John volunteered to give up one of his porters and in addition gave us some of his dwindling supply of rupees to pay the porters and make our way back to Kathmandu after the climb. Our ascent of Kwande was brilliantly enjoyable and successful but was only possible due to John's unselfishness and instinctive generosity. These qualities epitomized John's whole approach in the mountains and in life and it was a privilege to have known him.

John died at home in Winchmore Hill, Amersham on 24 February 2006 aged 82. His wife Joan died in 1995. They had had a long and happy marriage and are survived by their children, Peter and Anne, five grandchildren and a great grandchild.

John Edwards

Henry Arthur Osmaston 1922 - 2006

Two of my most enjoyable expeditions were made in the company of Henry Osmaston: the 1985 joint venture between the Alpine Club and Bombay Mountaineers to the Rimo massif in the East Karakoram, and the 1987 Shishapangma East Face expedition. Although he was an experienced mountaineer, Henry's presence on those trips resulted from his many other interests. He was a forester, dairy farmer and geographer who published well over a 100 academic papers during the course of a long and hugely varied career. His earliest childhood memories were of riding elephants amongst the Indian foothills of the Himalaya; one of his last field projects, aged 80, was a hydrological survey of the hill tarns of the Lake District; his proudest sporting achievement was to organise and participate in the 1958 Uganda Ski Championships on the Mountains of the Moon.

Forestry and a love of wild mountain country were his genetic inheritance. He was born in 1922 in Dehra Dun, where his father, Arthur Osmaston, was an officer in the Indian Forest Service; in his spare time Arthur wrote the first account of the birds of Garhwal and made a collection of 1500 botanical species, including two new discoveries named *osmastonii*. Two of Henry's uncles also worked in the Forest Service; a cousin, Gordon Osmaston, was Director of the Indian Military Survey and made several exploratory expeditions with Tenzing.

Like most boys in his position, at eight years old Henry was sent home to an English prep school, before going on to Eton, where he enjoyed fishing in the Fellows' Pond and bird watching at Slough sewage farm. During his first term at Worcester College, Oxford, in 1940, his interest in natural history prompted him to switch from chemistry to forestry, but those studies had soon to be combined with an intensive electronics course, as Oxford was interrupted by wartime service. He was commissioned into the Royal Electrical and Mechanical Engineers, starting in 1943 with a year's anti-aircraft duty in Suffolk, followed by four years in the Middle East. It was only in 1947 that he was demobbed with the rank of major and returned to Oxford to complete his Forestry degree, where his brother introduced him to Anna Weir, who was working at the Bodleian library. It was she who introduced Henry to climbing and they married at the end of 1948, shortly before Henry left to join the Uganda forestry service, followed a few weeks later by his bride.

Looking back recently on his 14 years service in Uganda, Henry commented, 'I had clear professional aims and sufficient independence to put them into practice. My colleagues, both British and African, were congenial and mostly were highly motivated. My family enjoyed life there as much as I did. What more could I ask?' He also compared his and Anna's rough simple life in Uganda to the pampered existence of the modern aid official, insulated inside his luxury hotel. And he became exasperated by the revisionist tendency of some modern commentators to denounce automatically the motives of former colonial officials. Under the Protectorate there was in fact an explicit aim of ultimate self-government; as Henry put it, 'it had been established from the beginning that the interests of the inhabitants were paramount'. In the specific area of forestry, by 1960 all the major areas of natural forests were protected for water catchment or timber production; further softwood plantations were created to cater for increased demand.

In their spare time Henry and Anna explored the wonderfully varied landscape of Uganda, in particular its mountains. On their first Easter leave they attempted the first ascent of a granite *inselberg* called Amiel. Henry almost trod on a puff adder, just as a rapidly approaching thunderstorm ended their attempt well short of the summit. They consoled themselves by naming their first daughter Amiel and in 1958 Henry finally returned to complete the first ascent with Andrew Stuart, who managed the rock climb despite being stung by a scorpion. Perhaps Henry's most satisfying posting was to Toro, close to the Rwenzori mountains, where he and Anna shared many treks and climbs, on one occasion being woken by a leopard entering their tent in the middle of the night (on another occasion Henry, alone in the bush, was very lucky to survive a buffalo attack). It was on that same 1949 trip that Anna discovered an old Huntley & Palmer biscuit tin in a cave and, on opening it, found inside the skull of a local Bakonzo tribesman, who had died of altitude sickness on an earlier expedition. Anna promptly developed a fever and had to be evacuated from the mountain, trussed up in a blanket slung from a pole.

In 1952 Henry took part in the Anglo-Belgian scientific expedition to the Rwenzori – the biggest since Alexander Wollaston's and the Duke of Abruzzi's pioneering ventures of 1906. It was whilst building the Elena

Hut in 1951, in preparation for the expedition, that Henry with Richard McConnell (he of McConnell's Prong, later climbed by Ian Howell) did the first recorded skiing on the then large snowy expanse of the Stanley Plateau; the first formal 'championship' followed in 1958.

Henry's Ugandan tour came to an end in 1963, soon after Independence. Reflecting 40 years later on the handover of power, he regretted that his British peers had not foreseen the speed and suddenness of Independence; he also felt that they had not coped successfully with the traditional dominance of the kingdom of Buganda. However, he felt generally proud of his achievements and from a distance watched in horror as one of the most stable, self-sufficient, well-governed countries in Africa was torn apart, first by Obote, then by Amin and then again by Obote.

Back in Britain, Henry Osmaston reinvented himself as a lecturer in Geography – a subject suited perfectly to his insatiable, eclectic curiosity. His entrée to academia was a DPhil thesis at Oxford, analysing past climate and vegetation changes from pollen samples in mud cores bored from the fathomless bogs of the Rwenzori. His supervisor said it was the best DPhil he had ever read and Bristol University offered Henry a job in its Geography department, where he remained a lecturer until his retirement in 1988.

As a geographer he had two paramount qualities. One was his love of real, physical, hands-on fieldwork, preferably in mountain environments; the other was the astonishing breadth of his interests, all backed up by copious research. A chance conversation with a colleague, John Crook, during a tedious departmental committee meeting, led to his being invited on Crook's 1980 Indian-British study of life in Zanskar, the inner kingdom of the northern Kashmir province of Ladakh, known traditionally as 'Little Tibet'. As Henry combined geography lecturing with running a dairy farm at Winford, near Bristol, he was invited to Zanskar as 'farming expert'. And to Zanskar he kept returning, often with teams of students, making comprehensive studies of traditional Tibetan-style agriculture, but also climbing peaks to embrace his geomorphological interests. This work culminated in 1994 with his publication, with John Crook, of the 1029 pages long *Himalayan Buddhist Villages: Environment, Resources, Society and Religious Life in Zanskar, Ladakh*.

On the 1985 Rimo expedition Henry could not fly out with the main party because he was still supervising exams in Bristol; from Leh I had to send a telegram announcing that, alas, he would not be able to join us: our mountains rose off a tributary of the Siachen glacier, where Indian and Pakistani artillery were busily shelling each other on the world's highest battlefield, and the Indian authorities were adamant that no-one outside the main, escorted, party could enter the war zone.

Henry ignored the telegram and, armed with a letter of introduction from cousin Gordon (the former military survey director) and a sheaf of US satellite photos (much coveted in those days of strained Indian-US relations) he bluffed, cajoled and charmed his way up through Kashmir, over the world's highest road pass, the Kardung La, into the restricted Nubra valley, onto the Siachen glacier, and then up the tributary North Terong glacier, surviving on an emergency supply of biscuits and Anna's home-made marmalade. Victor Saunders and I were returning one evening from our unsuccessful attempt on Rimo I, walking across the glacier towards base camp, when we stumbled across a traditional wood-shafted ice axe, labelled 'H.Osmaston', lying on the ice. A few moments later we met a tousled, grey-bearded gentleman, with battered spectacles held together by Araldite, who greeted us, 'Hello, do you happen to have seen an ice axe anywhere; I seem to have mislaid mine.' A few days later Henry left for Leh with Victor and Jim Fotheringham. It was dusk and we had been warned that any strangers approaching the Siachen army base after dark could be shot on sight. The three Englishman proclaimed their innocence by singing loudly; but as an extra precaution Henry offered nobly to go in front – reasoning that, as the eldest man, he was most expendable – holding aloft a white handkerchief on the end of his ice axe.

Two years later, in 1987, he was with us again, this time on Shishapangma in Tibet, supervising some of his Bristol students. A fierce October storm swept through the Himalaya, killing many people. We were all spared, but Henry and two students were caught out by the blizzard, shivering all night beside a boulder, half buried in a snowdrift (not the first time his students had suffered unplanned benightment on a field trip). After hours of shivering Henry was immensely relieved to see a brief glimmer of sunshine as his 65th birthday dawned and later that morning he and his students staggered into base camp. The storm seriously thwarted his researches and such rock and snow samples as he and his team had managed to secure were confiscated later by Chinese officials, who seemed determined to get our expedition out of Tibet as quickly as possible, in the wake of the recent brutally-crushed demonstrations in Lhasa.

Retirement from official duties in 1988 simply allowed Henry to work harder on his prodigious enthusiasms. In 1992 he and Anna sold the farm at Winford, and moved to Finsthwaite, near Lake Windermere, whence scientific papers continued to pour forth, even after Henry's 80th birthday. Prominent amongst them were his 2002 paper with George Kaser on the drastic dwindling of tropical glaciers and his 2005 paper on the Glaciation of the Bale Mountains, Ethiopia, based on a recent field trip. In 1996 he returned to Uganda as keynote speaker for a conference on the Rwenzori mountains. Typically, he made the effort to track down in Kampala the woman who had helped look after his children 40 years earlier; and in the Rwenzori he re-established contact with the Bakonzo people who had portered for his mountain expeditions. Despite the terrible problems of over-population, he was encouraged to see the country revitalised, 10 years after the end of Obote's murderous reign, and gratified to see some of his own forestry conservation measures still in place.

His last great project, completed just two weeks before he died, was a comprehensive revision of the definitive guidebook to the Rwenzori which he first published with David Pasteur in 1972. Both the book and the manner in which it was compiled were typical of the man. Although ostensibly a climbing guide, it is actually packed with fascinating information on the history, mythology, zoology, botany and glaciology of the region, reflecting Henry's abundant enthusiasms. The recent, drastic acceleration of glacial melting is recorded meticulously and a wealth of new colour photos has been added to the original monochrome collection. Assembling all this new material, as with all his other publications, Henry was tireless (and, when you were trying to cook supper, sometimes tire*some*) in badgering climbers, photographers, explorers and scientists all over the world, by telephone, by post and by email. His global network of friends and colleagues was as huge and varied as his range of interests. He loved life and pursued his interests right to the end, still as fascinated by the world as he had been as a child, when he asked his *mahout* to get the elephant he was riding to pick him interesting flowers and fruits.

Stephen Venables

Martin A Walker 1912 - 2005

Martin A Walker, or 'Johnnie' to everyone who knew him, died peacefully on 24 June 2005 aged 92. Johnnie loved life and certainly lived life to the full. He mountaineered, ran, skied, and climbed for just over 50 years. He put the same enthusiasm into the hills as into his work as manager of the Bexleyheath branch of Abbey National. He was always willing to help out in a crisis, and a colleague remembers a particular instance at the height of the troubles in Northern Ireland, when the company was struggling to get someone to manage the Belfast Branch. Johnnie stepped into the breach, and led the team through that most difficult period, only coming home at weekends so that he could go climbing.

Born in 1912, Johnnie began his working life for the Abbey Road Building Society at the age of 17 and continued to work for the same company through to retirement in 1973. In 1935 he met Doris Day his future wife, although their wedding was postponed for 46 years until he retired from both climbing and working.

In the early 1950s Johnnie climbed with fellow members of the London and Home Counties Branch of the Mountaineering Association. In those early years after the war, travel to the hills was difficult and time consuming. Coaches were organised for a weekend, when these stalwarts often spent more time on the coach than in the hills. However, the social side of club outings more than compensated for the tiredness on Mondays at work. In 1956 Johnnie and others broke away from the MA and formed the London Mountaineering Club.

Johnnie soon moved on to the Alpine scene, and for more than 20 years he climbed in the summer and skied during the winter months. In 1954 he was a member of the first MA course to the Dauphiné with Robin Collomb, traversing the Ecrins; not bad for a sprightly 42 year old. In the late 1950s notable excitements included being driven off the Rinderhorn in a storm and soft snow preventing a success on the Blumlisalphorn. His successes were of course more numerous. Subsequent summers saw him atop the Sustenhorn, Alphubel, Nadelhorn, Weissmies, Breithorn, Dufourspitze, Pigne d'Arolla, as well as the Mönch, Jungfrau, Matterhorn, Piz Bernina and Piz Palu. In France he climbed the Grande Casse and Mont Blanc. Johnnie also climbed in New Zealand.

A trip to Everest Base Camp in the early 1960s unfortunately ended for Johnnie at Namche Bazar when a companion with mountain sickness had to be taken down. Johnnie made the arrangements and stayed with his dying friend back to Lukla and on to Kathmandu hospital. He informed relatives back in England and arranged for burial in the grounds of the British Embassy. His practical compassionate care and loyalty for a climbing companion ranks as an example to us all.

In 1975 Johnnie went to East Africa, but failed on Mount Kenya and Kilimanjaro though he did get up Lenana. Probably his final goodbye to the bigger hills came in 1976 in the USA when with Robin Collomb and Tony Moulam he climbed Middle Teton, Teewinot and Fremont Peak.

Johnnie was renowned for being able to sort out problems and would always be on hand with cheerful advice and a witty quip. He was a member and past president of Blackheath Harriers Running Club as well as a founder member and president (1973-76) of the LMC. He was subsequently awarded honorary membership for his outstanding service to the LMC. Johnnie became a member of the Alpine Club in 1971.

Friends describe him as irrepressible, a jolly fellow, and a kind man, with a keen wit. Jim Nisbit, a regular partner and friend, said: 'As a climbing companion, he ranks amongst the finest for geniality, calm assurance, and reliability.' Others remember him as the perfect gentleman with a permanent smile, and of course that infectious laugh. Johnnie married his long time love, Doris Day, in 1981; she survives him.

The details for this obituary have been gathered mainly from one written for the LMC by Dave Langmead and from information provided by Robin Collomb, an early friend of Johnnie's.

Though I never climbed with Johnnie I had known him since 1960 and met him and his party in the Alps on a couple of occasions and frequently on club outings with the London Mountaineering Club to which I also belonged. As with everyone else I took great pleasure in his company.

Angel Vila

Group Captain George Cubby MBE 1920 - 2005

I first met George Cubby on a wet and windy weekend in 1960 at the hut of the London Mountaineering Club. I had been camping in Llanberis pass with a group of friends and most of our tents had been blown down during the night. Though only a temporary member of a few weeks I took all my friends and their soggy gear to the club hut and found only George and another member in residence. His imperturbability at our invasion ensured that the seeds of a life long friendship were sown.

George was a career officer in the RAF and at the time was working at the Air Ministry with the rank of squadron leader. He had joined the RAF in 1940 and during the war served in Bomber Command, completing two operational tours. He remained in the air force until 1971 when he retired with the rank of group captain. He became a Fellow of The Royal Meteorological Society in 1947. In 1953 he was awarded the MBE. He had many interests, but his passions were mountaineering and sailing.

After our meeting in Wales there were many trips together and an Alpine trip was planned for the following year with one of his friends, David Manns, and a friend of mine, Betty Seiffert, later to become George's wife. The trip duly took place, bringing many adventures, including climbing through storms on the Jaggigrat , bivouacking at 3900m on the Lagginhorn and its descent in a blizzard, and also an ascent of the Matterhorn in less than pleasant conditions.

Over subsequent Alpine seasons, some spent with me and some with mainly RAF friends, George took his tally of climbs over the requisite number to qualify for membership of the Alpine Club, joining in 1967. Amongst his summits were the Mönch, Jungfrau and Eiger by the splendid Mittelegi ridge.He climbed extensively in the UK, including winter climbing in Scotland and big Welsh walks such as the Welsh three thousanders.

During service in Singapore from 1963 to 1965, George climbed with the Far East Air Force Mountaineering Club. His main achievement there was taking part in the first ascent of a 2350ft peak on the island of Tiomen in Malaysia. It was the higher of twin-peaked mountain known as The Asses' Ears. The expedition, in October 1963, was led by AC member Norman Ridley (at the time a flight lieutenant) and took three days up and two days down, the team having to hack their way through thick jungle. The peak was eventually officially named Bukit Panjat Tuan.

After retirement from the RAF, George lived briefly in North Wales and whilst there climbed with friends in the Valley mountain rescue team. He worked as a planning inspector and eventually settled in Aldborough, North Yorkshire.

In 1974 on his way to the Alps, George was run over by a van in a German lay-by and ended up on a life support machine in hospital. He never quite recovered from this accident that left him unable to fully control the movement of his right foot. Though he returned to the Alps, most of his efforts were restricted to hut walks and lesser summits. However for many years he continued to walk over the British hills, his enthusiasm undiminished.

On 25 February 1980 Betty (also an AC member) and George were married. Mountain activities continued; indeed he and Betty continued to take an annual holiday walking in the Bernese Oberland for many years. Slowly however his health began to deteriorate, with Parkinson's disease adding to the legacy of his accident in Germany. He died on 11 June 2005.

I spent many unforgettable days on hill and mountain with George, kept going by his cheerful humour and his admonition every time I stopped for a breather that ... 'to rest is not to conquer'. He is sorely missed not only by Betty but also by his many friends.

Angel Vila

Michael Holton 1927-2006

Like many young men of the post-war era Mike gained his first experience of mountains through fell-walking in the Lakes, in his case with a favourite uncle. Called up for National Service, he joined the Air Force, trained as a radar mechanic, and later tried, without success, to get a posting to a station with a mountain rescue team. In 1948, however, the RAF Mountaineering Association was formed, open to all ranks. Mike enrolled at once and his apprenticeship in real mountaineering began. It was not long before he was on the committee, where he first experienced working with senior officers, who took leading roles. Also involved were veteran AC members such as Frank Smythe, Bentley Beauman, Bill Tilman and Graham Brown.

On demob Mike continued his RAFMA membership, entered the Civil Service and joined the Ministry of Food in Whitehall. Bored with his routine assignment, he asked for a job re-appraisal and was interviewed by George (later Sir George) Bishop. He too was a climber (AC member) and had risen through the Civil Service ranks, via scholarships to grammar school and the London School of Economics. Mike had a sympathetic hearing and Bishop arranged for him to transfer to the Minister's Private Office, as assistant secretary to the Principal Private Secretary. He also encouraged Mike to become an evening student at the LSE. This was in 1950, when my wife and I were active members of the School's Mountaineering Club. Mike, with his previous climbing experience, was an ideal recruit. Despite his day job, and reading for a degree in geography, he became an enthusiastic attender of meets and served the club as president in 1952-53.

It was, however, the RAFMA connection which was crucial for Mike's future life and career. Its chairman was Group Captain Tony Smyth, an experienced climber who had run the Aircrew Mountain Centre in Kashmir at the end of the war. From the club's inception they lobbied the Air Ministry to make use of the mountaineering expertise available in their ranks. The crash of a Lancaster on Beinn Eighe in March 1951 underlined deficiencies in equipment and mountaineering skills, particularly in winter conditions, of the local team and propelled the Ministry into taking action. An instruction manual was proposed and on Smyth's recommendation Mike was seconded to the Air Ministry to compile what was labelled AMP299. (Regularly updated, the seventh edition of the manual was published in 2005 with a new preface by Mike.)

For Mike it was an exciting assignment, involving visiting the stations, assessing the views of team leaders, arranging training courses and, perhaps more importantly, advising on the posting of known climbers to key positions. The result was a resounding success and the professionalism of the Valley and Kinloss mountain rescue teams became the benchmark by which all other teams would be judged during the next decade.

The officers of RAFMA then turned their attention to another project – the mounting of an expedition to the Himalayas. Again Mike found himself at the centre, acting as secretary and having a place on the team. Although hindered initially by bad weather, eight virgin peaks between 5500m and 6400m in the Kulti Himal of Lahul were climbed and Mike organised a photo-theodolite survey of the area.

By this time, 1955, Mike's abilities, both administrative and personal, had not gone unnoticed and he was promoted and posted permanently to the Air Ministry. Encouraged by Smyth, he now took on the job of honorary secretary of the fledgling British Mountaineering Council. Writing about it in 1996, he remarked, 'I must have been barmy'. The post was unpaid, secretarial help non-existent, and the business was conducted during the evenings and weekends from the sitting room at his home in Hampstead. It was a huge commitment for a young man recently married and starting a family, and without the support of Daphne, his wife at that time, would hardly have been possible.

Mike remained at the BMC for five years and meanwhile his career prospered. By the mid-sixties he was a Principal at the Air Ministry and then worked in Scotland for the next 10 years, first as Secretary of the new Countryside Commission for Scotland and then as Secretary to the UK Carnegie Trust. He retired in 1987 from the Air Staff Secretariat at the Ministry of Defence. In all these posts it is interesting to note how often the description 'Secretary' occurs. Mike was in fact the ideal Secretary and committee man. Firstly, because he was willing and capable of doing the sheer hard work involved, and secondly, because with his friendly personality he could charm a solution from the most controversial issues. Above all, his enthusiasm for mountains and love of the countryside shone through, and, with his infectious smile, he never seemed either to age or to lack energy.

There was another side to Mike's life of which I knew nothing until after his funeral. He was a committed member of the local Free Church, serving as a deacon and member of the choir. He took a keen interest in the history of Hampstead Garden Suburb and was active in the creation of a memorial to the suburb's civilian casualties during the war years.

Mike will be remembered not only as a valued friend, but as a true civil servant who served the community both at a national and local level – but particularly for his involvement in the formative years of the RAF Mountain Rescue teams, the British Mountaineering Council, and the Countryside Commission for Scotland.

Denis Greenald

Gillian Elizabeth Nisbet 1951-2006

Gill was elected to the Alpine Club in 1991. She had been an experimental officer in the University of Liverpool since graduating in genetics from the University of Leeds in the early 1970s. She started to climb in the early 1980s, as I discovered soon after my appointment as a professor at Liverpool around that time. She was initially fairly modest about her climbing activities, but when she returned from a weekend in Wales and mentioned that she had seconded *Helsinki Wall*, a climb on which I had been utterly gripped when seconding John Longland on the first ascent some 30 years previously, I realized that Gill was a very able rock-climber.

She started alpine climbing in 1986 with a trip that included an ascent of Mont Blanc. By the time of her election to the Club she had accomplished, with various companions, a substantial list of Alpine routes including the Matterhorn traverse and the north face of the Obergabelhorn. She was also in the Pinnacle Club. She was an all-rounder, with seven consecutive Karrimor Mountain Marathons and seven Saunders Mountain Marathons to her credit between 1985 and 1993, as well as several Nordic ski-mountaineering trips in Norway. Outside mountaineering she was a capable road runner, winning several prizes in her age category over distances from 10k to half marathons. She did the London Marathon (1993) in 3hr 29min. She once represented Cheshire at trampoline. She was a keen gardener, and sang in the Wirral Singers, a choir that won several awards at Llangollen.

In 1989 Gill supported me on the later stages of an attempt on the Bob Graham Round. I finished the Round outside the coveted 24-hour limit, but it was still a great outing, enhanced by Gill's capable and cheerful accompaniment. Thereafter I joined her group of rock-climbing friends and found the atmosphere to be most relaxed and friendly. There was no doubt that Gill was the group leader, proposing where and what to climb and constantly alert to safety. It occurred to me that she was ready for 'Cloggy and in the summer of 1990 we climbed three of the famous early classics, *Great Slab*, *Longlands* and *Curving Crack*, to her great pleasure. Also in 1990

Gill Nisbet 1951-2006

we did the first of three Saunders Marathons together (the fourth of her above-mentioned seven) and I joined briefly with her and a couple of her friends in Zermatt. Climbing in various combinations we each did a few peaks. Near the end, with only time for one hut-night, Gill wanted to do the Schallihorn. I had always thought of this peak as not quite 4000 metres and somewhat dwarfed by its bigger neighbours the Zinal Rothorn and Weisshorn. However, after the somewhat long approach from the Rothorn Hut and a distinct sense of being off the beaten track we found the Schallihorn to be an excellent and by no means trivial peak, overlooking wild tumbling glaciers and in close proximity to the Weisshorn's magnificent mass. Thus the Schallihorn was a wonderful summit with which to complete the Alpine trip.

Gill's interests were now extending to the Himalayas. She went on a trek to the Rolwaling valley in 1991, climbing Ramdung Go. The trek leader was the eminent Scottish climber, Andy Nisbet. They got on well together. Afterwards there began for Gill a period of frequent weekend drives to Scotland. Gill and Andy were married in 1993.

From their home in Boat of Garden they did a lot of climbing together in Scotland including some 40 new routes of up to E3 (summer) and V (winter) grades. They made several alpine visits, where their climbs encompassed many fine classics, including the Alphubel-Täschhorn-Dom traverse in difficult, largely de-iced conditions (1992), the Frontier Ridge of Mont Maudit (1993) and *Cassin Route* on the Badile (1995). In the Himalayas they climbed Mera Peak. Meanwhile back in Scotland Gill passed her Summer Mountain Leader in 1994 and her Winter Mountain Leader in 1995. She then became an experienced trek leader, leading treks to the Alps, Nepal and India. Of the Himalayan treks Andy recalls: 'She had the great skill of not getting too anxious when things went temporarily wrong, as they always do in these places, and getting on a treat with the local staff.'

When not climbing or tour leading she completed the Munros between 1993 and '96, and she and Andy completed the Corbetts together in 2000. She mentioned that in her opinion the Corbetts, being generally more isolated from each other and less well trodden than the Munros, are the tougher proposition. She had a good eye for a photograph, and several of her photos are in the Scottish Mountaineering Trust Munros and Corbetts guidebooks. She also wrote articles for climbing and walking magazines.

Some years ago Gill underwent surgery for a potentially serious condition. She made a full recovery, but afterwards her activities gradually shifted from mountaineering towards her love of natural history, and she embarked on a study of the distribution of bumble bees in parts of the Scottish Highlands. Early in 2004 complications arose from her previous illness, requiring chemotherapy. She put up a brave fight. During her periods of good health she and Andy took opportunities for holidays in Europe, and she kept up her work on the bumble bee project until achieving fulfilment with publication. She passed away in late summer 2006. Her funeral, on a beautiful day early in September, was attended by family and many friends, and was not so much a mourning as a celebration of a wonderfully full life. Andy said on the occasion that their years together had been the best years of his life. She also enriched the life of all her friends. We extend sympathy to Andy, to her mother Anne, and to her brothers Brian and Martin.

Ted Maden

Stanley Thomas 1915-2006

At the age of 81, in 1996, Stanley Thomas must have been one of the oldest applicants to join the Alpine Club. Son of a schoolmaster, he grew up in London, and won a scholarship to Imperial College where he met Eric Loewy who introduced him to the Climbers' Club in 1937. He became Secretary of the Imperial College Mountaineering Club, and climbed with them and with the Climbers' Club in Austria, the Julian Alps and Norway. After the war he teamed up with Tony Smyth to climb and ski in the Alps, where he often provided leads for Smyth's RAFMC meets.

Stanley's work as a Scientific Civil Servant took him, first to Woolwich Arsenal in 1939, and then, in 1946, to the National Chemical Laboratory at Teddington where he worked in many fields, and always at the cutting edge – work which over 30-plus years earned him the Imperial Service Order. Early in the 1950s he had done a tour of duty with the UK Scientific Mission in Washington, where he climbed both local and Rocky Mountain meets with the Appalachian Club.

He had met his wife in Sheffield just after the war, and when they moved south they both became active working for the BMC. Later, for some years, climbing took second place. However, after his wife died in 1980, Stanley returned to the mountains. He climbed in Chile with Steve Town, in Colorado with Frank Solari, and attended several AC meets as a guest. He trekked in the Himalaya with Alan Pullinger's parties, and later with Ashley Greenwood's, and it was with Ashley in Ladakh that he climbed Stok Kangri (6121m) at the age of 78. A couple of years later he did a Tour de Mont Blanc to celebrate his eightieth year.

Stanley was an extremely modest man who kept his life compartmentalized. His other interests – rugby, squash, theatre, ballet, opera, wine and gardening – gave him a wide circle of friends, very few of whom knew each other, and enabled him to live a remarkably active 91 years.

Eric Loewy wrote of him: 'His climbing was always meticulous and he was a staunch companion and valued friend.'

Livia Gollancz

Malcolm Neil Herbert Milne 1917-2006

Malcolm Milne, who died in the autumn of 2006, was born in April 1917 the son of Major G B Milne, a renowned horseman and Champion Gentleman Jockey in the 1890s. 'Gerry M', which won the 1912 Grand National, was named after him. Malcolm went to St Bee's School, Cumberland where he excelled academically as well as on the sporting field. He went on to St Catherine's College, Cambridge, where he was awarded the Kitchener Scholarship, and represented the university at rugger, squash and boxing, as well as having his first taste of flying with the university air squadron.

He joined the Colonial Service and was sent to Nigeria, but no sooner had he become assistant district officer in Onitsha, than the Second World War broke out and he joined the Royal West Africa Frontier Force. Appointed ADC to the general in Lagos, he met his future wife, Kat, one of the security staff at Government House. They married in 1941. Two years later, he was pressured into rejoining the Colonial Administration, it being deemed important that the colonies keep supplying the UK with vital commodities for the war effort. He was decorated with the Efficiency

Decoration, one of only two then awarded. Probably his most interesting period was in 1961 when he was involved in the handover of power to form the Republic of Cameroon, today one of the most stable of African countries.

A keen mountaineer, Malcolm kept in touch with numerous climbers who contributed towards his *Book of Modern Mountaineering*, for which Lord Hunt wrote the foreword. He was also a founder member of the Outward Bound organisation. After the Cameroons, Malcolm was invited to be secretary of the Ski Club of Great Britain, and he helped form the National Ski Federation which aimed to produce Olympic-class skiers. No mean skier himself, he won a Gold Medal at the Arlberg Kandahar course in Austria.

It was not long before Malcolm was offered the job of provincial planning officer in Kenya, funded by the Kenyan and UK governments; in 1968 he took up residence in Kisumu and bought a Cessna 182 aircraft for work and play, often flying people the 200 miles to Nairobi for medical attention. He took his flying instructor's aerobatic renewal test ten days after having both hips replaced. In the early 1980s, Malcolm and Kat moved back to Hampshire to be near their son John and his family, and spent the last 17 years of their lives together there, where Malcolm devotedly nursed Kat during her remaining years. He spent his own last three years in Norfolk, near his daughter, but finally opted to go into a nursing home, where he died in his ninetieth year.

Geoffrey Templeman
with information from John Milne

Keith John Miller 1932-2006

Keith John Miller travelled far from his humble origins in Blackburn, Lancashire, to become an academic of world standing and a remarkable explorer and mountaineer. Along his journey he became a Fellow of Trinity College, Cambridge, a Fellow of the Royal Academy of Engineering, a Founder's Gold Medallist of the Royal Geographical Society, and a Foreign Member of the Russian Academy of Science. He won countless other awards and honours, and made a huge number of real friends throughout the world; friends who held him in the greatest affection.

Born in 1932, he left Blackburn Grammar School aged 16 for an apprenticeship with Leyland Motors during which he took ONC and HNC evening courses, leading to a scholarship to read Mechanical Engineering at Imperial College. There he blossomed. He played tennis and football at a high level, became President of the Students' Union, got married and gained a First Class degree at a time when this was a considerable accolade. He initiated the Imperial College Expedition to the Karakoram in 1957,[1,2] demonstrating the tenacity and organizing skills which became his trademark in his later career. The expedition nearly floundered because of the delay in granting him a visa on account of suspected, but completely erroneous, communist sympathies. Keith enlisted the help of his local MP, the redoubtable Barbara Castle. The visa appeared. Eric Shipton, then going through a low period of his life after losing the leadership of the 1953 Everest expedition, was invited to be leader. Shipment of equipment and supplies was delayed because of the Suez crisis and, on eventual arrival in Scardu, news came through of the deaths of Herman Buhl on Chogolisa and of Bob Downes on Masherbrum. Despite all this, some six weeks were spent in the area of the great Lolofond and Siachen glaciers, surveys were made and several peaks were climbed.

Miller's academic career began at Rugby College of Technology (1958-60), from where he organised his second Karakoram[3, 4] expedition, to the Saltoro, during which a height of 7010m was reached on the west ridge of K12. He progressed to Amadu Bello University in Nigeria (1960-63), before his appointment as a lecturer at Queen Mary College, London, where he combined his duties with a PhD in metal fatigue, the topic that would occupy the rest of his life.

He moved to a Lectureship in Engineering at Cambridge University in 1968, and was elected to a Fellowship at Trinity College in 1970. In 1977 he was appointed to a Chair in Mechanical Engineering at the University of Sheffield, where he remained for the rest of his career. During his tenure in Cambridge he led a series of undergraduate mountaineering and scientific expeditions to the Staunings Alps in North East Greenland, a tradition he had started at Queen Mary College. On the first of this series in 1968, his presence in the field was curtailed when he was badly injured after falling into a crevasse and had to be evacuated to Iceland by helicopter and Catalina flying-boat. Whilst at Cambridge he led six further expeditions to this area, introducing scores of undergraduates to the Arctic and launching many successful careers. He developed radio-echo sounding techniques for measuring the depth of ice in glaciers,[5] and this he used on the Vatnajokull in Iceland [6, 7] in 1976-77. In 1975 he led a four-man team on the first north-south traverse of the Staunings, a hard and difficult journey of more than 170 miles across isolated and heavily glaciated mountains. This was probably the apogee of his mountaineering career, a truly magnificent performance overcoming huge logistical and not inconsiderable mountaineering difficulties in a very remote part of the world.[8]

But undoubtedly the crowning moment of his scientific exploration was his leadership of the 1980 Royal Geographical Society International Karakoram Project. This was a huge international scientific expedition with teams from many disciplines and countries, including China and Pakistan. His account, *Continents in Collision*,[9] transmits the flavour of the venture and some of the background political rumblings. He was accused by the Russians of being an agent of the CIA, a neat counterpoint of his visa difficulties 23 years previously. The extensive scientific results were published in two volumes following post-expedition conferences in Britain and Pakistan.[10] In recognition of his prodigious work he was awarded the Founder's Medal of the Royal Geographical Society. His pleasure during the expedition was marred by the death of a close friend: Jim Bishop who had been a member of the team that made the Staunings Alps traverse. This was the only fatality on Keith's many expeditions.

The term charismatic is much overused. However, Miller's lectures, talks and conversations defined this quality. Generations of undergraduates adored him; he filled public lecture halls to overflowing. His ability to transmit enthusiasm, it must be said sometimes at the expense of detail, was astonishing and inspiring. He was particularly caring of his graduate students, often finding funds to support their studies and always giving them guidance, encouragement, ambition and confidence. His neatness of presentation, stemming from his apprentice days, never deserted him. The meticulous care with which he prepared expedition reports on his return from the field was remarkable. All this came with some lovable quirks: he never learned to use a computer, neither did he seem to know how to look after a car, a strange omission for an engineer. Despite his organisation of Himalayan expeditions, the logistics of a simple trip to the Peak District or the Lakes often eluded him. His mountain apprenticeship was served in the Lakes, and although he had travelled in many parts of the world, he still loved the northern hills. I recall climbing with him on Gimmer when I was his research student, and some years ago we managed to combine to complete the Pennine Way together, an event which gave us both enormous pleasure.

Sadly, his life after (nominal) retirement was marred by ill health. He underwent a quadruple heart by-pass operation 11 years ago, and subsequently his ability to travel in mountainous regions was curtailed by various aliments. Although a member of the Alpine Club since 1975, his prodigious activities elsewhere, later combined with his ailing health, prevented him from significantly participating in its activities. Nevertheless, he continued working and produced several strong research papers in the last few years. He corresponded with friends and colleagues from all over the world. Two years ago before he died, he was told he had a rare form of cancer of the blood. He underwent the rigorous treatment that was needed stoically and bravely. He showed the same single-mindedness, grit and determination that had characterised his career. He suffered great discomfort without complaint and was comforted and cosseted by his wife, Catherine. Remarkably, he retained his humour, but he finally succumbed on 26 May 2006. He was completing the final chapter of a *magnum opus* on fatigue right to the end, which came just two weeks after he had attended the final game of the season at his beloved Blackburn Rovers.

Roderick A Smith

R E F E R E N C E S

1. E E Shipton, 'The Imperial College Karakoram Expedition, 1957' in *AJ* LXIII (297), 185-193, 1958.

2. K J Miller, 'The Imperial College Karakoram Expedition, 1957' in *HJ* XXI, 33-39, 1958.

3. K J Miller, 'Saltoro Expedition 1960' in *Climbers' Club Journal* XIII, New Series 2 (86), 176-182, 1961.

4. P J Stephenson, 'The Saltoro Expedition, 1960' in *HJ* XXIII, 71-79, 1961.

5. K J Miller, J S Halliday & J L Davis, 'Radio Echo Sounding of a Valley Glacier in East Greenland' in *Journal of Glaciology* 12 (64), 87-91, 1973.

6. K J Miller, H Bjornsson, R L Ferrari & G Owen, 'A 1976 Radio-Echo Sounding Expedition to the Vatnajokull Ice-cap' in *Polar Record* 18 (115), 375-377, 1977.

7. K J Miller, J F Bishop, A D G Cumming & R L Ferrari, 'Cambridge University Vatnajokull Expedition 1977' in *Polar Record* 19 (118), 51-54, 1978.

8. K J Miller, 'Traverse of the Staunings Alps' in *AJ* 81 (325), 143-153, 1976.

9. K J Miller, *Continents In Collision*. London: George Phillip, 1982.

10. K J Miller, *The International Karakoram Project*. 2 Vols., Cambridge University Press, 1984.

Alpine Club Notes

OFFICERS AND COMMITTEE FOR 2007

PRESIDENT	S Venables
VICE PRESIDENTS	C Watts
	P Wickens
HONORARY SECRETARY	R M Scott
HONORARY TREASURER (ELECT)	R N K Baron
HONORARY LIBRARIAN	D J Lovatt
HONORARY EDITOR OF THE *Alpine Journal*	S J Goodwin
HONORARY GUIDEBOOKS COMMISSIONING EDITOR	L N Griffin
COMMITTEE ELECTIVE MEMBERS	D R Buckle
	F E R Cannings
	J S Cleare
	M W H Day
	T A Gronlund
	A M Rickards
	A E Scowcroft
	A Stockwell

OFFICE BEARERS

LIBRARIAN EMERITUS	R Lawford
HONORARY ARCHIVIST	G D Hughes
HONORARY KEEPER OF THE CLUB'S PICTURES	P Mallalieu
HONORARY KEEPER OF THE CLUB'S ARTEFACTS	D J Lovatt
HONORARY KEEPER OF THE CLUB'S MONUMENTS	W A C Newsom
CHAIRMAN OF THE FINANCE COMMITTEE	R F Morgan
CHAIRMAN OF THE HOUSE COMMITTEE	R M Scott
CHAIRMAN OF THE ALPINE CLUB LIBRARY COUNCIL	H R Lloyd
CHAIRMAN OF THE MEMBERSHIP COMMITTEE	W G Thurston
CHAIRMAN OF THE GUIDEBOOKS EDITORIAL AND PRODUCTION BOARD	L N Griffin
GUIDEBOOKS PRODUCTION MANAGER	
ASSISTANT EDITORS OF THE *Alpine Journal*	P Knott
	G W Templeman
PRODUCTION EDITOR OF THE *Alpine Journal*	J Merz
NEWSLETTER EDITOR	R Turnbull

WEBSITE EDITOR	P Wickens
ASSISTANT HONORARY SECRETARIES:	
ANNUAL WINTER DINNER	W A C Newsom
LECTURES	M W H Day
MEETS	T A Gronlund
MEMBERSHIP	W G Thurston
BMC LIAISON	
TRUSTEES	M F Baker
	J G R Harding
	S N Beare
AUDITORS	Dixon Wilson

ALPINE CLIMBING GROUP

PRESIDENT	D Wilkinson
HONORARY SECRETARY	R A Ruddle

ALPINE CLUB NEW HONORARY MEMBERS

One of the most enjoyable duties of the president – with advice from the committee and from past presidents – is to appoint new honorary members. Over the last two years we have appointed three new honorary members:

J H EMLYN JONES

Emlyn Jones was on one of the first ever mountaineering expeditions to Nepal, getting close to the summit of Annapurna IV during the 1950 reconnaissance expedition led by Bill Tilman. He also led the first expedition to Ama Dablam in 1959, when Mike Harris and George Fraser disappeared near the top of the spectacular north ridge, having quite possibly made the first ascent of the mountain. He was also, of course, a reserve for Everest in 1953 – one of several volunteers who worked selflessly towards the expedition's success. However, this honorary membership is intended mainly as a big 'thank you' for Emlyn's very specific services to the Club. It was he who, in 1956, renegotiated our lease on 74 South Audley Street. To quote George Band in *Summit*, the terms included 'rent at a fixed price of £800 per annum, with the landlord still paying the rates, heating and maintenance. By 1990, the rates alone had risen to £6,740 per annum.' It was then, eleven years before the lease was due to expire, that Emlyn sold the remainder to the new landlord for £500,000 – a healthy return on the £2,500 the Club had paid in 1956 – giving us the capital to buy our own freehold in Charlotte Road.

PROFESSOR BRUNO MESSERLI

Bruno Messerli is one of the giants of mountain science. His working life has been centred at Bern University, where he was a professor from 1968, but has ranged over most of the world's mountains, with major studies focusing on the Mediterranean and African Mountains (1958-78), Himalaya and Bangladesh (1979-88) and the Arid Andes (1988-96). His many posts and honours include serving as President of the International Geographical Union. Now, at a time when climate change and other potential ecological threats press so urgently, it seems apt to be recognizing Bruno Messerli's contributions to the understanding of the mountain environments which are such delicate indicators of global change.

WALTER BONATTI

It seems extraordinary that we did not honour Italy's most famous modern mountaineer years ago. However, the delay did at least give us the chance of announcing Walter Bonatti's honorary membership as part of our 150th anniversary celebrations, right in front of the mountain where the great soloist made his historic winter swansong in 1965 – the Matterhorn. That epic solo of a new route up the north face was the climax to 15 years of ground-breaking exploration. Highlights included the first ascent, solo, of the 'Bonatti Pillar' on the Petit Dru, the East Face of the Grand Capucin, the Whymper Spur, the first winter ascent of the Walker Spur and, of course, many new routes on the south side of Mont Blanc, including no less than three on the Grand Pilier d'Angle. In the Karakoram it was Bonatti, with Carlo Mauri, who spearheaded Cassin's expedition to Gasherbrum IV, making the first ascent of what remains one of the hardest and most elusive of the world's highest summits. Walter Bonatti is one of the great pioneers. He pushed out the boundaries of alpinism, inspiring a whole generation with his vision and daring. On K2 in 1954 it was his selfless stoicism – labouring for many hours to carry up vital oxygen cylinders, then surviving an unplanned bivouac at 8000 metres, looking after his terrified Hunza companion Madhi – which made possible the summit success of Compagnoni and Lacedelli. Perhaps his greatest achievement was to know when to call a halt. The Matterhorn solo of 1965 ended his stint as an extreme alpinist, but it marked the start of a flourishing career as adventure photojournalist, travelling amongst the world's wildest places with an enthusiasm which is still undimmed. A fine example to us all.

Stephen Venables

SPIRIT OF MOUNTAINEERING COMMENDATION

At the 150th anniversary gathering in Zermatt, Doug Scott, on behalf of the Alpine Club, announced a scheme intended to give special recognition to unselfish acts in extreme situations in the mountains. It is to be known as *The Alpine Club Spirit of Mountaineering Commendation.*

The driving force behind the initiative has been Norman Croucher. He, along with others, felt ashamed at highly publicised instances where summit glory appeared to have been set above all else. Norman lobbied the Club committee and the scheme was duly adopted. It will be managed by a sub-committee comprising Norman, Frank Cannings and John Cleare. The President and Doug Scott are also closely involved. What follows is based on the press release drafted by John Cleare and issued by the Club during the Zermatt celebrations.

In the 2006 *AJ*, Doug wrote: 'A visit to a summit will be forever a hollow victory if we fail another in need.' He was reacting to a succession of well-authenticated instances when able-bodied mountaineers have ignored – have passed by – sick, injured or dying fellow climbers in their single-minded bid for 'summit glory'. Doug's warning echoed the so-called 'Rule of the Sea' obliging every mariner to aid another in distress. That this should also be second nature to all climbers was underlined by leading mountaineers in the Tyrol Declaration of 2002 which stated:

Helping someone in trouble has absolute priority over reaching the goals we set ourselves in the mountains. Saving a life or treating an injured person is far more valuable than the most prestigious of first ascents.

Background
Most of the incidents that alarmed Norman have occurred on 8000 metre peaks where guided commercial expeditions operate, most conspicuously on Everest. While not specifically castigating such expeditions, their pro-liferation and the competitive, must-prove-myself, get-my-money's-worth atmosphere engendered may easily blind ambitious expeditioners with little mountaineering background to the norms of long-accepted behaviour.

It has been argued that at the highest altitudes personality is distorted and a climber is not his usual rational self. While this may be true to an extent, it is no excuse to ignore a casualty. As the American climber Ed Viesturs pointed out: 'If you're strong enough to mount a summit attempt, you're strong enough to attempt a rescue.' (Viesturs was the first American to summit all fourteen 8000 metre peaks without bottled oxygen.)

One unfortunate result of these incidents is that the public perception of mountaineers and mountaineering has changed. Many now consider it a self-centred and dangerous do-or-die sport. Unlike Mallory, Hillary, Tenzing and others, Everest climbers of today are no longer perceived as pioneers in an heroic mould but as ambitious and callous achievers. 'Chivalry' is perceived to have no place.

The Alpine Club Spirit of Mountaineering Commendation will recognise unselfish acts in an extreme mountain situation. It is NOT an Award. Medals and awards are not Alpine Club tradition or policy. Rather is it a recognition – ultimately on behalf of mountaineers everywhere – of a self-sacrificing, Good Samaritan act in difficult conditions on a mountain.

It is hoped that any publicity attached to the Commendation will not only set an example to young and aspirant climbers but may counter the public perception of mountaineering as a callous, egocentric activity. To quote the Tyrol Declaration again: 'There is no morality free zone in mountaineering.'

The Criteria

In the true Spirit of Mountaineering, the person commended will have displayed unselfish devotion in rendering assistance to a fellow human being imperilled in the mountains. In so doing he / she will have sacrificed his / her own objective and possibly jeopardised his / her own personal safety.

It is a condition that the action should not be in the course of duty but should be while the commendee is climbing for his/her own purposes (for example, it would not apply to a member of a rescue team on call-out) and is sacrificing his/her own ambitions on behalf of the casualty.

The scheme is international in scope and the Commendation may be posthumous. It may be made to one person or to a rope or party. It will be made from time to time, when and as appropriate incidents come to the notice of the sub-committee charged with overseeing the scheme. Mountaineers all over the world are invited to inform the sub-committee of relevant happenings.

The Commendation

The actual Commendation will take the form of a beautifully crafted document, couched in the form of a letter signed by the current AC President, recognising the unselfish act and thanking the recipient for it on behalf of mountaineers everywhere.

Examples

Previous examples of the ethos it is aimed to recognise:

1962: On the Eigerwand, going strongly and hoping to make the first British ascent of this most formidable of alpine faces, Don Whillans and Chris Bonington aborted their attempt in order to rescue Brian Nally, also attempting the climb, whose companion has been killed.

1957: Attempting the first ascent of Haramosh in the Karokoram, Tony Streather repeatedly descended and reascended steep and dangerous avalanche slopes over several days in a courageous attempt to rescue the several fallen and badly injured members of his small expedition. Eventually he and one companion survived.

John Cleare

THE BOB LAWFORD COLLECTION

Throughout the history of the Club, members have been generous with their gifts of paintings which has meant that the art collection has gradually grown. These images were either their own efforts or mountain paintings they had collected. Some were by professional artists, many of whom were elected to the Club; others were records of members' own mountaineering endeavours in oil, watercolour or pencil.

Edward Whymper, E T Compton and Gabriel Loppé were leading alpinist/artists of their day. T H Somervell and Edward Norton were important Everest pioneers who painted extensively, while Charles Warren, also an Everest veteran, was an important collector and dedicated Keeper of Pictures who left us seven watercolour drawings by John Ruskin.

So how best to celebrate the Alpine Club's 150th anniversary from an artists point of view? My response was to write a book* about the 100 or so principal artists whose works (some 600 pictures) are found in the collection and to include some of the living artists (members and associates) very much active today. The idea also developed that perhaps these current artists could be persuaded to paint something especially to mark the occasion. The challenge to produce one A5 image was launched and, happily, accepted by 15 artists, to whom we are most grateful. The range is stimulating and diverse, professional painters towards the forefront of British Art and other artist/climbers who keep a pictorial record of their mountaineering activities. A full list of these artists together with the titles of their paintings is given below.

It was originally intended that after exhibitions at the John Mitchell Gallery in Old Bond St, the AC Lecture Room, the Kendal Mountain Festival and the NME at Rheged, Penrith, these drawings would be auctioned for the benefit of the AC Conservation Fund. However there was a further development when Anna Lawford proposed that, together with a suitable donation, the paintings could remain in the Club collection in perpetuity to be enjoyed by future generations, much in the spirit of the many earlier additions.

The Committee were delighted to accept her offer and decided that *The Bob Lawford Collection* would be an appropriate title to celebrate Bob's contribution during 35 years of dedicated work on behalf of the Club, in particular, and of the wider mountain scene in general. The diversity of his knowledge goes way beyond books, and the many climbers who consult him on the most obscure subjects rarely leave without complete satisfaction. This veritable sage of the dingy basement will be sadly missed when he finally decides to hang up his book-lists and crampons and 'retire'.

Peter Mallalieu
Keeper of Pictures

* *The Artists of the Alpine Club. A Biographical Dictionary* is reviewed on page 352.

THE BOB LAWFORD COLLECTION

All 15x20 or 20x15cm. All signed, titled and dated on verso.

1 JULIAN COOPER   *North Face of Kilash, Tibet*, 2006, oil

2 JIM CURRAN   *Storm over K2,* 2006, water colour

3 JOHN DUGGER   *Grand Teton,* 2006, oil

4 JAMES HART DYKE   *Stairway to Heaven, Himalaya,* 2006
                       water colour

5 JOHN FAIRLEY   *Nanda Ghunti, from N.W. near Kuari Pass,* 2006
                       water colour

6 HAMISH FULTON   *Death Zone: Climb to the Summit Plateau of
                       Cho Oyu at 8175m,* autumn 2000, pencil

7 ROWAN HUNTLEY   *Sunrise – The Matterhorn from Gornergrat,* 2006
                       chroma colour

8 JOHN INNERDALE   *Towers of Paine, Chile,* 2006, chroma colour

9 BILL NORTON   *Tirich Mir* (from a sketch of Aug 1995), 2006
                       water colour

10 ANDY PARKIN   *La Verte et La Face Nant Blanc,* 2006, pastel

11 ROB PIERCY   *Yr Wyddfa from Crib Goch,* 2006, water colour

12 SIMON PIERSE   *Dente del Gigante, Val Ferret, Aosta* 2006,
                       water colour and casein

13 TOM PRICE   *Mount Peterson, 7205ft. South Georgia,* 2006, oil

14 GEORGE ROWLETT   *Late afternoon light on Coniston Old Man from
                       Brantwood Shore,* 2006, oil

15 KIT SURREY   *Granite Handhold / Cormorant Promontory / West
                       Penwith,* 2006, graphite and conté

ALPINE CLUB LIBRARY ANNUAL REPORT 2006

In this 150th year of the Alpine Club, it is important to recollect that the Library was started in 1858, in the first year of the Club. Books, pictures, photographs and archives have been collected ever since. It is now a wonderful national heritage covering mountaineering from the golden years of Alpine exploration to current activities around all ranges in the World.

Mike Westmacott, previously a Chairman of the Library Council, reminds us: 'We do have a duty to keep faith with the many people who have generously contributed to the Library, making it the important collection we have today.' The Trustees of the Library Council heartily support this view and we thank all those members and volunteers who by their donations or hard work (and both) make the Library what it is today.

In particular, this year we welcome the new and significant financial help provided to the Club by the British Mountaineering Council. This is to assist the upkeep and development of the Library. In return, we now welcome to the Library every individual member of the BMC and grant them free access. The Library continues to grow with donations and bequests of numerous items; recent acquisitions of note are the archives and slide collections of Don Whillans and photos and film from Mike Banks.

The year also saw of the catalogue of archives held by us (diaries, news cuttings, letters, etc.) published on the Web under the 'A2A' (Access to Archives) site hosted by the National Archive Office at Kew: www.a2a.org.uk. This listing covers some 25,000 items and is a major achievement by Peter Berg and Margaret Pope, our retiring archivists; we are extremely grateful for their work. We now welcome Glyn Hughes as our new Hon Archivist, our Hon Librarian, Jerry Lovatt, continues to oversee the collection and day-to-day access to all books (and many other items) is managed by Yvonne Sibbald, our Chartered Librarian. The Himalayan Index – now available on the web at www.alpine-club.org.uk/hi – is run by Sally Holland.

The Photo Library is the next target for development. Anna Lawford, with help from Philip Pepper, has taken on the role of Hon Photo Curator and has embarked on the very large task of professionally cataloguing over 40,000 photographs that we now hold. Meanwhile, we do our best to respond to requests to provide images for reproduction in magazine articles and books. This is a very useful source of Library revenue but is hampered by the lack of a full searchable electronic illustrated catalogue; creating the start of this is a key priority for the next year.

Autumn 2006 saw the publication of *Summit: 150 years of the Alpine Club* by George Band (*see following page*), a beautifully written and illustrated book which show-cases around 120 splendid photos and drawings from the Library. If you have not yet purchased your copy, visit the Library for one at a special price.

Hywel Lloyd
Chairman of the Library Council

SUMMIT. 150 YEARS OF THE ALPINE CLUB

In 2003, while we were celebrating the anniversary of the first ascent of Everest, it was suggested that a book should be produced to mark an even more important anniversary coming up in 2007. The idea was for one of our members to be asked to write a history of the Club from its inauguration in 1857 up to the present day. But this would be a task of some magnitude and who could possibly carry it out in such a relatively short time? The obvious choice was George Band, whose book on Everest (*Everest. 50 Years on Top of the World*, HarperCollins, 2003) had just been published and had even briefly reached the best-seller lists; but surely George would not be willing to undertake this even greater task so soon after completing the last one? The question was put to him and, to our delight, George accepted the challenge.

The resulting large-format book, *Summit. 150 Years of the Alpine Club* (HarperCollins, 2006), is another fine demonstration of George's skill in marshalling a mass of material with order and accuracy while, at the same time, creating a heart-warming story of endeavour and achievement. The book, which is virtually the story of British mountaineering – most of the participants having been AC members – was launched at the Travellers Club on 9 November 2006 to great acclaim and by now most members own or have seen a copy. The final chapter, 'The Alpine Club At Home', is perhaps of especial interest to current members, as it describes the Club as it is today and profiles the major players in its many activities.

JM

THE ALPINE CLUB TIE AND LOGO

Now that the AC has acquired a new logo it seems timely to record the genesis of the old logo (yes, there actually was one) and of the old tie.

The question as to whether there should be 'a Club Badge or Colour' was raised in Committee by Geoffrey Winthrop Young in June 1909. The Committee, appearing cautious of the proposal, asked him to seek members' views at the following AGM. The AGM also appears to have taken a cautious line in that a postcard poll of all members was subsequently taken. Some two-thirds of respondents favoured the idea and the Committee was thus emboldened to take a further step by establishing an 'Emblem Sub-Committee', chaired by the President (Woolley), to consider the matter further. Its members comprised the Hon Sec (Withers), Sir Edward Davidson plus Messrs Farrar, Young and Stewart. Such a powerful body of mountaineers rapidly resolved that the Club should indeed adopt both an emblem (ie a button or badge which would nowadays be called a logo) and a colour (ie a tie). Whilst the design of the button/logo apparently presented them with no difficulty, that of the tie was less clear.

The main Committee's minutes record the Emblem Sub-Committee's detailed recommendations:

1) That the emblem should consist of a button and a colour
2) a. That the button should be of the material and design of the button now submitted with diameter of 7/8 of an inch. To be made in plain gunmetal. To bear the raised letters '**AC**'
   b. That one such button be issued to each member to be worn by him either on the lapel of his coat or as a top button of his coat as he should prefer.
3) That no suitable colour has as yet been decided upon and a further report will be submitted [to the main Committee] on this point in due course.

The last recommendation is a little strange in that the final meeting of the Emblem Sub-Committee apparently decided to present the following three alternative striped options for the tie to the main Committee for them to choose from:

a) tan or camels hair with dark red
b) dark blue with white (or gentian blue)
c) grey with blue and white

Unfortunately the notes from the Emblem Sub-Committee only spell out the intended significance of the latter option in which grey symbolised the rock, blue the sky and white the alpine snow. The significance of the other alternatives, particularly the first, remains far from clear.

The Committee readily accepted the design of the button, a few of which survive. However, despite the indecision of the Emblem Sub-Committee concerning the tie, the main Committee minutes record surprisingly that Winthrop Young and Stewart had unexpectedly, at the meeting, 'submitted a specimen colour of dark green with light green lines in it'. The Committee appears to have accepted this latter design without discussion (possibly in order to avoid the 'further report' threatened above ?)

Although the significance of the old button/logo with its bold letters **AC** was obvious, its styling was hardly innovative – at least by modern standards. The significance of the green and light-green sample tie produced at the Committee meeting remains unknown. Neither could it claim to be innovative in that I am informed that it was also the tie of a certain Church of England primary school in London. The more recent change from 'dark green with light green lines' to dark green with vivid yellow lines does, however, have a simple explanation. The old silk ties, stocked by Messrs Thresher and Glenny (just off The Strand), and obtainable only after the would-be purchaser's membership of the Club had been authenticated, were eventually deemed to be too expensive. A cheaper version made from a

synthetic material was thus selected from a chart of colours available from
another source where green with light green stripes was not an option.

It is interesting to compare the new logo with the old one. Unable to find
any documentation on the symbolism of the new one, it was left to my
unimaginative mind to fathom. To me it clearly represented a mountain
with a ring of cloud, but that was as far as I could get until it was pointed
out to me by one of the prime-movers of the design that the mountain and
cloud were … somewhat … in the shape of the letters '**A**' and '**C**'. So then
the new logo is really nothing more than a modernisation of the old Geoffrey
Winthrop Young **AC** button-hole! *Plus ça change, plus c'est la même chose!*

Mike Esten

THE MOUNTAIN LIBRARY IN POLAND

Margaret Ecclestone, the former AC librarian, in her article entitled
European Mountaineering Libraries (AJ 2004, p405) made no mention of
the library of the Polish Touring Association (PTTK). Perhaps I could add
to the European picture:

The Tatra Association (after 1919 titled the Polish Tatra Association –
PTT) has been accumulating a library since its formation in 1873 and has
had donations of books from other clubs, including the CAI and CAF, the
John Jullien bookshop of Geneva and private collections. In fact the
Association organized two libraries: the main was in Cracow and the
second, addressed to visitors, was in Zakopane (before the First World War,
the 'Casino' of the Tatra Association at Zakopane played the role of a social
centre in this small mountain village). Unfortunately this part of the
collection was destroyed by fire in 1900.

Significant development of the library in Cracow began in 1929. During
the Second World War the collection was partly included in the library of
the Cracow section of the DAV (Geman Alpine Club) and luckily survived.
After the war the library was augmented by the Mountaineering Club

collection. In 1950 the PTT and the Polish Country Lovers' Association united to become the PTTK, with the library operating under the patronage of its Mountain Tourism Committee. The library collection consists of 22,000 volumes, 1,200 maps and about 1,500 journal titles. Many of the books were acquired courtesy of the authors and publishers and a lot of journals by the way of exchange between the clubs and other libraries. Many titles of the collection are connected with the Carpathians. Rarities include *Medulla Geographiae Practicae* by D Frölich (1639), *Voyage en Hongrie* by R Townson (1801), *Voyage Mineralogique et Geologique en Hongrie* by F S Beudant (1818), and *Bemerkungen auf einer Reise im Jahre 1827* by A Sydow.

The library is situated in the centre of the Old Town in Cracow at 6 Jagiellonska St. The use of the library is free of charge and every year it receives 800-1000 visitors. The librarian since 1976 has been W A Wójcik who is also the chief editor of the *Wierchy* (*The Peaks*) yearbook.

Jerzy W Gajewski

THE BOARDMAN TASKER AWARD FOR MOUNTAIN LITERATURE 2006

In November 2006 the Boardman Tasker Award for Mountain Literature settled itself into a new berth as part of the Kendal Mountain Book Festival. From a record entry of 31 boooks, the judges, Ronnie Faux, Rob Collister and Julie Tait, drew up a shortlist of five titles, and this time festival-goers were able to have a good look at the authors involved as they were put through their paces in a lunchtime meet-the-shortlist session before the actual award reception.

In his adjudication, chair of judges, AC member and former *Times* correspondent Ronnie Faux, set out their judging criteria as asking 'whether a book added something new about a character or experience beyond a mere basic description. Did the book excite the imagination? Was this a book to which one could return again and again and draw something new?'

Turning to the individual titles: Graham Wilson was praised for the 'gentle wit and humility' with which his *A Rope of Writers* (Millrace) 'strung together the many pearls of writing about British mountaineering…thoughtful and entertaining and a valuable introduction to the genre.' Jimmy Cruickshank 'brought the rare talent and intellect of Robin Smith to life in his biography, *High Endeavours* (Canongate) and did 'a masterly job in editing a mass of material into a highly readable portrait'. Arlene Blum's autobiography, *Breaking Trail* (Scribner), 'cleverly juxtaposes the experience of mountaineering in an austerely male-dominated arena with flashback reflections on a difficult and unpredictable upbringing'. Jim Perrin was acclaimed as 'author of the most finely crafted mountain writing of his generation' and his latest collection, *The Climbing Essays*, reflected his continuing mastery.

Coming on to the least familiar name on the shortlist, Faux said: 'Charles Lind revives the perennial mystery of Mallory and Irvine on Everest. *An Afterclap of Fate* (The Ernest Press) is an extraordinary reconstruction in what Lind estimates could have been Mallory's own thoughts as the two climbers attempt the final lap to the summit ...This is a bold book; fact, fiction and fantasy rolled together in a refreshingly different approach. It concerns a most potent moment in mountaineering history and in Mallory one of the most fascinating and complex figures mountaineering has yet produced...The writing is powerful, superbly structured and Lind indeed casts the fine spell of words.'

Faux concluded: 'Delicate inquiries about the author revealed little more than he was a poet who lived in Hove. We should learn a lot more about him because he is unanimously judged to be the winner of this year's Boardman Tasker Prize.'

The full adjudication can be found on the Boardman Tasker website: www.boardmantasker.com

Maggie Body

Contributors

MALCOLM BASS lives with his partner Donna James on the edge of the North York Moors. He does most of his alpine climbing there amongst the soaring sandstone spires of Scugdale, but has been tempted abroad to put up new routes in Alaska and the Garhwal. Workwise he is sometimes a clinical psychologist and sometimes an NHS manager, depending on who is asking. His clinical speciality is working with people who self injure. There is absolutely no link whatsoever between his clinical interest and winter alpinism.

NICK BULLOCK was a PE instructor for the Prison Service until he became a nomadic full-time climber and writer in 2003. He discovered climbing in 1991 on a work-related course at Plas y Brenin since when he has established himself as one of Britain's leading alpinists. He has put up new routes in Wales, Scotland, the Alps, Peru and Nepal. He also rock climbs a bit.

ED DOUGLAS is a former honorary editor of the *Alpine Journal*. His books include *Tenzing*, published by National Geographic, and *Chomolungma Sings the Blues*, published by Constable, both prize winners at the Banff Mountain Book Festival. When not flogging his soul as a freelance journalist, he can be found on the gritstone edges near his home in Sheffield.

EVELIO ECHEVARRÍA was born in Santiago, Chile, and teaches Hispanic Literature at Colorado State University. He has climbed in North and South America, and has contributed numerous articles to Andean, North American and European journals.

JOHN EDWARDS is a retired RAF Wing Commander with a passion for adventure mountaineering. Has been climbing for 60 years (happily still is) and has completed the 61 Alpine 4000ers and climbed in Nepal, Kenya, Uganda, Tanzania, Canada, Norway, Ethiopia, Iran and South Africa. Second ascent (first British) of Kwande (Khumbu), two first ascents in the Ruwenzoris and eight in Zagros Mountains, Iran.

DEREK FORDHAM, when not dreaming of the Arctic, practises as an architect and runs an Arctic photographic library. He is secretary of the Arctic Club and has led 21 expeditions to the Canadian Arctic, Greenland and Svalbard to ski, climb or share the life of the Inuit.

JERZY GAJEWSKI is chairman of the Mountain Tourism Committee of the PTTK – Polish Touring Association. Born in Cracow, he has written several books and many articles in tourist journals, and has wandered through mountains in Eastern Europe, the Alps, the Caucasus, Asia and Africa.

TERRY GIFFORD is Director of the annual International Festival of Mountaineering Literature and Chair of the Mountain Heritage Trust. He is the author of *The Joy of Climbing* (Whittles, 2004) and *The Unreliable Mushrooms: New and Selected Poems* (Redbeck, 2003). He still seeks out the easier rock climbs in esoteric places. Profesor Honorario at the University of Alicante, Spain, he acted as porter for the making of Gill Round's walking guide, *Costa Blanca* (Rother, 2007).

PETER GILLMAN has been writing about mountaineering for 40 years. His biography of George Mallory, *The Wildest Dream*, co-authored with his wife Leni, won the Boardman Tasker prize in 2000. Other titles include *Eiger Direct* (written with Dougal Haston) and two editions of an Everest anthology. A devoted hill-walker, he completed the Munros in 1997.

STEPHEN GOODWIN renounced daily newspaper journalism on *The Independent* for a freelance existence in Cumbria, mixing writing and climbing. A precarious balance was maintained until 2003 when he was persuaded to take on the editorship of the *Alpine Journal* and 'getting out' became elusive again.

DENNIS GRAY began climbing at the age of 11 on Yorkshire gritstone. He subsequently visited more than 60 countries on the climbing trail, including eight visits to the Himalaya. He was the first National Officer and General Secretary of the BMC and after 18 years with the Council took early retirement to travel and write. He has published six books, most recently a novel *Todhra* (2005). Over the last decade he has concentrated on travels and lecturing in China, to which he has now made more than 30 visits.

LINDSAY GRIFFIN is currently serving what he hopes will be only a temporary sentence as an armchair mountaineer. However, he is still keeping up to speed on international affairs through his work with Mountain INFO and as Chairman of the MEF Screening and BMC International Committees.

GEOFF HORNBY is a consulting engineer now resident in the Italian Dolomites. He has made almost 300 first ascents in the mountains outside of the UK and is looking forward to 200 more, inshallah.

TONY HOWARD was a 1960s contributor to Gritstone and Limestone Peak District guidebooks, at which time he was a climbing instructor and BMC Guide. He was on the first ascent of Norway's Troll Wall in 1965 and wrote the now classic guide to *Climbs, Scrambles & Walks in Romsdal* where he was a guide. He was a founder of Troll climbing equipment and has opened new routes in Arctic Norway, Greenland, Canada and across North Africa and the Middle East from Morocco to Iran. He discovered Wadi Rum in Jordan in 1984 and wrote the guide to it, as well as guides to trekking in Jordan and Palestine. He has also been involved in trekking explorations in Nagaland.

GRAHAM HOYLAND is a BBC producer who specialises in Everest films. He has filmed on the mountain on eight expeditions and summited in October 1993. His other summits include Denali. He is planning an ambitious 'Seven Seas – Seven Summits' project, sailing around the world and climbing on each continent. It will be done in stages and Graham is keen to hear from AC members who would like to join in for one or more of the sail-climb legs.

DICK ISHERWOOD has been a member of the Alpine Club since 1970. His climbing record includes various buildings in Cambridge, lots of old fashioned routes on Cloggy, a number of obscure Himalayan peaks, and a new route on the Piz Badile (in 1968). He now follows Tilman's dictum about old men on high mountains and limits his efforts to summits just a little under 20,000 feet.

HARISH KAPADIA has climbed in the Himalaya since 1960, with ascents up to 6800m. He is Hon Editor of both the *Himalayan Journal* and the *HC Newsletter*. In 1993 he was awarded the IMF's Gold Medal and in 1996 was made an Hon Member of the Alpine Club. He has written several books including *High Himalaya Unknown Valleys, Spiti: Adventures in the Trans-Himalaya* and, with Soli Mehta, *Exploring the Hidden Himalaya*. In 2003 he was awarded the Patron's Gold Medal by the Royal Geographical Society.

PAUL KNOTT is a lecturer in business strategy at the University of Canterbury, New Zealand. He previously lived in the UK. He enjoys exploratory climbing in remote mountains, and since 1990 has undertaken eleven expeditions to Russia, Central Asia, Alaska and the Yukon. He has also climbed new routes in the Southern Alps and on desert rock in Oman and Morocco.

ROBERT MACFARLANE is the author of Mountains of the Mind (2003), and The Wild Places (2007). He is a Fellow of Emmanuel College, Cambriidge.

JOHANNA MERZ joined the Alpine Club in 1988 and has devoted most of her energies to the *Alpine Journal*, first as assistant editor, then as honorary editor from 1992 to 1998, and currently as production editor.

ADE MILLER currently lives, climbs and sometimes works in Redmond, Washington. He has visited and climbed in numerous mountain ranges but has spent the last few years climbing in the Washington, British Columbia, the Yukon Territories and Alaska. In the summer of 2007 he will be returning to South America to climb in Peru.

ERIK MONASTERIO is a Bolivian/New Zealand forensic psychiatrist and climber, currently living and working in NZ. Erik has climbed all over the world, but specializes in the Andes, where he has done more than 40 new alpine routes over ice, rock and mixed ground. He is involved in research into personality characteristics and accidents in climbers and base jumpers.

TAMOTSU NAKAMURA was born in Tokyo in 1934 and has been climbing new routes in the greater ranges since his first successes on technical peaks in the Cordillera Blanca of Peru in 1961. He has lived in Pakistan, Mexico, New Zealand and Hong Kong and in the last 17 years has made 28 trips to 'Alps of Tibet in East of the Himalaya' - the least-known mountains in East Tibet and the Hengduan mountains of Yunnan, Sichuan and East Tibet. He is currently editor of the *Japanese Alpine News*.

ANDY PARKIN is still pushing at frontiers as both artist and mountaineer. Active on the UK rock-climbing scene in the 1970s, he settled in the Chamonix valley, gaining a reputation for his painting and sculpting, along with hard routes such as *Beyond Good and Evil* on the Aiguille des Pèlerins. Andy is committed to exploratory mountaineering: Patagonia and Tierra del Fuego have become favourite locations.

IAN PARNELL is based in Sheffield and divides his time between his work as a freelance photographer and as *Climb* magazine's alpine editor. After several years learning his alpine craft with lightweight first and second ascents in Alaska he's recently concentrated his energies in the Himalaya.

SIMON RICHARDSON is a petroleum engineer based in Aberdeen. Experience gained in the Alps, Andes, Patagonia, Canada, Himalaya and Alaska is put to good use most winter weekends whilst exploring and climbing in the Scottish Highlands.

KEV REYNOLDS reckons he's the man with the world's best job, for as a guidebook writer he has the perfect excuse to spend several months each year in the mountains. He has climbed, trekked and walked in the Alps, Pyrenees, Himalaya, Andes, Atlas, Caucasus, and various other magical places, and is the author of more than 40 books.

C A RUSSELL, who formerly worked with a City bank, devotes much of his time to mountaineering and related activities. He has climbed in many regions of the Alps, in the Pyrenees, East Africa, North America and the Himalaya.

TONY RILEY has enjoyed photographing mountain areas for more than half a century. He qualified in Imaging Science with a dissertation on the measurement of colour difference in art reproduction and has a special interest in the digital preservation of heritage. Having spent most of his life as a mountaineering cameraman, professional photographer and lecturer, he now runs an art gallery in the Lake District.

BILL RUTHVEN has been Hon Secretary of the Mount Everest Foundation since 1985, and although 10 years in a wheelchair have had a somewhat limiting effect on his own activities, he has lost none of his enthusiasm for the world of mountains and expeditions, and is always happy to discuss ideas with individuals planning future trips.

DOUG SCOTT has made almost 40 expeditions to the high mountains of Asia. He has reached the summit of 30 peaks, of which half have been first ascents, and all were climbed by new routes or for the first time in lightweight style. Apart from his climb up the SW Face of Everest with Dougal Haston in 1975, he has made all his climbs in Alpine style without the use of supplementary oxygen. He has reached the highest peaks in all seven continents. He is a former President of the Alpine Club.

TIM SPARROW is a teacher of chemistry in Llandrindod Wells, the furthest point in Wales from any climbable rock, though only two hours from all of it. He has climbed in Central Asia on four occasions, twice to the Tien Shan, once to the Caucasus with the AC and most recently to the Pamirs. After a respectful break from expeditions for parenting, he hopes to resume action. He suspects that this is the first time Llandrindod Wells has ever been mentioned in the AJ but would love to be proved wrong.

GORDON STAINFORTH is best known for his award-winning books *Eyes to the Hills, Lakeland, The Cuillin* and *The Peak: Past and Present*. Before becoming a full-time photographer and writer he worked in the TV and film industry as a film editor, having graduated from the RCA Film School in 1975. He has designed all his own books, co-edited *The Owl & the Cragrat* in 2004, and has recently acquired a reputation for his state-of-the-art website designs. Gordon has climbed irregularly, and not always very competently, in Britain, the Alps, Norway, France and America for more than 40 years.

JOHN STARBUCK is an experienced mountaineer who has completed many expeditions including Greenland (12), Antarctica (1), India, Nepal (2), Alaska (2), Canada (2), Ecuador (2), Argentina (2), Peru, Colombia, Kenya, Uganda, Tanzania and Russia, along with numerous other outings in the mountains of Scandinavia and mainland Europe. He has made more than 50 first ascents in Greenland. In 2001 he made the first all-overland unsupported traverse of Spitsbergen (AJ 2002). He lives in Cumbria.

OSAMU TANABE was born in 1961 and is a member of the Japanese Alpine Club's Tokai section. Since making the first ascent of Labuche Kang, 7367m (Tibet) in 1987 he has been on 20 expeditions to Nepal, Pakistan and Tibet-China. He has summited six 8000m peaks, including a first winter ascent of Everest's south-west face. He organized and led three winter expeditions to the south face of Lhotse, completing the first winter ascent of the face in 2006.

GEOFFREY TEMPLEMAN, a retired chartered surveyor, has greatly enjoyed being an Assistant Editor of the *Alpine Journal* for the past 30 years. A love of mountain literature is coupled with excursions into the hills which are becoming less and less energetic.

JOHN TOWN is Registrar and Secretary at Loughborough University. He has climbed in the Alps, Caucasus, Altai, Andes, Turkey and Kamchatka, and explored little known mountain areas of Mongolia, Yunnan and Tibet. He is old enough to remember the days without GPS and satellite phones.

MARK WATSON works for the New Zealand Alpine Club as editor of both *The Climber* magazine and the *New Zealand Alpine Journal*. Mostly found hanging out at various crags, he can also been seen in the mountains from time to time. Mark's favourite New Zealand area is the Darran Mountains, a wonderland of deep diorite valleys and alpine rock. He has also rock-climbed extensively in the USA, UK, Western Europe and Australia.

KEN WILSON climbs regularly and maintains a keen interest in mountaineering history, politics and ethics. As a mountain book publisher (and a sometime architectural photographer and climbing magazine editor) he brings a strong visual emphasis to his books. His adaptation of Blödig's *Die Viertausender der Alpen* (as *The High Mountains of the Alps*, 1993) has been adopted by the original German publishers (Rother) and published in Italian, French, Spanish, Polish and American editions. Amongst more recent publications, in 2002 he prepared Huber's and Zak's *Yosemite* (Rother) for UK/US British publication. Bill Murray's autobiography *The Evidence of Things Not Seen* (2002) won the Banff Grand Prize and Mick Fowler's *On Thin Ice* (2005) won the Banff Mountain Literature Prize. All three books have been shortlisted for the Boardman Tasker Award.

DAVE WYNNE-JONES used to teach before he learnt his lesson. He has spent more than 30 years exploring the hills and crags of Britain and climbed all but one of the Alpine 4000m peaks. By the 1990s annual Alpine seasons had given way to explorative climbing further afield, including Jordan, Morocco, and Russia, though ski-mountaineering took him back to the Alps in winter. Expeditions to Pakistan, Peru, Alaska, the Yukon, Kyrgyzstan, Nepal and China have yielded a respectable tally of ascents.

SIMON YATES has, over the last 25 years, climbed and travelled from Alaska in the west to New Zealand in the east, from the Canadian Arctic in the north to the tip of South America. He is the author of two books, *Against The Wall* and *The Flame of Adventure*. As well as writing, Simon runs his own commercial expedition company (www.mountaindream.co.uk) and is a popular lecturer.

Index 2007

2007 Vol 112

Abraham, George & Ashley: and
The Crux exhibition, 98-99
Aconcagua: 188
Ala Dag (Turkey): 291
Alaska: art. 'The Ascent of South
Walsh', 47, in art. 'North America
2006', 330
Allain, Pierre: 143
Allen, Rick: in art. 'Top Marx in
Pamirs for AC climbers', 27
Alpine Climbing Group: 145, 146, 407
Alpine Club: 77, 80, 128, 139, 142,
Officers & Committee, 406, Office
Bearers, 406, new Honorary
Members, 407, The Bob Lawford
Collection, 411, *Summit. 150 Years
of the Alpine Club*, 414
Alpine Club Library: report, 413
Alpine Club Spirit of Mountaineering
Commendation: 408
Alpine Club Tie and Logo: 414
Alpen, Die: 77
Alpine Journal, The: viii, 139, 142,
extracts from in art. 'One Hundred
Years Ago', 256
Alps, European: art. 'Resisting the
Appeasers', 77
Alps, The: art. 'The Alps 2006', 263
America, North & Central: art. 'North
America 2006', 330, MEF report,
336
America, South & Antarctica: MEF
report, 337
American Alpine Journal: 83
Anderson, Vince: 129
Annapurna, the S face: and The
Crux exhibition, 118, *photo*, 118;
E ridge, 307
Archer, Harry: *photo*, 238
Area Notes: 262-335
Arunachal Pradesh: 297
Asia, Central & The Far East: 343

Baillie, Rusty: 106-107, 112-113
Band, George: 89, obit of Joy Hunt,
385, and *Summit: 150 Years of the
Alpine Club*, 413, 414
Banks, Mike: 413
Bass, Malcolm: art. 'Haizi Shan ~ A
lot to be grateful for', 40, *photo*, 41
Beatty, John: *photo*, 138
Ben Nevis: 145, 152, 284
Bernese Oberland: 267
Bernina: 268
Bey Daglari (Turkey): 295
Bishop, Peter: 293, *photo*, 293
Bloody Slab: and The Crux
exhibition, 108, *photo*, 109
Boardman, Peter: 86, 89, 120, *photo*,
122
Boardman Tasker Memorial Award:
417
Bob Lawford Collection: 411
Body, Margaret: her report 'The
Boardman Tasker Award', 417-8
Bolivia: art. 'Bolivia 2006', 323,
map, 326
Bolts, the spread of: in art.
'Resisting the Appeasers', 76; 290
Bonatti, Walter: 87, 122, is made an
Honorary Member of the AC, 408,
photo: back cover
Bonington, Chris: 110, 112, 120, 148
Borman, Kevin: poem, 'Stac Pollaid',
220
Botoi Tsangpo (Tibet): *map*, 168
Bourdillon, Tom: 143
Bracey, Jon: in art. 'Silent Scream',
11, *photos*, 13, 15; 340
Bregaglia-Masino: 267
Brice, Russell: 245
British Mountaineering Council: 135,
143, 413
Brocherel, Alexis and Henri: and
first ascent of Trisul (7120m) with
T G Longstaff, 257

Bruce, C G: 257
Brown, Joe: 89; and The Crux exhibition, 104-105; 144
Buckle, Derek: in arts. 'Top Marx in Pamirs for AC climbers', 27, 'Celestial Touring. Ski-mountaineering in the Tien Shan', 54
Bullock, Nick: art. 'Silent Scream ~ A year in the life of ... ', 3; 80, 129, 337, 340, biography, 419

Cairngorms: 154, 287
Cairns, Alastair: in art. 'Celestial Touring. Ski-mountaineering in the Tien Shan', 54
Canada: 332
Carrington, Rab: 91, 152
Cassin, Riccardo: 143
Caucasus: 272
Cave, Andy: 80
Cenotaph Corner: and The Crux exhibition, 106, photo, 107; 143
Central Asia & The Far East: MEF report,
Central Buttress, Scafell: 98, photo, 99
Cerro Torre: 132
Cesen, Tomo: 67, 88, 90
Chamonix: 143
China: art. 'China & Tibet, MEF report, 341
Cleare, John: photos, iv (frontispiece), 106-107; 409
Clogwyn d'ur Arddu: 108
Clough, Ian: 118, 150
Clyma, Julie Ann: and British North Sikkim expedition, 340
Compagnoni, Achille: 87
Continental United States: 334
Cooper, Bob: poem, 'Watching Finches', 221
Cooper, Julian: and the Bob Lawford Collection, 412
Cordillera Blanca (Peru): 337
Cordillera Central, Argentina: 184, Province of San Juan: map, 185
Province of Mendoza: map, 186

Cordillera Darwin: 68
Cox, David: 143
Craig, David: poem, 'The Height of Great Moss', 223
Creagh Dhu, the: 142, 145
Crimea: 273
Croucher, Norman: and 'AC Spirit of Mountaineering Commendation', 408-9
Cubby, George, MBE: obituary by Angel Vila, 395
Cunningham, Andy: 145, 155
Curran, Jim: 84, 183,his review of Brotherhood of the Rope, 344, and the Bob Lawford Collection, 412

Dhaulagiri: 121
Davison, Brian: 294--5
Deavoll, Pat: in art. 'Haizi Shan ~ A lot to be grateful for', 40
Dedigol Daglari: 292
Dent du Géant (4013m): 82, 264
Destivelle, Catherine: 124
Dickinson, Leo: 115, 133
Diemberger: 91, photo: back cover
Digital technology: art. 'Preserving our Mountain Art', 204
Dolomites: 269
Douglas, Ed: vii, art. 'Soul Traders: 150 Years of Peddling Adventures', 124, obit of Bradford Washburn, 382, biography, 420
Dream of White Horses, A: and The Crux exhibition, 114, photo, 115
Drummond, Ed: 115
Dugger, John: and the Bob Lawford Collection, 412
Durrer, Bruno: 79
Dylan, Bob: 77, 79

Echevarría, Evelio: art. 'Cordillera Central, Argentina', 184, maps, 185, 186, 374, biography, 419
Edwards, John: art. 'The Eiger of Africa', 229, photos, 234, 236, his obit. of John Whyte, 387, biography, 419

Eiger Direct: the Central Pillar and The Crux exhibition, 110, *photo*, 111

Emmett, Tim: in art. 'Confounding the Colonel on Kedar Dome', 17; 301

Esten, Mike: and 'The Alpine Club Tie and Logo', 414, *photos*, 416

Ethiopia: 343

Everest (see Mount Everest)

Faarland, Nils: 82

Fairley, John: and the Bob Lawford Collection, 412

Far East & Central Asia, The MEF report, 343

Farrar, J P: 83, 257

Faux, Ronnie: 361-3

Foraker, Mt (Alaska): 330, *photo*, 331

Fordham, Derek: art. 'Greenland 2006', 279 ; biography, 419

Fowler, Mick: 80, 129, 153, 316

Freshfield, D W: 141, 258

Fuchs, Arved: 282

Fulton, Hamish: and the Bob Lawford Collection, 412

Gajewski, Jerzy: and the Mountain Library in Poland, 416, biography, 419

Gallop, Nigel: 191, *photo*, 190

Garhwal: art. 'Confounding the Colonel on Kedar Dome', 17, *photo*, 18; in art. 'India 2006', 300

Gifford, Terry: art. 'The Charged Silence of a Summit' in contemporary mountaineering poetry, 211; 348-351, 353-356

Gillman, Peter: vii, art. 'Climbing Controversies', 131, biography, 420

Glenmore Lodge: 151, 154, 284

Gollancz, Livia: her obituary of Stanley Thomas, 400

Gombu, Nawang: 85

Goodwin, John: in art. 'Celestial Touring. Ski-mountaineering in the Tien Shan', 54

Goodwin, Stephen: Foreword, vii, reviews, 364, 367-370, 372, 376-7, biography, 421, *photo*: back cover

Grandes Jorasses (4208m): 141, 264, *photo*, 265

Gray, Dennis: art. 'The Rise and Fall of the Working Class Climber', 142, poem, 'A Summit Gained', 223, biography, 420

Green, Kai: in art. 'Top Marx in Pamirs for AC climbers', 27

Greenland: art. 'Greenland 2006', 279, MEF report, 339

Greenald, Denis: obit. of Michael Holton, 396

Grenier, Philippe (Chamonix guide): 122

Griffin, Lindsay: 83, arts. 'The Alps 2006', 263, 'Pakistan 2006', 308, biography, 420

Gronlund, Toto: *photo*: back cover

Grylls, Bear: and *Born Survivor*, 137

Gunnbjørnsfjeld, 3693m (Greenland): art. 'Mad Dogs?' (first winter ascent), 173-183; 281

Habeler, Peter: 86

Haizi Shan, 5833m (Tibet): first ascent via the 1100m north face by Malcolm Bass and Pat Deavoll, 40, *photo*, 41

Hardie, Norman: 89

Hargreaves, Alison: 87, 121

Harrison, Ginette: 1211

Hart Dyke, James: and the Bob Lawford Collection, 412

Haston, Dougal: 85; *photo*, 119

Hawker, Lizzie: in art. 'Celestial Touring. Ski-mountaineering in the Tien Shan', 54, *photo*, 59; 360, 372

Heckmair, Anderl: 143

Helliker, Matt: in art. 'Silent Scream', 7, 337

Herbert, Sir Edwin: 80

Herford, Siegfried: and The Crux exhibition, 100-101

Hillary, Edmund: 85
Himachal Pradesh: 302
Himalaya: arts. 'Confounding the
    Colonel on Kedar Dome', 17,
    'Recent Himalayan History' 83,
    and 'The Highest Peaks', 84-90,
    'India 2006', 296, MEF report, 339
Hinks, A R: 128
Holton, Michael: obituary by Denis
    Greenald, 396
Hornbein, Tom: 85
Hornby, Geoff: art. 'Turkey 2002-
    2006', 291
Houlding, Leo: 123, *photo*, 122
House, Steve: 129
Howard, Tony: art. 'Wadi Rum &
    Jordan', 288, biography, 420
Hoyland, Graham: art. 'Testing
    Mallory's Clothes on Everest', 243
Huantsán, Cordillera Blanca (Peru):
    7, 337
Hughes, Glyn: 413
Hunt, John: viii, 85, 127
Hunt, Joy: obituary by George Band,
    385
Hunt, Steve: in art. 'Top Marx in
    Pamirs for AC climbers', 27, *photo*,
    38
Huntley, Rowan: watercolour, *The
    Matterhorn from Sunnegga*, front
    cover; and the Bob Lawford
    Collection, 412

India: art. 'India 2006', 296; MEF
    report, 339
Innerdale, John: and the Bob
    Lawford Collection, 412
Irvine, Sandy: 100, 103; in art.
    'Testing Mallory's Clothes on
    Everest', 243
Isherwood, Dick: art. 'Nepal 2006',
    305, biography, 421

Japanese Alpine Club: 61
Jefferson, Thomas: and the price of
    freedom, 83

Jones, Eric: 133
Jones, J H Emlyn: made an Honorary
    Member of the AC, 407
Jordan: art.. 'Wadi Rum and Jordan',
    288

K2/Chogiri (8611m): in 'The Highest
    Peaks. Notable attempts, ascents,
    repeats, trends, incidents.', 87
Kangchenjunga (8586m): in 'The
    Highest Peaks. Notable attempts,
    ascents, repeats, trends, incidents',
    89; 123, 145
Kangri Garpo (Tibet): 165, *map*, 164
Kapadia, Harish: art. 'India 2006',
    296, biography, 421
Karakoram: arts. 'Pakistan 2006',
Karakoram, East: 302
Karakoram, West: 308
Karl Marx (6736m), Pik: in 'Top Marx
    in Pamirs for AC climbers', 39
Kedar Dome (6830m): 17, 301
Keep, Toby: 10
Kendal Mountain Film Festival: 93
Kenyon, Ron: 363-4
Khumbhakarna (Jannu) 7710m:
    (important Kangchenjunga satellite
    peak, 47th in the listings) in 'The
    Highest Peaks. Notable attempts,
    ascents, repeats, trends, incidents',
    91
Kielkowski, Jan: 84
Kingdon-Ward, F: 161
Kirkpatrick, Andy: 336
Knott, Paul: viii, arts. 'The Ascent of
    South Walsh', 47, Area Notes
    collected by, 261, 'Russia & Central
    Asia 2006-7', 272, biography, 421
Kool, Kenton: 80
Kor, Layton: 110-111

Lacedelli, Lino: 87
Ladies' Alpine Club: formation, 258
    Lawford, Anna: and the Bob
    Lawford Collection, 411, *photo*:
    back cover

Lawford, Bob: and the Bob Lawford Collection, 411

Le Blond, Mrs Aubrey: first President of the Ladies Alpine Club, 258

Lenartowicz, Steve: 351-2

Lhotse (8516m), south face: art. 'Lhotse South Face Winter Ascent', 61; 307

Lincoln's Inn: and the AC Ju bilee Winter Dinner, 258

Lindlblade, Andrew: 129

Lhotse (8516): art. 'Lhotse South Face Winter Ascent – The Dream Comes True', 61, *photo*, 64, in 'The Highest Peaks. Notable attempts, ascents, repeats, trends, incidents', 91

Littlejohn, Pat: 79, 80

Lloyd, Hywel (Chairman of the AC Library Council): his ACL Annual Report 2006, 413

Lochnagar (Scotland): 148

Longland, Jack: 143

Longstaff, T G: and the first ascent of Trisul, 256

Lovatt, Jerry: 413

Luchsinger, Fritz: 91

Lunn, Arnold: on pegs and pitons, 80

McCallum, Keith: 131

MacIntyre, Alex: 121

MacLeod, Dave: 158

Macfarlane, Robert: vii, art. 'All one might wish of wisdom', 137, biography, 421

McGowan, Pete: *photo*, 238

McHaffie, James ('Caff'): 5

MacInnes, Hamish: 145, 148

Maden, Ted: obit. of Gillian Nisbet, 398

Maestri, Cesare: 132

Mallalieu, Peter: 411

Mallory, George: and The Crux, 100-101, 103; 128; in art. 'Testing Mallory's Clothes on Everest', 243

Martindale, Kym: poem, 'Tigers and Summits', 222

Matterhorn: watercolour *The Matterhorn from Sunnegga* by Rowan Huntley: front cover; 81, *engraving*, 'A Cannonade on the Matterhorn', 94-95; 141

Mawenzi (Tanzania): first ascent of E face, in art. 'The Eiger of Africa', 229, *map*, 232, *photo*, 233

Mazur, Dan: 306

Merz, Johanna: viii, biography, 422

Mesmer, Stefan: vii, his bronze mountaineer at Zermatt (*photo*), iv

Messerli, Professor Bruno: made an Honorary Member of the AC, 408

Messner, Günther: 135

Messner, Reinhold: 78, 86, 88, 90, 92, 128, 135

Miller, Ade: art. 'North America 2006', 330

Miller, Keith John: obituary by Roderick A Smith, 402

Milne, Malcolm Neil Herbert: obituary by Geof Templeman, 401

Monasterio, Erik: art. 'Bolivia 2006', 323, biography, 421

Mont Blanc: 130

Mont Blanc range: 82, 144, 257

Mont Maudit: *illustration*, 195; 257

Monte Iorana I & II, Cordillera Darwin: 74

Mort, Graham: *poem*, 'Bidean nam Bian', 224

Mountain Heritage Trust: 246

Mountain Library in Poland, The: 416

Mount Everest: *photo*, 66, in 'The Highest Peaks. Notable attempts, ascents, repeats, trends, incidents', 85; and NNE Ridge, 120, *photo*, 121; 128, 145, in art. 'Testing Mallory's Clothes on Everest', 243, in art. 'Nepal 2006', 305

Mount Everest Foundation Expedition Reports: 336-343

Mumm, A L: 257

Mummery, A F: vii, 130

Murray, W H: 141, 145

Nakamura, Tamotsu: art. 'Further Travels in Eastern Tibet', 161, biography, 422
Nanga Parbat (8125m):
Neill, Tim: in art. 'Silent Scream ~ A year in the life of ... ', 3,
Nepal: arts. 'Silent Scream', 11, 'Nepal 2006', 305, MEF report, 340
New Zealand: art. 'New Zealand 2006-2007', 318
Ngawang Tenzi Sherpa: 92
Nimlin, Jock: 78
Nicol, Graeme: 146
Nisbet, Andy: 154
Nisbet, Gillian Elizabeth: obituary by Ted Maden, 398, photo, 399
Norton, Bill: and the Bob Lawford Collection, 412
Norton, Edward: 85; and The Crux exhibition, 103, photo, 102; 208
Norway, retro-bolting in: 82
Nyainqentanglha (Tibet): 316

Obituaries: 381-405
Odell, Noel: 100
Old Man of Hoy, The: and The Crux exhibition, 112-113
Osmaston, Henry Arthur: 303, obituary by Stephen Venables, 389

Pakistan: art. 'Pakistan 2006', 308, MEF report, 342
Pamir mountains: art. 'Top Marx in Pamirs for AC climbers', 27; 275
Pamir Ali: 273
Parkin, Andy: xiii, in art. 'A Good Day', 68, photo, 73; 80; cartoons: 'A Night on Les Droites', 197-203; illustrations: 1, 75, 159, 195, 227, 261; and the Bob Lawford Collection, 412
Parnell, Ian: art. 'Confounding the Colonel on Kedar Dome', 17; 80, 129, 285, 301, biography, 422
Passage to Freedom, The, El Capitan: and The Crux exhibition, 123, photo, 122

Patey, Tom: 147
Payne, Roger: 79-82, and British North Sikkim expedition, 340
Pearce, Dave: 115
Pedley, Adrian: in art. 'Mad Dogs?', 173
Pen y Gwryd Hotel: 145
Peru: in art. 'Silent Scream', 7-9
Peter, Libby: 3
Piercy, Rob: and the Bob Lawford Collection, 412
Pierse, Simon: 349, and the Bob Lawford Collection, 412
Plaisir Climbing: 78
Price, Tom: and the Bob Lawford Collection, 412
Pyrenees: art. 'Prophets of Pyrénéisme', 247

Qu Yin Hua: 85

Ramsden, Paul: 316, 336
Ravier, Jean and Pierre: in art. 'Prophets of Pyrénéisme', 247, photos, 249, 253
Reiss, Ernst: 91
Retiche (Alps): 268
Reynolds, Kev: art. 'Prophets of Pyrénéisme', 247, 358-9, biography, 422
Renshaw, Dick: and Everest, 118, photo, 119, 146

Reviews: 344-380
Brotherhood of the Rope. The Biography of Charles Houston by Bernadette McDonald, reviewed by Jim Curran, 344. Khangchendzonga: Sacred Summit by Pema Wangchuk and Mita Zulca, reviewed by Simon Pierse, 346. The Climbing Esssays by Jim Perrin, reviewed by Terry Gifford, 349. Safety, Risk & Adventure in Outdoor Activities by Bob Barton, reviewed by Steve Lenartowicz, 351. The Artists of the Alpine Club by Peter Mallalieu,

reviewed by Ben Tufnell, 352. *'Art at the Rockface: The Fascination of Stone'*, exhibition catalogue edited byAndrew Moore and Nigel Larkin, reviewed by Terry Gifford, 354. *'The Mountaineer and the Artist'*, the Alpine Club of Canada Centennial Exhibition reviewed by Terry Gifford, 355. *The Boys of Everest* by Clint Willis, reviewed by Val Randall, 356. *Jean & Pierre Ravier: 60 ans de Pyrénéisme* by Jean-François Labourie & Rainier Munsch, reviewed by Kev Reynolds, 358. *High Infatuation. A Climber's Guide to Love and Gravity*, by Steph Davis, reviewed by Lizzie Hawker, 359. *Himalaya: Personal Stories of Grandeur, Challenge, and Hope*, edited by Richard C Blum, Erica Stone, and Broughton Coburn, reviewed by Mikel Vause, 359. *The Mountaineer's Pontiff* by William Lowell Pontiff, reviewed by Ronnie Faux, 361. *Wasdale Climbing Book. A History of Early Climbing in the Lake District* by Michael Cocker, reviewed by Ron Kenyon, 363. *The Avalanche Handbook* by David McClung and Peter Schaerer, reviewed by Stephen Goodwin, 364. *An Afterclap of Fate* by Charles Lind, reviewed by Dave Wynne-Jones, 366. *Reconnecting with John Muir. Essays in post-pastoral practice* by Terry Gifford, reviewed by Stephen Goodwin, 367. *Hostile Habitats. Scotland's Mountain Environment,* edited by Nick Kempe & MarkWrightham, reviewed by Stephen Goodwin, 368. *Scottish Hill Names. Their origin and meanng* by Peter Drummond, reviewed by Stephen Goodwin, 369. *Northern Highlands South. SMC Climbers' Guide* by Andy Nisbet and Noel Williams, reviewed by

Stephen Goodwin, 370. *A History of the Association of British Members of the Swiss Alpine Club* by James Bogle, reviewed, 370. *And Nobody Woke up the Dead. The Life & Times of Mabel Barker, Climber & Educational Pioneer,* by Jan Levi, reviewed by Lizzie Hawker, 371. *The Eiger Obsession. Facing the Mountain That Killed My Father* by John Harlin III, reviewed byStephen Goodwin, 372. *El Macizo del San Lorenzo* by Silvia Metzeltin Buscaini, reviewed by Evelio Echevarría, 373. *Travels in Far-Off Places* by Michael Clarke, reviewed, 374. *Guide to the Rwenzori. Mountains of the Moon* by Henry Osmaston, reviewed, 374. *Exploring the Highlands of Himalaya* Harish Kapadia, reviewed, 375. *The Alps. A Cultural History* by Andrew Beattie, reviewed, 375. *The Last Blue Mountain* by Ralph Barker, reviewed, 375. *Into the Untravelled Himalaya. Travels, Treks and Climbs* by Harish Kapadia; *Touching Upon the Himalaya. Excursions and Enquiries* by Bill Aitken; *Adventure Travels in the Himalaya* by John Angelo Jackson, reviewed, 375-376. *Mountain Area Research and Management. Integrated Approaches,* edited by Martin F Price, reviewed, 376. *Kilimanjaro & East Africa. A Climbing and Trekking Guide* (2nd Edition) by Cameron M Burns, reviewed, 377. *Meetings with Mountains* by Stephen Venables, reviewed, 378. *Fontainebleau. Bouldering "Off Piste" at Grade 6 and above* by Jo and Françoise Montchaussee & Jacky Godoffe, reviewed, 378. *Walks and Scrambles in Norway* by Anthony Dyer, John Baddeley and Ian H Robertson, reviewed, 378. *One More Step* byM S Kohli, reviewed,

379. *Climb Every Mountain. A Journey to the Earth's most spectacular High Altitude Locations* by Colin Monteath, reviewed, 379.
Holding On. A Story of Love and Survival by Jo Gambi, reviewed, 380.

Right Unconquerable, The: and The Crux exhibition, 105, *photo*, 104
Richardson, Simon: arts. 'Scottish Winter Climbing: the last 50 years', 147, 'Scottish Winters 2006-2007', 283; biography, 422
Rickards, Alex: in art. 'Top Marx in Pamirs for AC climbers', 27, *photo*, 38
Riley, Tony: art. 'Preserving our Mountain Art. Digital Technology: a new imaging landscape', 204
Roberts, Barry: in art. 'Mad Dogs?', 173
Rock and Ice Club: 144
Rouse, Al: 91, 152, 153
Rowbotham, Graham: in art. 'The Ascent of South Walsh', 47
Rowlett, George: and the Bob Lawford Collection, 412
Royal Geographical Society: 145, 257
Russell, C A: art. 'One Hundred Years Ago', 256, biography, 422
Russia: in art. 'Russia & Central Asia 2006-7', 272
Ruthven, Bill: and MEF Expedition Reports, 336, biography, 422

St Elias range, Alaska: 47
Saunders, Victor: 153
Scoop, The: and The Crux exhibition, 117, *photo*, 116
Scotland: arts. 'Scottish Winter Climbing: the last 50 years', 147, 'Scottish Winters 2006-2007', 283
Scott, Doug: viii, art. 'Resisting the Appeasers', 77; 86, 89; and The Crux exhibition, 116-117, 119; 408-9, biography, 423, *photo*: back cover

Scottish Mountaineering Trust: 369
Seale, Anna: in art. 'Celestial Touring. Ski-mountaineering in the Tien Shan', 54, *photo*, 55
Sewell, John: poem, 'The Ascent of Skiddaw from Dead Crags', 218
Shakdara range, Tajikistan: *map*, 26
Sharp, Mike: in art. 'Celestial Touring. Ski-mountaineering in the Tien Shan', 54
Shipton, Eric: 129
Siberia: 278
SMC Journal: 78
Smith, Albert: 126
Smith, Roderick A: obituary of Keith John Miller, 402
Snotty's Gully, Phari Lapcha (Machermo Peak), Nepal: 11, *photo*, 14; 340
Somervell, T Howard: 85, 103, 243
South Walsh, St Elias range, Alaska: first ascent by Paul Knott and Graham Rowbotham, 47, *photo*, 48
Sparrow, Tim: art. 'Top Marx in Pamirs for AC climbers', 27, *map*, 26
Stainforth, Gordon: art. 'The Crux', 93, biography, 423
Starbuck, John: art. 'Mad Dogs?', 173, biography, 423
Streather, Tony: 89
Streetly, John: 108
Strutt, E L: 83
Sunday Times, The: 131
Surrey, Kit: and the Bob Lawford Collection, 412
Swiss Alpine Club: 77

Tajikistan: art. 'Top Marx in Pamirs for AC climbers', 27
Tanaba, Osamu: art. 'Lhotse South Face Winter Ascent', 61; 87, 92
Tasker, Joe: 89, 120, *photo*, 121
Templeman, Geoffrey: viii, reviews compiled by, 344, obituaries compiled by, 381, obituary of Malcolm Neil Herbert Milne, 401, biography, 423

Tenzing Norgay: 85
Thomas, Stanley: obituary by Livia
    Gollancz, 400
Thompson, Tommy: in art. 'The Eiger
    of Africa', 229
Tibet: arts. 'Haizi Shan ~ A lot to be
    grateful for', 40, art. 'Further
    Travels in Eastern Tibet', 161,
    MEF report, 341
Tien Shan: art. 'Celestial Touring.
    Ski-mountaineering in the
    Tien Shan', 54; 275
Tierra del Fuego, Chilean: 68, 74
Tomasson, Beatrice: and The Crux
    exhibition, 96, *photo*, 97
Town, John: art. 'China & Tibet
    2006', 315, biography, 424
Trisul (7120m): first ascent by T G
    Longstaff and party, 258, *photo*, 259
Tufnell, Ben: 354
Turkey: art. 'Turkey 2002-2006', 291
Tyrol Declaration, The: 76

Unsoeld, Willi: 85
UIAA: 77, and Mountain Code, 290
Uttarakhand: 299

Valais Alps: 266
Vause, Mikel: 360-1
Venables, Stephen: 87, 378, obit of
    Henry Osmaston, 389; 408, *photo*:
    back cover
Vila, Angel: obits. of Martin A
    Walker, 393, and George Cubby,
    MBE, 395
Vines, Stuart: 188

Wadi Rum: art. 'Wadi Rum and
    Jordan', 288
Walker, Martin A ('Johnnie'):
    obituary by Angel Vila: 393
Walker, Paul: in art. 'Mad Dogs?', 173
Wang Fu-Chou: 85
Washburn, Henry Bradford: obituary
    by Ed Douglas, 382, *photo*, 383

Watkins Mts: *map*, 172; 281
Watson, Mark: art. 'New Zealand
    2006-2007', 318, biography, 424
Westmacott, Mike: 413
Whillans, Don: 128, 144-5, 413
Whimp, Athol: 129
Whitby, Chris: poem, 'Breaking
    Silence', 221
Whymper, Edward: and The Crux
    exhibition, 94-95; 130
Whyte, John Stuart, CBE: obituary by
    John Edwards, 387
Wickens, Phil: in art. 'Top Marx in
    Pamirs for AC climbers', 27
Wilson, Ken: viii, arts. 'Recent
    Himalayan History', 84, and 'The
    Highest Peaks' 85-92; in art.
    'Resisting the Appeasers', 77; 117,
    131, biography, 424
Wrangham, E A: 108
Wynne-Jones, Dave: art. 'Celestial
    Touring', 54, *photo*, 59; 367,
    biography, 424

Yalung Kang, 8420m
    (Kangchenjunga's W Summit; the
    7th highest peak): in 'The Highest
    Peaks: notable attempts, ascents,
    repeats, trends, incidents', 90
Yamaguchi, Takahiro: 63, 67, 92
Yamamoto, Toshio: in art. 'Lhotse
    South Face Winter Ascent', 61
Yates, Simon: art. 'A Good Day', 68;
    80, biography, 424
Yi'ong Tsampo (Tibet): in art.
    'Further Travels in Eastern Tibet',
    161
Young, Geoffrey Winthrop: 100, 126,
    143, 257

Zermatt: vii, 81, 141
Zmutt Ridge: vii, 81

NOTES FOR CONTRIBUTORS

The *Alpine Journal* records all aspects of mountains and mountaineering, including expeditions, adventure, art, literature, geography, history, geology, medicine, ethics and the mountain environment.

Articles Contributions in English are invited. They should be sent to the Hon Editor, Stephen Goodwin, 1 Ivy Cottages, Edenhall, Penrith, Cumbria CA11 8SN (e-mail: sg@stephengoodwin.demon.co.uk). Articles should preferably be sent on a disk with accompanying hard copy or as an e-mail attachment (in Word) with hard copy sent separately by post. They will also be accepted as plain typed copy. Their length should not exceed 3000 words without prior approval of the Editor **and may be edited or shortened at his discretion.** It is regretted that the *Alpine Journal* is unable to offer a fee for articles published, but authors receive a complimentary copy of the issue of the *Alpine Journal* in which their article appears.

Articles and book reviews should not have been published in substantially the same form by any other publication.

Maps These should be well researched, accurate, and finished ready for printing. They should show the most important place-names mentioned in the text. It is the authors' responsibility to get their maps redrawn if necessary. This can be arranged through the Production Editor if required.

Photographs Colour transparencies are preferable. These should be originals (not copies) in 35mm format or larger. Prints (any size) should be numbered (in pencil) on the back and accompanied by captions on a separate sheet (see below). Images on CD are acceptable but must have been scanned at high resolution and must be accompanied by numbered captions that match the serial numbers on the CD.

Captions Please list these **on a separate sheet** and give title and author of the article to which they refer.

Copyright It is the author's responsibility to obtain copyright clearance for text, photographs and maps, to pay any fees involved and to ensure that acknowledgements are in the form required by the copyright owner.

Summaries A brief summary, helpful to researchers, may be included with 'expedition' articles.

Biographies Authors are asked to provide a short biography, in about 60 words, listing the most noteworthy items in their climbing career and anything else they wish to mention.

Deadline: copy and photographs should reach the Editor by 1 January of the year of publication.

thirsty?

ether you've got a taste for hydration or adventure, there's a Nalgene that's up to the
'lenge. There are just as many Nalgene container designs as there are real-life situations
: call for them, so feel free to stock up. We've created different styles to suit the pack,
cup holder, the hip pocket and the stroller. Wherever and whenever, we're standing by
dy to quench. Drink in all the possibilities at **www.nalgene-outdoor.com.**

MADE IN USA

www.nalgene-outdoor.com

st Ascent
: **01629 580484** Web: **www.firstascent.co.uk**

Rathbones welcomes
private investors

Discretionary portfolio management

How often do you receive a truly personal service today?

At Rathbones we offer a bespoke service with a dedicated investment manager from £100,000, including SIPPS.

We also welcome directly invested portfolios when some other investment managers may insist on a restricted list of unit trusts.

We listen to your needs and plan your strategy together.

Rathbones manages the investment funds for **The Alpine Club, The Alpine Club Library and the Mount Everest Foundation.**

Drake Davis
Investment Director

Tel: 020 7399 0000
drake.davis@rathbones.com
www.rathbones.com

Rathbone Investment Management Limited is authorised and regulated by the Financial Services Authority. Registered office: Port of Liverpool Building, Pier Head, Liverpool L3 1NW. Registered in England No. 1448919.

RATHBONES
Established 1742

THE ART OF COMFORT

...mfort. At Therm-a-Rest,® it's as much a state of mind as a brand promise. It's about ...tting off-trail, bedding down amid the rocks and needles.

And it's the foundation of our new puncture-resistant ToughSkin™ a rugged, multilayer backpacking mattress that stands up to even the thorniest Trek & Travel™ adventure.

From the brand that pioneered outdoor comfort.

THERMAREST®
go to www.thermarest.com

Go to www.firstascent.co.uk or call 01629 580484 for more information.

IN GUIDES' HANDS

Weight: 103 g
Suggested retail
price: £19.99

- Guide Mode with
  lowering capabilities

- High Friction Belay
  and Rappel Mode

- Regular Friction
  Belay and
  Rappel Mode

www.BlackDiamondEquipment.com
info@firstascent.co.uk
01629 580484

LENGTH 50, 57, 64 cm
WEIGHT 493 g (50 cm tool without leash)
SUGGESTED RETAIL PRICE £ 99.99

VENOM
MAXIMUM PERFORMANCE

Get after it with the high performance and super lightweight new Venom piolet. An **Interchangeable 4340 CrMo steel pick, curved 7075-T6 aluminium shaft, dual-density grip** and a **Lockdown Leash** give it just the right features for **blazing up steep couloirs** or **descending bulletproof neve**. So, pick a line and get going with the Venom, knowing you'll get the maximum performance from this lightweight piolet if things get steep.

www.BlackDiamondEquipment.com
info@firstascent.co.uk
01629 580484

◆ Black Diamond™

Lowe alpine®

**Shared
Alpine
Experience**

The Alpine Club is Britain's
oldest and most respected
institution for sharing alpine
experiences and knowledge.
For more than 40 years Lowe
Alpine has been dedicated to
making great alpine gear.
We are pleased to therefore
share and support this
**150th Anniversary of the
Alpine Club.**

Photo: John Norris

For more information
contact Lowe Alpine on
01539 740 840 or email
info@lowealpine.co.uk
www.lowealpine.com

Lowe Alpine.
Helping climbers
achieve their dreams.

© 2006 Cascade Designs, Inc.®

THE MSR REACTOR:

THE FASTEST, MOST EFFICIENT ALL-CONDITION STOVE SYSTEM. EVER.

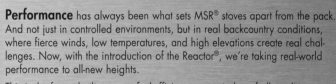

Performance has always been what sets MSR® stoves apart from the pack. And not just in controlled environments, but in real backcountry conditions, where fierce winds, low temperatures, and high elevations create real challenges. Now, with the introduction of the Reactor®, we're taking real-world performance to all-new heights.

This is the fastest-boiling, most fuel-efficient, most windproof all-condition stove system ever made, capable of boiling one liter of water in just three minutes. It combines a patent-pending canister stove and a high-efficiency 1.7-liter pot into one compact, easy-to-use unit. And its internal pressure regulator ensures consistent flame output throughout the life of the canister and in even the most challenging conditions—where performance really matters.

Go to www.firstascent.co.uk
or call 01629-580484 for more information.

MSR®

GEAR THAT PERFORMS—FOR LIFE.

MOUNTAIN SAFETY RESEARCH®

www.msrgear.com

1945   Zinalrothorn E Face ... 1946   Batian SW Ridge ...   1947   Lloy

1950   Bandar Punch (Kashmir) ... 1951   Mt Everest Reconnaissance ...

1955   Kangchenjunga ... 1956   Muztagh Tower ... 1957   Pumasillc

1960   Trivor (Karakoram) ... 1961   Ama Dablam ... 1962   Monte D

1964   Kulu Pumori ... 1965   RH Pillar of Brouillard ... 1966   Eiger

1969   Ali Ratna Tibba (Kulu) ... 1970   Annapurna S Face ... 1971   B

1973   Koh-I-Mondi N Face (Hindu Kush) ...   1974   Changabang

1976   Trango Nameless Tower (Karakoram) ... 1977   The Ogre (Kara

1979   Kangchenjunga N Ridge ... 1980   Mt Huntingdon SE Face (A

1983   Kishtwar Shivling ... 1984   Chamlang E Summit (Nepal) ... 19

1987   Golden Pillar of Spantik (Karakoram) ... 1988   Everest Kangshur

1991   Kusum Kangguru SW Face (Nepal) ... 1992   Central Tower of Pa

1995   Taweche NE Pillar (Nepal) ... 1996   Kullu Eiger (Himachal P

1998   Drohmo S Spur (Nepal) ... 1999   Citadel (Baffin Island) ... 200

2002   Siguniang N Face (Sichuan Province, China) ... 2003   Mt Grosve

2006   Haizi Shan (Tibet) ... 2007   AC 150 (Garhwal)

Königspitze   *Photogravure from a painting by E. T. Comp*